1,000,000 Books

are available to read at

---

www.ForgottenBooks.com

Read online
Download PDF
Purchase in print

ISBN 978-0-260-92042-3
PIBN 11113176

This book is a reproduction of an important historical work. Forgotten Books uses state-of-the-art technology to digitally reconstruct the work, preserving the original format whilst repairing imperfections present in the aged copy. In rare cases, an imperfection in the original, such as a blemish or missing page, may be replicated in our edition. We do, however, repair the vast majority of imperfections successfully; any imperfections that remain are intentionally left to preserve the state of such historical works.

Forgotten Books is a registered trademark of FB &c Ltd.
Copyright © 2018 FB &c Ltd.
FB &c Ltd, Dalton House, 60 Windsor Avenue, London, SW19 2RR.
Company number 08720141. Registered in England and Wales.

For support please visit www.forgottenbooks.com

1 MONTH OF FREE READING

at

www.ForgottenBooks.com

By purchasing this book you are eligible for one month membership to ForgottenBooks.com, giving you unlimited access to our entire collection of over 1,000,000 titles via our web site and mobile apps.

To claim your free month visit:

www.forgottenbooks.com/free1113176

* Offer is valid for 45 days from date of purchase. Terms and conditions apply.

English
Français
Deutsche
Italiano
Español
Português

www.forgottenbooks.com

Mythology Photography **Fiction**
Fishing Christianity **Art** Cooking
Essays Buddhism Freemasonry
Medicine **Biology** Music **Ancient Egypt** Evolution Carpentry Physics
Dance Geology **Mathematics** Fitness
Shakespeare **Folklore** Yoga Marketing
Confidence Immortality Biographies
Poetry **Psychology** Witchcraft
Electronics Chemistry History **Law**
Accounting **Philosophy** Anthropology
Alchemy Drama Quantum Mechanics
Atheism Sexual Health **Ancient History**
Entrepreneurship Languages Sport
Paleontology Needlework Islam
Metaphysics Investment Archaeology
Parenting Statistics Criminology
Motivational

CENTRAL CIRCULATION AND BOOKSTACKS
The person borrowing this material is responsible for its renewal or return before the **Latest Date** stamped below. **You may be charged a minimum fee of $75.00 for each non-returned or lost item.**

Theft, mutilation, or defacement of library materials can be causes for student disciplinary action. All materials owned by the University of Illinois Library are the property of the State of Illinois and are protected by Article 16B of *Illinois Criminal Law and Procedure.*

TO RENEW, CALL (217) 333-8400.
University of Illinois Library at Urbana-Champaign

When renewing by phone, write new due date below previous due date. L162

THE

EIGHTEENTH ANNUAL CATALOGUE

OF THE

OFFICERS AND STUDENTS

IN

HANOVER COLLEGE.

1849–50.

THE

EIGHTEENTH

ANNUAL CATALOGUE

OF THE

OFFICERS AND STUDENTS

IN

HANOVER COLLEGE.

1849–50.

....

PRINTED FOR HANOVER COLLEGE:
BY JOHN D. THORPE, FOURTH STREET, CINCINNATI.
1850.

CORPORATION.

REV. JOHN FINLEY CROWE, D. D., President.
REV. JAMES BROWN, of Madison.
REV. DANIEL LATTIMORE, of Vernon.
REV. JOHN H. NEVIUS, of Decatur.
REV. THOS. E. THOMAS, of Hanover.
REV. SAMUEL TAYLOR, of Waveland.
WILLIAM A. BULLOCK, ESQ., of Vernon.
REV. J. G. MONFORT, of Greensburgh.
REV. WILLIAM SICKLES, of Canaan.
REV. JOHN H. BONNER, of Hanover.
GEORGE A. IRVIN, ESQ., of Hanover.
WILLIAM McKEE DUNN, ESQ., of Madison.
REV. THOS. S. CROWE, of Hanover.
REV. N. L. RICE, D. D., of Cincinnati.
REV. DAVID V. SMOCK, of Franklin.
REV. DAVID M. STEWART, of Rushville.
REV. SAMUEL R. WILSON, of Cincinnati.
REV. C. LEAVENWORTH, of Indianapolis.
ALEXANDER GUY, M. D., of Cincinnati.
A. R. FORSYTH, ESQ., of Greensburgh.
JOHN L. SCOTT, ESQ., of Cincinnati.
HON. WILLIAMSON DUNN, of Hanover.
REV. P. D. GURLEY, of Dayton.
REV. DANIEL STEWART, of New Albany.

PROF. S. H. THOMPSON, Secretary.
REV. THOS. S. CROWE, Treasurer.
REV. JOHN C. EASTMAN, Agent.

FACULTY.

THOMAS EBENEZER THOMAS,
PRESIDENT;
Professor of Biblical Instruction, and Intellectual and Moral Philosophy.

JOHN FINLEY CROWE, D. D.,
VICE PRESIDENT;
And Professor of Rhetoric, Logic, Political Economy, and History.

SAMUEL HARRISON THOMSON, A. M.,
Professor of Mathematics, and Mechanical Philosophy.

MINARD STURGUS, A. M.,
Professor of Languages, and Alumni Professor of English Literature.

JARED MERWIN STONE, A. M.,
Professor of Natural Science.

ABSALOM C. KNOX, A. M.,
Adjunct Professor of Languages, and Principal of the Preparatory Department.

SAMUEL CLARKE MERCER,
Tutor.

HENRY SEYMOUR KRITZ,
Tutor.

CATALOGUE OF STUDENTS.

SENIOR CLASS.

William Maxwell Blackburn,	*Byron, Ia.*
Joshua Selby Brengle,	*Palmyra, Ia.*
Avery Williams Bullock,	*Vernon, Ia.*
John Simpson Frierson,	*Mt. Sylvan, Miss.*
Samuel David Hawthorn,	*Princeton, Ky.*
John Alexander Kimmons,	*Oxford, Miss.*
Claudius Buchanan Henry Martin,	*Livonia, Ia.*
Samuel Clarke Mercer,	*Hanover, Ia.*
Robert Symington Reese,	*Hanover, Ia.*
William Harvey Rice,	*Waveland, Ia.*
William Walton Sickles,	*Pleasant P. O., Ia.*
Alexander Stuart Walker,	*New Ross, Ia.*
Benjamin Rush Whitney,	*Madison, Ia.*
William Alexander Martin Young,	*Hanover, Ia.*

SENIORS, 14.

JUNIOR CLASS.

Joseph W. Aikin,	*Greensburgh, Ky.*
James Madison Alexander,	*Paris, Ill.*
Henry Martyn Bayless,	*Charleston, Ia.*
Joseph Boon,	*Pleasant Hill, Miss.*
James Bruce,	*New Brighton, Pa.*
James W. Brummal,	*Greensburgh, Ky.*
James Huston Burns,	*Dunlap, O.*
Jacob Cooper,	*Somerville, O.*
Bennett H. Davis,	*El Dorado, Ark.*
Theophilus Wilson Guy,	*Cincinnati, O.*
James Simpson Jones,	*Madison. Ia.*
James McEwen Kimmons,	*Oxford, Miss.*
Alexander Mayne,	*Auburn, Mo.*
Archibald V. McKee,	*Greensburgh, Ia.*
William James MacKnight,	*Denmark, Tenn.*
Uriah Millsaps,	*Hargraves, Miss.*
Edward Ethel Porter,	*Memphis, Tenn.*
Benjamin Niles Sawtelle,	*Memphis, Tenn.*
Joseph Gaston Symmes,	*Symmes' Corner, O.*
Robert Francis Taylor,	*Waveland, Ia.*
Joseph Greene Wells,	*Waveland, Ia.*
John Jackson Wheat,	*Hargraves, Miss.*

JUNIORS, 22.

SOPHOMORE CLASS.

Robert Allison,	*Macomb, Ill.*
Joseph Mayo Batchelder,	*Peoria, Ill.*
Stephen James Bovell,	*Paris, Ill.*
Henry Michael Giltner,	*Waveland, Ia.*
Thomas Hibben,	*Hillsboro, O.*
Samuel Hibben,	*Hillsboro, O.*
Thomas Maise Hopkins,	*Ripley, O.*
James Asa Hughes,	*Somerville, O.*
Alexander Martin,	*Salem, Ia.*
James Matlack Scovel,	*Hanover, Ia.*
Sylvester Fithian Scovel,	*Hanover, Ia.*
George Shannon,	*Hanover, Ia.*
Leander Joseph Sherrill,	*Covington, Tenn.*
Francis Marion Symmes,	*Symmes' Corner, O.*
Paddock Storrs Turner,	*Franklin, O.*
Daniel Price Young,	*Nicholasville, Ky.*

SOPHOMORES, 16.

FRESHMAN CLASS.

Lyman Beecher Andrews,	*Northfield, O.*
John Clayton Bell,	*Hanover, Ia.*
George Washington Brackenridge,	*Boonville, Ia.*
Lewis Isaac Drake,	*Springdale, O.*
Jeremiah Mead Drake,	*Springdale, O.*
Otho Evans,	*Franklin, O.*
James D. Fort,	*Richland, Miss.*
Joshua Bolles Garritt,	*Delphi, Ia.*
John Henry Gaster,	*Frankfort, Ia.*
Michael Herold,	*Cincinnati, O.*
Henry Seymour Kritz,	*Buena Vista, Ia.*
Harvey Lamb,	*Galena, Ia.*
Charles Lee,	*Hanover, Ia.*
William Pope Lemaster,	*Memphis, Tenn.*
John Hancock McRae,	*Pensacola, Flor.*
James Alexander McWhorter McRee,	*Somerville, Tenn.*
Joseph Warren Mahan,	*Neville, O.*
William Henry Mahin,	*Crawfordsville, Ia.*
Sidney Jonathan Mayhew,	*Hamilton, O.*
William Wright Millsaps,	*Hargraves, Miss.*
Joseph Potts Moreland,	*Owensboro, Ky.*
Alexander William Reese,	*Hanover, Ia.*
Joseph Clendennin Ross,	*Twenty Mile Stand, O.*
Henry Spencer Scovel,	*Hanover, Ia.*
James Leonard West,	*Franklin, Ky.*
William Wheat,	*Hargraves, Miss.*
James Jolly Wilson,	*Cynthiana, O.*

FRESHMEN, 27.

PREPARATORY DEPARTMENT.

SENIOR CLASS.

James Barnes Craig,	*Danville, Ky.*
Stephen Crane,	*Symmes' Corner, O.*
Isaac Watts Elsey,	*Rockville, Ia.*
John Hollins,	*Pensacola, Flor.*
Joseph Sterritt Hollins,	*Pensacola, Flor.*
William Hall Huston,	*Symmes' Corner, O.*
Nathaniel Field Lemaster,	*Memphis, Tenn.*
James Moore Loughborough,	*Louisville, Ky.*
James Brown Payne,	*Lexington, Ky.*
Albert E. Riddles,	*Orleans, Ia.*
John William Sickles,	*Utica, N. Y.*
William Rondeau Sim,	*Golconda, Ill.*

SENIORS, 12.

JUNIOR CLASS.

Parker Thomas Beall,	*Deersville, O.*
James Elijah Bright,	*Brownsville, Tenn.*
David Graham Bruce,	*New Brighton, Pa.*
Paul Huston Burns,	*Dunlap, O.*
Robert Alexander Mitchel Campbell,	*Paoli, Ia.*
James Brown Cannon,	*Louisville, Ky.*
William Coffin,	*Paoli, Ia.*
John Corrie,	*Hanover, Ia.*
Madison Evans,	*Taylorsport, Ia.*
Christopher Elison Frith,	*Liberty, Miss.*
Barsabas Giltner,	*N. Washington, Ia.*
Henry Brown Graham,	*Symmes' Corner, O.*
James Graham,	*Symmes' Corner, O.*
David Burr Hood,	*Ft. Wayne, Ia.*
John McClanahan Irwin,	*Providence, N. C.*
Robert Calvin Irwin,	*Hanover, Ia.*
Henry Lagow,	*Princeton, Ia.*
Walter Lawrence,	*Cincinnati, O.*
James McCarty,	*Frankfort, Ia.*
Thomas Black McChord,	*Hillsboro, Ill.*
Alexander MacGregor,	*Cannelton, Ia.*
Henry MacGregor,	*Cannelton, Ia.*
Cornelius Wycoff Hall McNiel,	*Symmes' Corner, O.*
Alexander McMechan,	*Collinsville, O.*
Zachariah McCutchen Mahorney,	*Hanover, Ia.*
John Minor Millikin,	*Hamilton, O.*
William Jackson Millsaps,	*Hargraves, Miss.*
Martin Van Buren Owens,	*Springville, Ia.*
John L. Reed,	*Cynthiana, O.*
John R. Ritchie,	*Smyrna, Ia.*

Leander Armistead Riely,	*Orleans, Ia.*
Francis Sim,	*Golconda, Ill.*
Thomas Shannon,	*Hanover, Ia.*
Abner Lowry Shannon,	*Hanover, Ia.*
Isaac Newton Stevens,	*Canal Fulton, O.*
Elijah Willis Still,	*Hanover, Ia.*
Thomas Thorn Swan,	*Hanover, Ia.*
John Lindsay Swan,	*Saluda, Ia.*
William Bloomer Truax,	*Paoli, Ia.*
Thomas Wallace,	*Springdale, O.*
Isaac G. Webb,	*Dover, Mo.*
John Alexander Woodward,	*Hanover, Ia.*
John Milton Youart,	*Troy, O.*

JUNIORS, 43.

IRREGULARS.

Thomas Alexander Beverley,	*Henderson, Ky.*
Patrick Henry Bland,	*Louisville, Ky.*
Joseph Cilley,	*Cleves, O.*
William Coleman,	*Colemansville, Ky.*
James Guthrie Cox,	*Bardstown, Ky.*
James C. Finley,	*Laporte, Ia.*
Richard Henry George,	*Simpsonville, Ky.*
David Graham,	*Reynoldsburgh, O.*
David C. Herrider,	*Cleves, O.*
Columbus Clay Kalfus,	*Shepherdsville, Ky.*
William Winchester Locke,	*Harmony Landing, Ky.*
James Irwin Lodge,	*Madison, Ia.*
George Washington McCague,	*Snow Hill, Ky.*
John McEnery,	*Monroe, La.*
David Felter Marshall,	*Twenty Mile Stand, O.*
Robert Shannon,	*Hanover, Ia.*
William Jones Smith,	*Newcastle, Ky.*
George B. Sparks,	*Cincinnati, O.*
James Dunn Spear,	*Logansport, Ia.*
John C. Stephens,	*Newtown, Ia.*
Anthony Symmes,	*Hamilton, O.*
Joseph L. Thornton,	*Logansport, Ia.*
William Carley Vallette,	*Cincinnati, O.*
David Perine Vinton,	*Lafayette, Ia.*
Stephen J. Wade,	*Venice, O.*
Joseph Martin Windsor.	*N. Washington, Ia.*

IRREGULARS, 26.

SUMMARY.

UNDERGRADUATES.
    Seniors, - - - - - - - - 14
    Juniors, - - - - - - - - 22
    Sophomores, - - - - - - 16
    Freshmen, - - - - - - - 27
                                 — 79

PREPARATORY.
    Seniors, - - - - - - - - 12
    Juniors, - - - - - - - - 43
                                 — 55

Irregulars, - - - - - - - 26

TOTAL, - - - - - - - - 160

PROPORTION FROM DIFFERENT STATES.

Indiana, - - - 63	Missouri, - - 2
Ohio, - - - 41	Pennsylvania, - - 2
Kentucky, - - 19	New York, - - 1
Mississippi, - - 11	N. Carolina, - - 1
Tennessee, - - 8	Louisiana, - - 1
Illinois, - - 7	Arkansas, - - 1
Florida, - - - 3	

ADMISSION.

CANDIDATES for admission into the Freshman Class are examined in Arithmetic; Geography, ancient and modern; Algebra; the English, Latin, and Greek Grammars; Bullions' Greek Reader, or an equivalent; Cæsar's Commentaries, select Orations of Cicero, and Sallust. They must also furnish testimonials of good moral character; and if from another College, must bring certificates of honorable dismission. Candidates for a higher standing are examined in that part of the course already studied by the class which they propose to enter.

"Before any student shall be admitted to actual standing in any class, he shall present to the President a written receipt from the Treasurer of the corporation, showing that he has complied with the statutes relating to College charges and scholarships; after which he shall be matriculated."

Course of Instruction.

PREPARATORY DEPARTMENT.

JUNIOR CLASS.

WINTER TERM.
- Andrews and Stoddard's Latin Grammar, Reader and Exercises.
- Bullions' Greek Grammar and Reader.
- Robinson's Algebra.
- Watts and Shimeall's Scripture History.

SUMMER TERM.
- Cæsar's Commentaries, Andrews' edition.
- Bullions' Greek Reader.
- Robinson's Algebra.
- Watts and Shimeall's Scripture History.

SENIOR CLASS.

WINTER TERM.
- Andrews' Sallust.
- Bullions' Greek Reader.
- Mitchel's Classical Geography.
- Watts and Shimeall's Scripture History.
- Exercises in Latin and Greek composition, and in written translations.

SUMMER TERM.
- Cicero's Orations, (Zumpt and Schmidt's series).
- Coleman's Biblical Geography.
- Robinson's Algebra reviewed.
- Bullions' Greek Reader.
- Exercises in Latin and Greek composition, and in written translations.

COLLEGE PROPER.

FRESHMAN CLASS.

WINTER TERM.
- Cooper's Virgil.
- Xenophon's Anabasis, Owen's edition.
- Davies' Plane Geometry, Mensuration, and Plane Trigonometry.
- Greek Testament (Gospels and Acts).
- Horne's Biblical Antiquities, abridged edition.
- Bojesen's Manual of Roman antiquities.

SUMMER TERM.
- Cooper's Virgil.
- Homer's Odyssey, Owen's edition.
- Davies' Surveying and Solid Geometry.
- Greek Testament (Epistles).
- Bojesen's Manual of Grecian Antiquities.

SOPHOMORE CLASS.

WINTER TERM.
- Lincoln's Livy.
- Homer's Odyssey.
- Davies' Spherical Trigonometry, and its applications.
- Davies' Analytical Geometry.
- Greek Testament (Epistles finished).
- Taylor's Manual of Ancient History.

SUMMER TERM.
- Cicero de Senectute, and de Amicitia, Dillaway's edition.
- Xenophon's Memorabilia, Anthon's edition.
- Davies' Analytical Geometry.
- Blair's Rhetoric.
- Taylor's Manual of Modern History.
- Ecclesiastical History.

JUNIOR CLASS.

WINTER TERM.
- Horace.
- Demosthenes de Corona, Champlin's edition.
- Olmstead's Natural Philosophy, 1st vol.
- Upham's Intellectual Philosophy.
- Horne's Evidences of Christianity, and Sacred Criticism, abridged edition.
- Cutter's Anatomy and Physiology.

SUMMER TERM.
- Germania and Agricola of Tacitus.
- Plato's Gorgias, Woolsey's edition.
- Olmstead's Natural Philosophy, 2d vol.
- Wayland's Political Economy.
- Wayland's Moral Philosophy.
- Woods' Botany.

SENIOR CLASS.

WINTER TERM.
- Nordheimer's Hebrew Grammar and Chrestomathy.
- Hebrew Bible.
- Olmstead's Astronomy.
- Silliman's Chemistry.
- Whately's Logic.
- Paley's Natural Theology, Paxton's edition.
- Tusculan Questions, Dillaway's edition.
- Woolsey's Greek Plays.

SUMMER TERM.
{
Hebrew Bible.
Lowth's Lectures on Hebrew Poetry.
Shaw's English Literature.
Butler's Analogy with Wilson's Criticisms.
Hitchcock's Geology.
Mineralogy.
Elements of Political Science.
}

The preceding course is so arranged as to require of every class four recitations, of one hour each, daily, excepting Saturday. These recitations are attended between the hours of 8 and 12, A. M.; leaving the remainder of the day for study and recreation. Exercises in declamation and composition are required throughout the whole course.

Changes of the particular authors recited may sometimes be introduced; but they will not affect *the amount* of study required. Except where such changes are made, students will be required to furnish themselves with *the editions* mentioned

Besides the text-book recitations in Anatomy, Physiology, Chemistry and Geology, courses of Lectures, accompanied with illustrations and experiments, will be delivered by Prof. Stone.

There is a private examination of all the class, at the close every month, except the last in each session; when the *public* examinations are held by a Committee of the Board. Reports of the conduct and progress of each student are forwarded to parents or guardians in March, August and December.

The PUBLIC COMMENCEMENT takes place on the second Thursday in August; after which there is a vacation until the last Monday in September. The winter term closes with the last Thursday in March; and is followed by a vacation until the last Monday in April. It is *particularly important* that the students attend *from the very beginning* of the session. *In most cases, the loss of a few weeks, or even days, seriously affects the future standing of a pupil in his class.* No student is allowed to be absent, without special leave, except in vacations.

RELIGIOUS EXERCISES AND INSTRUCTION.

It will be seen, from the course of study above laid down, that *a daily recitation in the Holy Scriptures*, in English, Greek or Hebrew, or something directly connected with them, is attended by every student, whether in the College or Preparatory Department. By this means, the historical portions of the Old Testament, Biblical Geography, the New Testament in Greek, Ecclesiastical History, the evidences of Christianity, sacred Criticism, portions of the Hebrew Bible, Natural Theology, and the Analogy of Religion natural and revealed to the constitution and course of nature, are carefully and faithfully studied. In addition to this, there is a Sabbath recitation, by classes, in the Assembly's catechism, or the Bible; a public, Sabbath service appropriated to the students; and daily prayers in the Chapel. The students are also expected to attend the Sabbath morning service of the congregation worshipping in the Chapel, or of some congregation in the vicinity, if their parents prefer any of the latter. The Methodist, Associate Reformed, and Associate Churches have regular service in or near the village.

EXPENSES.

The entire annual expenditures of a student need not exceed $100 or $120, viz:

Tuition, (winter term $15, summer do. $10,)	$25 00
Contingent fee,	1 00
Boarding with families, in a furnished room, at $1 50 to $1 75, per week,	$60 to 70
Fuel, lights, washing, &c.,	10 to 15
Text-books, &c.,	5 to 10

Boarding in clubs will cost from 50 cents to 75 cents per week; and many board themselves at a lower rate. The other expenses, for clothing, &c., will, of course, vary with the taste and habits of the student. Although Hanover presents few temptations to extravagance, yet parents are *earnestly advised* to require of their sons a detailed account of their expenditures. The laws of the Institution require that every pupil under fourteen years of age, be placed under the care of some member of the Faculty, without whose written permission the boy can make no purchases. The younger portion of the students are also required to board where the Faculty may direct, and where they may exercise a more careful and frequent supervision. A limited number will be received into the family of Prof. Stone.

SCHOLARSHIPS.

The endowment of this Institution, so far as it has been secured, is in the form of scholarships; a part ot which are under the control of the corporation, and a part at the disposal of the donors. The following rules were adopted at the last meeting of the Board, in reference to these scholarships; to which the particular attention of the parties concerned is requested.

"*Every person applying for admission as a beneficiary of a scholarship under the control of the donors, shall present to the Treasurer, at the beginning of each session,* A WRITTEN CERTIFICATE, *from those controlling the scholarship, of his right to such benefit; when,* AFTER PAYING WHATEVER INTEREST MAY BE DUE ON SAID SCHOLARSHIP, *he shall receive an acknowledgment of his right, which he shall lodge with the President.*"

"*The scholarships subject to the disposal of the Corporation, may be occupied by such applicants as the Faculty shall select, after satisfactorly inquiry into their circumstances, character and attainments; the preference being given, (cæteris paribus,) to those who give the best evidence of scholarship.*"

"*There shall at no time be more than one student upon each scholarship.*"

Indigent and deserving young men, placed upon scholarships by the Faculty, are relieved, wholly or in part, from the payment of tuition fees.

SOCIETIES, LIBRARIES, ETC.

There are two societies connected with the College,—the *Union Literary* and the *Philalethean*, whose libraries number about *fifteen hundred* volumes apiece. The *Society of Inquiry* has also begun to collect a Library, maps, &c. The College Library, which comprises nearly *two thousand* well selected volumes, is accessible to all the students. The Cabinet contains several hundred specimens in Mineralogy and Geology. The Laboratory is supplied with the apparatus most necessary for chemical experiments.

GENERAL REMARKS.

The village of Hanover is situated upon an elevated bluff of the Ohio river, six miles below Madison, Indiana; in a region of remarkable salubrity and beauty. The village and neighborhood are characterized by morality, and the absence of all ordinary temptations to vice and idleness. Intoxicating liquors have never been sold in the township; the traffic being prohibited by popular vote. The Ohio river, and the railways from Madison and Cincinnati, place Hanover within twenty-four hours of all the principal points in Indiana, and western Ohio.

Hanover College is controlled by a Board of Trustees, one half of whom are appointed by the Presbyterian Synods of Indiana and Northern Indiana. All its officers are Ministers or members of the Presbyterian Church. Since the publication of our last Catalogue, the Board has purchased a farm, lying between the village and the Ohio; upon a beautiful point of which, overlooking the river, and commanding a view of its course for fifteen or twenty miles, it is proposed to erect a new College building, so soon as the necessary funds can be obtained. The friends of the College will be glad to learn that its permanent endowment from scholarships already exceeds *forty thousand dollars;* some *seven thousand* of which have been secured since last November.

THE

NINETEENTH

ANNUAL CIRCULAR

OF

HANOVER COLLEGE;

COMPRISING THE

CATALOGUE, COURSE OF STUDY, ETC.

AUGUST, 1851.

PRINTED FOR HANOVER COLLEGE:
BY JOHN D. THORPE, FOURTH STREET, CINCINNATI.
1851.

BOARD OF TRUSTEES.

Rev. JOHN FINLEY CROWE, D. D., President.

BY WHOM ELECTED.		TERM EXPIRES.
Bd.	Rev. JAMES BROWN, of Madison,	A. D. 1851.
Bd.	Rev. WILLIAM SICKLES, of Switzerland Co.,	"
Bd.	Rev. MOSES ARNOTT, of Hanover,	"
Bd.	W. McKEE DUNN, Esq., of Madison,	
Bd.	WM. A. BULLOCK, Esq., of Vernon,	"
S. S.	Rev. J. G. MONFORT, of Greensburg,	"
S. S.	Rev. THOMAS S. CROWE, of Hanover,	"
S. S.	Rev. JAMES A. McKEE, of Franklin,	"
Bd.	Rev. N. L. RICE, D. D., of Cincinnati, O.,	1852.
Bd.	Rev. S. R. WILSON, of Cincinnati, O.,	"
Bd.	Rev. SAMUEL STEEL, D. D., of Hillsboro, O.,	"
Bd.	ALEX. GUY, M. D., of Cincinnati, O.,	
S. S.	Rev. D. V. SMOCK, of Crawfordsville,	
S. S.	Rev. D. M. STEWART, of Rushville,	
S. S.	Rev. C. LEAVENWORTH, of Indianapolis,	"
S. S.	Rev. H. H. CAMBERN, of Charleston,	"
Bd.	Rev. JOHN FINLEY CROWE, D. D., of Hanover,	1853.
Bd.	JOHN L. SCOTT, Esq., of Cincinnati, O.,	"
Bd.	A. R. FORSYTH, of Greensburg,	"
Bd.	JOHN P. BANTA, of Franklin,	
S. S.	Rev. P. D. GURLEY, D. D., of Dayton, O.,	
S. S.	Rev. DANIEL STEWART. D. D., of N. Albany,	
S. S.	Hon. WILLIAMSON DUNN, of Hanover,	
S. S.	JESSE D. CARMICHAEL, of Greensburg,	
N. S.	Rev. W. C. HOLLIDAY, of Indianapolis,	"
N. S.	S. D. MAXWELL, of Frankfort,	"
Bd.	Rev. THO. E. THOMAS, D. D, of Hanover,	1854.
Bd.	Rev. JNO. M. STEVENSON, of N. Albany,	"
Bd.	Rev. DANIEL LATTIMORE, of Vernon,	"
Bd.	JAMES BLAKE, Esq., of Indianapolis,	
S. S.	Rev. D. D. McKEE, of Fairfield,	
S. S.	Rev. JNO. F. SMITH. of Vincennes,	
S. S.	ROBERT HAMILTON, of Greensburg,	
S. S.	JAMES M. RAY, Esq., of Indianapolis.	
N. S.	Rev. WM. Y. ALLEN, of Rockville,	
N. S.	ISAAC COE, M. D., of Indianapolis.	

Prof. S. H. THOMSON,   Secretary,
Rev. THOMAS S. CROWE,   Treasurer,
Rev. JNO. C. EASTMAN,   Financial Agent.

FACULTY
AND INSTRUCTORS.

Rev. THOMAS EBENEZER THOMAS, D. D., President,
    Professor of Biblical Instruction, and Intellectual and Moral Philosophy.

Rev. JOHN FINLEY CROWE, D. D., Vice President,
    Professor of Rhetoric, Logic, Political Economy, and History.

Rev. JARED MERWIN STONE, A. M.,
    Professor of Natural Science.

SAMUEL HARRISON THOMSON, A. M.,
    Professor of Mathematics and Mechanical Philosophy.

MINARD STURGUS, A. M.,
    Professor of Languages, and Alumni Professor of English Literature.

ABSALOM C. KNOX, A. M.,
    Adjunct Professor of Languages, and Principal of the Preparatory Department.

M. PIEDFOURCK,
    Teacher of the French Language.

JOSEPH GREENE WELLS,
    Tutor.

HENRY SEYMOUR KRITZ,
    Tutor.

RESIDENT GRADUATES.

Samuel Emmett Barr, A. B.,	Hanover, Ind.
Williamson Dunn Symington, A. B.,	Hanover, Ind.

UNDERGRADUATES.

SENIOR CLASS.

James Madison Alexander,	Paris, Ill.
Henry Martyn Bayless,	Charleston, Ind.
Joseph Boon,	Pleasant Hill, Miss.
James Bruce,	N. Brighton, Pa.
James Huston Burns,	Dunlap, O.
Bennett Hillsman Davis,†	Eldorado, Ark.
Theophilus Wilson Guy,	Cincinnati, O.
Edmund Goforth Hallowell,†	Lexington, Ind.
James Simpson Jones,	Madison, Ind.
James McEwen Kimmons,	Oxford, Miss.
Cornelius McCain,	Delphi, Ind.
Hugh Mac Hatton,	Clark's Run, O.
Archibald McKee,	Greensburgh, Ind.
William James McKnight,	Denmark, Tenn.
Alexander Mayne,	Auburn, Mo.
Uriah Millsaps,†	Hargraves, Miss.
Edward Ethel Porter,	Memphis, Tenn.
Benjamin Niles Sawtell,	Memphis, Tenn.
Joseph Gaston Symmes,	Symmes' Corner, O.
Robert Francis Taylor,	Waveland, Ind.
Joseph Greene Wells,	Waveland, Ind.
John Jackson Wheat,†	Hargraves, Miss.

SENIORS, 22.

†Left before Graduating.

JUNIOR CLASS.

Robert Alison,	*Macomb, Ill.*
Joseph Mayo Batchelder,	*Peoria, Ill.*
Stephen James Bovell,	*Paris, Ill.*
Jonathan Turner Carthel,	*Trenton, Tenn.*
John McCutchen Coyner,	*S. Salem, O.*
Benjamin Parke Dewey,	*Charleston, Ind.*
Robert Chrystie Galbraith,	*Frankfort, O.*
Henry Michael Giltner,	*Waveland, Ind.*
Thomas Hibben,	*Hillsboro, O.*
Thomas Mayse Hopkins,	*Ripley, O.*
Joseph Mac Hatton,	*Clark's Run, O.*
Alexander Martin,	*Salem, Ind.*
James Matlack Scovel,	*Hanover, Ind.*
Leander Joseph Sherrill,	*Covington, Tenn.*
Francis Marion Symmes,	*Symmes' Corner, O.*
Paddock Storrs Turner,	*Franklin, O.*
Daniel Price Young,	*Nicholasville, Ky.*

JUNIORS, 17.

SOPHOMORE CLASS.

Lyman Beecher Andrews,	*Northfield, O.*
James Morrison Bodine,	*Fairfield, Ky.*
Francis Willard Bristol,	*Lexington, Ky.*
James Guthrie Cox,	*Bardstown, Ky.*
Lewis Isaac Drake,	*Springdale, O.*
Jeremiah Mead Drake,	*Springdale, O.*
Joshua Bolles Garritt,	*Delphi, Ind.*
Henry Seymour Kritz,	*Buena Vista, Ind.*
Harvey Lamb,	*Galena, Ind.*
Charles Lee,	*Hanover, Ind.*
William Pope Lemaster,	*Memphis, Tenn.*
David Tilford McCampbell,	*Charleston, Ind.*
John Hancock McRae,	*Pensacola, Flor.*
James Alexander McRee,	*Somerville, Tenn.*
Joseph Warren Mahan,	*Newville, O.*
William Henry Mahin,	*Crawfordsville, Ind.*
William Right Millsaps,	*Hargaves. Miss.*
William Green Millsaps,	*Hargraves, Miss.*
James Sanderson Rankin,	*Hanover, Ind.*
Henry Spencer Scovel,	*Hanover, Ind.*
Sylvester Fithian Scovel,	*Hanover, Ind.*
Jackson Jay Smith,	*Simpsonville, Ky.*
James Leonard West,	*Franklin, Ky.*
William Wheat,	*Hargraves, Miss.*
Spottswood Leland Wills,	*High Grove, Ky.*
James Jolly Wilson,	*Cynthiana, O.*
Jared Ryker Woodfill,	*Bryantsburg, Ind.*

SOPHOMORES, 27.

FRESHMAN CLASS.

Stephen Cromwell Adair,	*Morganfield, Ky.*
Andrew Witherspoon Adams,	*Troy, O.*
William Martin Alexander,	*Carpentersville, Ind.*
Reuben Bell Berry,	*Versailles, Ky.*
James Elijah Bright,	*Brownsville, Tenn.*
Robert Alexander Mitchell Campbell,	*Paoli, Ind.*
Thomas Marquis Coen,	*Rensselaer, Ind.*
Stephen Crane,	*Symmes' Corner, O.*
James D. Fort,	*Richland, Miss.*
John Henry Gaster,	*Frankfort, Ind.*
Barsabas Giltner,	*N. Washington, Ind.*
Samuel Newell Goodhue,	*Paris, Ind.*
Michael Herold,	*Cincinnati, O.*
William Hall Huston,	*Symmes' Corner, O.*
Robert Irwin,	*Muncie, Ind.*
Nathaniel Field Lemaster,	*Memphis, Tenn.*
James Irwin Lodge,	*Madison, Ind.*
Duncan D. McLean,	*Franklin, Ind.*
Gideon Blackburn McLeary,	*Covington, Tenn.*
Alexander McMechan,	*Collinsville, O.*
John Minor Millikin,	*Hamilton, O.*
Webster Millsaps,	*Hargraves, Miss.*
Isaac Brown Moore,	*Monticello, Ind.*
Edward Hubbard Rutherford,	*Brownsville, Tenn.*
John William Sickles,	*Utica, N. Y.*
William Rondeau Sim,	*Golconda, Ill.*
William Bloomer Truax,	*Paoli, Ind.*
Thomas Wallace,	*Springdale, O.*
Joseph Glass Wilson,	*Bardstown, Ky.*
John Milton Youart,	*Troy, O.*

FRESHMEN, 30.

PREPARATORY DEPARTMENT.

SENIOR CLASS.

Henry Brown Graham,	*Hamilton, O.*
Thomas Ainsworth Holliday,	*Gallatin, Miss.*
Joseph Kennedy,	*Covington, Ky.*
Thomas Black McChord,	*Hillsboro, Ill.*
Robert Clark McGee,	*Charleston, Ind.*
Thomas Elijah Millsaps,	*Hargraves, Miss.*
Thomas Jefferson Millsaps,	*Hargraves, Miss.*
John Samuel Park,	*Memphis, Tenn.*
Francis Sim,	*Golconda, Ill.*
Edward Mackintosh Watson,	*Hargraves, Miss.*
Reuben Franklin Wheat,	*Hargraves, Miss.*

SENIOR PREPARATORY, 11.

JUNIOR CLASS.

James Bailie Adams,	*Pleasant, Ind.*
John Campbell Anderson,	*Lexington, Ky.*
Tiba King Ashby,	*Bedford, Ky.*
William George Bayne,	*Louisville, Ky.*
Taylor Becket,*	*Rossville, O.*
David Campbell,	*Lexington, Ind.*
James Brown Cannon,	*Louisville, Ky.*
Celestin Octave Carlin,	*Tigerville, La.*
William Brown Chamberlain,	*Hanover, Ind.*
Erastus Spaulding Close,	*Springdale, O.*
William Coffin,	*Paoli, Ind.*
Hiram Baxter Collins,	*Vincennes, Ind.*
Allen Cullen,	*Patriot, Ind.*
John Williamson Dunn,	*Frankfort, Ind.*
Dyer Burgess Eastman,	*Hanover, Ind.*
Charles Thomas Elliott,	*Dayton, Ind.*
Samuel Newell Fisher,	*Orleans, Ind.*
Thomas Curtis Gilpin,	*Mt. Carmel, Ind.*
Levin Elliott Goslee,	*Campbellsburg, Ky.*
Henry Washington Green,	*Vicksburg, Miss,*
Samuel Brown Holcombe,	*Madison, Ind.*
Alfred William Hynes,	*Hanover, Ind.*
John Chandler Irwin,	*Mansfield, O.*
Robert Calvin Irwin,	*Hanover, Ind.*
Henry Keigwin,	*Louisville, Ky.*
William Job Klapp,	*Scipio, Ind.*
Joseph Winslow Levett,	*Memphis, Tenn.*
William Campbell McCaskey,	*Canton, Ind.*
David Mac Dill,	*Sparta, Ill.*
James Charlott McElroy,	*Greenecastle, Ind.*
Cornelius Wikoff Hall McNeil,	*Symmes' Corner, O.*
William Jackson Millsaps,	*Hargraves, Miss.*
Robert Daniel Morris,	*Milton, Ky.*
John Morrison,	*Tigerville, La.*
James Kennedy Patterson,	*Elizabethtown, Ind.*
Joseph Allen Porter,	*Lodiana, Northern India.*
Benjamin Rankin,	*Hanover, Ind.*
John Ritchie,	*Smyrna, Ind.*
Robert Rogers,	*Wheeling, Va.*

*Deceased.

Charles Fary Ross,	*Jefferson, Ind.*
Joseph Franklin Saunders,	*Cross Roads, Ky.*
Thomas Shannon,	*Hanover, Ind.*
John Dorth Shannon,	*Hanover, Ind.*
Nelson Smith,	*New Castle, Pa.*
John McLain Stalker,	*Salem, Ind.*
Isaac Newton Stevens,	*Canal Fulton, O.*
Thomas Thorn Swan,	*Hanover, Ind.*
John Lindsay Swan,	*Saluda, Ind.*
George Patton Talbot,	*Louisville, Ky.*
James Harvey Tedford,	*Pittsburgh, Ind.*
Conrad Varner,	*New Hope, Ind.*
John Henry Webb,	*Cordova, Ky.*
Benjamin Dubois Wikoff,	*Franklin, O.*
Francis George Wilson,	*New Frankfort, Ind.*
Samuel Gregg Woodfill,	*Bryantsburg, Ind.*

JUNIOR PREPARATORY, 55.

ENGLISH AND SCIENTIFIC DEPARTMENT.

William Goforth Armstrong,	*Jeffersonville, Ind.*
Allen Thomas Barnes,	*Hanover, Ind.*
Clayton Curl Bell,	*Hanover, Ind.*
John Valentine Bland,	*Louisville, Ky.*
William Bland,	*Louisville, Ky.*
John Williamson Brough,	*Madison, Ind.*
Paul Huston Burns,	*Dunlap, O.*
Josiah Brown,	*Montgomery, O.*
David Charlton,	*Pleasant, Ind.*
Daniel Field Clark,	*Golconda, Ill.*
John Field,	*Golconda, Ill.*
Harvey Bassett Foster,	*Madison, Ind.*
Richard Henry George,	*Simpsonville, Ky.*
William Addison Gilliland,	*Ripley, O.*
William Riley Hathway,	*Owensboro, Ky.*
John Hervey,	*Wheeling, Va.*
James Samuel Lewis,	*West Point, Ky.*
Richard Claiborn Longest,	*Louisville, Ky.*
William Wesley Moore,	*Fishersville, Ky.*
James Newton Pogue,	*Hanover, Ind.*
George Washington Saunders,	*Shepherdsville, Ky.*
Jesse Forer Scott,	*Campbellsburg, Ky.*
Abner Lowry Shannon,	*Hanover, Ind.*
Benjamin Franklin Slocumb,	*Vicksburg, Miss.*
Henry Warren Snapp,	*Snow Hill, Ky.*
William Frederick Snapp,	*Snow Hill, Ky.*
William Snoddy,	*Dayton, Ind.*
Anthony Lockwood Symmes,	*Covington, Ky.*
John Logan Townsend,	*Winonia, Ky.*
William Vannice,	*Morefield, Ind.*
Guy William Vinyard,	*Golconda, Ill.*
David Perine Vinton,	*Lafayette, Ind.*
Archibald Cameron Voris,	*Bennington, Ind.*
Allen Fletcher West,	*Hanover, Ind.*

IRREGULARS, 34.

ADMISSION.

Candidates for admission into the Freshman Class are examined in Arithmetic; Geography, ancient and modern; the English, Latin, and Greek Grammars; Bullions' Greek Reader, or an equivalent; Cæsar's Commentaries; Select Orations of Cicero, and Sallust. They must furnish testimonials of good moral character; and, if from another College, must bring certificates of honorable dismission. Candidates for a higher standing are examined upon that part of the course already studied by the class which they propose to enter.

"Before any student shall be admitted to actual standing in any class, he shall present to the President a written receipt from the Treasurer of the Corporation, showing that he has complied with the statutes relating to College charges and scholarships."

The last two days in each vacation are the stated time for examining such as seek admission into the College classes.

SUMMARY.

Resident Graduates,	2
Undergraduates—	
Seniors,	22
Juniors,	17
Sophomores,	27
Freshmen,	30
	— 96
Preparatory,	66
Irregulars,	34
Total,	198

REPRESENTATION FROM THE SEVERAL STATES, &C.

Indiana,	78	Virginia,	2
Ohio,	34	Louisiana,	2
Kentucky,	34	Florida,	1
Mississippi,	17	Missouri,	1
Tennessee,	13	N. York,	1
Illinois,	11	Arkansas,	1
Pennsylvania,	2	Northern India,	1

Average age of the students, *nineteen* years.

COURSE OF INSTRUCTION.

PREPARATORY DEPARTMENT.

JUNIOR CLASS.

I.

Bullions' Latin Grammar, with praxis.
Bullions' Greek Grammar, with praxis.
Arithmetic reviewed.
Historical portions of the Old Testament.

II.

Bullions' Latin Grammar and Reader.
Bullions' Greek Grammar and Reader.
Robinson's Algebra.
Historical portions of the Old Testament.

III.

Bullions' Latin Grammar and Reader.
Bullions' Greek Grammar and Reader.
Robinson's Algebra.
Historical portions of the Old Testament.

SENIOR CLASS.

I.

Bullions' Cæsar.
Bullions' Greek Reader.
Robinson's Algebra.
Historical portions of the New Testament.

II.

Sallust.
Bullions' Greek Reader.
Mitchell's Classical Geography.
Historical portions of the New Testament.

III.

Cicero's Orations.
Bullions' Greek Reader.
Robinson's Algebra reviewed.
Coleman's Biblical Geography.

COLLEGE.

FRESHMAN CLASS.

I.

Cooper's Virgil.
Owen's Anabasis.
Davies' Plane Geometry.
Murray's English Grammar, 8 vo. edition.
Robinson's Harmony of the Gospels.
Horne's Biblical Antiquities. (Abridged edition.)
Bojesen's Roman Antiquities.

II.

Cooper's Virgil.
Owen's Anabasis.
Davies' Plane Trigonometry and Surveying.
English Grammar and Composition.
Robinson's Harmony of the Gospels.
Horne's Biblical Antiquities.
Bojesen's Roman and Grecian Antiquities.

III.

Cooper's Virgil.
Owen's Anabasis.
Davies' Surveying and Navigation.
Robinson's Harmony of the Gospels.
Bojesen's Grecian Antiquities.
Blair's Rhetoric.

SOPHOMORE CLASS.

I.

Lincoln's Livy.
Owen's Odyssey.
Davies' Solid Geometry.
Taylor's Manual of Ancient History.

II.

Lincoln's Livy.
Owen's Odyssey.
Davies' Spherical Trigonometry, and Applications.
Taylor's Modern History.
Horne's Evidences of Christianity, and Lectures.

III.

Cicero De Senectute et De Amicitia.
Xenophon's Memorabilia.
Davies' Analytical Geometry.
Ecclesiastical History.
Wood's Botany, and Lectures on Botany and Zoology.

JUNIOR CLASS.

I.

Horace.
Champlin's Demosthenes De Corona.
Olmstead's Natural Philosophy. 1st vol.
Upham's Intellectual Philosophy.
Cutter's Anatomy and Physiology, with Lectures.

II.

Horace.
Demosthenes De Corona.
Olmstead's Natural Philosophy. 1st vol.
Upham's Intellectual Philosophy.
Paley's Natural Theology.

III.

Germania and Agricola of Tacitus.
Woolsey's Plato's Gorgias.
Olmstead's natural Philosophy. 2nd Vol.
Wayland's Political Economy.
Wayland's Moral Philosophy.

SENIOR CLASS.

I.

Nordheimer's Hebrew Grammar.
Hebrew Bible.
Olmstead's Astronomy.
Silliman's Chemistry, with Lectures.
Whately's Logic.

II.

Hebrew.
Silliman's Chemistry.
Epistles of the Greek Testament.
Dillaway's Tusculan Disputations.

III.

Hebrew.
Hitchcock's Geology, and Lectures on Mineralogy.
Butler's Analogy of Natural and Revealed Religion to the Constitution and Course of Nature.
Shaw's English Literature.

The preceding course is so arranged as to require of every class *four re-citations* of one hour each, *daily*, excepting Saturday. These recitations are attended between the hours of 8 and 12 A. M.; leaving the remainder of the day for study and recreation. Changes of the particular authors recited may sometimes be introduced; but they will not affect the *amount* of study required. Except where such changes are made, students will be required to furnish themselves with *the editions* mentioned.

Besides the text-book recitations in Anatomy, Physiology, Chemistry, and Geology, courses of lectures, accompanied with illustrations and experiments, will be delivered by Prof. Stone.

As it often happens that young men not only enter but leave College without a thorough knowledge of their mother tongue, a careful review and philosophical investigation of English Grammar, preparatory to the study of rhetoric, has been introduced into the College course.

At the close of each Term, the several classes are examined upon the studies of that Term. The examination for degrees is upon all the studies of the course. A report of the conduct and progress of each student is forwarded to his parents or guardian in March, August and December.

The collegiate year is divided into *three terms*, of *thirteen weeks* each, and *three vacations*. The *first term* begins on *the fourth Wednesday in September;* the *second,* on the *first Wednesday in January;* and *the third* on the *first Wednesday in May,* closing with THE FIRST WEDNESDAY IN AUGUST, *which is* COMMENCEMENT DAY. It is of great importance that students attend from *the very begining* of the term; especially since so considerable a portion of time is allotted to vacations. *In most cases the loss of a few weeks, or even days, seriously affects the future standing of a pupil.* Absence during term-time, without special leave, is prohibited.

RELIGIOUS EXERCISES

AND

INSTRUCTION.

It will be seen from the course of study above presented, that *a daily recitation in the Holy Scriptures, in English, Greek, or Hebrew,* or something directly connected with them, *is attended by every student,* whether in the College or Preparatory Department. Proficiency in these, as in other studies, is tested by the usual examinations. By this means the historical portions of the Old and New Testaments, Biblical Geography and Antiquities, the New Testament in Greek, Ecclesiastical History, the Evidences of Christianity, portions of the Hebrew Bible, Natural Theology, and the Analogy of Religion, natural and revealed to the constitution and course of nature, are carefully and faithfully studied. In addition to this, there is a Bible or Catechetical recitation on Sabbath morning; a public service on Sabbath afternoon, appropriated to the students;—and daily, morning prayers. The students are also expected to attend the Sabbath morning service of the congregation worshipping in the chapel, or of some congregation in the vicinity, if their parents prefer any of the latter. The Methodist, Associate Reformed, and Associate Churches have regular service in or near the village.

EXPENSES.

The entire annual expenditures of a student need not exceed $125; viz:

Tuition and contingent fee, $10 per term,	$30 00
Boarding with private families, and a furnished room, at $1 50 to $1 75 per week,	$60 to 70 00
Fuel, light, washing, &c.,	10 to 15 00
Books, &c.,	5 to 10 00

Boarding in clubs will cost from *fifty* to *seventy-five cents* per week; and many board themselves at a lower rate. The expense of clothing and pocket-money will of course vary with the taste and habits of the student. Although Hanover presents few temptations to extravagance, yet parents are *earnestly advised* to require of their sons a detailed account of their expenditures. It is also recommended that the funds of young pupils be deposited with some member of the Faculty; without whose written order the boy should make no purchases. The younger class of students are required to board where the Faculty may direct, and where they may exercise a more careful and frequent supervision.

SCHOLARSHIPS.

The endowment of this Institution, so far as it has been secured, is in the form of *Scholarships;* of which the Board has established several sorts. The sum of $400, paid, or secured to the Corporation by note payable within five years, and bearing six per cent. interest in advance upon principal remaining unpaid,—purchases for the owner, his heirs and assigns, a perpetual right to the tuition of one scholar, in Hanover College. The sum of $200, paid, or subscribed under similar conditions, secures a right to twenty years' tuition; after which time, the scholarship is subject to the disposal of the Board for the gratuitous education of candidates for the Gospel Ministry. A church scholarship of $200 secures to the church so contributing, a perpetual right to the tuition of one student, who shall be a member of that church, and appointed by the Session. A Presbyterial scholarship of $200 secures a similar right to a Presbytery, in behalf of pupils who shall be candidates for the Ministry under its care. The *principal* paid on these scholarships is invested by the Corporation in some safe and productive stock; and the *interest only* can be expended for the support of the college.

The sum of $100, *paid within two years at farthest*, with interest in advance on unpaid principal, purchases a right to ten years' tuition within twenty years from the date of subscription. Both principal and interest of this scholarship may be employed for contingent purposes; and the scholarship expires with the owner's right to its use.

The Board has adopted the following rules in reference to scholarships; particular attention to which, by the parties interested, is invited:

"*Every person applying for admission as a beneficiary of a scholarship under the control of the donors, shall present to the Treasurer, at the beginning of each term,* A WRITTEN CERTIFICATE. *from those controlling the scholarship, of his right to such benefit; when, after paying whatever interest may be due on said scholarship, he shall receive an acknowledgment of his right, which he shall lodge with the President.*"

"*The scholarships subject to the disposal of the Corporation may be occupied by such applicants as the Faculty may select, after inquiry into their circumstances, character and attainments; the preference being,* (cæteris paribus,) *to those who give the best evidence of scholarship.*"

"There shall at no time be more than one student upon each scholarship."

N. B. Students placed upon scholarships by the Faculty, are relieved, in part, or wholly, as the case may require, from the payment of tuition fees.

SOCIETIES, LIBRARIES, &C.

There are two Societies connected with the College,—the *Union Literary*, and the *Philalethean*, whose libraries number about *fifteen hundred* volumes apiece. *The Society of Inquiry* has also begun to collect a Library, Maps, &c. The College Library, which comprises nearly *two thousand* well selected volumes, is accessible to the students. The Cabinet contains several thousand specimens in Mineralogy and Geology. The Laboratory is supplied with the apparatus most necessary for chemical experiments.

GENERAL REMARKS.

The village of Hanover is situated upon an elevated bluff of the Ohio river, six miles below Madison, Indiana; in a region of remarkable salubrity and natural beauty. The village and neighborhood are characterized by morality, and the absence of all ordinary temptations to vice and idleness. Intoxicating liquors have never been sold in the township; the traffic being prohibited, annually, by popular vote. The Ohio river, and the railways from Madison and Cincinnati, place Hanover within twenty-four hours of all the principal points in Indiana, and western Ohio. A plank-road from Madison to Hanover, now nearly completed, renders the village easy of access in all seasons of the year.

Hanover College is controlled by a Board of Trustees, one half of whom are appointed by the Board itself, and the other half by the Synods of Indiana and Northern Indiana. All its officers are Ministers or members of the Presbyterian Church.

The Board has recently purchased a farm of 200 acres, lying between the village and the Ohio; upon a beautiful point of which, overlooking the river from an elevation of four hundred feet, and commanding a view of its course for fifteen or twenty miles, it is proposed to erect a new college building, as soon as the necessary funds can be obtained. The friends of the College will be glad to learn that its permanent fund from scholarships already exceeds *forty thousand dollars*.

THE

TWENTIETH

ANNUAL CIRCULAR

OF

HANOVER COLLEGE;

COMPRISING THE

TRIENNIAL AND ANNUAL CATALOGUES,

THE TWENTIETH ANNUAL CIRCULAR

OF

HANOVER COLLEGE;

COMPRISING THE

TRIENNIAL AND ANNUAL CATALOGUES,
COURSE OF STUDIES, &C.

AUGUST, 1852.

PRINTED FOR HANOVER COLLEGE,
BY JOHN D. THORPE, FOURTH STREET, CINCINNATI.
1852.

BOARD OF TRUSTEES.

BY WHOM ELECTED.		TERM EXPIRES.
S. S.	Rev. D. V. SMOCK, Crittenden, Ky.,	A. D. 1852.
S. S.	Rev. D. M. STUART, Rushville,	"
S. S.	Rev. C. LEAVENWORTH, Indianapolis,	"
S. S.	Rev. H. H. CAMBERN, Charleston,	"
Bd.	Rev. JOHN FINLEY CROWE, D. D. Hanover,	1853.
Bd.	JOHN L. SCOTT, Esq. Cincinnati, O.,	"
Bd.	A. R. FORSYTH, Greensburg,	"
Bd.	JOHN P. BANTA, Franklin,	"
S. S.	Rev. P. D. GURLEY, D. D. Dayton, O.,	"
S. S.	Hon. WILLIAMSON DUNN, Hanover,	"
N. S.	Rev. W. C. HOLLIDAY, Indianapolis,	"
N. S.	S. D. MAXWELL, Frankfort,	"
Bd.	Rev. THOMAS E. THOMAS, D. D. Hanover,	1854.
Bd.	Rev. JOHN M. STEVENSON, New Albany,	"
Bd.	Rev. DANIEL LATTIMORE, Vernon,	"
Bd.	JAMES BLAKE, Indianapolis,	"
S. S.	Rev. D. D. McKEE, Fairfield,	"
S. S.	JAMES M. RAY, Indianapolis,	"
N. S.	Rev. WM. Y. ALLEN, Rockville,	"
N. S.	ISAAC COE, M. D. Indianapolis,	"
Bd.	JOHN KING, Madison,	1855.
Bd.	Rev. WM. SICKELS, Switzerland Co.,	"
Bd.	W. McKEE DUNN, Esq. Madison,	"
Bd.	WM. A. BULLOCK, Esq. Vernon,	"
S. S.	Rev. J. G. MONFORT, Greensburg,	"
S. S.	Rev. THOS. S. CROWE, Hanover,	"
N. S.	Rev. JOHN C. EASTMAN, Hanover,	"
N. S.	Rev. SAMUEL N. EVANS, Thorntown,	"
Bd.	Rev. N. L. RICE, D. D. Cincinnati. O.,	1856.
Bd.	Rev. S. R. WILSON, Cincinnati. O.,	"
Bd.	ALEX. GUY, M. D. Cincinnati, O.,	"
Bd.	Rev. W. W. HILL, D. D. Louisville, Ky.,	"

OFFICERS AND STANDING COMMITTEES OF THE BOARD.

Rev. JOHN FINLEY CROWE, *President,*
Rev. THOMAS E. THOMAS, *Secretary,*
Rev. THOMAS S. CROWE, *Treasurer,*
Rev. JOHN C. EASTMAN, *Agent for Building Fund.*

EXECUTIVE COMMITTEE.

Rev. THOMAS E. THOMAS, Hon. WILLIAMSON DUNN,
Rev. THOS. S. CROWE, W. McKEE DUNN, Esq.,
JOHN L. SCOTT, Esq.

AUDITING COMMITTEE.

JAMES BLAKE, Esq., JAMES M. RAY, Esq.

EXAMINING COMMITTEE.

Rev. JOHN M. STEVENSON, Rev. FREDERIC T. BROWN,
W. McKEE DUNN, Esq.

FACULTY.

Rev. THOMAS E. THOMAS, D. D. *President,*
Professor of Biblical Instruction, Psychology, and Moral Philosophy.

Rev. JOHN FINLEY CROWE, D. D. *Vice President,*
Professor of Rhetoric, Logic, History, and Political Economy.

Rev. JARED M. STONE, A. M.
Professor of Natural Science.

S. HARRISON THOMSON, A. M.
Professor of Mathematics and Mechanical Philosophy.

Rev. WILLIAM BISHOP, A. M.
Professor of the Greek Language and Literature.

Rev. WILLIAM HAMILTON, A. M.
Professor of the Latin Language and Literature.

M. PIEDFOURCK,
Instructor in French.

ALUMNI.

CLASS OF 1834.
*Rev. William H. Bruner, A. M.
*Selby Harney,
Rev. John M. McChord, A. M.
Isaac McCoy, A. M.
Rev. Isaac N. Shepherd, A. M.
Rev. Charles K. Thompson, A. M.

CLASS OF 1835.
Rev. Robert S. Bell,
Rev. James Brown, A. M.
Rev. Jonathan Edwards, A. M.
Rev. Robert Simpson, A. M.
Prof. Middleton Goldsmith, A. M., M. D. *Vermont Medical College.*
*James A. Watson, *Tutor in Nashville University,* 1838.

CLASS OF 1836.
Rev. Samuel J. P. Anderson, A. M.
Prof. Noble Butler, A. M., *Han. Coll.* 1836—'39.
Rev. Josiah Crawford,
Rev. David H. Cummins, A. M.
Andrew Fulton, M. D.
Rev. Thos. W. Hynes, A. M. *Prof. Han. Coll.* 1838—'43.
Rev. Wm. W. McLain,
Rev. Samuel F. Morrow, A. M.
Rev. Samuel Newell, A. M.
Rev. David E. Y. Rice, A. M.
Rev. Amos H. Rogers,
*Rev. Nathaniel Schillinger,
Prof. Minard Sturgus, A. M., *Han. Coll.* 1841—'52.
Rev. Samuel R. Wilson, A. M.

CLASS OF 1837.
Rev. Thomas H. Alderdice,
Rev. Franklin Berryhill,
Rev. James Black,
Rev. Samuel N. Evans, A. M.
Edmund W. Hawkins, Esq. A. M.
Rev. John M. Hoge,
Rev. Braxton D. Hunter,

*Deceased.

Rev. Sylvanus Jewett,
Rev. John W. McCormick,
Rev. James A. McKee, A. M.
Rev. Asahel Munson,
Rev. William C. Scott,
Rev. Josiah D. Smith, A. M.
Prof. S. Harrison Thomson, A. M. *Han. Coll.*
James F. Wood.

CLASS OF 1838.

Rev. George B. Armstrong,
William Blair,
James E. Blythe, Esq, A. M. *Member Indiana Constitutional Convention.*
Rev. William K. Brice, A. M.
Alexander M. Brown, Esq. A. M.
Rev. William M. Cheever, A. M.
Rev. James B. Crowe, A. M.
Rev. Thomas S. Crowe, A. M.
Rev. Joseph F. Fenton, A. M.
James J. Gardiner, A. M.
Robert A. Gibson, Esq. A. M.
Rev. Abram T. Hendricks, A. M.
John Jones,
James W. Matthews, A. M.
Rev. George F. Whitworth, A. M.

CLASS OF 1839.

Samuel S. Crowe, A. M.
David S. Dunn, Esq.
William W. Gilliland, Esq. A. M.
*Philander Hamilton, Esq. A. M.
Rev. Ephraim K. Lynn, A. M.
Rev. Fielding G. Strahan, A. M.

CLASS OF 1840.

Rev. Harleigh Blackwell, A. M.
Samuel G. Haas,
Prof. A. C. Knox, A. M. *Han. Coll.* 1844—'52.
Rev. Robert C. Matthews, A. M.
Rev. Robert Symington, A. M.

CLASS OF 1841.

Charles M. Hays, Esq.
John L. King, Esq. *Member Ia. Legislature.*
George C. Lyen.

*Deceased.

CLASS OF 1842.

Alexander M. Johnston, A. M., M. D.
*Thomas C. McCutchen, A. M.
Rev. Alexander McHatton, A. M.
*Rev. George McMillan, A. M.
Rev. James N. Saunders, A. M.
*Rev. William W. Simonson, A. M.
Zebulon B. Sturgus, A. M.

CLASS OF 1843.

Daniel L. Fouts,
*Rev. James G. Hopkins, A. M. *Missionary*,
George A. Irwin, A. M.
Samuel B. Keys, Esq., A. M.
Joseph C. McKibbin, Esq.
Rev. F. P. Montfort, A. M.
John F. Read, Esq. A. M.
John F. Trenchard, A. M., M. D.

CLASS OF 1844.

John C. Greer.

CLASS OF 1845.

David R. Thompson, Esq.
William T. Robinson, Esq. A. M.

CLASS OF 1846.

William H. G. Butler, A. M.
John A. Frazer, Esq.
Rev. Samuel C. Logan, A. M.

CLASS OF 1847.

Rev. Samuel E. Barr, A. M.
Rev. Fauntleroy Senour, A. M.

CLASS OF 1848.

Addison W. Bare, A. M.
John W. Blake, Esq. A. M.
Rev. John C. Caldwell, Esq., A. M.
Rev. Moses S. Coulter, A. M. *Missionary to China*.
Robert G. Jackson, A. M.
Robert S. Shannon, A. M.
Samuel C. Taggart, A. M., M. D.
Rev. James H. L. Vannuys, A. M.

CLASS OF 1849.

Rev. Samuel C. Baldridge, A. M.
Jesse Y. Higbee, A. M., M. D.
Rev. Nathan S. Palmer, A. M.
Xenophon B. Sanders, Esq., A. M.

*Deceased.

Rev. Williamson D. Symington, A. M.
John W. Taylor, A. M.
Rev. Henry E. Thomas, A. M.

CLASS OF 1850.

William Maxwell Blackburn,
Joshua Selby Brengle,
Avery Williams Bullock,
John Simpson Frierson,
*Samuel David Hawthorn,
John Alexander Kimmons,
Claudius Buchanan Henry Martin,
Samuel Clark Mercer,
Robert Symington Reese,
William Harvey Rice,
William Walton Sickels,
Alexander Stuart Walker,
Benjamin Rush Whitney,
William Alexander Martin Young.

CLASS OF 1851.

James Madison Alexander,
Henry Martyn Bayless,
Joseph Boon,
James Bruce,
James Huston Burns,
Theophilus Wilson Guy,
James Simpson Jones,
James McEwen Kimmons,
Cornelius McKain,
Hugh MacHatton,
Archibald McKee,
William James McKnight,
Alexander Mayne,
Edward Ethel Porter,
Benjamin Niles Sawtell,
Joseph Gaston Symmes,
Robert Francis Taylor,
Joseph Greene Wells.

CLASS OF 1852.

Joseph Mayo Batchelder,
Stephen Jefferson Bovell,
Jonathan Turner Carthel,
John McCutchen Coyner,
Benjamin Parke Dewey,

*Deceased.

Henry Michael Giltner,
Thomas Mayse Hopkins,
Alexander Martin,
Robert Langdon Neeley,
James Matlack Scovel,
Francis Marion Symmes,
Daniel Price Young.

SUMMARY.

Whole number of Alumni,	152
In the Ministry, (Two Missionaries,)	61
Law,	17
Teachers,	12
Professors,	5
Physicians,	5
Merchants,	2
Farmers,	2
Unknown,	4
Engaged in Professional Studies,	44
Of whom, Theological Students,	30

UNDERGRADUATES.

SENIOR CLASS.

Joseph Mayo Batchelder,	*Peoria, Ill.,*
Stephen Jefferson Boyell,	*Paris, Ill.,*
Jonathan Turner Carthel,	*Trenton, Tenn.,*
John McCutchen Coyner,	*S. Salem, O.,*
Benjamin Parke Dewey,	*Charleston,*
Henry Michael Giltner,	*Waveland,*
Thomas Mayse Hopkins,	*Ripley, O.,*
Alexander Martin,	*Salem,*
Robert Langdon Neeley,	*Denmark, Tenn.,*
James Matlack Scovel,	*Hanover,*
Francis Marion Symmes,	*Symmes' Corner, O.,*
Daniel Price Young,	*Nicholasville, Ky.,*

SENIORS, 12.

JUNIOR CLASS.

Lyman Beecher Andrews,	*Northfield, O.,*
James Andrew Cunningham,	*Madison,*
Lewis Isaac Drake,	*Springdale, O.,*
Jeremiah Mead Drake,	*Springdale, O.,*
Robert Chrystie Galbraith,	*Frankfort, O.,*
Joshua Bolles Garritt,	*Delphi,*
Edward John Hamilton,	*Cincinnati, O.,*
Henry Seymour Kritz,	*Buena Vista,*
Harvey Lamb,	*Galena,*
Charles Lee,	*Hanover,*
William Pope LeMaster,	*Memphis, Tenn.,*
David Tilford McCampbell,	*Charleston,*
Gideon Blackburn McLeary,	*Covington, Tenn.,*
John Hancock McRae,	*Victoria, Texas,*
James Alexander McRee,	*Somerville, Tenn.,*
Joseph Warren Mahan,	*Neville, O.,*
William Right Millsaps,	*Hargraves, Mi.,*
William Green Millsap,	*Hargraves, Mi.,*
Henry Thomas Morton,	*Shelbyville, Ky.,*
Henry Spencer Scovel,	*Hanover,*
Sylvester Fithian Scovel,	*Hanover,*

Jackson Jay Smith, *Simpsonville, Ky.,*
William Wheat, *Hargraves, Mi.,*
Jared Ryker Woodfill, *Bryantsburg.*

JUNIORS, 24.

SOPHOMORE CLASS.

Stephen Cromwell Adair, *Morganfield, Ky.,*
Andrew Witherspoon Adams, *Troy, O.,*
William Martin Alexander, *Carpentersville,*
Robert Mitchell Campbell, *Paoli,*
Stephen Crane, *Symmes' Corner, O.,*
James D. Fort, *Richland, Mi.,*
John Henry Gaster, *Frankfort,*
Barsabas Giltner, *N. Washington,*
Samuel Newell Goodhue, *Paris,*
David Gilkeson Herron, *Willettville, O.,*
William Hall Huston, *Symmes' Corner, O.,*
Robert Irwin, *Wheeling,*
Robert Alexander Johnston, *Batavia, O.,*
Nathaniel Field LeMaster, *Memphis, Tenn.,*
Duncan McLean, *Franklin,*
John Minor Millikin, *Hamilton, O.,*
Webster Millsaps, *Hargraves, Mi.,*
Isaac Brown Moore, *Monticello,*
Samuel William Rankin, *Henderson, Ky.,*
Edwin Hubbard Rutherford, *Brownsville, Tenn.,*
John William Sickels, *Utica, N. Y.,*
Edward Cooke Sickels, *Pleasant,*
William Rondeau Sim, *Golconda, Ill.,*
William Bloomer Truax, *Paoli,*
Thomas Wallace, *Springdale, O.,*
Joseph Glass Wilson, *Bardstown, Ky.,*
James Edwards Wilson, *Allahabad, N. India.*

SOPHOMORES, 27.

FRESHMAN CLASS.

John Crothers Allen, *Rockville,*
James Cyrus Alexander, *Paris, Ill.,*
Michael Montgomery Fisher, *Russell's Mills,*
John Hervey, *Wheeling, Va.,*
John Chandler Irwin, *Mansfield, O.,*
Thomas Black McChord, *Hillsboro, Ill.,*
Robert Clark McGee, *Charleston,*

Thomas Ainsworth Holliday, Gallatin, Mi.,
John Quincy McKeehan, Queensville,
Thomas Jefferson Millsaps, Hargraves, Mi.,
Robert Daniel Morris, Milton, Ky.,
John Samuel Park, Memphis, Tenn.,
Charles Hopkins Park, Jerseytown, Pa.,
David Henry Ruffner, Louisville, Ky.,
William Addison Sample, Covington, Tenn.,
William Stanley, Fairfield, Ky.,
James Harvey Tedford, Pittsburgh,
Thomas Marion Tucker, N. Philadelphia,
Archibald Cameron Voris, Bennington,
Edward Mackintosh Watson, Hargraves, Mi.,
Reuben Franklin Wheat, Hargraves, Mi.

FRESHMEN, 21.

GRAMMAR SCHOOL.

SENIOR CLASS.

William Wilberforce Andrew, La Porte,
James Baillie Adams, Pleasant,
William Washington Berry, Springdale, O.,
David Charlton, Pleasant,
Erastus Spaulding Close, Springdale, O.,
Hiram Baxter Collins, Vincennes,
Dyer Burgess Eastman, Hanover,
Charles Fais, Louisville, Ky.,
Samuel Newell Fisher, Orleans,
James Cleland Hamilton, Cincinnati, O.,
William Wilberforce Hamilton, Cincinnati, O.,
James Hendron, Palestine, Ill.,
Robert Calvin Irwin, Hanover,
George Madison Johnston, Pittsburgh,
Henry Keigwin, Louisville, Ky.,
Joseph Kennedy, Covington, Ky.,
Thomas Prentice Killen, Dover, Del.,
Joseph Winslow Levitt, Memphis, Tenn.,
George Logan, Greenfield, O.,
Stephen Daniel Lyon, Newark, N. J.,
James Charlott McElroy, Greencastle,
John Morrison, Tigerville, La.,

James Kennedy Patterson,	*Elizabethtown,*
Charles Fary Ross,	*Jeffersonville,*
Abner Lowry Shannon,	*Hanover,*
John Worth Shannon,	*Hanover,*
Benjamin Franklin Slocumb,	*Vicksburgh, Mi.,*
Nelson Smith,	*New Castle, Pa.,*
Samuel Van Meter,	*Lexington, Ky.,*
Benjamin Dubois Wikoff,	*Franklin, O.,*
Francis George Wilson,	*N. Frankfort,*
Luther Halsey Wilson,	*Allahabad, N. India,*
Edward Wolfe,	*Rushville.*

SENIOR GRAMMAR SCHOLARS, 33.

JUNIOR CLASS.

John Wallace Bain,	*Swanville,*
Andrew James Baxter,	*Cincinnati, O.,*
William McConnell Blake,	*Indianapolis,*
William Brent,	*Campbellsburg, Ky.,*
James Henry Bruce,	*Lancaster, Ky.,*
John Aleneth Byers,	*Long Creek, Mi.,*
Robert Charlton,	*Pleasant,*
Francis Marion Decell,	*Hargraves, Mi.,*
James Walter Elliott,	*Madison,*
Charles Thomas Elliott,	*Dayton,*
Milo Ellis,	*N. Bethel,*
Theodore Brigham Fisher,	*Cincinnati, O.,*
Israel Sylvester Hogeland,	*Lafayette,*
Theodore Dudley Johnson,	*Madison,*
Cyrus Alexander Johnson,	*Memphis, Tenn.,*
Benjamin Letcher,	*Lancaster, Ky.,*
William Brackenridge List,	*Franklin,*
Simon Lott,	*Madison,*
James Love,	*Cincinnati, O.,*
Samuel McComb,	*Columbus, O.,*
William Campbell McCoskey,	*Canton,*
James McNeel,	*Sloanville,*
Joseph Millikin,	*Hamilton, O.,*
James Newton Pogue,	*Hanover,*
Joseph Allen Porter,	*Lodiana, N. India,*
Lewis Ruffner,	*Louisville, Ky.,*
James R. Shean,	*West Point, Ky.,*
Benjamin Livingston Smith,	*Paris,*
Thomas Thorn Swan,	*Hanover.*
David Taylor,	*Hibernia, O.,*
William Wirt Thomson,	*McLeod's, Mi.,*

John Lowrie Wilson, *Allahabad, N. India,*
Samuel Gregg Woodfill, *Bryantsburgh,*
John Brown Wright, *Logansport.*

JUNIOR GRAMMAR SCHOOL, 34.

SCIENTIFIC DEPARTMENT.

Lewis Alexander, *N. Liberty, Ky.,*
Fielding Alexander, *N. Liberty, Ky.,*
William Goforth Armstrong, *Jeffersonville,*
Clayton Curl Bell, *Hanover,*
John Reed Bigham, *Hamilton, O.,*
Hiram Davis Blankenbaker, *Louisville, Ky.,*
John Williamson Brough, *Madison,*
Paul Huston Burns, *Dunlap, O.,*
William Perritt Campbell, *Patriot,*
Alexander Hamilton Connor, *Noblesville,*
Allen Cullen, *Patriot,*
Andrew Culver, *Jeffersonville,*
John Edward Dixon, *Henderson, Ky.,*
Simeon Addison Gaar, *Louisville, Ky.,*
William Addison Gilliland, *Ripley, O.,*
Alfred William Hynes, *Hanover,*
Henry Frederic Kalfus, *Shepherdsville, Ky.,*
Henry Clay Lockett, *Henderson, Ky.,*
James Irwin Lodge, *Madison,*
Cornelius Wycoff Hall McNeil, *Symmes' Corner, O.,*
John Puge Page, *Madison,*
John Benner Pence, *Frankfort,*
Thomas Lloyd Posey, *Henderson, Ky.,*
William Siller, *Springdale, O.,*
Leven Sprigg, *Boston, Ky.,*
William Snoddy, *Dayton,*
Alfred Nevin Snoddy, *Dayton,*
John McLain Stalker, *Salem,*
Francis Strader, *Madison,*
Benjamin Franklin Van Meter, *Winchester, Ky.,*
William Vannice, *Morefield,*
Allen Fletcher West, *Hanover,*
James Wilcox, *Shelbyville, Ky.*

SCIENTIFIC DEPARTMENT, 33.

SUMMARY.

Undergraduates,—Seniors,	12	
Juniors,	24	
Sophomores,	27	
Freshmen,	21	
	—	84
Grammar School,—Senior Class,	33	
Junior Class,	34	
	—	67
Scientific Department,	33	
Total,		184

REPRESENTATION FROM THE SEVERAL STATES, &C.

Indiana,	79	New York,	1
Ohio,	34	New Jersey,	1
Kentucky,	29	Delaware,	1
Mississippi,	13	Virginia,	1
Tennessee,	11	Louisiana,	1
Illinois,	6	Texas,	1
Pennsylvania,	2	Northern India,	4

ADMISSION.

CANDIDATES for admission into the Freshman Class are examined in Arithmetic; Ancient and Modern Geography; the English, Latin and Greek Grammars; Bullions' Greek Reader; Cæsar's Commentaries; four Orations of Cicero, and Sallust. They must furnish testimonials of good character; and, if from another College, must bring certificates of honorable dismission. Candidates for a higher standing, are examined upon that part of the course already studied by the class which they propose to enter.

No one can be admitted to the Freshman Class till he has completed his fourteenth year; nor to an advanced standing without a proportional increase of age.

"*Before any student shall be admitted to actual standing in any class, he shall present to the President a written receipt from the Treasurer, showing that he has complied with the statutes relating to College charges and Scholarships.*"

N. B. The last two days in each vacation, are the stated time for examining such as seek admission into the College Classes.

COURSE OF STUDIES.

GRAMMAR SCHOOL.

Bullions' Latin and Greek Grammars, with praxis; Bullions' Latin and Greek Readers; Bullions' Cæsar; Bullions' Cicero; Schmidtz and Zumpt's Sallust; Higher Arithmetic; Robinson's Algebra, University edition; Mitchell's Classical Geography; Coleman's Biblical Geography; Historical portions of the Old and New Testaments.

SCIENTIFIC DEPARTMENT.

FIRST YEAR.

Review of Higher Arithmetic; Algebra; Plane Geometry; Plane Trigonometry; Surveying and Navigation; Ancient, Modern and Ecclesiastical History.

SECOND YEAR.

Higher Algebra; Ancient and Biblical Geography; Solid Geometry; Spherical Trigonometry, and its applications; Analytical Geometry; Natural Philosophy and Astronomy; Rhetoric; Logic, and Political Economy.

THIRD YEAR.

Anatomy and Physiology; Zoology; Botany; Chemistry; Natural Theology; Butler's Analogy; Psychology and Moral Philosophy.

COLLEGE.

FRESHMAN CLASS.

I.

Robinson's Harmony of the Gospels.
Horne's Biblical Antiquities, (abridged edition.)
Cooper's Virgil.
Owen's Anabasis.
Bajesen's Roman Antiquities.
Davies' Plane Geometry.

II.

Robinson's Harmony.
Cooper's Virgil.
Owen's Anabasis.
Roman, Grecian and Biblical Antiquities.
Davies' Plane Trigonometry and Surveying.

III.

Robinson's Harmony.
Cooper's Virgil.
Xenophon's Memorabilia.
Grecian and Biblical Antiquities.
Davies' Surveying and Navigation.

SOPHOMORE CLASS.

I.

Acts of the Apostles, (Owen's edition,)
Lincoln's Livy.
Anthon's Homer's Iliad.
Eschenburgh's Manual of Classical Literature.
Davies' Solid Geometry.
Taylor's Manual of Ancient History.

II.

Epistles of the New Testament.
Lincoln's Livy.
Homer's Iliad.
Davies' Spherical Trigonometry, and applications.
Taylor's Modern History.

III.

Epistles continued.
Cicero de Senectute et de Amicitia.
Herodotus.
Davies' Analytical Geometry.
Ecclesiastical History.

JUNIOR CLASS.

I.

Hebrew Grammar, (Stuart's Rœdiger.)
Genesis.
Horace.
Champlin's Demosthenes de Corona.
Olmstead's Natural Philosophy, Vol. 1st.
Blair's Rhetoric.

II.

Hebrew Grammar—Genesis.
Horace.

Demosthenes de Corona.
Olmstead's Natural Philosophy, Vols. 1st. and 2nd.
Whately's Logic.

III.

Hebrews—Psalms.
Tyler's Germania and Agricola of Tacitus.
Woolsey's Plato's Gorgias.
Olmstead's Natural Philosophy, Vol. 2nd.
Olmstead's Astronomy.
Wayland's Political Economy.

SENIOR CLASS.

I.

Select portions of the Hebrew Bible, with Lectures.
Psychology—Walker's edition of Reid.
Stockhardt's Chemistry.
Cutter's Anatomy and Physiology, with Lectures.
Wood's Botany, with Lectures.
Prometheus Vinctus of Æschylus.

II.

Select Hebrew, and Lectures.
Psychology.
Chemistry.
Paley's Natural Theology.
Chase's Tusculan Disputations, and Somnium Scipionis.

III.

Select Hebrew, and Lectures.
Butler's Analogy of Natural and Revealed Religion to the Constitution and Course of Nature.
Moral Philosophy; (Walker's edition of Stuart & Wayland.)
Mineralogy.
Hitchcock's Geology.

DISTRIBUTION OF RECITATIONS, &C.

	DEPARTMENT OF Bibl. Instruction, & Philos. THE PRESIDENT.	DEPARTMENT OF Rhetoric, History, Logic. Dr. CROWE.	DEPARTMENT OF Natural Science. Prof. STONE.	DEPARTMENT OF Mathematics & Nat. Phil. Prof. THOMSON.	DEPARTMENT OF Greek Lang. & Literature. Prof. BISHOP.	DEPARTMENT OF Latin Lang. and Literature. Prof HAMILTON.
	I.	I.	I.	I.	I.	I.
J. G. S.	....	....	....	Arithmetic,........	Greek Grammar,........	Latin Grammar,........
S. G. S.	....	....	Algebra,........	....	Bullions' Greek Reader, ..	Bullions' Cæsar,........
F.	½ Harmon. of Gospels,......	....	....	Plane Geometry, ...	Anabasis,........	Virgil,........
So.......	½ Acts,........	Ancient History,........	....	Sol. Geometry,........	½ Iliad,........	½ Livy,........
J.	Hebrew,........	½ Rhetoric........	....	Natural Philosophy........	½ De Corona,........	½ Horace. ....
Sen......	½ Heb. & Lect. Psychology.	....	Chemistry, ½ Anat. Phys.	....	Prometh. Vinct........	....
	II.	II.	II.	II.	II.	II.
J. G. S.	....	....	....	Algebra, ...	Greek Reader,........	Latin Reader,........
S. G. S.	....	....	Classical & Bibl. Geog. ..	....	Greek Reader,........	Orations of Cicero,........
F.......	½ Harmon. Gospels, ...	....	....	Plane Trigonometry, ...	Anabasis,........	Virgil,........
So.......	½ Epistles, ...	Modern History........	....	Spher. Trig. and Appl...	½ Iliad,........	½ Livy,........
J.	Hebrew,........	½ Logic........	....	Natural Philosophy........	½ De Corona........	½ Horace,........
Sen......	½ Heb. & Lect. Psychology.	....	Chemistry, ½ Nat. Theol..	....	....	Cicero's Tusc. Disp........
	III.	III.	III.	III.	III.	III.
J. G. S.	....	....	....	Algebra, ...	Greek Reader,........	Latin Reader,........
S. G. S.	....	....	Algebra,........	....	Greek Reader,........	Sallust,........
F.......	½ Harmon. Gospels,........	....	....	Surveying & Navigation.	Memorabilia,........	Virgil,........
So.......	½ Epistles,........	Eccl. History,........	....	Anal. Geometry,........	½ Herodotus, ...	½ Cicero de Sen. et Amicit.
J.	Hebrew,........	½ Political Economy........	....	Nat. Phil., Astronomy....	½ Plato's Gorgias.	½ Tacit. Germ, et Agric....
Sen......	½ Heb. & Lectures; Moral Philosophy.	....	Butler's Anal. ½ Geology and Mineralogy.	....	....	....

Permanent Recitation Hours in all Departments.

A. M.

8	½ Seniors,........	Sophomores,........	½ Seniors,........	Juniors,........	Sen. Gram. Sch....	Freshmen,........
9	Juniors,........	....	Seniors,........	Sophomores,........	Freshmen,........	Sen. Gram. Sch....
10	Seniors,........	....	Sen. Gram. Sch. ..	Freshmen,........	½ Sophs. & Juniors...	½ Sophs. & Juniors...
11	½ Fresh. & Sophs...	½ Juniors........	....	Jun. Gram. Sch...	....	....

PERMANENT RECITATION HOURS---SCIENTIFIC DEPARTMENT.

A. M.	FIRST CLASS.	SECOND CLASS.	THIRD CLASS.
8.	History.	Nat. Philos. and Astron.	Nat. Sci. & Nat. The.
9.		Mathematics.	Chem. & Butl. Anal.
10.	Mathematics.	Alg. & Anct. & Bib. Geog.	Psychol. & Mor. Phil.
11.	Arith. & Algeb.	½ Rhet. Log. Pol. Econ.	

The preceding course is so arranged, in all departments, as to require from every Class, except the Senior, an average of *three hours and a half* in recitations, *daily,* excepting Saturday. These recitations are attended, without loss of time, between the hours of 8 and 12 A. M.; leaving the remainder of the day for study and recreation.

SCIENTIFIC DEPARTMENT.

The Board of Trustees, at their recent meeting, established the Department of English, Mathematical and Scientific Instruction above presented; and adopted a course of study which enables the student to acquire, in three years, all that is included in the Collegiate scheme, except the Classical branches. To those who have obtained a respectable common-school education, and who have not time or opportunity to pursue the Classical course, this system of studies will, it is hoped, commend itself, as solid, comprehensive and practical. Those who shall complete the prescribed Scientific course, will receive a Diploma, exhibiting the extent of their attainments.

COLLEGE YEAR—EXAMINATIONS.

The Collegiate Year is divided into *three Terms* of *thirteen weeks* each, and *three Vacations.* The *First Term* begins on the *Fourth Wednesday in September;* the *Second,* on the *First Wednesday in January;* and the *Third,* on the *First Wednesday in May,* closing with THE FIRST WEDNESDAY IN AUGUST, which is COMMENCEMENT DAY. It is of great importance that Students attend from *the very beginning* of the term; especially since so considerable a portion of time is allotted to vacations. *In most cases, the loss of a few weeks, or even days, seriously affects the future standing of a pupil.* Absence during term-time, without special leave, is prohibited.

Public examinations will be held, hereafter, only at the close of the College Year; when the Freshman and Junior classes will be examined on the studies of the preceding year; and the Sophomore and Senior classes, upon those of the two preceding years. These last examinations will be *final,* for the studies pursued in those years. All the examinations will be *thorough* and *rigid;* and will be conducted, chiefly, by the use of *written questions,* prepared by the Faculty and the Examining Committee, covering the whole field of study prosecuted during a given period, and entirely unknown to the Student until the moment of examination. These questions must be answered in writing before the Committee; and correct answers to a definite portion of them will be the passport of admission to a higher standing. Similar examinations, of a briefer and less decisive character, however, and by way of preparation for the final trial, may be conducted privately, at the pleasure of the Faculty.

The Board of Trustees, having sanctioned the distribution of honorary and pecuniary rewards, the average standing of every pupil will hereafter be posted up in some conspicuous place, at the end of the year; and suitable prizes will be conferred upon the most deserving.

RELIGIOUS EXERCISES AND INSTRUCTION.

The attention of a Christian community is respectfully invited to the system of Biblical Instruction which forms a characteristic feature of our course of study. The Grammar School Classes recite daily in the English Bible; and every College Class has a daily, or tri-weekly, recitation in the Greek Testament, or the Hebrew. Proficiency in these, as in other studies, is tested by the usual examinations. In addition to this, Biblical Geography and Antiquities, Ecclesiastical History, Natural Theology, and the Analogy, or Religion Natural and Revealed to the constitution and course of nature, are carefully and faithfully studied. There is also a Bible or Catechetical exercise on Sabbath mornings; a public service on Sabbath afternoons, appropriated to the Students; and daily morning prayers. The Students are expected to attend the Sabbath morning service of the congregation worshipping in the chapel, or of some other congregation in the vicinity, if their parents prefer any of the latter. The Methodist, Associate, and Associate Reformed Churches have regular service in or near the village.

An experiment of three years in this Institution, has established the fact that the daily study of God's word by no means interferes with, but rather promotes, sound and comprehensive attainments in other branches of knowledge. Some, indeed, have questioned the expediency of adding *Hebrew* to an already overburdened curriculum; especially since the Theological Students may acquire it in the Seminary, and non-theologians are unlikely to make any practical use of such an acquisition. Our confident answer is,—*First,* that Theological Students need more acquaintance with Hebrew than with Greek, when they enter the Seminary; since familiarity with the Old Testament is more rare and difficult than with the New:— *Secondly,* that the mental discipline secured by this study is fully equal to that obtained from any other:—*Thirdly,* that a knowledge of Hebrew, as connected with the Indo-European tongues, greatly contributes to the students' mastery of the latter:—*Fourthly*, that non-theological students are as likely to cultivate the Hebrew, when once acquired, as the higher Mathematics and the Classics:—*Fifthly*, that the Hebrew Scriptures contain more valuable, practical truth, than all the pagan classics put together: and *lastly*, that the day is to be dreaded when ability to peruse the Sacred Volume, in the originals, shall be the exclusive property of the Clergy.

EXPENSES.

The entire annual expenditures of a student need not exceed $125; viz:

Tuition and contingent fee, $10 per term,	$30 00
Boarding with private families, and a furnished room, at $1 50 to $1 75 per week,	$60 to 70 00
Fuel, light, washing, &c..	10 to 15 00
Books, &c.,	5 to 10 00

Boarding in clubs will cost from *fifty* to *seventy-five cents* per week; and many board themselves at a lower rate. The expense of clothing and pocket-money will of course vary with the taste and habits of the student. Although Hanover presents few temptations to extravagance, yet parents are *earnestly advised* to require of their sons a detailed account of their expenditures. It is also recommended that the funds of young pupils be deposited with some member of the Faculty; without whose written order the boy should make no purchases. The younger class of students are required to board where the Faculty may direct, and where they may exercise a more careful and frequent supervision.

SCHOLARSHIPS.

The endowment of this Institution, so far as it has been secured, is in the form of *Scholarships;* of which the Board has established several sorts. The sum of $400, paid, or secured to the Corporation by note payable within five years, and bearing six per cent. interest in advance upon principal remaining unpaid,—purchases for the owner, his heirs and assigns, a perpetual right to the tuition of one scholar, in Hanover College. The sum of $200, paid, or subscribed under similar conditions, secures a right to twenty years' tuition; after which time, the scholarship is subject to the disposal of the Board for the gratuitous education of candidates for the Gospel Ministry. A church scholarship of $200 secures to the church so contributing, a perpetual right to the tuition of one student, who shall be a member of that church, and appointed by the Session. A Presbyterial scholarship of $200 secures a similar right to a Presbytery, in behalf of pupils who shall be candidates for the Ministry under its care. The *principal* paid on these scholarships is invested by the Corporation in some safe and productive stock; and the *interest only* can be expended for the support of the College.

The sum of $100, *paid within two years at farthest*, with interest in advance on unpaid principal, purchases a right to ten years' tuition within twenty years from the date of subscription. Both principal and interest of this scholarship may be employed for contingent purposes; and the scholarship expires with the owner's right to its use.

The Board has adopted the following rules in reference to scholarships; particular attention to which, by the parties interested, is invited:

"*Every person applying for admission as a beneficiary of a scholarship under the control of the donors, shall present to the Treasurer, at the beginning of each term,* A WRITTEN CERTIFICATE, *from those controlling the scholarship, of his right to such benefit; when, after paying whatever interest may be due on said scholarship, he shall receive an acknowledgment of his right, which he shall lodge with the President.*"

"*The scholarships subject to the disposal of the Corporation may be occupied by such applicants as the Faculty may select, after inquiry into their circumstances, character and attainments; the preference being, (cæteris paribus,) to those who give the best evidence of scholarship.*"

"*There shall at no time be more than one student upon each scholarship.*"

N. B. Students placed upon scholarships by the Faculty, are relieved, in part, or wholly, as the case may require, from the payment of tuition fees.

SOCIETIES, LIBRARIES, &C.

There are two Societies connected with the College,—the *Union Literary*, and the *Philalethean*, each of whose Libraries number about *fifteen hundred* volumes. *The Society of Inquiry* has also begun to collect a Library, Maps, &c. The College Library, which comprises nearly *two thousand* well selected volumes, is accessible to the students. The Cabinet contains several thousand specimens in Mineralogy and Geology. The Laboratory is supplied with the apparatus most necessary for chemical experiments.

Three hundred volumes of valuable books have been added to the College Library, within the year, by donation. Similar contributions will be thankfully received.

GENERAL REMARKS.

The village of Hanover is situated upon an elevated bluff of the Ohio river, six miles below Madison, Indiana; in a region of remarkable salubrity and natural beauty. The village and neighborhood are characterized by morality, and the absence of all ordinary temptations to vice and idleness. Intoxicating liquors have never been sold in the township; the traffic being prohibited, annually, by popular vote. The Ohio river, and the railways from Madison and Cincinnati, place Hanover within twenty-four hours of all the principal points in Indiana, and western Ohio. A plank road from Madison to Hanover, now nearly completed, renders the village easy of access in all seasons of the year.

Hanover College is controlled by a Board of Trustees, one-half of whom are appointed by the Board itself, and the other half by the Synods of Indiana and Northern Indiana. All its officers are Ministers or members of the Presbyterian Church.

The Board purchased, some three years since, a farm of two hundred acres, lying between the village and the Ohio river; upon a beautiful point of which, overlooking the river from an elevation of four hundred feet, and commanding a view of its course for fifteen or twenty miles, they are now erecting a new College edifice. Several thousand dollars have been collected, as a building fund; and the Agent, Rev. JNO. C. EASTMAN, has been directed to devote his labors, exclusively, to the completion of that fund.

THE TWENTY-FIRST ANNUAL CIRCULAR

OF

HANOVER COLLEGE;

COMPRISING THE

CATALOGUE, COURSE OF STUDY, &c.

AUGUST, 1853.

PRINTED FOR HANOVER COLLEGE:
BY JOHN D. THORPE, 74 FOURTH STREET,
CINCINNATI.
1853.

THE TWENTY-FIRST ANNUAL CIRCULAR

OF

HANOVER COLLEGE;

COMPRISING THE

CATALOGUE, COURSE OF STUDY, &c.

AUGUST, 1853.

PRINTED FOR HANOVER COLLEGE:
BY JOHN D. THORPE, 74 FOURTH STREET,
CINCINNATI.
1853.

BOARD OF TRUSTEES.

BY WHOM ELECTED.		TERM EXPIRES.
Bd.	Rev. JOHN FINLEY CROWE, D. D., Hanover,	1853.
Bd.	JOHN L. SCOTT, Esq., Cincinnati, O.,	"
Bd.	A. R. FORSYTH, Greensburg,	"
Bd.	JOHN P. BANTA, Franklin,	"
S. S.	Rev. P. D. GURLEY, D. D., Dayton, O.,	"
S. S.	Hon. WILLIAMSON DUNN, Hanover,	
N. S.	Rev. W. C. HOLLIDAY, Indianapolis,	
N. S.	S. D. MAXWELL, Frankfort,	"
Bd.	Rev. THOMAS E. THOMAS, D. D., Hanover,	1854.
Bd.	Rev. JNO. M. STEVENSON, New Albany,	"
Bd.	Rev. DANIEL LATTIMORE, Vernon,	"
Bd.	JAMES BLAKE, Indianapolis,	"
S. S.	Rev. D. D. McKEE, Fairfield,	"
S. S.	JAMES M. RAY, Indianapolis,	"
N. S.	Rev. WM. Y. ALLEN, Rockville,	"
N. S.	ISAAC COE, M. D., Galena, Ill.,	"
Bd.	JOHN KING, Madison,	1855.
Bd.	Rev. WM. SICKELS, Pleasant,	"
Bd.	W. McKEE DUNN, Esq., Madison,	"
Bd.	WM. A. BULLOCK, Esq., Vernon,	"
S. S.	Rev. J. G. MONFORT, D. D., Greensburgh,	"
S. S.	Rev. THO. S. CROWE, Hanover,	"
N. S.	Rev. JOHN C. EASTMAN, Hanover,	"
N. S.	Rev. SAMUEL N. EVANS, Waveland,	"
Bd.	Rev. N. L. RICE, D. D., St. Louis, Mo.,	1856.
Bd.	Rev. S. R. WILSON, Cincinnati, O.,	"
Bd.	ALEX. GUY, M. D., Cincinnati, O.,	"
Bd.	Rev. W. W. HILL, D. D., Louisville, Ky.,	"
S. S.	Rev. D. M. STEWART, Rushville,	
S. S.	Rev. C. LEAVENWORTH, New Albany,	"
N. S.	Rev. F. P. CUMMINS, La Porte,	"
N. S.	Rev. ROBERT IRWIN, Wheeling,	"

OFFICERS OF THE BOARD.

Rev. J. F. CROWE, *President.*
Rev. T. E. THOMAS, *Secretary.*
Rev. T. S. CROWE, *Treasurer.*
Rev. D. LATTIMORE, *Financial Agent.*

FACULTY.

REV. THOMAS E. THOMAS, D. D., *President*,
    Professor of Biblical Instruction, Psychology, and Moral Philosophy.

REV. JOHN FINLEY CROWE, D. D.,
    Professor of Rhetoric, Logic, History, and Political Economy

REV. JARED M. STONE, A. M.,
    Professor of Natural Science.

S. HARRISON THOMSON, A. M.,
    Professor of Mathematics and Mechanical Philosophy.

REV. WILLIAM BISHOP, A. M.,
    Professor of the Greek Language and Literature.

REV. WILLIAM HAMILTON, A. M.,
    Professor of the Latin Language and Literature.

M. J. J. H. PIEDFOURCK,
    Instructor in French.

UNDERGRADUATES.

SENIOR CLASS.

Lyman Beecher Andrews,	Northfield, O.,
James Andrew Cunningham,	Madison,
Lewis Isaac Drake,	Springdale, O.;
Jeremiah Mead Drake,	Springdale, O.,
Joshua Bolles Garritt,	Delphi,
Edward John Hamilton,	Hanover,
Henry Seymour Kritz,	Waveland,
Charles Lee,	Hanover,
William Pope LeMaster,	Memphis, Tenn.,
Gideon Blackburn McLeary,	Covington, Tenn.,
†John Hancock McRae,	Victoria, Texas,
James Alexander McRee,	Somerville, Tenn.,
Joseph Warren Mahan,	Neville, O.,
*William Right Millsaps,	Hargraves, Mi.,
*William Green Millsaps,	Hargraves, Mi.,
Henty Thomas Morton,	Shelbyville, Ky.,
Henry Spencer Scovel,	New Albany,
Sylvester Fithian Scovel,	New Albany,
Jackson Jay Smith,	Simpsonville, Ky.,
William Wheat,	Hargraves, Mi.

JUNIOR CLASS.

Stephen Cromwell Adair,	Morganfield, Ky.,
Stephen Crane,	Symmes' Corner, O.,
David Gilkeson Herron,	Willettville, O.,
Robert Irwin,	Wheeling,
Robert Alexander Johnston,	Mt. Carmel, O.,
Harvey Lamb,	Hanover,
Duncan McLean,	Franklin,
*Webster Millsaps,	Hargraves, Mi.,
Isaac Brown Moore,	Monticello,
Edwin Hubbard Rutherford,	Brownsville, Tenn.,
Edward Cooke Sickels,	Pleasant,
William Rondeau Sim,	Golconda, Ill.,
Thomas Wallace,	Springdale, O.,
James Edward Wilson,	Hanover.

†Died, 8th Dec., 1852, lamented by all who knew him.
*Honorably dismissed, April, 1853.

SOPHOMORE CLASS.

John Crothers Allen,	Rockville,
James Cyrus Alexander,	Paris, Ill.,
Robert Mitchel Campbell,	Paoli,
John Hervey,	Wheeling, Va.,
William Hall Huston,	Symmes' Corner, O.,
Nathaniel Field LeMaster,	Memphis, Tenn.,
Robert Clark McGee,	Charleston,
John Quincy McKeehan,	Queensville,
Thaddeus Mac Rae,	De Kalb, Mi.,
Thomas Jefferson Millsaps,	Hargraves, Mi.,
Robert Daniel Morris,	Milton, Ky.,
Charles Hopkins Park,	Jerseytown, Pa.,
Samuel William Rankin,	Henderson, Ky.,
William Addison Sample,	Covington, Tenn.,
William Bloomer Truax,	Paoli,
Thomas Marion Tucker,	N. Philadelphia,
Archibald Cameron Voris,	Bennington,
Nathaniel Warner,	Jamesport, L. I.,
Reuben Franklin Wheat,	Hargraves, Mi.

FRESHMAN CLASS.

James Baillie Adams,	Pleasant,
William Washington Berry,	Springdale, O.,
David Charlton,	Pleasant,
Erastus Spaulding Close,	Springdale, O.,
Dinsmore Cramer,	Plymouth, Mich.,
Dyer Burgess Eastman,	Hanover,
James Cleland Hamilton,	Hanover,
William Wilberforce Hamilton,	Hanover,
James Hendron,	Palestine, Ill.,
Robert Brown Herron,	Willettville, O.,
William Rogers Irwin,	Wheeling,
Robert Calvin Irwin,	Hanover,
Henry Keigwin,	Louisville, Ky.,
Stephen Daniel Lyon,	Newark, N. J.,
Thomas Jefferson McConnell,	Simpsonville, Ky..
Thomas Black McCord,	Hillsboro', Ill.,
James Charlott McElroy,	Greencastle,
Stephen Woodruff Markley,	Mt. Carmel, O.,
John Morrison,	Tigerville, La.,
James Kennedy Patterson,	Elizabethtown,
Josiah Richardson,	Louisville, Ky.,
Abner Lowry Shannon,	Hanover,

John Worth Shannon,	*Hanover,*
Benjamin Franklin Slocumb,	*Vicksburgh, Mi.,*
Nelson Smith,	*Sharpsburgh, Pa.,*
Richmond Kelly Smoot,	*Huntingdon, Tenn.,*
James Harvey Tedford,	*Pittsburgh,*
Benjamin Dubois Wikoff,	*Franklin, O.,*
Luther Halsey Wilson,	*Hanover,*
Edward Wolfe,	*Rushville.*

SCIENTIFIC DEPARTMENT.

SENIOR CLASS.

John McLain Stalker,	*Salem,*
William Stanley,	*Fairfield, Ky.*

MIDDLE CLASS.

George McDowell Caldwell,	*Nicholasville, Ky.,*
Alexander Hunter,	*Bardstown, Ky.,*
Alfred William Hynes,	*Hanover,*
James Irwin Lodge,	*Madison,*
Cornelius Wycoff Hall McNeil,	*Symmes' Corner, O.,*
David Henry Ruffner,	*Louisville, Ky.*

JUNIOR CLASS.

William McConnell Blake,	*Indianapolis,*
John Roach Blanchard,	*Louisville, Ky.,*
John Williamson Brough,	*Madison,*
Thaddeus Smith Chester,	*Columbus, O.,*
Elmore Corry,	*Cincinnati, O.,*
Gabriel Davis,	*Uniontown, Ky.,*
Edward Hugh Dobyns,	*New Orleans, La.,*
William Webster Eastman,	*Hanover,*
Charles Haggin,	*Louisville, Ky.,*
William Morgan Higgins,	*Louisville, Ky.,*
Thomas Hobbs Hammond,	*Bardstown, Ky.,*
William Daniel Hantsch,	*Indianapolis,*
William Beard Hoke,	*Fisherville, Ky.,*
William Harvey Robbins Irwin,	*Greenfield, O.,*
James Samuel Jones,	*Hanover,*
Theodore Judge,	*Frankfort, Ky.,*

William Wesley Moore, Fisherville, Ky.,
Benjamin O'Neal, Carrollton, Ky.,
James Newton Pogue, Hanover,
Robert James Prather, Louisville, Ky.,
Samuel Robeson, Dayton,
Francis Marion Robinson, Waterford, Ky.,
Lewis Joseph Sloan, Fairfield, Ky.,
Milton White Smith, Hanover,
Charles Albert Smith, Hanover,
Abner Crothers Smith, Hanover,
Alfred Nevin Snoddy, Dayton,
Homer Chenoweth Stucky, Jeffersontown, Ky..
William Vannice, Morefield,
Thomas Marquis Wallace, London, O.,
William Owens Watts, Bardstown, Ky.,
Allen Fletcher West, Hanover.

GRAMMAR SCHOOL.

SENIOR CLASS.

Leonard Fisk Andrews, Northfield, O.,
Charles Dorsey Armstrong, Louisville, Ky.,
Andrew James Baxter, Cincinnati, O.,
William Allison Carmichael, Rushville,
Robert Charlton, Pleasant,
Jacob Ditzler, Saltillo, Ky..
Milo Ellis, New Bethel,
Joshua Bradley Fisher, Bayou Rouge, La.,
Cyrus Alexander Johnson, Memphis, Tenn.,
Theodore Dudley Johnson, Madison,
James Warren Lanham, Buena Vista,
Alexander Williamson Lattimore, Vernon,
Finley Crowe Lattimore, Vernon,
William Baty Laughlin, Rushville,
William Brackenridge List, Franklin,
George Logan, Greenfield, O.,
Simon Lott, Madison,
James Love, Cincinnati, O.,
Samuel Vigo McKee, Vincennes,
James McNeel, Sloanville,
Joseph Allen Porter, Lodiana, N. India,
Thomas Thorn Swan, Hanover,
David MacKnight Williamson, Logansport,

Francis George Wilson, *N. Frankfort,*
John Lowrie Wilson, *Hanover,*
John Brown Wright, *Logansport.*

JUNIOR CLASS.

David McIlvain Allen, *Owensboro, Ky.,*
John Wallace Bain, *Swanville,*
William Peter Baker, *Ft. Wayne,*
Marshall D. Bowman, *Vincennes,*
William Brown, *Sharpsburgh, Ky..*
John Aleneth Byers, *Long Creek, Mi.,*
John Gilkeson Clark, *Jefferson,*
William Thomas Covert, *Franklin,*
John Wesley Dean, *Worthville, Ky.,*
Joseph McClelland Douglas, *Wesley Chapel,*
Theodore Brigham Fisher, *Cincinnati, O.,*
Robert Harvey Gilmore, *Manhattan,*
Sylvester Franklin Gilmore, *Manhattan,*
Henry Lyter Giltner, *Milton, Ky.,*
John William Gordon, *Jeffersonville,*
James Hendricks, *Shelbyville,*
Israel Sylvester Hogeland, *Lafayette,*
Charles Cornelius Hoke, *Fisherville, Ky.,*
Simon White Huddleston, *Olympus, Tenn.,*
William Wallace Jamieson, *Rising Sun,*
William Coleman Jones, *Fairfield, Ky.,*
John David McClintock, *Greensburgh,*
John Miller, *Greensburgh,*
David William Moffat, *Madison,*
Gideon Elijah Moncrief, *Vernon,*
Robert Starr Moore, *Kingsbury,*
James Alexander Piper, *Byron,*
Robert Blair Smith, *Sharpsburgh, Pa.,*
Benjamin Sterritt, *Cincinnati, O.,*
David Taylor, *Hibernia, O.,*
William Wirt Thomson, *MacLeod's, Mi.,*
James Harvey Vannuys, *Franklin,*
C. Pleasant Voris, *Bennington,*
John Warden Wilson, *Crawfordsville.*

SUMMARY.

Undergraduates—Seniors,	20
Juniors,	14
Sophomores,	19
Freshmen,	30
	83
Scientific Students,	40
Grammar Scholars,	60
Total,	183

CALENDAR.

1853.
Sept. 19, Examination of candidates for admission, *Monday and Tuesday.*
" 21, First Term begins, - - - - - - *Wednesday.*
Dec. 20, First Term ends, - - - - - - *Tuesday.*

WINTER VACATION OF TWO WEEKS.

1854.
Jan. 4, Second Term begins, - - - - - *Wednesday.*
April 3, Exhibition of the Philalethean Society, - *Monday evening.*
" 4, " " Union Literary Society, *Tuesday evening.*
" 4, Second term ends.

SPRING VACATION OF FOUR WEEKS.

May 3, Third Term begins, - - - - - *Wednesday.*
July 12, Biennial Examination, Senior Class, begins, - *Wednesday.*
" 17, Examination for Honors in College Classes begins, *Monday.*
" 19, Biennial Examination, Sophomore Class, begins, *Wednesday.*
" 24, Annual Examination, Junior Class, begins, - *Monday.*
" 26, " " Freshman Class, begins, *Wednesday.*
" 31, " " Grammar School, begins, *Monday.*
Aug. 1, Anniversary of the Literary Societies, - - *Tuesday.*
" 2, Commencement, - - - - - - *Wednesday.*

SUMMER VACATION OF SEVEN WEEKS.

Sept. 18, Examination of Candidates for admission, *Monday and Tuesday.*
" 20, First Term begins, - - - - - *Wednesday.*

ADMISSION.

CANDIDATES for admission into the Freshman Class are examined in Arithmetic, and Algebra through Quadratic Equations; Ancient and Modern Geography; the English, Latin and Greek Grammars; Cæsar's Commentaries; four Orations of Cicero; the first three books of Virgil's Æneid; Arnold's Latin Prose Composition; Bullions' Greek Reader, and the Anabasis of Xenophon. They must furnish testimonials of good character; and if from another College, must bring certificates of honorable dismission. Candidates for a higher standing are examined upon that part of the course already studied by the class which they propose to enter.

No one can be admitted to the Freshman Class until he has completed his fourteenth year; nor to an advanced standing, without a proportional increase of age.

"*Before a student shall be admitted to actual standing in any class, he shall present to the President a receipt from the Treasurer, showing that he has complied with the statutes relating to College charges and Scholarships.*"

N. B. The regular examination for admission into College, commences on the Monday preceding the beginning of each term.

COURSE OF INSTRUCTION.

GRAMMAR SCHOOL.

Bullions' Latin and Greek Grammars, with praxis; Bullions' Latin and Greek Readers; Bullions' Cæsar, and Cicero; Cooper's Virgil; Arnold's Latin Prose Composition, first XII. chapters; Owen's Anabasis, with Boise's Greek Prose Compositions; Higher Arithmetic; Robinson's Algebra, University edition; Mitchell's Classical Geography; Coleman's Biblical Geography; Historical portions of the Old and New Testaments.

SCIENTIFIC SCHOOL.

FIRST YEAR.

Algebra, completed; Plane Geometry; Plane Trigonometry; Surveying and Navigation; Ancient, Modern and Ecclesiastical History.

SECOND YEAR.

Solid Geometry; Spherical Trigonometry, and its applications; Analytical Geometry; Natural Philosophy, and Astronomy; Rhetoric, Logic, and Political Economy.

THIRD YEAR.

Anatomy and Physiology; Zoology; Botany; Chemistry; Natural Theology; Butler's Analogy; Psychology, and Moral Philosophy.

COLLEGE.

FRESHMAN CLASS.

I.

Robinson's Greek Harmony of the Gospels.
Horne's Biblical Antiquities, (abridged edition.)
Cooper's Virgil, with the study of Prosody.
Xenophon's Memorabilia of Socrates, (Robbins' edition.)
Roman Antiquities, (Bojesen,)
Arnold's Greek Composition.
Robinson's Algebra, completed, (University edition.)

II.

Robinson's Harmony.
Lincoln's Livy.
Memorabilia, continued.
Herodotus, (Leipsic edition,) begun.
Roman, Grecian, and Biblical Antiquities.
Davies' Plane Geometry.

III.

Robinson's Harmony.
Lincoln's Livy, continued.
Herodotus, continued.
Grecian and Biblical Antiquities.
Davies' Plane Trigonometry, and Surveying.

SOPHOMORE CLASS.

I.

Acts of the Apostles, (Owen's edition.)
Cicero de Amicitia and de Senectute.
Homer's Iliad, (Owen's edition.)
Davies' Solid Geometry.
Weber's Manual of Ancient History.

II.

Epistolary portion of the New Testament, in Greek.
Horace, with study of the Horatian metres.
Homer's Iliad continued; Plato's Gorgias begun.
Davies' Spherical Trigonometry, and applications.
Weber's Modern History.

III.

Epistles, continued.
Horace, continued.
Plato's Gorgias, (Woolsey's edition.)
Davies' Analytical Geometry.
Ecclesiastical History.

JUNIOR CLASS.

I.

Hebrew Grammar, (Stuart's Rœdiger.)
Genesis.
Tacitus' Germania and Agricola, (Tyler's edition.)
Æschines against Ctesiphon, (Champlin's edition.)
Olmstead's Natural Philosophy, Vol. 1st.
Blair's Rhetoric.

II.

Hebrew—Genesis.
Cicero de Oratore.
Æschines, continued; Demosthenes de Corona begun.
Olmstead's Natural Philosophy, Vols. 1st and 2nd.
Whately's Logic.

III.

Hebrew—Psalms.
Cicero de Oratore, continued.
Demosthenes de Corona, (Champlin's edition,) finished.
Olmstead's Astronomy.
Wayland's Political Economy.

SENIOR CLASS.

I.

Select portions of the Hebrew Bible, with Lectures.
Psychology, (Walker's edition of Reid.)
Silliman's Chemistry.
Anatomy and Physiology, with Lectures.
Wood's Botany, with Lectures.
Cicero's Tusculan Disputations, &c., (Chase's edition.)

II.

Select Hebrew.
Psychology.
Chemistry.
Paley's Natural Theology.
Greek Tragedies; Lectures on Grecian Art, Literature, &c.

III.

Select Hebrew.
Butler's Analogy of Religion, natural and revealed, to the Constitution and Course of Nature.
Moral Philosophy, (Walker's edition of Stewart, and Alexander.)
Mineralogy.
Hitchcock's Geology.

DISTRIBUTION OF RECITATIONS, &c.

	DEPARTMENT OF Bibl. Instruction, & Philos. THE PRESIDENT.	DEPARTMENT OF Rhetoric, History, Logic. Dr. CROWE.	DEPARTMENT OF Natural Science. Prof. STONE.	DEPARTMENT OF Mathematics and Nat. Phil. Prof. THOMSON.	DEPARTMENT OF Greek Lang. and Literature. Prof. BISHOP.	DEPARTMENT OF Latin Lang. and Literature. Prof. HAMILTON.
	I.	**I.**	**I.**	**I.**	**I.**	**I.**
J. G. S.	½ Harmon. of Gospels,...	Ancient History,...	Algebra,...	Algebra, finished,...	Greek Grammar,...	Latin Grammar,...
S. G. S.	½ Acts,...	½ Rhetoric,...		Solid Geometry,...	Bullions' Greek Reader,...	Bullions' Caesar,...
F.	½ Hebrew, Psychology,...			Nat. Philosophy,...	Memorabilia,...	Virgil, continued,...
So.					½ Iliad,...	½ De Amicit. and de Senec.
J.			Chemistry, ½ Anat. Phys.		½ Æschines,...	½ Tacit Germ. and Agric.
S.						½ Tusculan Disputations...
	II.	**II.**	**II.**	**II.**	**II.**	**II.**
J. G. S.	½ Harmon. Gospels,...	Modern History,...	Algebra,...	Plane Geometry,...	Greek Reader,...	Latin Reader,...
S. G. S.	½ Epistles,...	½ Logic,...		Spher. Trig. and Applic.	Anabasis,...	Cicero's Orations,...
F.	½ Hebrew, Psychology.			Nat. Philosophy,...	Memor. and Herodotus,...	Livy,...
So.					¼ Iliad and Gorgias,...	½ Horace,...
J.			Chemistry, ½ Nat. Theol.		¼ Æsch. and Demosthenes,	½ Cic. De Oratore,...
S.					½ Greek Tragedies,...	
	III.	**III.**	**III.**	**III.**	**III.**	**III.**
J. G. S.	½ Harmon. Gospels,...	Eccles. History,...	Algebra,...	Plane Trig. & Surveying.	Greek Reader,...	Latin Reader,...
S. G. S.	½ Epistles,...	½ Pol. Economy.		Analyt. Geometry,...	Anabasis,...	Virgil,...
F.	½ Hebrew,...			Astronomy,...	Herodotus,...	Livy,...
So.					½ Gorgias,...	½ Horace,...
J.	½ Hebrew, Mor. Philosophy.		Butler's Anal., ½ Mineral, and Geology		½ Demosthenes,...	½ Cic. De Oratore,...

PERMANENT RECITATION HOURS IN ALL DEPARTMENTS.

A. M.				
8	½ Seniors,...	Sophomores,...	½ Seniors,...	Juniors,...	Sen. Gram. Sch....	Freshmen,...
9	Juniors,...		Seniors,...	Sophomores,...	Freshmen,...	Sen. Gram. Sch....
10	Seniors,...		Sen. Gram. Sch....	Freshmen,...	½ Sophs. and Juniors,...	½ Soph. and Juniors....
11	½ Fresh. and Sophs.	½ Juniors....				

PERMANENT RECITATION HOURS—SCIENTIFIC DEPARTMENT.

A. M.	FIRST CLASS.	SECOND CLASS.	THIRD CLASS.
8.	History.	Nat. Philos. and Astron.	Nat. Sci. & Nat. The.
9.		Mathematics.	Chem. & Butl. Anal.
10.	Mathematics.		Psychol. & Mor. Phil.
11.		½ Rhet. Log. Pol. Econ.	

The preceding course is so arranged, in all departments, as to require from every class, except the Senior, an average of *three hours and a half* in recitations, *daily*, excepting Saturday. These recitations are attended, without loss of time, between the hours of 8 and 12 A. M.; leaving the remainder of the day for study and recreation.

SCIENTIFIC DEPARTMENT.

The *three years' course* of English, Mathematical and Scientific instruction, pursued in this Department, embraces *all that is included in the Collegiate scheme*, except the Classical languages. Such as desire it, however, may pursue the study of *Latin*, or *French*, in connection with a scientific course. We do not recommend it as *in any sense an equivalent* for a thorough Classical course; nor is it intended for *mere boys;* since the subjects which it includes are entirely above their capacity; but to *young men*, who have obtained *a respectable common school education*, including the elements of Algebra, and who have not time or means to prosecute the Classical course, this system of studies, will, it is hoped, commend itself as solid, comprehensive, and practical. Those who shall complete the prescribed Scientific course, will receive a Diploma, certifying the extent of their attainments.

COLLEGE YEAR—EXAMINATIONS.

The Collegiate Year is divided into *three Terms* of *thirteen weeks* each, and *three Vacations*. The *First Term* begins on the *Third Wednesday in September;* the *Second*, on the *First Wednesday in January;* and the *Third*, on the *First Wednesday in May*, closing with THE FIRST WEDNESDAY IN AUGUST, which is COMMENCEMENT DAY. It is of great importance that Students attend from *the very beginning* of the term; especially since so considerable a portion of time is allotted to vacations. *In most cases, the loss of a few weeks, or even days, seriously affects the future standing of the pupil.* Absence during term time, without special leave, is prohibited.

Public *examinations* will be held, hereafter, only at the close of the College Year; when the Freshman and Junior Classes will be examined on the studies of the preceding year, and the Sophomore and Senior Classes, upon those of the two preceding years. These last examinations will be *final*, for the studies pursued in those years. All the examinations will be *thorough* and *rigid;* and will be conducted, chiefly, by the use of *written questions*, prepared by the Faculty and the Examining Committee, covering the whole field of study prosecuted during a given period, and entirely unknown to the Student until the moment of examination. These questions must be answered in writing before the Committee; and correct answers to a definite portion of them will be the passport of admission to a higher standing. Similar examinations, of a briefer and less decisive character, however, and by way of preparation for the final trial, may be conducted privately, at the pleasure of the Faculty.

The Board of Trustees, having sanctioned the distribution of honorary and pecuniary rewards, the average standing of every pupil will hereafter be posted up in some conspicuous place, at the end of the year; and suitable prizes will be conferred upon the most deserving.

RELIGIOUS INSTRUCTION AND SERVICES.

The attention of a Christian community is respectfully invited to the system of Biblical Instruction which forms a characteristic feature of our course of study. The Grammar School Classes recite daily in the English Bible; and every College Class has a daily, or tri-weekly, recitation in the Greek Testament, or the Hebrew. Proficiency in these, as in other studies, is tested by the usual examinations. In addition to this, Biblical Geography and Antiquities, Ecclesiastical History, Natural Theology, and the Analogy of Religion Natural and Revealed to the constitution and course of nature, are carefully and faithfully studied. There is also a Bible or Catechetical exercise on Sabbath mornings; a public service on Sabbath afternoons, appropriated to the Students; and daily morning prayers. The Students are expected to attend the Sabbath morning service of the congregation worshipping in the chapel, or of some other congregation in the vicinity, if their parents prefer any of the latter. The Methodist, Associate, and Associate Reformed Churches, have regular service in or near the village.

An experiment of four years in this Institution, has established the fact that the daily study of God's word by no means interferes with, but rather promotes, sound and comprehensive attainments in other branches of knowledge. Some, indeed, have questioned the expediency of adding *Hebrew* to an already overburdened curriculum; especially since Theological Students may acquire it in the Seminary, and non-theologians are unlikely to make any practical use of such an acquisition. Our confident answer is,—*First*, that Theological Students need more acquaintance with Hebrew than with Greek, when they enter the Seminary; since familiarity with the Old Testament is more rare, and more difficult of attainment, than familiarity with the New:—*Secondly*, that the mental discipline secured by this study is fully equal to that obtained from any other:—*Thirdly*, that a knowledge of Hebrew, as connected with the Indo-European tongues, greatly contributes to the students' mastery of the latter:—*Fourthly*, that non-theological students are as likely to cultivate the Hebrew, when once acquired, as the higher Mathematics and the Classics: —*Fifthly*, that the Hebrew Scriptures contain more valuable, practical truth, than all the pagan classics put together:—and *lastly*, that the day is to be dreaded when ability to peruse the Sacred Volume, in the originals, shall be the exclusive property of the Clergy.

EXPENSES.

The entire annual expenditures of a Student need not exceed $130, viz:

Tuition and contingent fee, $10 per term,	$30 00
Boarding with private families, and a furnished room, at $1.50 to $2.00 per week,	$60 to $80 00
Fuel, light, washing, &c.,	10 to 15 00
Books, &c.,	5 to 10 00

Boarding in clubs will cost from *fifty* to *seventy-five cents* a week; and some board themselves at even a lower rate. The cost of clothing, and the amount spent as pocket-money, will vary with the taste and habits of the student, and with the wishes of parents. As a general rule, the more money is allowed to a young man, beyond what is *strictly necessary*, the less likely is he to reflect honor upon his parents and instructors. Although Hanover presents comparatively few temptations to extravagance, yet parents are *earnestly advised* to require of their sons a detailed account of their expenditures, and peremptorily to refuse the payment of any debt incurred by them without a *written permission*. It is also recommended that the funds of young pupils be deposited with some one of the Faculty, and expended under his direction. The younger students are required to board where the Faculty may direct, and where they may exercise a more careful and frequent supervision.

N. B. Students placed upon Scholarships by the Faculty, are relieved, in part, or wholly, as the case may require, from the payment of tuition fees.

SCHOLARSHIPS.

The endowment of this Institution, so far as it has been secured, is in the form of *Scholarships;* of which the Board has established several sorts. The sum of $400, paid, or secured to the Corporation by note payable within five years, and bearing six per cent. interest in advance upon principal remaining unpaid—purchases for the owner, his heirs and assigns, a perpetual right to the tuition of one scholar, in Hanover College. The sum of $200, paid, or subscribed under similar conditions, secures a right to twenty years' tuition; after which time, the scholarship is subject to the disposal of the Board for the gratuitous education of candidates for the Gospel Ministry. A church scholarship of $200 secures to the church so contributing, a perpetual right to the tuition of one student, who shall be a member of that church, and appointed by the Session. A Presbyterial scholarship of $200 secures a similar right to a Presbytery, in behalf of pupils who shall be candidates for the Ministry under its care. The *principal* paid on these scholarships is invested by the Corporation in some safe and productive stock; and the *interest only* can be expended for the support of the College.

The sum of $100, *paid within two years, at farthest*, with interest in advance on unpaid principal, purchases a right to ten years' tuition within twenty years from the date of subscription. Both principal and interest of this scholarship may be employed for contingent purposes; and the scholarship expires with the owner's right to its use.

The sum of $100, *paid* into the building fund; or the sum of $50 *paid* in like manner, secures a right to ten, or five, years' tuition of one student.

"*Every person applying for admission as a beneficiary of a scholarship under the control of the donors, shall present to the Treasurer, at the beginning of each term,* A WRITTEN CERTIFICATE, *from those controlling the scholarship, of his right to such benefit; when, after paying whatever interest may be due on said scholarship, he shall receive an acknowledgment of his right, which he shall lodge with the President.*

"*The scholarships subject to the disposal of the Corporation may be occupied by such applicants as the Faculty may select, after inquiry into their circumstances, character and attainments; the preference being, (cœteris paribus,) to those who give the best evidence of scholarship.*"

"*There shall at no time be more than one student upon each scholarship.*"

SOCIETIES, LIBRARIES, &c.

There are two Societies connected with the College,—the *Union Literary*, and the *Philalethean*, each of whose Libraries number about *fifteen hundred* volumes. *The Society of Inquiry* has also begun to collect a Library, Maps, &c. The College Library, which comprises nearly *two thousand* well selected volumes, is accessible to the students. The Cabinet contains several thousand specimens in Mineralogy and Geology. The Laboratory is supplied with the apparatus most necessary for chemical experiments.

A number of valuable books have been added to the College Library, within the year, by donation. Similar contributions will be thankfully received.

GENERAL REMARKS.

The village of Hanover is situated upon an elevated bluff of the Ohio river, six miles below Madison, Indiana; in a region of remarkable salubrity and natural beauty. The village and neighborhood are characterized by morality, and the absence of all ordinary temptations to vice and idleness. Intoxicating liquors have never been sold in the township, the traffic being prohibited, annually, by popular vote. The Ohio river, and the railways from Madison and Cincinnati, place Hanover within twenty-four hours of all the principal points in Indiana, and western Ohio. A plank road from Madison to Hanover, renders the village easy of access in all seasons of the year.

Hanover College is controlled by a Board of Trustees, one-half of whom are appointed by the Board itself, and the other half by the Synods of Indiana and Northern Indiana. All its officers are Ministers or members of the Presbyterian Church.

The Board purchased, some four years since, a farm of two hundred acres, lying between the village and the Ohio river; upon a beautiful point of which, overlooking the river from an elevation of four hundred feet, and commanding a view of its course for fifteen or twenty miles, they are now erecting a new College edifice, which, it is hoped, will be completed during the ensuing year.

THE
TWENTY-SECOND
ANNUAL CIRCULAR

OF

HANOVER COLLEGE,

COMPRISING THE

CATALOGUE, COURSE OF STUDY, &c.

AUGUST, 1854.

INDIANAPOLIS:
INDIANA STATE JOURNAL STEAM PRESS.
1854.

HANOVER COLLEGE.

THE
TWENTY-SECOND
ANNUAL CIRCULAR
OF
HANOVER COLLEGE,

COMPRISING THE

CATALOGUE, COURSE OF STUDY, &c.

AUGUST, 1854.

PRINTED FOR HANOVER COLLEGE.

INDIANAPOLIS.
INDIANA STATE JOURNAL STEAM PRESS.
1854.

HANOVER COLLEGE.

BOARD OF TRUSTEES.

BY WHOM ELECTED.		TERM EXPIRES.
Bd.	Rev. THOMAS E. THOMAS, D. D., Hanover,	1854.
Bd.	Rev. JOHN M. STEVENSON, New Albany,	"
Bd.	Rev. DANIEL LATTIMORE, Vernon,	"
Bd.	Hon. JAMES BLAKE, Indianapolis,	"
S. S.	Rev. D. D. McKee, Dunlapsville,	"
S. S.	JAMES M. RAY, Esq., Indianapolis,	"
N. S.	Rev. WM. Y. ALLEN, Rockville,	"
N. S.	ISAAC COE. M. D., Galena, Ill.,	"
Bd.	JOHN KING, Esq., Madison,	1855.
Bd.	Rev. WM. SICKELS, Pleasant,	"
Bd.	WM. McKEE DUNN, Esq., Madison,	"
Bd.	Judge WM. A. BULLOCK, Vernon.	"
S. S.	Rev. J. G. MONTFORT, D. D., Greensburgh.	"
S. S.	Rev. THOS. S. CROWE, Hanover.	"
N. S.	Rev. JNO. C. EASTMAN, Hanover,	"
N. S.	Rev. SAMUEL N. EVANS, Waveland,	"
Bd.	Rev. JOHN A. McCLUNG, Indianapolis.	1856.
Bd.	Rev. S. R. WILSON, Cincinnati, O.,	"
Bd.	ALEXANDER GAY, M. D., Oxford, O.,	"
Bd.	Rev. W. HILL, D. D., Louisville, Ky.,	"
S. S.	Rev. D. M. STEWART, Rushville,	"
S. S.	Rev. C. LEAVENWORTH, Richmond,	"
N. S.	Rev. F. P. CUMMINS, La Porte,	"
N. S.	Rev. ROBERT IRWIN, Wheeling,	"
Bd.	Rev. JOHN FINLEY CROWE, D. D., Hanover,	1857.
Bd.	A. R. FORSYTH, Esq., Greensburgh,	"
Bd.	JESSE L. WILLIAMS, Esq., Fort Wayne,	"
Bd.	JNO. L. SCOTT, Esq., Cincinnati, O.,	"
S. S.	Rev. PHILIP LINDSLEY, D. D. L. L. D., New Albany.	"
S. S.	Hon. WILLIAMSON DUNN, Hanover,	"
N. S	Rev. E. W. WRIGHT, Delphi,	"
N. S.	Hon. S. HANNA, Ft. Wayne.	"

OFFICERS OF THE BOARD.

Dr. JOHN F. CROWE, *President.*
Dr. THOS. E. THOMAS, *Secretary,*
Rev. JNO. C. EASTMAN, *Treasurer.*
Rev. DANIEL LATTIMORE, } *Agents.*
Rev. H. H. CAMBERN,

FACULTY.

REV. THOMAS E. THOMAS, D. D., *President.*
PROFESSOR OF BIBLICAL INSTRUCTION, PSYCHOLOGY, AND MORAL PHILOSOPHY.

REV. JOHN FINLEY CROWE, D. D.,
PROFESSOR OF RHETORIC, LOGIC, HISTORY, AND POLITICAL ECONOMY.

REV. JARED M. STONE, A. M.,
PROFESSOR OF NATURAL SCIENCE.

S. HARRISON THOMPSON, A. M.,
PROFESSOR OF MATHEMATICS AND POLITICAL ECONOMY.

REV. WM. BISHOP, A. M.,
PROFESSOR OF THE GREEK LANGUAGE AND LITERATURE.

*REV. WILLIAM HAMILTON, A. M.,
PROFESSOR OF THE LATIN LANGUAGE AND LITERATURE.

C. B. H. MARTIN, A. B., *Tutor in Latin and Greek.*

DAVID G. HERRON, *Tutor in Mathematics.*

JAMES K. PATTERSON, *Tutor in Latin.*

---

*Professor Hamilton's resignation was accepted by the Board in April; and the Chair will be filled in August.

RESIDENT GRADUATES.

CHARLES LEE, A. B.	Hanover,	Student of Theology.
HENRY THOMAS MORTON, A. B.,	Shelbyville, Ky.,	" " "
ROBERT SYMINGTON REESE, A. B.,	Hanover,	" " "
AUSTIN WARNER, A. B.,	Hanover,	" " "

UNDERGRADUATES.

SENIOR CLASS.

STEPHEN CROMWELL ADAIR,	Morganfield, Ky.
DAVID GILKESON HERRON,	Willettville, O.
ROBERT IRWIN,	Wheeling,
ROBERT ALEXANDER JOHNSTON,	Mt. Carmel, O.
ISAAC BROWN MOORE,	Monticello.
EDWIN HUBBARD RUTHERFORD,	Brownsville. Tenn.
EDWARD COOKE SICKELS,	Pleasant.
WILLIAM RONDEAU SIM,	Golconda, Ill.
THOMAS WALLACE,	Springdale, O.
JAMES EDWARD WILSON,	Madisonville, Tenn.
JARED RYKER WOODFILL,	Belleville.

JUNIOR CLASS.

JOHN CYRUS ALLEN,	Rockville.
JAMES CYRUS ALEXANDER,	Paris, Ill.
JAMES ROBINSON EVANS,	Hillsboro, O.
MICHAEL MONTGOMERY FISHER,	Russell's Mills.
THOMAS BENTON HENLEY,	San Francisco, Cal.
JAMES HOLLISTER HUNTER,	Marysville, O.
WILLIAM HALL HUSTON,	Symmes' Corner.
HARVEY LAMB,	Hanover.
NATHANIEL FIELD LEMASTER,	Memphis, Tenn.
ROBERT CLARK McGEE,	Charleston.
JOHN QUINCY McKEEHAN,	Charleston.
THADDEUS MAC RAE	De Kalb, Miss.

Charles Hopkins Park, ...Jerseytown, Pa.
Samuel William Rankin, ...Henderson, Ky.
William Addison Sample, ...Memphis, Ten.
William Bloomer Truax, ...Paoli,
Thomas Marion Tucker, ...N. Philadelphia.
Archibald Cameron Voris, ...Pleasant.
Nathaniel Warner, ...Jamesport, L. I.

SOPHOMORE CLASS.

James Baillie Adams, ...Pleasant,
James William Allison, ...Grand View, Ill.
William Washington Berry, ...Spring Dale, O.
Robert Little Brooks, ...Paris, Ill.
Robert Mitchel Campbell, ...Paoli.
David Charlton, ...Pleasant.
James Hendron, ...Palestine, Ill.
Robert Brown Herron, ...Willetville, O.
Henry Keigwin, ...Louisville, Ky.
Robert Daniel Morris, ...Milton, Ky.
James Kennedy Patterson, ...Madison.
Josiah Richardson, ...Louisville, Ky.
John Worth Shannon, ...Hanover.
Abner Lowry Shannon, ...Hanover.
Benjamin Franklin Slocumb, ...Vicksburgh, Mis.
Richmond Kelly Smoot, ...Huntingdon, Ten.
James Harvey Tedford, ...Pittsburgh.
Benjamin DuBois Wikoff, ...Franklin, O.
Luther Halsey Wilson, ...Madisonville, Ten.

FRESHMAN CLASS.

Leonard Fisk Andrews, ...Northfield, O.
Isaac Hall Christian, ...Grand View, Il.
Jacob Ditzler, ...Saltillo, Ky.
Dyer Burgess Eastman, ...Hanover.
Milo Ellis, ...N. Bethel.
John Hanna Gray, ...Raleigh, Tenn.
James Cleland Hamilton, ...Hanover.
William Wilberforce Hamilton, ...Hanover,
Theodore Dudley Johnston, ...Madison.
James Warren Lanham, ...Buena Vista.
Alexander Williamson Lattimore, ...Vernon.
William Batty Laughlin, ...Rushville.

Simon Lott,	Madison.
James Charlott McElroy,	Greencastle.
Samuel Vigo McKee,	Vincennes.
William Mack Moore,	Portersville, Tenn.
John Samuel Park,	Memphis, Tenn.
Junius Philander Sample,	Raleigh, Tenn.
Nelson Smith,	Sharpsburgh, Pa.
David McKnight Williamson,	Logansport.
John Lowry Wilson,	Madisonville, Tenn.

SCIENTIFIC DEPARTMENT.

SENIOR CLASS.

ALEXANDER HUNTER,	Bardstown, Ky.
ALFRED WILLIAM HYNES	Hanover.
WILLIAM HARVEY ROBBINS IRWIN.	Greenfield, O.
WILLIAM MCFADDEN,	Boggstown.

MIDDLE CLASS.

THOMAS HOBBES HAMMOND,	Bardstown, Ky.
ALFRED NEVIN SNODDY,	Dayton.
WILLIAM VANNICE;	Morefield,
THOMAS MARQUIS WALLACE.	London. O.

JUNIOR CLASS.

ROBERT LONG ADAMS,	Pleasant.
SAMUEL LEE BEACH,	Jeffersonville.
DAVID SHELLEY BLACKBURN,	Paris, Ill.
JOHN WESLEY BONTA	Franklin.
DANIEL WILLIAM BOWEN,	Ft. Wayne.
ROBERT NICHOLSON BROADBENT,	Raysville.
JACOB ARMSTRONG BRUNER,	Hanover.
CYRUS FINLEY BUTLER,	Flemingsburg, Ky.
ALEXANDER SHANNON BUTLER,	Richland.
RICHARD STRADER COLLUM,	Jeffersonville.
LORD BYRON CONWAY,	Springfield, O.
WILLIAM HARRISON COPELAND,	Canaan.
WILLIAM CURTIS COWELL,	Vernon.
GEORGE WASHINGTON COX,	Bardstown, Ky.
JOHN WESLEY DEAN,	Westville, Ky
JOHN SCHENCK DENISE,	Franklin, O.
JOHN WILLIAM FISH,	Florence, Ky.
SAMUEL NEWELL FISHER,	Orleans.
GEORGE SPARHAWK GARRETT,	High Grove, Ky.
WILLIAM PENFIELD GARRET,	Delphi.
ARMSTRONG GIBSON,	Fairland.
BEN GULLION,	West Point, Iowa.
SAMUEL HERRON,	Westville, Ky.

Simon White Huddleston,	Olympus, Tenn.
Franklin Brown Hunt,	Knoxville, Mi.
Robert Calvin Irwin,	Hanover.
Cyrus Alexander Johnson,	Memphis, Tenn.
George Washington MacCawley,	Cross-roads, Ky.
John Thomas McClure,	Crittenden, Ky.
William Thomas McCoughtry,	Raleigh, Ky.
John Thomas McMillan,	Hanover.
James Harvey Marshall,	Kent.
Gideon Elijah Moncrief,	Vernon.
John Samuel Park,	Louisville, Ky.
James Edwin Rankin,	Henderson, Ky.
James Ritchie,	Smyrna.
James William Roberts.	Christiansburgh, Ky.
Samuel Robeson,	Dayton.
Thomas Shannon,	Hanover.
George Haynes Simmons,	Bardstown, Ky.
Milton White Smith,	Hanover.
Charles Albert Smyth,	Hanover.
David Taylor,	Hibernia, O.
James Nathaniel Taylor.	Smith's Mill, Ky.
John Taylor,	Swanville.
Robert Taylor.	Swanville.
William Nathaniel Thompson,	Vincennes.
Salathiel Boone Voris,	Christiansburgh, Ky.
William Owen Watts,	Bardstown, Ky.
John William Ward,	Indianapolis.
Isidore Wellington,	Bardstown, Ky.
James Alexander Wildman,	Madison.
Wallace Woodward,	Hanover.
John Brown Wright,	Logansport.

GRAMMAR SCHOOL.

SENIOR CLASS.

William Wilberforce Andrew,	La Porte.
David McIlvaine Allen,	Owensboro, Ky.
Cornelius Bailey,	Henderson, Ky.
William Peter Baker,	Fort Wayne.
James Ray Blake,	Indianapolis.
Marshall Bowman,	Vincennes.
Robert Harvey Gilmore,	Manhattan.
Samuel Telford Hanna,	Fort Wayne.
Horace Hovey Hanna,	Fort Wayne.

Israel Sylvester Hogeland, ...Lafayette.
Charles Cornelius Hoke, ...Fisherville, Ky.
William Brackenridge List, ...Franklin.
John David McClintock, ...Greensburgh.
Thomas Michael McIlwrath, ...Madison.
James McNeel, ...Sloansville.
Nathan Amzi Means, ...Northfield, O.
John Miller. ....Greensburgh.
David William Moffat, ...Madison.
Robert Starr Moore, ...Kingsbury.
Joseph Allen Porter, ...Lodiana, N. India.
James Alexander Piper, ...Byron.
Chauncey Sabin, ...Union Mills.
Isaac Coe Sickels, ...Pleasant.
George Martin Shaner, ...Apple Creek, Mo.
Thomas Thorn Swan, ...Hanover.
Augustus Taylor, ...Ft. Madison, Iowa.
William Wirt Thomson, ...McLeods, Mi.
James Harvey Vannuys, ...Franklin.
C. Pleasant Voris, ...Pleasant.
William Baty Warren, ...Louisville, Ky.

JUNIOR CLASS.

John Newton Abernathy, ...Knightstown.
Myron Andrews, ...Vernon.
George Robert Bright, ...Madison.
Charles William Brown, ...Raysville.
John Aleneth Byers, ...Long Creek, Mi.
Samuel Montgomery Cambern, ...Hanover.
Charles Chauncey Colting, ...Hanover.
William Thomas Covert, ...Franklin.
William Irwin Craddock, ...Louisville, Ky.
George Washington Craft, ...Raysville.
Edward Hugh Dobbins, ...N. Orleans, La.
William Webster Eastman, ...Hanover.
Benjamin Franklin Elder, ...Knightstown.
Sylvester Franklin Gilmore, ...Manhattan.
David Alfred Gilpin, ...Hanover.
Samuel John Gilpin, ...Hanover.
James Hall, ...Knightstown.
Nathaniel Lewis Howard, ...Knightstown.
William Wallace Jamieson, ...Rising Sun.
Robert Newman John, ...Harrison, O.
Robert Lenington, ...Kokomo.
Thomas Armstrong Long, ...Washington.
Samuel Thompson McClure, ...Vincennes.
Samuel Finley McKeehan, ...Vernon.
William Kennedy Patterson, ...Madison.
James Newton Pogue, ...Hanover.

HANOVER COLLEGE. 11

John Calvin Riddle, ...Knightstown.
John Addison Ryman, ...Lawrenceburg.
Robert Blair Smith, ...Sharpsburgh, Pa.
Austin Lowry Thomson, ...Kingston.
John Bacon Vawter, ...Worthsville.
Charles Whitesel, ...Knightstown.
John Ward Wilson, ...Crawfordsville
Francis George Wilson, ...N. Frankfort.

SUMMARY.

Resident Graduates, ... 4
Undergraduates, Seniors, ... 11
      Juniors, ... 20
      Sophomores, ... 20
      Freshmen, ... 21
      Scientific Students, ... 63
                     — 135
Grammar Scholars, ... 64

 Total, ... 203

CALENDAR.

1854.

Sept. 18, 19, Examination of candidates for admission,···Monday and Tuesday.
" 20, First term begins,··Wednesday.
Dec. 19, First term begins,···Tuesday.

WINTER VACATION OF TWO WEEKS.

1855.

Jan. 3, Second term begins,··Wednesday.
April 2, Exhibition of the Union Literary Society,················Monday.
" 3, Exhibition of the Philalethean Society.·····················Tuesday.
" 3, Second term ends,··Tuesday.

SPRING VACATION OF FOUR WEEKS.

May 2, Third term begins,··Wednesday.
July 9, Biennial Examination, Senior Class, begins,···············Monday.
" 18, Biennial Examination, Sophomore Class, begins,·······Wednesday.
" 23, Annual Examination, Junior Class, begins, ················Monday.
" 25, Annual Examination, Freshman Class, begins,··········Wednesday.
" 30, Annual Examination, Grammar School, begins,·········Wednesday.
" 31, Anniversary of the Literary Societies, ·····················Tuesday.
Aug. 1, COMMENCEMENT DAY, ··Wednesday.

SUMMER VACATION OF SEVEN WEEKS.

Sept. 17, Examination of candidates for admission,···Monday and Tuesday.
" 19, First term begins, ··Wednesday.

ADMISSION.

CANDIDATES for admission into the Freshman Class are examined in Arithmetic, and Algebra through Quadratic Equations; Ancient and Modern Geography; the English, Latin and Greek Grammars; Cæsar's Commentaries; four Orations of Cicero; the first three books of Virgil's Æneid; Arnold's Latin Prose Composition; Bullion's Greek Reader, and the Anabasis of Xenophon. They must furnish testimonials of good character; and if from another College, must bring certificates of honorable dismission. Candidates for a higher standing are examined upon that part of the course already studied by the class which they propose to enter.

No one can be admitted to the Freshman Class until he has completed his fourteenth year; nor to an advanced standing, without a proportional increase of age.

"Before a student shall be admitted to actual standing in any class, he shall present to the President a receipt from the Treasurer, showing that he has complied with the statutes relating to College charges and Scholarships."

N. B. The regular examination for admission into College, commences on the Monday preceding the beginning of each term.

COURSE OF INSTRUCTION.

GRAMMAR SCHOOL.

Bullions' Latin and Greek Grammars, with praxis; Bullions' Latin and Greek Readers; Bullions' Cæsar, and Cicero; Cooper's Virgil; Arnold's Latin Prose Composition, first XII. chapters; Owen's Anabasis, with Boise's Greek Prose Composition; Higher Arithmetic; Robinson's Algebra, University edition; Mitchell's Classical Geography; Coleman's Biblical Geography; Historical portions of the Old and New Testaments.

SCIENTIFIC SCHOOL.

FIRST YEAR.

Algebra, completed; Plane Geometry; Plane Trigonometry; Surveying and Navigation; Ancient, Modern and Ecclesiastical History.

SECOND YEAR.

Solid Geometry; Spherical Trigonometry, and its applications; Analytical Geometry; Natural Philosophy, and Astronomy; Rhetoric, Logic, and Political Economy.

THIRD YEAR.

Anatomy and Physiology; Zoology; Botany; Chemistry; Natural Theology; Butler's Analogy; Psychology, and Moral Philosophy.

COLLEGE.

FRESHMAN CLASS.

I.

Robinson's Greek Harmony of the Gospels.
Horne's Biblical Antiquities, (abridged edition.)
Cooper's Virgil, with the study of Prosody.
Xenophon's Memorabilia of Socrates, (Robbins' edition.)
Roman Antiquities, (Bojesen.)
Arnold's Greek Composition.
Robinson's Algebra, completed, University edition.)

II.

Robinson's Harmony.
Lincoln's Livy.
Memorabilia, continued.
Herodotus, (Leipsic edition,) begun.
Roman, Grecian, and Biblical Antiquities.
Davies's Plane Geometry.

III.

Robinson's Harmony.
Lincoln's Livy, continued.
Herodotus, continued.
Grecian and Biblical Antiquities.
Davies' Plane Trigonometry, and Surveying.

SOPHOMORE CLASS.

I.

Acts of the Apostles, (Owen's edition.)
Cicero de Amicitia and de Senectute.
Homer's Iliad, (Owen's edition.)
Davies' Solid Geometry.
Weber's Manual of Ancient History.

II.

Epistolary portion of the New Testament, in Greek.
Horace, with study of the Horatian metres.
Homer's Iliad continued; Plato's Gorgias begun.
Davies' Spherical Trigonometry, and applications.
Weber's Modern History.

III.

Epistles, continued.
Horace, continued.
Plato's Gorgias, (Woolsey's edition.)
Davies' Analytical Geometry.
Ecclesiastical History.

JUNIOR CLASS.

I.

Hebrew Grammar. (Stuart's Rœdiger.)
Genesis.
Tacitus' Germania and Agricola, (Tyler's edition.)
Æschines against Ctesiphon, (Champlin's edition.)
Olmstead's Natural Philosophy, Vol. 1st.
Blair's Rhetoric.

II.

Hebrew—Genesis.
Cicero de Oratore.
Æschines, continued; Demosthenes de Corona begun.
Olmstead's Natural Philosophy, Vols. 1st and 2nd.
Whately's Logic.

III.

Hebrew—Psalms.
Cicero de Oratore, continued.
Demosthenes de Corona, (Champlin's edition,) finished.
Olmstead's Astronomy.
Wayland's Political Economy.

SENIOR CLASS.

I.

Select portions of the Hebrew Bible, with Lectures.
Psychology, (Walker's edition of Reid.)
Silliman's Chemistry.
Anatomy and Physiology, with Lectures.
Wood's Botany, with Lectures.
Cicero's Tusculan Disputations, &c., (Chase's edition.)

II.

Select Hebrew.
Psychology—Philosopy of Sir Wm. Hamilton, (Wight's edition.)
Chemistry.
Paley's Natural Theology.
Greek Tragedies; Lectures on Grecian Art, Literature, &c.

III

Select Hebrew.
Butler's Analogy of Religion, Natural and Revealed, to the Constitution and Course of Nature.
Moral Philosophy, (Walker's edition of Stewart, and Alexander.)
Mineralogy.
Hitchcock's Geology.

N. B. The text-books needed for any part of the College Course, may be procured of Mr. Lee, Bookseller, Hanover, at Cincinnati and Louisville prices.

DISTRIBUTION OF RECITATIONS, &c.

	DEPARTMENT OF Bibl. Instruction, & Phil. THE PRESIDENT.	DEPARTMENT OF Rhetoric, Hist., Logic, Dr. CROWE.	DEPARTMENT OF Natural Science. Prof. STONE.	DEPARTMENT OF Mathematics & Nat. Phil. Prof. THOMPSON.	DEPARTMENT OF Greek Lang. & Literature. Prof. BISHOP.	DEPARTMENT OF Latin Lan. & Literature. Prof. HAMILTON.
	I.	**I.**	**I.**	**I.**	**I.**	**I.**
J. G. S.	Hebrew, Psychology,...	Rhetoric,...	Algebra,...	Algebra, finished,...	Greek Grammar,...	Latin Grammar,...
S. G. S.	Acts,...	Ancient History,...	Algebra,...	Solid Geometry,...	Bullion's Greek Reader,...	Bullions' Caesar,...
F.	Harmon. of Gospels,...			Nat. Philosophy,...	Memorabilia,...	Virgil, continued,...
So.	Hebrew,...				Iliad,...	De Amicit. & de Senec.
J.					Æschines,...	Tacit Germ. and Agric.
S.						Tusculan Disputations,
	II.	**II.**	**II.**	**II.**	**II.**	**II.**
J. G. S.	Hebrew, Psychology,...	Rhetoric,...	Chemistry, ½ Anat. Phys.		Greek Reader,...	Latin Reader,...
S. G. S.	Harmon. Gospels,...	Modern History,...	Algebra,...	Plane Geometry,...	Anabasis,...	Cicero's Orations,...
F.	Epistles,...	Logic,...	Algebra,...	Spher. Trig. and Applic.	Memor. and Herodotus,	Livy,...
So.	Hebrew,...			Nat. Philosophy,...	Iliad and Gorgias,...	Horace,...
J.					Æsch. & Demosthenes,	Æsch. & Demosthenes,...
S.					Greek Tragedies,...	Cic. De Orat.,...
	III.	**III.**	**III.**	**III.**	**III.**	**III.**
J. G. S.	Hebrew, Mor. Philos...	Eccles. History,...	Butler's Anal. ½ Miner-		Greek Reader,...	Latin Reader,...
S. G. S.	Harmon. Gospels,...	Pol. Economy,...	al, and Geology.	Algebra,...	Anabasis,...	Virgil,...
F.	Epistles,...		Chemistry, ½ Nat. Theol.	Plane Trig. & Surveying	Herodotus,...	Livy,...
So.	Hebrew,...			Analyt. Geometry,...	Gorgias,...	Horace,...
J.	Hebrew, Mor. Philos...			Astronomy,...	Demosthenes,...	Cic. De Oratore,...

PERMANENT RECITATION HOURS IN ALL DEPARTMENTS.

A. M.			
8	½ Seniors,...	½ Sophomores,...	½ Juniors,...
9	½ Juniors,...	½ Seniors,...	½ Sophomores,...
10	½ Seniors,...	Sen. Gram. Sch...	½ Freshmen,...
11	½ Fresh. and Sophs...	½ Juniors,...	Sen. Gram. Sch...
			½ Soph. and Juniors,...

PERMANENT RECITATION HOURS—SCIENTIFIC DEPARTMENT.

A. M.	FIRST CLASS.	SECOND CLASS.	THIRD CLASS.
8.	History	Nat. Philos. and Astron.	Nat. Sci. & Nat. The.
9.		Mathematics.	Chem. & Butl. Anal.
10.	Mathematics.		Psychol. & Mor. Phil.
11.		‡ Rhet. Log. Pol. Econ.	

The preceding course is so arranged, in all departments, as to require from every class, except the Senior, an average of *three hours and a half* in recitations, *daily*, excepting Saturday. These recitations are attended, without loss of time, between the hours of 8 and 12 A. M.; leaving the remainder of the day for study and recreation.

SCIENTIFIC DEPARTMENT.

The three year's course of English, Mathematical and Scientific instruction pursued in this Department, embraces all that is included in the Collegiate scheme, except the Classical languages. Such as desire it, however, may pursue the study of Latin, or French, in connection with a scientific course. We do not recommend it as in any sense an equivalent for a thorough, Classical course; nor is it intended for mere boys; since the subjects which it includes are entirely above their capacity; but to young men, who have obtained a respectable common school education, including the elements of Algebra, and who have not time or means to prosecute the Classical course, this system of studies, will, it is hoped, commend itself as solid, comprehensive, and practical. Those who shall complete the prescribed Scientific course, will receive a Diploma, certifying the extent of their attainments.

COLLEGE YEAR.—EXAMINATIONS.

The Collegiate Year is divided into three Terms of thirteen weeks each, and three Vacations. The First Term begins on the Third Wednesday in September; the Second, on the First Wednesday in January; and the Third, on the First Wednesday in May, closing with the First Wednesday in August, which is Commencement Day. It is of great importance that Students attend from the very beginning of the term; especially since so considerable portion of time is allotted to vacations. In most cases, the loss of a few weeks, or even days, seriously affects the future standing of the pupil. Absence during term time, without special leave, is prohibited.

Public examinations will be held, hereafter, only at the close of the College year; when the Freshmen and Junior Classes will be examined on the studies of the preceding year, and the Sophomore and Senior Classes, upon those of the two preceding years. These last examinations will be *final*, for the studies pursued in those years. All the examinations will be *thorough* and *rigid;* and will be conducted, chiefly, by the use of written questions, prepared by the Faculty and the Examining Committee, covering the whole field of study prosecuted during a given period, and entirely unknown to the Student until the moment of examination These questions must be answered in writing before the Committee; and correct answers to a definite portion of them will be the passport of admission to a higher standing. Similar examinations, of a briefer and less decisive character, however, and by way of preparation for the final trial, may be conducted privately, at the pleasure of the Faculty.

The Board of Trustees, having sanctioned the distribution of honorary and pecuniary rewards, the average standing of every pupil will hereafter be posted up in some conspicuous place, at the end of the year; and suitable prizes will be conferred upon the most deserving.

RELIGIOUS INSTRUCTION AND SERVICES.

The attention of a Christian community is respectfully invited to the system of Biblical Instruction which forms a characteristic feature of our course of Study. The Grammar School Classes recite daily in the English Bible; and every College Class has a daily or tri-weekly, recitation in the Greek Testament, or the Hebrew. Proficiency in these, as in other studies, is tested by the usual examinations. In addition to this, Biblical Geography and Antiquities, Ecclesiastical History, Natural Theology, and the Analogy of Religion, Natural and Revealed, to the constitution and course of nature, are carefully and faithfully studied. There is also a Bible or Catechetical exercise on Sabbath mornings; a public service on Sabbath afternoons, appropriated to the Students; and daily morning prayers. The Students are expected to attend the Sabbath morning service of the congregation worshipping in the chapel, or of some other congregation in the vicinity, if their parents prefer any of the latter. The Methodist, Associate, and Associate Reformed Churches, have regular service in or near the village.

An experiment of four years in this Institution, has established the fact that the daily study of God's word by no means interferes with, but rather promotes, sound and comprehensive attainments in other branches of knowledge. Some, indeed, have questioned the expediency of adding *Hebrew* to an already overburdened curriculum; especially since Theological Students may acquire it in the Seminary, and non-theologians are unlikely to make any particular use of such an acquisition. Our confident answer is,—*First*, that Theological Students need more acquaintance with Hebrew than with Greek, when they enter the Seminary; since familiarity with the Old Testament is more rare, and more difficult of attainment, than familiarity with the New:—*Secondly*, that the mental discipline secured by this study is fully equal to that obtained from any other:—*Thirdly*, that a knowledge of Hebrew, as connected with the Indo-European tongues, greatly contributes to the students' mastery of the latter:—*Fourthly*, that non-theological students are as likely to cultivate the Hebrew, when once acquired, as the higher Mathematics and the Classics:—*Fifthly*, that the Hebrew Scriptures contain more valuable, practical truth, than all the pagan classics put together:—and *lastly*, that the day is to be dreaded when ability to peruse the Sacred Volume, in the originals, shall be the exclusive property of the Clergy.

EXPENSES.

The entire annual expenditures of a Student need not exceed $140, viz:

Tuition and contingent fee, $10 per term,	$30 00
Boarding with private families, and a furnished room, at $1 75 to $2 25 per week,	$70 to 90 00
Fuel, light, washing, &c.,	10 to 15 00
Books, &c.,	5 to 10 00

Boarding in clubs will cost from *fifty* to *seventy-five cents* a week; and some board themselves even at a lower rate. The cost of clothing, and the amount spent as pocket-money, will vary with the taste and habits of the student, and with the wishes of parents. As a general rule, the more money is allowed to a young man beyond what is *strictly necessary*, the less likely is he to reflect honor upon his parents and instructors. Although Hanover presents comparatively few temptations to extravagance, yet parents are *earnestly advised* to require of their sons a detailed account of their expenditures, and peremptorily to refuse the payment of any debt incurred by them without a written permission. It is also recommended that the funds of young pupils be deposited with some one of the Faculty, and expended under his direction. The younger students are required to board where the Faculty may direct, and where they may exercise a more careful and frequent supervision.

N. B. Students placed upon Scholarships by the Faculty, are relieved in part, or wholly, as the case may require, from the payment of tuition fees.

SCHOLARSHIPS.

The endowment of this Institution, so far as it has been secured, is in the form of *Scholarships;* of which the Board has established several sorts. The sum of $400, paid, or secured to the Corporation by note payable within five years, and bearing six per cent. interest in advance upon principal remaining unpaid—purchases for the owner, his heirs and assigns, a perpetual right to the tuition of one scholar, in Hanover College. The sum of $200, paid, or subscribed under similar conditions, secures a right to twenty years' tuition; after which time, the scholarship is subject to the disposal of the Board for the gratuitous education of candidates for the Gospel Ministry. A church scholarship of $200 secures to the church so contributing, a perpetual right to the tuition of one student, who shall be a member of that church, and appointed by the session. A Presbyterial scholarship of $200 secures a similar right to a Presbytery, in behalf of pupils who shall be candidates for the Ministry under its care. The *principal* paid on these scholarships is invested by the Corporation in some safe and productive stock; and the *interest only* can be expended for the support of the College.

The sum of $100, *paid within two years at farthest,* with interest in advance on unpaid principal, purchases a right to ten years' tuition within twenty years from the date of subscription. Both principal and interest of this scholarship may be employed for contingent purposes; and the scholarship expires with the owner's right to its use.

The sum of $100 *paid* into the building fund; or the sum of $50 *paid* in like manner, secures a right to ten, or five years' tuition of one student.

"Every person applying for admission as a beneficiary of a scholarship under the control of the donors, shall present to the Treasurer, at the beginning of each term, *a written certificate*, from those controlling the scholarship, of his right to such benefit; when, after paying whatever interest may be due on said scholarship, he shall receive an acknowledgment of his right, which he shall lodge with the President.

"The scholarships subject to the disposal of the Corporation may be occupied by such applicants as the Faculty may select, after inquiry into their circumstances, character and attainments; the preference being, (cœteris paribus,) to those who give the best evidence of scholarship."

"There shall at no time be more than one student upon each scholarship."

SOCIETIES, LIBRARIES, &c.

There are two Societies connected with the College,—the *Union Literary*, and the *Philalethean*, each of whose Libraries number about *fifteen hundred* volumes. *The Society of Inquiry* has also begun to collect a Library, Maps, &c. The College Library, which comprises nearly *two thousand* well selected volumes, is accessible to the students. The Cabinet contains several thousand specimens in Mineralogy and Geology. The Laboratory is supplied with the apparatus most necessary for chemical experiments.

A number of valuable books have been added to the College Library, within the year, by donation. Similar contributions will be thankfully received.

LOCATION, BUILDING, &c.

The village of Hanover is situated upon an elevated bluff of the Ohio river, six miles below Hanover, Indiana, in a region of remarkable salubrity and natural beauty. The village and neighborhood are characterized by morality, and the absence of all ordinary temptations to vice and idleness. Intoxicating liquors have never been sold in the township; the traffic being prohibited, annually, by popular vote. The Ohio river, and the Railways from Madison, New Albany, and Cincinnati, place Hanover within twenty-four hours of all the principal points in Indiana, Western Ohio, and Eastern Illinois. A Plank Road from Madison to Hanover, renders the village easy of access at all seasons of the year.

Hanover College is controlled by a Board of Trustees; one half of whom are appointed by the Board itself, and the other half by the Synods of Indiana and Northern Indiana. All its officers are Ministers, or members, of the Presbyterian church.

The Board purchased, some five years ago, a farm of two hundred acres, lying between the village and the Ohio river, upon a beautiful point of which, overlooking the river from an elevation of four hundred feet, they have erected a commodious College edifice, now nearly completed. The new College, a sketch of which accompanies this Catalogue, consists of a centre building, nearly 80 feet square, with lateral and transverse wings. The whole length is about 200 feet. It contains no dormitories for students; (an undesirable provision;) but affords ample and convenient halls, library, cabinet, lecture and recitation rooms, and a spacious chapel. Its entire cost, when finished, will not exceed thirty thousand dollars.

The property of the College, including scholarship notes, is estimated at seventy thousand dollars.

HANOVER COLLEGE.

THE
Twenty-Third Annual Circular,

OF

HANOVER COLLEGE,

COMPRISING THE

CATALOGUE, COURSE OF STUDY, &c.

AUGUST, 1855.

MADISON.
COURIER STEAM PRINTING ESTABLISHMENT.
1855.

BOARD OF TRUSTEES.

BY WHOM ELECTED.		TERM EXPIRES
Bd.	JOHN L. KING, Esq., Madison,	1855.
Bd.	Rev. WM. SICKLES, Indianapolis,	"
Bd.	WM. McKEE DUNN, Esq., Madison,	"
Bd.	Judge WM. A. BULLOCK, Vernon,	
S. S.	Rev. J. G. MONTFORT, D. D., Greensburg,	"
S. S.	Rev. THOS. S. CROWE, Hanover,	"
N. S.	Rev. JNO. C. EASTMAN, Hanover,	"
N. S.	Rev. SAMUEL N. EVANS, Waveland,	"
Bd.	Rev. JOHN A. McCLUNG, Indianapolis,	1856.
Bd.	Rev. S. R. WILSON, Cincinnati, O.	"
Bd.	ALEXANDER GUY, M. D., Oxford, O.	"
S. S.	Rev. D. M. STEWART, Rushville,	"
S. S.	Rev. C. LEAVENWORTH, Richmond,	"
N. S.	Rev. F. P. CUMMINS, La Porte,	"
N. S.	Rev. ROBERT IRWIN, Wheeling,	"
Bd.	Rev. J. L. HALSEY, D. D., Louisville, Ky.	"
Bd.	Rev. JOHN FINLEY CROWE, D. D., Hanover.	1857.
Bd.	A. R. FORSYTH, Esq., Greensburg,	"
Bd.	JESSE L. WILLIAMS, Esq., Fort Wayne,	"
Bd.	Rev. J. B. MORTON, Middletown, O.,	"
S. S.	Rev. J. F. SMITH, Vincennes,	"
S. S.	Rev. J. M. STEVENSON, D. D., New Albany,	"
N. S.	Rev. E. W. WRIGHT, Delphi,	
N. S.	Hon. S. HANNA, Fort Wayne,	"
Bd.	Rev. H. H. CAMBERN, Rushville,	1858.
Bd.	Rev. THOMAS E. THOMAS, New Albany,	"
Bd.	Rev. DANIEL LATTIMORE, Vernon,	"
Bd.	Hon. JAMES BLAKE, Indianapolis,	"
N. S.	Rev. CHARLES K. THOMSON, Darlington,	"
N. S.	Rev. SAMUEL C. LOGAN, Constantine, Mich.	"
S. S.	Rev. D. D. McKEE, Dunlappsville	"
Bd.	JAMES M. RAY, Esq., Indianapolis.	"

OFFICERS OF THE BOARD.

Dr. JOHN F. CROWE, President.
Rev. THOMAS S. CROWE, General Agent.
Prof. S. H. THOMSON, Treasurer.

FACULTY.

REV. JONATAAN EDWARDS, A. M., *President.*
PROFESSOR OF BIBLICAL INSTRUCTION, PSYCHOLOGY AND MORAL PHILOSOPHY.

REV JOHN FINLEY CROWE, D. D.,
PROFESSOR OF RHETORIC, LOGIC, HISTORY AND POLITICAL ECONOMY.

REV. S. HARRISON THOMSON, A. M.,
PROFESSOR OF MATHEMATICS AND ASTRONOMY.

REV. J. M. STONE, A. M.,
PROFESSOR OF NATURAL SCIENCE.

REV. WM. BISHOP., A. M.
PROFESSOR OF GREEK LANGUAGE AND LITERATURE.

HENRY R. LOTT, A. M., M. D.;
PROFESSOR OF LATIN LANGUAGE AND LITERATURE.

MICHAEL M. FISHER, *Tutor in Mathematics.*

JOHN Q. McKEEHAN, *Tutor in Greek.*

ROBERT J. L. MATTHEWS, *Tutor in Latin.*

UNDERGRADUATES.

Senior Class.

James Robinson Evans,	Hillsboro, O.
Michael Montgomery Fisher,	Russel's Mills.
James Hollister Hunter,	Point Prescot, Wis.
William Hall Huston,	Symms' Corner, O.
Robert Clarke McGee,	Charleston.
John Quincy McKeehan,	Queensville.
Robert John Louis Matthews,	New Albany.
Charles Hopkins Park,	Jerseytown, Pa.
William Addison Sample,	Memphis, Tenn.
William Bloomer Truax,	Paoli.
Thomas Marion Tucker,	New Philadelphia.
Archibald Cameron Voris,	Bennington.

Junior Class.

James Baillie Adams,	Pleasant.
James William Allison,	Grand View, Ill.
Robert Little Brooks,	Paris, Ill.
William Means Crozier,	Iowa City, Ia.
Dinsmore Cramer,	Plymouth, Mich.
Robert Brown Herron,	Willettville, O.
Henry Keigwin,	Louisville, Ky.
D. F. Marshall,	Franklin, O.
James Kennedy Patterson,	Madison.
Josiah Rickardson,	Louisville, Ky.
Benjamin Franklin Slocumb,	Vicksburg, Miss.

Richard Kelly Smoot,......................Huntingdon, Tenn.
James Harvey Tedford,.....................Pittsburg.
Benjamin DuBois Wykoff,...................Franklin, O.
Luther Halsey Wilson,.....................Madisonville, Tenn.

Sophomore Class.

Leonard Fisk Andrews,.....................Northfield, O.
Isaac Hall Christian,.....................Grand View, Ill.
John Collerick,...........................Fort Wayne.
*John Hanna Gray,.........................Raleigh, Tenn.
James Clelland Hamilton,..................N. Y. City.
William Wilberforce Hamilton,.............N. Y. City.
Homer Hill,...............................Newburg.
Alexander Williamson Lattimore,...........Vernon.
James Charlott McElroy,...................Greencastle.
Samuel Vigo McKee,........................Vincennes.
John McMurray,............................New Concord, O.
John Samuel Park,.........................Memphis, Tenn.
Nelson Orville Wendell,...................Oreonta, N. Y.
David McKnight Williamson,................Logansport.

*Deceased.

Freshman Class.

William Peter Baker,......................Fort Wayne.
Marshall D. Bowman........................Vincennes.
William Cochrane,.........................Cincinnati, O.
Alexander Miller Crawford,................Graysville.
Dyer Burgess Eastman,.....................Hanover.
Robert Harvey Gilmore,....................Manhattan.
Samuel Telford Hanna,.....................Fort Wayne.

Horace Hovey Hanna,........................Fort Wayne.
George Herschell Hill,......................Newburg.
John David McClintock,....................Hanover.
Robert Campbell McKinney,.................Sullivan.
Thomas Michael McElwrath,.................Madison.
Abraham David Matthews,...................Hanover.
Nathan Amzi Means,........................Northfield, O.
John Miller,...............................Greensburg.
David William Moffat,......................Madison.
Robert Starr Moore,........................Kingsboro.
James Alexander Piper,....................Laporte.
George West Richardson,...................Madison.
Robert Gaines Ross,.......................Twenty Mile Stand, O.
Chauncey Sabin,...........................Union Mills.
George Martin Shaner,.....................Apple Creek, Mo.
John L. Scott,............................Shelbyville, Ky.
Isaac Coe Sickles,........................Indianapolis.
William Wirt Thomson,.....................McLeod's P.O. Miss.
James Harvey Vaunuys,.....................Franklin.
Cornelius Pleasant Voris,.................Bennington.
William Warren,...........................Louisville, Ky.
Henry Clay Warren,........................Louisville, Ky.
Jesse Peet Williams,......................Fort Wayne.
Gavin Easton Wiseman,.....................Williamsburg, O.

SCIENTIFIC DEPARTMENT.

Senior Class.

Alfred Nevin Snoddy,.......................Dayton.

Middle Class.

Robert Long Adams,........................Pleasant.
Jacob Armstrong Bruner,....................Hanover.
Cyrus Finley Butler,..........................Flemmingsburg, Ky
George Washington McCawley,..............Louisville, Ky.
John Thomas McClure,......................Crittenden, Ky.
William Penfield Garritt,....................Delphi.
John Adam Goodlett,........................Bedford.
Robert Calvin Irwin,.........................Hanover.
Cyrus Alexander Johnson,...................Memphis, Tenn.
James Edwin Rankin,........................Henderson, Ky.
George Wherry Rutherford,..................Batesville, Ark.

Junior Class.

Gavan Alves,................................Henderson, Ky.
William Louis Bence,........................Fishpool, Ky.
Hiram Francis Braxtan,......................Paoli.
John Robison Brown,........................Montgomery, O.
Marshal Stanley Brown,......................Boston, Ky.
Richard Penrose Conner,....................Bardstown, Ky.
Milo Ellis,..................................N. Bethel.
George Washington Felter,..................Montgomery, O.
William Fenwick,...........................Frankfort, Ky.
George Richardson Fitch,...................York, Ill.
Thomas Fontaine,...........................Batesville, Ark.
James Hall,.................................Knightstown.
Robert Andrew Hamilton,...................Louisville, Ky.

William Johnson Harned,......................Boston, Ky.
Howard Hathaway,..........................Bardstown, Ky.
Nathaniel Louis Howard,....................Knightstown.
Charles Absalom Hunt,......................Hartford.
Franklin Brown Hunt,.......................Knoxville, Miss.
Isaac Newton Jones,........................Montgomery, O.
William Pinckney Nason,....................Starkville, Miss.
William Dodd O'Bannon,....................Eminence, Ky.
Martin Scott Patterson,.....................Kokomo.
Milton White Smith,........................Hanover.
David Taylor,..............................Hibernia, O.
John Newton Voris,.........................Bennington.
John Thomas Tenney Waters.................Louisville, Ky.
Charles Park Whitesell,.....................Knightstown.
James Lowry Whitesell,.....................Knightstown.
Joseph Wallace,............................Madison.
Willis Woodward,..........................Hanover.
Milas Young,..............................Hanover.

GRAMMAR SCHOOL.

Senior Class.

Myron Andrews,............................Vernon.
Samuel Montgomery Cambern,................Rushville.
James Evans Cooper,........................Newcastle, Ky.
William Irwin Craddock,....................Louisville, Ky.
Benjamin Franklin Elder,....................Knightstown.
Sylvester Franklin Gilmore,..................Manhattan.
Albert Newton Keigwin,.....................Louisville, Ky.
Robert Lennington,.........................Kokomo.
Samuel Finley McKeehan,....................Vernon.
James McBeth,.............................Urbana, O.
William Kennedy Patterson,..................Madison.

John William Rabb,..............................Rising Sun.
James David Rabb,.............................Carrollton, Ky.
Robert Blair Smith,............................Sharpsville, Pa.
Austin Lowry Thomson,.........................Kingston.
John Bacon Vawter,............................Worthsville.
Alpha Walter,.................................Charlestown.
John Warden Wilson,...........................Crawfordsville.
George Francis Wilson,........................Frankfort.

Junior Class.

John Newton Abernathy,........................Knightstown.
Preston Loughborough Bland,...................Louisville, Ky.
John McKnight Blass,..........................New Philadelphia.
Ezra Ebenezer Chester,........................Columbus, O.
William S. Coulter,...........................Hanover.
John Parmer Darnall,..........................Flemingsburg, Ky.
John Fox,.....................................Bruceville.
Samuel Henry Howe,............................Flemingsburg, Ky.
Alexander Guy Huey,...........................Jacksonville, Ill.
John Humphrey,................................Crown Point.
Columbus DeWitt Huston,.......................New Philadelphia.
Robert Calvin Irwin,..........................Walnut Bend, Ark.
Samuel Emmett Key,............................Newburg.
James David Knox,.............................Louisville, Ky.
Albert A. C. Martyn,..........................Franklin.
Reuben Franklin Middleton,....................Frankfort, Ky.
John Andrew Moore,............................Granville, Ill.
Ebenezer Muse,................................Hanover.
Benjamin Franklin McCawley,...................Fishpool, Ky.
Ezra Fitch Paboddy,...........................Vernon.
George Talifaro Shackleford,..................Richmond, Ky.
Edmund James Shackleford,.....................Richmond, Ky.
Benjamin Simpson,.............................Vernon.
Francis Simpson,..............................Vernon.
Edward Livingston Taylor,.....................Hibernia, O.
Aaron Vawter,.................................Worthsville.

SUMMARY.

Undergraduates—Seniors, ...12
      Juniors, ...15
      Sophomores, ...14
      Freshmen, ...31
      Scientific Students, ...43
               — 115
Grammar Scholars, ... 45

  Total 160

CALENDAR.

1855.

Sept. 17, 18. Examination of candidates for admission, ... Monday and Tuesday.
" 19, First term begins, ... Wednesday.
Dec. 18, First term ends, ... Tuesday.
    WINTER VACATION OF TWO WEEKS.

1856.

Jan. 2, Second term begins, ... Wednesday.
March 31, Exhibition of the Philalethean Society, ... Monday.
April 1. Exhibition of the Union Literary Society, ... Tuesday.
"   1 Second term ends, ... Tuesday.
    SPRING VACATION OF FOUR WEEKS.
April 30. Third term begins, ... Wednesday.
July 7, Biennial Examination, Senior Class, begins, ... Monday.
" 30, Examination of the remaining classes, begun, ... Wednesday.
" 31, Continued, ... Thursday.
Aug. 1, Closed, ... Friday.
" 4, Annual Examination of the Grammar School, ... Monday.
" 5, Anniversary of the Literary Societies, ... Tuesday.
" 6, COMMENCEMENT DAY, ... Wednesday.
    SUMMER VACATION OF SEVEN WEEKS.
Sept. 22, 23, Examination of candidates for admission, ... Monday and Tuesday.
" 24, First term begins, ... Wednesday.

ADMISSION.

CANDIDATES for admission into the Freshman Class are examined in Arithmetic, and Algebra, through Quadratic Equations; Ancient and Modern Geography; the English, Latin and Greek Grammars; Cæsar's Commentaries; four Orations of Cicero; the first three books of Virgil's Æneid; Arnold's Latin Prose Composition; Bullion's Greek Reader, and the Anabasis of Xenophon. They must furnish testimonials of good character; and if from another College, must bring certificates of honorable dismission. Candidates for a higher standing are examined upon that part of the course already studied by the class which they propose to enter.

No one can be admitted to the Freshman Class until he has completed his fourteenth year; nor to an advanced standing, without a proportional increase of age.

"Before a student shall be admitted to actual standing in any class, he shall present to the President a receipt from the Treasurer, showing that he has complied with the statutes relating to College charges and Scholarships."

N. B. The regular examination for admission into College, commences on the Monday preceding the beginning of each term.

COURSE OF INSTRUCTION.

GRAMMAR SCHOOL.

Bullion's Latin and Greek Grammars, with praxis; McClintock's 1st and 2nd Latin and Greek books; Bullion's Cæsar, and Cicero; Cooper's Virgil; Arnold's Latin Prose Composition, first XII. chapters; Owen's Anabasis, with Boise's Greek Prose Composition; Higher Arithmetic; Robinson's Algebra, University edition; Mitchell's Classical Geography; Coleman's Biblical Geography; Historical portions of the Old and New Testaments.

SCIENTIFIC SCHOOL.

FIRST YEAR.

Algebra, completed; Plane Geometry; Plane Trigonometry; Surveying and Navigation; Ancient, Modern and Ecclesiastical History.

SECOND YEAR.

Solid Geometry; Spherical Trigonometry, and its applications; Analytical Geometry; Natural Philosophy, and Astronomy; Rhetoric, Logic, and Political Economy.

THIRD YEAR.

Anatomy and Physiology; Zoology; Botany; Chemistry; Natural Theology; Butler's Analogy; Psychology, and Moral Philosophy.

COLLEGE.

FRESHMAN CLASS.

I.

Robinson's Greek Harmony of the Gospels.
Horne's Biblical Antiquities, (abridged edition.)
Virgil's Æneid, with the study of Prosody.
Xenophon's Memorabilia of Socrates, (Robbins' edition.),
Roman Antiquities, (Bojesen..)
Arnold's Greek Composition.
Robinson's Algebra, completed, (University edition.)

II.

Robinson's Harmony.
Lincoln's Livy.
Memorabilia, continued.
Herodotus, (Leipsic edition,) begun.
Roman, Grecian, and Biblical Antiquities.
Davies' Plane Geometry.

III.

Robinson's Harmony.
Lincoln's Livy, continued:
Grecian and Biblical Antiquities.
Davies' Plane Trigonometry, and Surveying.

SOPHOMORE CLASS.

I.

Acts of the Apostles, (Owen's edition.)
Cicero de Amicitia and de Senectute.
Homer's Iliad. (Owen's edition.)
Davies' Solid Geometry.
Weber's Manual of Ancient History.

II.

Epistolary portion of the New Testament, in Greek.
Horace, with study of the Horatian metres.
Homer's Iliad, continued; Plato's Gorgias begun.
Davies' Spherical Trigonometry, and applications.
Weber's Modern History.

III.

Epistles, continued.
Horace, continued.
Plato's Gorgias, (Woolsey's edition.)
Davies' Analytical Geometry.
Ecclesiastical History.

JUNIOR CLASS.

I.
Hebrew Grammar, (Stuart's Rœdiger.)
Genesis.
Tacitus' Germania and Agricola, (Tyler's edition.)
Æschines against Ctesiphon, (Champlin's edition.)
Olmstead's Natural Philosophy, Vol. 1st.
Blair's Rhetoric.

II.
Hebrew—Genesis.
Cicero de Oratore.
Æschines, continued; Demosthenes de Corona, begun.
Olmstead's Natural Philosophy, Vols. 1st and 2d.
Whately's Logic.

III.
Hebrew—Psalms.
Cicero de Oratore, continued.
Demosthenes de Corona, (Champlin's edition,) finished.
Olmstead's Astronomy.
Wayland's Political Economy.

SENIOR CLASS.

I.
Select portions of the Hebrew Bible, with Lectures.
Psychology, (Walker's edition of Reid.)
Silliman's Chemistry.
Anatomy and Physiology, with Lectures.
Wood's Botany, with Lectures.
Cicero's Tusculan Disputations, &c.,(Chase's edition.)

II.
Select Hebrew.
Psychology—Philosophy of Sir Wm. Hamilton, (Wight's edition.)
Chemistry.
Paley's Natural Theology.
Greek Tragedies; Lectures on Grecian Art, Literature, &c.

III.
Select Hebrew.
Butler's Analogy of Religion, Natural and Revealed, to the Constitution and Course of Nature.
Moral Philosophy, (Walker's edition of Stewart and Alexander.)
Mineralogy.
Hitchcock's Geology.

N. B. The text-books needed for any part of the College Course, may be procured of Mr. LEE, Bookseller, Hanover, at Cincinnati and Louisville prices.

DISTRIBUTION OF RECITATIONS, &c.

	DEPARTMENT OF Bibl. Instruction & Phil. THE PRESIDENT.	DEPARTMENT OF Rhetoric, Hist., Logic. Dr. CROWE.	DEPARTMENT OF Netural Science. Prof. STONE.	DEPARTMENT OF Mathematics & Nat. Phil. Prof. THOMPSON.	DEPRATMENT OF Greek Lang. & Literature Prof. BISHOP.	DEPARTMENT OF Latin Lang. & Literature Prof. LOTT.
	I.	I.	I.	I.	I.	I.
J. G. S.					Greek Grammar,	Latin Grammar,
S. G. S.			Algebra,		Bullion's Greek Reader	Bullion's Cæsar,
F	½ Harmon. of Gospels,			Algebra, finished,	Memorabilia,	Virgil, continued,
So	½ Acts,	Ancient History,		Solid Geometry,	½ Iliad,	½ De Amicit. & de Senec.
J.	Hebrew,	½ Rhetoric,		Nat. Philosophy,	½ Æschines,	½ Tacit Germ. & Agric.
S.	½ Hebrew, Psychology,		Chemistry, ½ Anat. Phys.			½ Tusculan Disputations,
	II.	II.	II.	II.	II.	II.
J. G. S.					Greek Reader,	Latin Reader,
S. G. S.			Algebra,		Anabasis,	Cicero's Orations,
F	½ Harmon. Gospels			Plane Geometry,	Memor. and Herodotus	Livy
So	½ Epistles,	Modern History,		Spher. Trig. & Applic.	½ Iliad and Gorgias,	½ Horace,
J.	Hebrew,	½ Logic,		Nat. Philoosphy,	½ Æsch. & Demosthenes	½ Cicero de Oratore,
S.	½ Hebrew, Psychology,		Chemistry, ½ Nat. Theol.		½ Greek Tragedies,	
	III.	III.	III.	III.	III.	III.
J. G. S.					Greek Reader,	Latin Reader,
S. G. S.			Algebra,		Anabasis,	Virgil,
F	½ Harmon, Gospels,			Plane Trig., Surveying,	Herodotus,	Livy,
So	½ Epistles,	Eccles. History,		Analyt. Geometry,	½ Gorgias,	½ Horace,
J	Hebrew,	½ Pol. Economy,		Astronomy,	¾ Demosthenes,	½ Cicero de Oratore,
S.	½ Hebrew, Mor. Philos.		Butler's Anal., ½ Mineral and Geology,			

PERMANENT RECITATION HOURS IN ALL DEPARTMENTS.

A. M.						
8	½ Seniors,	Sophomores,	½ Seniors,	Juniors,	Senior Gram. Sch.	Freshmen,
9	Juniors,		Seniors,	Sophomores,	Freshmen,	Senior Gram. Sch.
10	Seniors,		Seniors Gram. Sch.,	Freshmen,	½ Sophs. and Juniors,	½ Sophs. and Juniors.
11	½ Fresh. and Sophs.	½ Juniors,				

PERMANENT RECITATION HOURS----SCIENTIFIC DEPARTMENT.

A. M.	FIRST CLASS.	SECOND CLASS.	THIRD CLASS.
8.	History.	Nat. Philos. and Astron.	Nat. Sci. and Nat. Theol.
9.		Mathematics.	Chem. and Butl. Anal.
10.	Mathematics.		Psychol. and Mor. Phil.
11.		½ Rhet, Log. Pol. Econ.	

The preceding course is so arranged, in all departments, as to require from every class, except the Senior, an average of THREE HOURS AND A HALF in recitations DAILY, excepting Saturday. These recitations are attended, without loss of time, between the hours of 8 and 12, A. M.; leaving the remainder of the day for study and recreation.

CLASSICAL DEPARTMENT.

In connection with the daily recitations, constant reference is made to Bullion's Latin and Greek Grammars, Leverett's or Andrew's Latin Lexicon, Liddell and Scott's Greek Lexicon, Anthon's Classical Dictionary, Bojesen's Roman and Greek Antiquities, and Mitchell's Atlas of Ancient Geography.

The following works are recommended for more extended consultation by the student in private: Zumpt's Latin Grammar, Kuhner's and Crosby's Greek Grammars, Crusius' Homeric Lexicon, Munk's Greek and Latin Metres, Eschenburg's Manual of Classical Literature, and Smith's Dictionary of Greek and Roman Antiquities.

SCIENTIFIC DEPARTMENT.

The three years' course of English, Mathematical and Scientific instruction pursued in this department, embraces all that is included in the Collegiate scheme, except the Classical languages. Such as desire it, however, may pursue the study of Latin or French, in connection with a Scientific course. We do not recommend it as in any sense an equivalent for a thorough, Classical course; nor is it intended for mere boys, since the subjects which it includes are entirely above their capacity; but to young men, who have obtained a respectable common school education, including the elements of Algebra, and who have not time nor means to prosecute the Classical course, this system of studies, will, it is hoped, commend itself as solid, comprehensive, and practical. Those who shall complete the prescribed Scientific course, will receive a Diploma, certifying the extent of their attainments.

COLLEGE YEAR.—EXAMINATIONS.

The Collegiate Year is divided into three Terms of thirteen weeks each, and three Vacations. The First Term begins on the Third Wednesday in September; the Second, on the First Wednesday in January; and the Third, on the First Wednesday in May, closing with the First Wednesday in August, which is Commencement Day. It is of great importance that Students attend from the very beginning of the term; especially since so considerable portion of time is allotted to vacations. In most cases, the loss of a few weeks, or even days, seriously affects the future standing of the pupil. Absence during term time, without special leave, is prohibited.

PUBLIC EXAMINATIONS will be held, hereafter, only at the close of the college year; when the Freshmen and Junior Classes will be examined on the studies of the preceding year, and the Sophomore and Senior Classes, upon those of the two preceding years. These last examinations will be FINAL, for the studies pursued in those years. All the examinations will be THROUGH and RIGID; and will be conducted, chiefly, by the use of written questions, prepared by the Faculty and the Examining Committee, covering the whole field of study prosecuted during a given period, and entirely unknown to the Student until the moment of examination. These questions must be answered in writing before the Committee; and correct answers to a definite portion of them will be the passport of admission to a higher standing. Similar examinations, of a briefer and less decisive character, however, and by way of preparation for the final trial, may be conducted privately, at the pleasure of the Faculty.

The Board of Trustees, having sanctioned the distribution of honorary and pecuniary rewards, the average standing of every pupil will hereafter be posted up in some conspicuous place, at the end of the year; and suitable prizes will conferred upon the most deserving.

RELIGIOUS INSTRUCTION AND SERVICES.

The attention of a Christian community is respectfully invited to the system of Biblical Instruction which forms a characteristic feature of our course of Study. The Grammar School Classes recite daily in the English Bible; and every College Class has a daily or tri-weekly, recitation in the Greek Testament, or the Hebrew. Proficiency in these, as in other studies, is tested by the usual examinations In addition to this, Biblical Geography and Antiquities, Eclesiastical History, Natural Theology, and the Analogy of Religion, Natural and Revealed, to the constitution and course of nature, are carefully and faithfully studied. There is also a Bible or Catechetical exercise on Sabbath mornings; a public service on Sabbath afternoons, appropriated to the Students; and daily morning prayers. The Students are expected to attend the Sabbath morning service of the congregation worshipping in the chapel, or of some other congregation in the vicinity, if their parents prefer any of the latter. The Methodist, Associate, and Associate Reformed Churches, have regular services in or near the village.

An experiment of five years in this Institution, has established the fact that the daily study of God's word by no means interferes with, but rather promotes, sound and comprehensive attainments in other branches of knowledge. Some, indeed, have questioned the expediency of adding Hebrew to an already overburdened curriculum; especially since Theological Students may acquire it in the Seminary, and non-theologians are unlikely to make any particular use of such an acquisition. Our confident answer is,—FIRST, that Theological Students need more acquaintance with Hebrew than with Greek, when they enter the Seminary; since familiarity with the Old Testament is more rare, and more difficult of attainment, than familiarity with the New:—SECONDLY, that the moral discipline secured by this study is fully equal to that obtained from any other:—THIRDLY, that a knowledge of Hebrew, as connected with the Indo-European tongues, greatly contributes to the student's mastery of the latter:—FOURTHLY, that non-theological students are as likely to cultivate the Hebrew, when once acquired, as the higher Mathematics and the Classics:—FIFTHLY, that the Hebrew Scriptures contain more valuable, practical truth, than all the pagan classics put together:—and LASTLY, that the day is to be dreaded when ability to peruse the Sacred Volume, in the originals, shall be the exclusive property of the Clergy.

EXPENSES.

The entire annual expenditures of a Student need not exceed $140, viz:
Tuition and contingent fee, $10 per term,............................$30 00
Boarding with private families, and a furnished room, at $1 75 to
  $2 25 per week,...$70 to 90 00
Fuel, light, washing, &c.,..10 to 15 00
Books, &c.,..5 to 10 00*

Boarding in clubs will cost from fifty to seventy-five cents a week; and some board themselves even at a lower rate. The cost of clothing, and the amount spent as pocket-money, will vary with the taste and habits of the Student, and with the wishes of parents. As a general rule, the more money is allowed to a young man beyond what is strictly necessary, the less likely is he to reflect honor upon his parents and instructors. Although Hanover presents comparatively few temptations to extravagance, yet parents are earnestly advised to require of their sons a detailed account of their expenditures, and peremptorily to refuse the payment of any debt incurred by them without a written permission. It is also recommended that the funds of young pupils be deposited with some one of the Faculty, and expended under his direction. The younger Students are required to board where the Faculty may direct, and where they may exercise a more careful and frequent supervision.

N. B. Students placed upon Scholarships by the Faculty, are relieved in part, or wholly, as the case may require, from the payment of tuition fees.

---

* This may be taken as a fair estimate of expenses in ordinary years. During the last year, the price of boarding has, indeed, considerably exceeded the amount here presented; but, in all probability, it will soon return to the usual standard.

DISCIPLINE AND GENERAL RULES.

A record is kept by the Faculty, in which are entered weekly, the grade of scholarship of the student, his absences from the exercises of the Institution, and such other facts as are worthy of notice with respect to his General Deportment. From this record a report is made out at the end of each session and sent to the Parent or Guardian of each Student. In case of deficiency in scholarship, negligence in study, irregularity in attendance upon the exercises of the Institution, or improper conduct, the Student will be privately admonished, and the Parent or Guardian will be promptly informed of the fact.

It is the object of this arrangement to keep Parents and Guardians accurately informed with regard to their sons and wards in this Institution, and thus to secure their co-operation with the Faculty in a mild system of discipline. Whenever it is ascertained that a Student is deriving no advantage from his connection with the Institution, or is pursuing courses injurious to himself, or fellow-students, the Faculty will take decisive action, and his Parent or Guardian will be promptly addressed on the subject, and requested to remove him from the Institution.

SCHOLARSHIPS.

The endowment of this Institution, so far as it has been secured, is in the form of Scholarships; of which the Board has established several sorts. The sum of $400, paid, or secured to the Corporation by note payable within five years, and bearing six per cent. interest in advance upon principal remaining unpaid—purchases for the owner, his heirs and assigns, a perpetual right to the tuition of one scholar, in Hanover College. The sum of $200, paid, or subscribed under similar conditions, secures a right to twenty years' tuition; after which time, the scholarship is subject to the disposal of the Board for the gratuitous education of candidates for the Gospel Ministry. A church scholarship of $200 secures to the church so contributing, a perpetual right to the tuition of one student, who shall be a member of that church, and appointed by the session. A Presbyterial scholarship of $200 secures a smilar right to a Presbytery in behalf of pupils who shall be candidates for the Ministry under its care. The PRINCIPAL, paid on these scholarships is invested by the Corporation in some safe and Productive stock; and the INTEREST ONLY can be expended for the support of the College.

The sum of $100, PAID WITHIN TWO YEARS AT FARTHEST, with interest in advance on unpaid principal, purchases a right to ten years' tuition within twenty years from the date of subscription. Both principal and interest of this scholarship may be employed for contingent purposes; and the scholarship expires with the owner's right to its use.

The sum of $100 PAID into the building fund; or the sum of $50 PAID in like manner, secures the right to ten, or five years' tuition of one student.

Every person applying for admission as a beneficiary of a scholarship under the control of the donors, shall present to the Treasurer, at the beginning of each term, A WRITTEN CERTIFICATE from those controlling the scholarship, of his right to such benefit; when, after paying whatever interest may be due on said scholarship, he shall receive an acknowledgment of his right, which he shall lodge with the President.

"The scholarships subject to the disposal of the Corporation, may be occupied by such applicants as the Faculty may select, after inquiry into their circumstances, character and attainments; the preference being, (cœteris paribus,) to those who give the best evidence of scholarship.

"There shall at no time be more than one student upon each scholarship."

SOCIETIES, LIBRARIES, &c.

There are two Societies connected with the College,—the UNION LITERARY, and the PHILALETHEAN, each of whose Libraries numbers about fifteen hundred volumes. The SOCIETY OF INQUIRY has also begun to collect a Library, Maps, &c. The College Library, which comprises nearly two thousand well selected volumes, is accessible to the students. The Cabinet contains several thousand specimens in Mineralogy and Geology. The Laboratory is supplied with the apparatus most necessary for chemical experiments.

A number of valuable books have been added to the College Library, within the year, by donation. Similar contributions will be thankfully received.

LOCATION, BUILDING, &c.

The village of Hanover is situated upon an elevated bluff of the Ohio river, six miles below Madison, Indiana, in a region of remarkable salubrity and natural beauty. The village and neighborhood are characterized by morality, and the absence of all ordinary temptations to vice and idleness. Intoxicating liquors have never been sold in the township; the traffic being prohibited, annually, by popular vote. The Ohio river, and the Railways from Madison, New Albany, and Cincinnati, place Hanover within twenty-four hours of all the principal points in Indiana, Western Ohio, and Eastern Illinois. A Plank Road from Madison to Hanover, renders the village easy of access at all seasons of the year.

Hanover College is controlled by a Board of Trustees; one half of whom are appointed by the Board itself, and the other half by the Synods of Indiana and Northern Indiana. All its officers are Ministers, or members, of the Presbyterian church.

The Board purchased, some five years ago, a farm of two hundred acres, lying between the village and the Ohio river, upon a beautiful point of which, overlooking the river from an elevation of four hundred feet, they have erected a commodious College edifice, now nearly completed. The new College, a sketch of which accompanies this Catalogue, consists of a centre building, nearly 80 feet square, with lateral and transverse wings. The whole length is about 200 feet. It contains no dormitories for Students; (an undesirable provision;) but affords ample and convenient halls, library, cabinet, lecture and recitation rooms, and a spacious chapel. Its entire cost, when finished, will not exceed thirty thousand dollars.

The property of the College, including scholarship notes, is estimated at seventy thousand dollars.

THE TWENTY-FOURTH

Annual Catalogue & Circular

OF

Hanover College,

AND

EIGHTH TRIENNIAL

Catalogue of the Alumni,

AUGUST, 1856.

LOUISVILLE:
Hull & Brother, Printers, 497 Main Street.
1856.

THE TWENTY-FOURTH

Annual Catalogue & Circular

OF

HANOVER COLLEGE,

INCLUDING THE

EIGHTH TRIENNIAL

CATALOGUE OF THE ALUMNI.

AUGUST, 1856.

LOUISVILLE:
HULL & BROTHER PRINTERS, 497 MAIN STREET.
1856.

Board of Trustees.

	Term Expires.		Term Expires.
*REV. J. G. SYMMES, Madison,	1856.	*REV. H. H. CAMBERN, Rushville	1858.
*REV. J. EDWARDS, So. Hanover	1856.	*REV. T. E. THOMAS, D. D., N. Albany	1858.
*ALEXANDER GUY, M. D., Oxford, O.	1856.	*REV. DANL. LATTIMORE, Vernon	1858.
*REV. L. J. HALSEY, D. D., Louisville	1856.	*HON. JAMES BLAKE, Indianapolis	1858.
†REV. D. M. STEWART, Rushville	1856.	‡REV. C. K. THOMPSON, Darlington	1858.
†REV. C. LEAVENWORTH, Cambridge, Ill.	1856.	‡REV. S. C. LOGAN, Constantine, Mich.	1858.
‡REV. F. P. CUMMINS, LaPorte	1856.	†REV. D. D. McKEE, Marion, Iowa	1858.
‡REV. ROBERT IRWIN, Wheeling	1856.	*JAMES M. RAY, Indianapolis	1858.
*REV. J. F. CROWE, D. D., So. Hanover	1857.	*JOHN KING, Esq., Madison	1859.
*A. R. FORSYTH, Esq., Greensburg	1857.	*REV. WM. SICKELS, Indianapolis	1859.
*J. L. WILLIAMS, Esq., Fort Wayne	1857.	*W. M. DUNN, Esq., Madison	1859.
*REV. J. B. MORTON, Middletown, O.	1857.	*W. A. BULLOCK, Esq., Vernon	1859.
†REV. J. F. SMITH, Richmond	1857.	†REV. J. G. MONFORT, D. D., Cin'ti, O.	1859.
†REV. J. M. STEVENSON, D.D., N. Albany	1857.	†REV. T. S. CROWE, So. Hanover	1859.
‡REV. E. W. WRIGHT, Delphi	1857.	‡REV. I. N. SHANNON, Terre Haute	1859.
‡HON. S. HANNA, Fort Wayne	1857.	‡REV. J. C. BROWN, Valparaiso	1859.

* Appointed by the Board.
† Appointed by the Synod of Indiana.
‡ Appointed by the Synod of Northern Indiana.

Officers of the Board.

REV. J. FINLEY CROWE, D. D., President.
REV. T. S. CROWE, Sec. and General Agent.
PROF. S. H. THOMSON, Treasurer.

Executive Committee.

REV. J. EDWARDS...REV. J. F. CROWE.
REV. T. S. CROWE....W. M. DUNN,
JNO. KING.

Faculty.

REV. JONATHAN EDWARDS, D. D.,
President, and Professor of Biblical Instruction, Psychology and Ethics.

REV. JOHN FINLEY CROWE, D. D.,
Professor of Rhetoric, Logic, History, and Political Economy.

REV. S. HARRISON THOMSON, A. M.,
Professor of Mathematics and Mechanical Philosophy.

*REV. J. M. STONE, A. M.,
Professor of Natural Science.

REV. WILLIAM BISHOP, A. M.,
Professor of the Latin and Greek Languages and Literature.

JOHN QUINCY McKEEHAN, A. B.,
Principal of the Preparatory Department.

PROF. WM. BISHOP,
Librarian.

* PROFESSOR STONE has also during the year given instruction to the Freshman Class in Latin, to the Junior Class in Hebrew, and to the Senior Class in Political Philosophy.

Alumni.

1834.

NAME.	PROFESSION.	RESIDENCE.
*Wm. H. Bruner, A. M.	Minister, A. M.	
*Selby Harney	Teacher	
John M. McChord, A. M.	Minister	Bruceville Ind.
Isaac McCoy, A. M.	Teacher	
Isaac N. Shepherd, A. M.	Minister	Marion, O.
Chas. K. Thompson, A. M.	Minister	Darlington, Ind.

1835.

Robt. S. Bell, A. M.	Minister	Washington, Va.
James Brown, A. M.	Minister	Keokuk, Iowa.
†Jonathan Edwards, D. D.	Minister	So. Hanover Ind.
Robert Simpson, A. M.	Minister	Newton, Ill.
‡Middleton Goldsmith, A. M., M. D.	Physician	New York City.
*James A. Watson	Teacher	

1836.

Sam'l J. P. Anderson, D. D.	Minister	St. Louis, Mo.
§Noble Butler, A. M.	Teacher	Louisville, Ky.
Josiah Crawford, A. M.	Minister	Polk Run, Ind.
D. H. Cummins, A. M.	Minister	Mountain, Tenn.
*Andrew Fulton, M. D.	Physician	
‖Thos. W. Hynes, A. M.	Minister	Greenville, Ill.
*Wm. Wylie McLain	Minister	
Sam'l F. Morrow, A. M.	Minister	Albany, N. Y.
Sam'l Newell	Minister	Paris, Ill.
*David E. Y. Rice, A. M.	Minister	
Amos H. Rogers	Minister	Waynesville, Ill.
*Nath'l S. Schillinger	Minister	
¶Minard Sturgus	Teacher	Monroe, O.
S. Ramsay Wilson, D. D.	Minister	Cincinnati, O.

* Deceased.
† President Hanover College, 1855.
‡ Professor Vermont Medical College.
§ Professor Hanover College, 1836–1839.
‖ Professor Hanover College, 1838–1843.
¶ Professor Hanover College, 1841–1852.

ALUMNI.

1837.

NAME.	PROFESSION.	RESIDENCE.
T. H. Alderdice	Minister	Scaffold Prairie, Ind.
Franklin Berryhill	Minister	Bellbrook, O.
James Black	Minister	Blue Ball, O.
Sam'l N. Evans, A. M.	Minister	Stillwater, Min. Ter.
Edmund W. Hawkins, A. M.	Lawyer	Warsaw, Ky.
John M. Hoge	Minister	Mt. Holly, Ark.
Braxton D. Hunter	Minister	
Sylvanus Jewett	Minister	Roscoe, Ill.
*John W. McCormick	Minister	
James A. McKee, A. M.	Minister	Franklin, Ind.
Asahel Munson	Minister	Jackson, Mo.
*Wm. C. Scott	"	
Josiah D. Smith, A. M.	"	Columbus, O.
†S. H. Thomson, A. M.	Teacher	So. Hanover, Ind.
Jas. F. Wood	Physician	Greenbury, Penn.

1838.

Geo. B. Armstrong	Minister	Crittenden, Ky.
Wm. Blair	"	Brown County, O.
‡James E. Blythe, A. M.	Lawyer	Evansville, Ind.
Wm. K. Brice, A. M.	Minister	Pleasant, O.
A. M. Brown, A. M.	Lawyer	Paris, Ky.
Wm. M. Cheever, A. M.	Minister	Terre Haute.
Jas. B. Crowe, A. M.	"	Crawfordsville, Ind.
Thos. S. Crowe, A. M.	"	So. Hanover, Ind.
Jos. F. Fenton, A. M.	"	Kirkwood, Mo.
Jas. J. Gardiner, A. M.	Teacher	Cape Girardeau, Mo.
Rob't A. Gibson, A. M.		——, Ill.
Abram T. Hendricks, A. M.	Minister	Petersburgh, Ind.
John Jones		
James W. Matthews, A. M.	Teacher	Macomb, Ill.
Geo. F. Whitworth, A. M.	Minister	Olympia, Wash. Ter.

1839.

Samuel S. Crowe, A. M.	Lawyer	New Lexington, Ind.
David M. Dunn	Lawyer	Logansport, Ind.
Wm. W. Gilliland, A. M.	Lawyer	New Albany, **Ind.**
*Philander Hamilton	Lawyer	
E. K. Lynn, A. M.	Minister	Urbana, Ill.
F. G. Strahan, A. M.	"	Hopkinsville, Ky.

1840.

Harleigh Blackwell, A. M.	Minister	Eagle Fork, Mo.
Samuel J. Haas	Business	Valparaiso, Ind.
¿Absalom C. Knox, A. M.	Teacher	California.

* Deceased.
† Professor Hanover College, 1844.
‡ Member Indiana Constitutional Convention.
¿ Professor Hanover College, 1844–1852.

ALUMNI.

NAME.	PROFESSION.	RESIDENCE.
Robert C. Matthews, A. M.	Minister	Monmouth, Ill.
Robert S. Symington, A. M.	"	Pleasant Hill, Mo.

1841.

Chas. M. Hays	Lawyer	Pittsburgh, Penn.
John L. King	Lawyer	Chicago, Ill.
Geo. C. Lyen		

1842.

A. M. Johnson, A. M., M. D.	Physician	Cincinnati, O.
*Thomas C. McCutchen, A. M.	Farmer	
Alex. McHatton, A. M.	Minister	Cedarville, O.
*George McMillan, A. M.	"	
J. N. Saunders, A. M.	"	Bloomfield, Ky.
*Wm. W. Simonson, A. M.	"	
Zeb. B. Sturgus, A. M.	Teacher	Charlestown, Ind.

1843.

Daniel L. Fouts	Lawyer	California.
*James G. Hopkins, A. M.	Minister	
George A. Irvin, A. M.	Teacher	Fort Wayne, Ind.
Samuel B. Keys, A. M.	Lawyer	Cincinnati, O.
Joseph C. McKibbin	Lawyer	
F. P. Monfort, A. M.	Minister	Highland, Kan. Ter.
John F. Read	Lawyer	Jeffersonville, Ind.
John F. Trenchard, A. M., M. D.	Physician	Philadelphia, Penn.

1844.

John C. Greer	Planter	———, Tenn.

1845.

David R. Thompson	Lawyer	Amite County, Miss.
Wm. T. Robinson, A. M.	Lawyer	Amite County, Miss.

1846.

*Wm. H. G. Butler, A. M.	Teacher	
John A. Frazer	Lawyer	California.
Samuel C. Logan, A. M.	Minister	Constantine, Mich.

1847.

Samuel E. Barr, A. M.	Minister	Livonia, Ind.
F. Senour, A. M.	Minister	Louisville, Ky.

1848.

Addison W. Bare, A. M.	Physician	Clark County, Ind.
John W. Blake, A. M.	Lawyer	Frankfort, Ind.
John C. Caldwell, A. M.	Minister	Shelbyville, Ind.
*†M. S. Coulter, A. M.	Minister	

* Deceased.
† Missionary to China.

ALUMNI.

NAME.	PROFESSION.	RESIDENCE.
*Robert G. Jackson, A. M.	Teacher	
Robert S. Shannon, A. M.	Physician	———, Texas.
Samuel C. Taggart, A. M., M. D.	Physician	Charlestown, Ind.
James H. L. Vannuys, A. M.	Minister	Goshen, Ind.

1849.

Samuel C. Baldridge, A. M.	Minister	Friendsville, Ill.
Jesse Y. Higbee, A. M., M. D.	Physician	
N. S. Palmer, A. M.	Minister	Grandview, Ill.
X. B. Sanders, A. M.	Lawyer	
W. D. Symington, A. M.	Teacher	Independence, Mo.
John W. Taylor, A. M.	Lawyer	Waco Village, Texas.
Henry E. Thomas, A. M.	Minister	Georgetown, Ky.

1850.

W. M. Blackburn	Minister	Erie, Penn.
J. S. Brengle	Physician	Carlisle, Ind.
A. W. Bullock	Lawyer	Vernon, Ind.
J. S. Frierson	Minister	Oxford, Miss.
*S. D. Hawthorn		
John A. Kimmons	Minister	
C. B. H. Martin	Minister	Corydon, Ind.
Samuel C. Mercer	Editor	Hopkinsville, Ky.
Robert S. Reese	Teacher	Independence, Mo.
Wm. A. Rice	Minister	———, Texas.
Wm. W. Sickels	Minister	Bedford, Ind.
Alex. S. Walker	Lawyer	———, Texas.
Austin Warner	Minister	Ladoga, Ind.
Benj. R. Whitney	Engineer	Madison, Ind.
Wm. A. M. Young	Surveyor	Hanover.

1851.

Jas. M. Alexander	Minister	
Henry M. Bayless		
Joseph Boon	Minister	
James Bruce		
James Huston Burns	Minister	Monroe, O.
Theophilus W. Guy	Farmer	Oxford, O.
*James S. Jones	Lawyer	
James McEwen Kimmons		
Cornelius McKain	Teacher	
Hugh McHatton	Minister	Washington, Iowa.
Archibald McKee	Lawyer	Troy, Mo.
Wm. J. McKnight	Minister	Danville, Ky.
Alexander Mayne	Teacher	Shelbyville, Ky.
Edward E. Porter	Minister	
Benjamin N. Sawtell	Minister	
Joseph G. Symmes	Minister	Madison, Ind.
Robert F. Taylor	Minister	Waco Village, Texas.
Jos. Greene Wells	Minister	———, Arkansas.

* Deceased.

ALUMNI.

1852.

NAME.	PROFESSION.	RESIDENCE.
Jos. M. Bachelder	Minister	———, Ill.
Stephen J. Bovell	Farmer	Paris, Ill.
Jonathan T. Carthel	Lawyer	Trenton, Tenn.
John M. Coyner	Teacher	Waveland, Ind.
Benjamin P. Dewey	Lawyer	Charlestown, Ind.
Henry M. Giltner	Minister	Nebraska City.
Thos. M. Hopkins	Minister	Enon, Ohio.
Alexander Martin	Engineer	Salem, Ind.
Robt. L. Neely	Minister	———, Tenn.
James M. Scovel	Lawyer	Camden, N. J.
Francis Marion Symmes	Minister	Pleasant, Ind.
Danl. P. Young	Minister	Nicholasville, Ky.

1853.

Lyman B. Andrews	Teacher	Cape Girardeau, Mo.
Jas. A. Cunningham	Business	Madison, Ind.
Lewis I. Drake	Minister	F't Desmoines, Iowa.
Jer. M. Drake	Minister	Maineville, Ohio.
Josh. B. Garritt	Minister	Delphi, Ind.
Edward J. Hamilton	Teacher	New Brunswick, N.J.
Henry Kritz	Teacher	Waveland, Ind.
Charles Lee	Minister	Dupont, Ind.
Wm. P. Lemaster	Stud. Theol.	Danville, Ky.
Gideon B. McLeary	Lawyer	———, Tenn.
Jas. A. McRee	Minister	Versailles, Ind.
Jos. W. Mahan		
Henry T. Morton	Teacher	Princeton, Ind.
*Henry S. Scovel	Stud. Theol.	
S. Fithian Scovel	Stud. Theol.	New Albany, Ind.
Jackson J. Smith	Lawyer	Taylorsville, Ky.
William Wheat	Minister	———, Miss.

1854.

Stephen C. Adair	Lawyer	Morganfield, Ky.
David G. Herron	Teacher	Bardstown, Ky.
Robert Irwin	Minister	Clermont, Ind.
Robert A. Johnson	Lawyer	Batavia, O.
Isaac B. Moore	Stud. Theol.	New Albany, Ind.
Edwin H. Rutherford	Minister	Danville, Ky.
Edward C. Sickels	Minister	Indianapolis, Ind.
Wm. R. Sim	Stud. Theol.	Danville, Ky.
Thos. Wallace	Teacher	Middletown, O.
Jas. E. Wilson	Stud. Theol.	———, S. C.
Jared R. Woodfill	Teacher	Edinburg, Ind.

1855.

Jas. R. Evans	Teacher	
†M. M. Fisher	Teacher	Fulton, Mo.
Jas. H. Hunter	Teacher	Prescott, Wis.

* Deceased.
† Professor Westminster College, 1855.

ALUMNI.

NAME.	PROFESSION.	RESIDENCE.
Wm. H. Huston	Farmer	Hamilton, O.
Robert J. L. Mathews	Stud. Theol	New Albany, Ind.
Robert C. McGee	Teacher	Lexington, Ky.
J. Q. McKeehan	Teacher	So. Hanover, Ind.
Chas. H. Park	Stud. Theol	Princeton, N. J.
Wm. A. Sample	Stud. Theol	Danville, Ky.
Wm. B. Truax	Teacher	Carrollton, Ky.
Thos. M. Tucker	Physician	Shelbyville, Ind.
Arch'd C. Voris	Teacher	Bedford, Ind.

1856.

James Balie Adams............James Kennedy Patterson.
James William Allison.........James Sanderson Rankin.
Robert Brown Herron...........Richmond Kelly Smoot.
Henry Keigwin.................James Harvey Tedford.
Harvey Lamb...................Benjamin Du Bois Wikoff.

Summary of Alumni.

Whole number Alumni	203
Ministers	91
Lawyers	29
Teachers, (eight Professors in College)	33
Physicians	10
Engineers and Surveyors	3
Farmers	5
Editor	1
Business	2
Unknown	3
Students of Theology	8
Present Class	10

Undergraduates.

Senior Class.

James Bailie Adams	Pleasant.
James William Allison	Grand View, Ill.
Robert Brown Herron	Hillsborough, O.
Henry Keigwin	Louisville, Ky.
Harvey Lamb	Hanover.
James Kennedy Patterson	Madison.
James Sanderson Rankin	Hanover.
William Washington Shelby	Henderson, Ky.
Richmond Kelly Smoot	Huntingdon, Tenn.
James Harvey Tedford	Delphi.
Benjamin Du Bois Wikoff	Franklin, O.

Seniors................11.

Junior Class.

Leonard Fisk Andrews	Northfield, O.
Isaac Hall Christian	Grand View, Ill.
William Cochrane	Cincinnati, O.
John Colerick	Fort Wayne.
William Means Crozier	Iowa City, Iowa.
Samuel Vigo McKee	Vincennes.
John McMurray	New Concord, O.
David McKnight Williamson	Logansport.

Juniors................8.

Sophomore Class.

William Peter Baker	Fort Wayne.
Alexander Miller Crawford	Graysville.
Samuel Telford Hanna	Fort Wayne.
Horace Hovey Hanna	Fort Wayne.
John David McClintock	Millersburg, Ky.
James Baird McClure	Vincennes.
Thomas Johnston McElrath	Madison.
Robert Campbell McKinny	Sullivan.
Nathan Amzi Means	Northfield, O.
David William Moffat	Madison.
James Alexander Piper	LaPorte.
Robert Gaine Ross	Twenty-mile Stand, O.
Isaac Coe Sickels	Indianapolis.
Augustus Taylor	Fort Madison, Iowa

CATALOGUE OF

James Harvey Vannuys..Franklin.
Cornelius Pleasant Voris..Bennington.
William Bates Warren..Louisville, Ky.
Henry Clay Warren...Louisville, Ky.
Edward Peet Williams..Fort Wayne.

Sophomores:..............19.

Freshman Class.

Robert Long Adams...Pleasant.
Jacob Armstrong Bruner..Hanover.
Samuel Montgomery Cambern...Rushville.
James Evans Cooper..New Castle, Ky.
William Irwin Craddock..Louisville, Ky.
Thomas Cleland Cunningham...Madison.
James William Edie..Stewartstown, Penn.
John Fox..Bruceville.
Sylvester Franklin Gilmore..Manhattan.
Dwight B. Hervey..Martinsburg, O.
Columbus De Witt Huston...New Philadelphia.
Albert Newton Keigwin...Louisville, Ky.
Robert Lenington..Kokomo.
William Kennedy Patterson...Madison.
John William Rabb...Rising Sun.
James David Rabb..Carrollton, Ky.
Chauncey Sabin..Westville.
Robert Blair Smith..Social Circle, Ga.
Worsley Smith...Louisville, Ky.
William George Thomas...Indian Creek, Va.
Samuel Finley Thompson..Darlington.
John Bacon Vawter...Franklin.
Francis George Wilson...Austin.

Freshmen:..............23.

Scientific Department.

Third Year.

Cyrus Alexander Johnson...Memphis, Tenn.
George Washington McCawley..Louisville, Ky.
James Edwin Rankin..Henderson, Ky.

Second Year.

Gavin Alves...Henderson, Ky.
Hiram Francis Braxtan...Paoli.
James Hall..Knightstown.
Thomas Soaper...Henderson, Ky.
David Taylor..Hibernia, O.
John Newton Voris...Pleasant.

HANOVER COLLEGE.

First Year.

Norwood Alves	Henderson, Ky.
Preston Loughborough Bland	Louisville, Ky.
Nettleton David	Uniontown, Ky.
John Randolph Erringer	Jeffersonville.
William Schenck Evans	Franklin, O.
Charles Foley	Indianapolis.
James Leander Furgason	Knightstown.
Alonzo Hatfield	Uniontown, Ky.
Samuel Henry	Pleasant.
Julius Azor Huntington	Richmond.
Charles Henry Montgomery	Fishpool, Ky.
Jacob Fullinwider Mount	Shannondale.
James Riley Paddock	Terre Haute.
James Butler Smith	Rising Sun.
William Franklin Standiford	Fishpool, Ky.
John Thomas Waters	Louisville, Ky.
Charlie Pyle Wiggins	Richmond.
Jonathan Clinton Wood	Bardstown, Ky.
John Benton Wood	Bardstown, Ky.
Joseph Putnam Wood	Bardstown, Ky.

Scientifics............29.

Preparatory Department.

Senior Class.

John Newton Abernathy	Knightstown.
John McKnight Bloss	New Philadelphia.
Ezra Ebenezer Chester	Columbus, O.
William S. Coulter	New Manchester, Va.
William Robert Davidson	Madison.
Nathaniel Fields	Jeffersonville.
Cyrus Hull Higginson	Uniontown, Ky.
Samuel Henry Howe	Flemingsburgh, Ky.
Robert Calvin Irwin	Austin, Miss.
Benjamin Franklin McCawley	Louisville, Ky.
Reuben Franklin Middleton	Frankfort, Ky.
Ebenezer Muse	Milton, Ky.
Ezra Fitch Pabody, Jr.	Vernon.
John Steele Paxton	Grand View, Ill.
Benjamin Simpson	Vernon.
Francis Tweedie Simpson	Vernon.
Edward Livingston Taylor	Hibernia, O.
William Colclough Thompson	Coleraine, Ireland.
Samuel Demaree Voris	Bennington,
Alpha Walter	Charleston.
James Wilson	Hanover.

Sen. Prep............21.

Junior Class.

John William Baldwin	Louisville, Ky.
Anthony Caldwell	Cincinnati, O.
George Washington Cummings	Logansport.
Solomon Frederick Denton	Cincinnati, O.
Samuel Patterson Dillon	Cincinnati, O.
George Washington Ewing, Jr	Fort Wayne.
George Monfort Gilchrist	Franklin.
William Hays	Louisville, Ky.
William Heath	La Fayette.
Joseph Henry Innis	Cross Plains.
Stephen Paul Lee	Hanover.
Thomas Jefferson Lindley	New Centreville.
Joseph Glass Marshall	Madison.
Albert A. C. Martin	Wash'tn, Daviess co.
Henry Venable Martin	Livonia.
Samuel Edgar McIlhenny	Bean Blossom.
Oliver Bright McIntire	Madison.
William Rush Patton	Palestine, Ill.
Aaron Vawter	Franklin.
John Terry Warner	Jamesport, L. I.
Milas Bestor Young	Hanover.

Jun. Prep....................21.

Summary.

Seniors	11
Juniors	8
Sophomores	19
Freshmen	23
Scientific Department	29
Preparatory Department	42
Total	132

Recapitulation.

Indiana	71
Kentucky	31
Ohio	15
Illinois	4
Virginia	2
Iowa	2
Tennessee	2
Mississippi, Georgia, Pennsylvania, Long Island, Ireland, each one	5
Total	132

Calender.

1856.

SEPT. 22, 23.	—Examination of candidates for admission,	Monday and Tuesday.
SEPT. 24.	—First term begins	Wednesday.
DEC. 24.	—First term ends	Wednesday.

WINTER VACATION OF TWO WEEKS.

1857.

JANUARY 7.	—Second term begins	Wednesday.
APRIL 7.	—Exhibition of the Union Literary Society	Tuesday.
APRIL 8.	—Exhibition of the Philalethean Society	Wednesday.
APRIL 8.	—Second term ends	Wednesday.

SPRING VACATION OF FOUR WEEKS.

MAY 6.	—Third term begins	Wednesday.
JULY 5.	—Biennial Examination, Senior Class, begins	Monday.
JULY 28.	—General Examination begins	Wednesday.
AUGUST 1.	—Baccalaureate Sermon	Sabbath.
AUGUST 3.	—Examination closes	Tuesday.
AUGUST 4.	—Anniversary of the Literary Societies	Wednesday.
AUGUST 5.	—COMMENCEMENT DAY	Thursday.

SUMMER VACATION OF SEVEN WEEKS.

SEPT. 20, 21.	—Examination of candidates for admission	Monday and Tuesday.
SEPT. 22.	—First term begins	Wednesday.

Admission.

CANDIDATES for admission into the Freshman Class are examined in Arithmetic, and Algebra through Quadratic Equations ; Ancient and Modern Geography ; the English, Latin and Greek Grammars ; Cæsar's Commentaries , four Orations of Cicero ; the first three books of Virgil's Æneid ; Arnold's Prose Composition ; Bullion's Greek Reader, and the Anabasis of Xenophon, or what is equivalent to these attainments. They must furnish testimonials of good character ; and, if from another College, must bring cirtificates of honorable dismission. Candidates for a higher standing, are examined upon that part of the course already studied by the class which they propose to enter.

No one can be admitted to the Freshman Class until he has completed his fourteenth year ; nor to an advanced standing, without a proportional increase of age.

"Before a student shall be admitted to actual standing in any class, he shall present to the President a receipt from the Treasurer, showing that he has complied with the statutes relating to College Charges and Scholarships."

N. B. The regular examination for admission into College, commences on the Monday preceding the beginning of each term.

Course of Instruction.

Preparatory Department.

Bullion's Latin and Greek Grammars, with praxis; Bullion's Latin and Greek Readers; Bullion's Cæsar, Sallust; Cooper's Virgil; Arnolds Latin Prose Composition, first XII, chapters; Owen's Anabasis, with Boise's Greek Prose Composition; Higher Arithmetic; Robinson's Algebra, University edition; Mitchell's Classical Geography; Coleman's Biblical Geography; Historical portions of the Old and New Testaments.

Scientific Department.

First Year.

Algebra, completed; Plane Geometry; Plane Trigonometry; Surveying and Navigation; Ancient, Modern and Ecclesiastical History.

Second Year.

Solid Geometry; Spherical Trigonometry, and its applications; Analytical Geometry; Natural Philosophy, and Astronomy; Rhetoric, Logic, and Political Economy.

Third Year.

Anatomy and Physiology; Zoology; Geology; Botany; Chemistry; Natural Theology Butler's Analogy; Psychology, and Moral Philosophy.

College Proper.

Freshman Class.

I.

Robinson's Greek Harmony of the Gospels.
Biblical Antiquities,
Virgil's Æneid, with the study of Prosody.
Xenophon's Anabasis, Completed.
Roman Antiquities, (Bojesen.)

Arnold's Greek Composition.
Robinson's Algebra, completed, (University edition.)

II.

Robinson's Harmony.
Lincoln's Livy.
Herodotus, (Leipsic edition,) begun.
Grecian History.
Roman, Grecian, and Biblical Antiquities,
Davies' Plane Geometry.

III.

Robinson's Harmony.
Lincoln's Livy, continued :
Herodotus, continued :
Grecian History, continued :
Grecian and Biblical Antiquities,
Davies' Plane Trigonometry, and surveying.

Sophomore Class.

I.

Greek Testament, (Acts.)
Cicero de Amicitia and de Senectute.
Homer's Iliad. (Owen's edition.)
Davies' Solid Geometry.
Roman History.

II.

Greek Testament, (Epistles.)
Horace, with study of the Horatian metres.
Homer's Iliad, continued ; Plato's Gorgias begun.
Davies' Spherical Trigonometry, and applications.
English History.

III.

Epistles, continued.
Horace, continued.
Plato's Gorgias, (Woolsey's edition.)
Davies' Analytical Geometry.
American History.

Junior Class.

I.

Hebrew Grammar, (Stuart's Rœdiger.)
Genesis.
Tacitus' Germania and Agricola, (Tyler's edition.)
Æschines against Ctesiphon, (Champlin's edition.)
Olmstead's Natural Philosophy, Vol. 1st.
Blair's Rhetoric.

II.

Hebrew—Genesis.
Cicero de Oratore.
Æschines, continued ; Demosthenes de Corona, begun.
Olmstead's Natural Philosophy, Vols. 1st. and 2d.
Whately's Logic.

III.

Hebrew—Psalms.
Cicero de Oratore, continued.
Demosthenes de Corona,(Champlin's edition,) finished.
Olmstead's Astronomy,
Wayland's Political Economy.

Senior Class.

I.

Select portions of the Hebrew Bible, with Lectures.
Psychology, (Walker's edition of Reid,) with Lectures.
Silliman's Chemistry.
Anatomy and Physiology, with Lectures.
Wood's Botany, with Lectures.
Cicero's Tusculan Disputations, &c., (Chase's edition.)

II.

Select Hebrew.
Psychology—Philosophy of Sir Wm. Hamilton, (Wight's edition.)
Chemistry.
Paley's Natural Theology.
Greek Tragedies ; Lectures on Grecian Art, Literature, &c.

III.

Select Hebrew.
Butler's Analogy of Religion, Natural and Revealed, to the Constitution and Course of Nature.
Moral Philosophy, Alexander, (with Lectures.)
Mineralogy.
Hitchcock's Geology.

N. B. The text-books needed for any part of the College Course, may be procured at the Hanover Book Store, at Cincinnati and Louisville prices.

Distribution of Recitations, &c.

	Department of Bibl. Instruction and Phil. The PRESIDENT.	Department of Rhetoric, Hist., Logic. Dr. CROWE.	Department of Natural Science. Prof. STONE.	Department of Mathematics & Nat. Phil. Prof. THOMPSON.	Department of Greek Lang. & Literature. Prof. BISHOP.	Department of Latin Lang. & Literature. Prof. LOTT.
	I	I.	I.	I.	I.	I.
J.P.		Bible			Greek Grammar	Latin Grammar
S.P.		Bible		Algebra	Bullion's Greek Reader	Bullion's Cæsar
F.	½ Harmon. of Gospels			Algebra, finished	Memorabilia	Virgil, continued
So.	½ Acts	Ancient History		Solid Geometry	½ Iliad	½ De Amicit. & de Senec.
J.	Hebrew	½ Rhetoric		Nat. Philosophy	½ Æschines	½ Tacit Germ. & Agric.
S.	½ Hebrew, Psychology		Chemistry. ½ Anat. Phys.			½ Tusculan Disputations.
	II	II.	II.	II.	II.	II.
J.P.		Bible			Greek Reader	Latin Reader
S.P.		Bible	Algebra		Anabasis	Cicero's Orations
F.	½ Harmon. of Gospels			Plane Geometry	Memor. and Herodotus	½ Livy
So.	½ Epistles	Modern History		Spher. Trig. and Applic.	½ Iliad and Georgias	½ Horace
J.	Hebrew	½ Logic		Nat. Philosophy	½ Æsch. & Demosthenes.	½ Cicero de Oratore
S.	½ Hebrew. Psychology		Chemistry, ½ Nat. Theol.		½ Greek Tradegies	
	III.	III.	III.	III.	III.	III.
J.P.		Bible			Greek Reader	Latin Reader
S.P.		Bible	Algebra		Anabasis	Virgil
F.	½ Harmon, Gospels			Plane. Trig. Surveying	Herodotus	Livy
So.	½ Epistles	Eccles. History		Analyt. Geometry	½ Georgias	½ Horace
J.	Hebrew	½ Pol. Economy,		Astronomy	½ Demosthenes	½ Cicero de Oratore
S.	½ Hebrew, Mor. Philos.		Butler's Anal. ½ Mineral and Geology			

Permanent Recitation Hours in all Departments.

A. M.						
8	½ Seniors	Sophomores	½ Seniors	Juniors	Sen. Prep.	Freshmen
9	Juniors		Seniors	Sophomores	Freshmen	Sen. Prep.
10	Seniors	Sen. and Jun. Prep.		Freshmen	½ Sophs. and Junior	Sophs. and Juniors
11	½ Fresh. and Sophs.	½ Juniors		Sen. Prep.		

Permanent Recitation Hours—Scientific Department.

A. M.	FIRST CLASS.	SECOND CLASS.	THIRD CLASS.
8	History	Nat. Philos. and Astron	Nat. Sci. and Nat. Theol.
9		Mathematics	Chem. and Butl. Anal.
19	Mathematics		Psychol. and Mor. Phil.
11		½ Rhet., Log., Pol, Econ	

The preceding course is so arranged, in all departments, as to require from every class, except the Senior, an average of THREE HOURS AND A HALF in recitations DAILY, excepting Saturday. These recitations are attended without loss of time between the hours of 8 and 12 A. M.; leaving the remainder of the day for study and recreation.

Classical Department.

In connection with the daily recitations, constant reference is made to Bullion's Latin and Greek Grammars Leverett's or Andrew's Latin Lexicon, Liddell and Scott's Greek Lexicon Anthon s Classical Dictionary, Bojesen's Roman and Greek Antiquities, and Mitchell's Atlas of Ancient Geography.

The following works are recommended for more extended consultation by the student in private: Zumpt's Latin Grammar, Kuhner's and Crosby's Greek Grammars, Crusius' Homeric Lexicon, Munk's Greek and Latin Metres, Eschenburg's Manual of Classical Literature, and Smith's Dictionary of Greek and Roman Antiquities.

Scientific Department.

The three years' course of English, Mathematical and Scientific instruction pursued in this department embraces all that is included in the Collegiate scheme, except the Classical languages. Such as desire it however may pursue the study of Latin or French, in connection with a Scientific Course. We do not recommend it as in any sense an equivalent for a thorough Classical course; nor is it intended for mere boys since the subjects which it includes are entirely above their capacity; but to young men, who have obtained a respectable common school education, including the elements of Algebra and who have not time nor means to prosecute the Classical course, this system of studies, will, it is hoped, commend itself as solid, comprehensive, and practical. Those who shall complete the prescribed Scientific course, will receive a Diploma, certifying the extent of their attainments.

College Year—Examinations.

THE COLLEGIATE YEAR is divided into three Terms of thirteen weeks each, and three Vacations. The First Term begins on the Fourth Wednesday in September; the Second, on the First Wednesday in January; and the Third, on the First Wednesday in May, closing with the First Thursday in August, which is commencement Day

It is of great importance that Students attend from the very beginning of the term; especially since so considerable portion of time is allotted to vacations. In most cases, the loss of a few weeks or even days, seriously affects the future standing of the pupil. Absence during term time, without special leave, is prohibited.*

Public examinations will be held, hereafter, only at the close of the college year, when the Freshmen and Junior Classes will be examined on the studies of the preceding year, and the Sophomore and Senior Classes,-upon those of the two preceding years. These last examinations will be final for the studies pursued in those years. All the examinations will be thorough and rigid; and will be conducted chiefly by the use of written questions, prepared by the Faculty and the Examining Committee, covering the whole field of study prosecuted during a given period, and entirely unknown to the Student until the moment of examination. These questions must be answered in writing before the Committee; and correct answers to a definite portion of them will be the passport of admission to a higher standing. Similar examinations of a briefer and less decisive character however, and by way of preparation for the final trial may be conducted privately, at the pleasure of the Faculty.

Religious Instruction and Services.

The attention of a Christian community is respectfully invited to the system of Biblical Instruction which forms a characteristic feature of our course of Study. The Grammar School Classes recite statedly in the English Bible; and every College Class has a daily or triweekly recitation in the Greek Testament or the Hebrew. Proficiency in these, as in other studies, is tested by the usual examinations. In addition to this, Biblical Geography and Antiquities, Ecclesiastical History, Natural Theology, and the Analogy of Religion Natural and Revealed to the constitution and course of nature, are carefully and faithfully studied. There is also a Bible or Catechetical exercise on Sabbath mornings; a public service on Sabbath-afternoons appropriated to the Students; and daily morning prayers. The Students are expected to attend the Sabbath morning service of the congregation worshiping in the chaple or of some other congregation in the vicinity, if their parents prefer any of the latter. The Methodist, Associate, and Associate Reformed Churches, have regular services in or near the village.

An experiment of several years in this Institution, has established the fact that the daily study of God's word by no means interferes with, but rather promotes sound and comprehensive attainments in other branches of knowledge. Some, indeed, have questioned the expediency of adding Hebrew to an already overburdened curriculum; especially since Theological Students may acquire it in the Seminary and non-theologians are unlikely to make any particular use of such an acquisition. Our confident answer is,—First, that Theological Students.

---

* Parents are respectfully advised to give their sons no such permission to be absent, except in cases of necessity.

need more acquaintance with Hebrew than with Greek, when they enter the Seminary, since familiarity with the Old Testament is more rare, and more difficult of attainment, than familiarity with the New :—SECONDLY, that the moral discipline secured by this study is fully equal to that obtained from any other:— THIRDLY, that a knowledge of Hebrew, as connected with the Indo-European tongues, greatly contributes to the Student's mastery of the latter :—FOURTHLY. that non-theological students are as likely to cultivate the Hebrew, when once acquired, as the higher Mathematics and the Classics :—FIFTHLY, that the Hebrew Scriptures contain more valuable, practical truth, than all the pagan classics put together :—and LASTLY, that the day is to be dreaded when ability to peruse the Sacred Volume, in the originals, shall be the exclusive property of the Clergy.

Expenses.

The entire annual expenditures of a Student need not much exceed **$150**, viz:
  Tuition and contingent fee, $10 per term,.....................$30 00
  Boarding with private families, and a furnished room, at
    $2 50 per week,...$97 50
  Fuel, light, washing, &c.,...$15 00
  Books, &c.,.. 5 to $10

Boarding in clubs will cost from seventy-five cents to one dollar twenty-five cents a week; and some board themselves even at a lower rate. The cost of clothing, and the amount spent as pocket-money, will vary with the taste and habits of the Student, and with the wishes of parents. As a general rule, the more money allowed to a young man beyond what is strictly necessary, the less likely is he to reflect honor upon his parents and instructors. Although Hanover presents comparatively few temptations to extravagance, yet parents are earnestly advised to require of their sons a detailed account of their expenditures, and peremptorily to refuse the payment of any debt incurred by them without a written permission. It is also recommended that the funds of young pupils be deposited with some one of the Faculty, and expended under his direction. The younger Students are required to board where the Faculty may direct, and where they may exercise a more careful and frequent supervision.

N. B. Students placed upon Scholarships by the Faculty, are relieved in part, or wholly, as the case may require, from the payment of tuition fees.

Discipline.

A record is kept by the Faculty, in which are entered weekly, the grade of scholarship of the student, his absences from the exercises of the Institution, and such other facts as are worthy of notice with respect to his General Deportment. From this record a report is made out at the end of each session and sent to the Parent or Guardian of each Student. In case of deficiency in scholarship, negligence in study, irregularity in attendance upon the exercises of the Institution, or improper conduct, the Student will be privately admonished, and the Parent or Guardian will be promptly informed of the fact.

It is the object of this arrangement to keep Parents and Guardians accurately informed with regard to their sons and wards in this Institution, and thus to secure their co-operation with the Faculty in a mild system of discipline. Whenever it is ascertained that a Student is deriving no advantage from his connection with the Institution, or is pursuing courses injurious to himself, or fellow-students, the Faculty will take decisive action, and his Parent or Guardian will be promptly addressed on the subject, and requested to remove him from the Institution.

Scholarships.

The endowment of this Institution, so far as it has been secured, is in the form of Scholarships; of which the Board has established several sorts. The sum of $400 paid, or secured to the Corporation by note payable within five years, and bearing six per cent. interest in advance upon principal remaining unpaid—purchases for the owner, his heirs and assigns, a perpetual right to the tuition of one scholar, in Hanover College. The sum of $200 paid, or subscribed under similar conditions, secures a right to twenty years tuition; after which time, the scholarship is subject to the disposal of the Board for the gratuitous education of candidates for the Gospel Ministry. A church scholarship of $200 secures to the church so contributing, a perpetual right to the tuition of one student, who shall be a member of that church, and appointed by the session. A Presbyterial scholarship of $200 secures a similar right to a Presbytery in behalf of pupils who shall be candidates for the Ministry under its care. The PRINCIPAL paid on these scholarships is invested by the Corporation in some safe and productive stock; and the INTEREST ONLY can be expended for the support of the College.

The sum of $100, PAID WITHIN TWO YEARS AT FARTHEST, with interest in advance on unpaid principal, purchases a right to ten years' tuition within twenty years from the date of subscription. Both principal and interest of this scholarship may be employed for contingent purposes; and the scholarship expires with the owner's right to its use.

The sum of $100 PAID into the building fund; or the sum of $50 PAID in like manner, secures the right to ten, or five years' tuition of one student.

Every person applying for admission as a beneficiary of a scholarship under the control of the donors, shall present to the Treasurer, at the beginning of each term, A WRITTEN CERTIFICATE from those controlling the scholarship, of his right to such benefit; when, after paying whatever interest may be due on said scholarship, he shall receive an acknowledgment of his right, which he shall lodge with the President.

"The scholarships subject to the disposal of the Corporation, may be occupied by such applicants as the Faculty may select, after inquiry into their circumstances, character and attainments; the preference being, (cœteris paribus,) to those who give the best evidence of scholarship.

"There shall at no time be more than one student upon each scholarship."

Accommodations.

The community system of Boarding in Commons, or of rooming in large Lodging Halls, is not adopted in Hanover. Arrangements are made to accommodate the students with Board and Rooms in respectable private families, where the number together can never be large, and where all hall be brought under domestic influence.

Settlement of Accounts.

No Diploma nor Honorable Dismission shall be granted until the student shall exhibit a Receipt of Settlement of all his Bills for Boarding, Room and Washing.

Degrees.

No Degrees are conferred in course. Candidates for Literary Honors are reported to the Board upon their ascertained or acknowledged merits.

Societies, Libraries, &c.

There are two Societies connected with the College, the UNION LITERARY and the PHILALETHEAN, whose Libraries number each about fifteen-hundred volumes.

There is also a SOCIETY OF RELIGIOUS INQUIRY which has begun to collect a Library, Maps, &c., and which in connection with another association formed for the purpose. sustains a valuable Reading Room.

The College Library contains two thousand well selected volumes, and is accessible to the Students.

The Cabinet contains several thousand specimens in Mineralogy and Geology.

The friends of the College are advised that contributions to the Library, to the Cabinet, or to or for the Laboratory are much needed and will be thankfully received.

Prohibited Secret Societies.

The following order was passed by the Board of Trustees in July 1855, viz:

"*Resolved*, That this Board disapprove of the existence among the Students of Hanover College of any Society or Association of which the Faculty are not ex-officio members; and will not permit the public exhibition of any such Society."

Location, Building, &c.

The village of Hanover is situated upon an elevated bluff of the Ohio river, six miles below Madison, Indiana, in a region of remarkable salubrity and natural beauty. The village and neighborhood are characterized by morality, and the absence of all ordinary temptations to vice and idleness Intoxicating liquors have never been publicly sold in the township; the traffic being prohibited, annually. by popular vote. The Ohio river, and the Railways from Madison, New Albany, and Cincinnati place Hanover within twenty-four hours of all the principal points in Indiana, Kentucky, Western Ohio, and Eastern Illinois. A Plank Road from Madison to Hanover, renders the village easy of access at all seasons of the year.

Hanover College is controlled by a Board of Trustees; one half of whom are appointed by the Board itself, and the other half by the Synods of Indiana and Northern Indiana. All its officers are Ministers, or members, of the Presbyterian Church.

The Board purchased, some years ago, a farm of two hundred acres lying between the village and the Ohio river, upon a beautiful point of which overlooking the river from an elevation of four hundred feet, they have erected a commodious College edifice, now nearly completed. The new College consists of a center building, nearly eighty feet square, with lateral and transverse wings. The whole length is about two hundred feet. It contains no dormitories for Students; (an undesirable provision;) but affords ample and convenient halls, library. cabinet lecture and recitation rooms, and a spacious chapel.

The building commands an exceedingly diversified view of the river, for six miles up, and ten miles down its course.

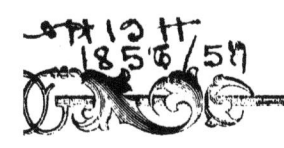

THE TWENTY-FIFTH

Annual Catalogue & Circular,

OF

HANOVER COLLEGE.

AUGUST 1857.

MADISON, IND.
Courier Job Office print, West street.
1857.

THE TWENTY-FIFTH

Annual Catalogue & Circular,

OF

HANOVER COLLEGE,

AUGUST 1857.

MADISON, IND.
Courier Job Office print, West street.
1857.

BOARD OF TRUSTEES.

	Term Expires.
*REV. J. F. CROWE, D. D., HANOVER,	1857.
*A. R. FORSYTH, GREENSBURG,	1857.
*J. L. WILLIAMS, FORT WAYNE,	1857.
*REV. J. B. MORTON, MIDDLETOWN, O.,	1857.
†REV. J. F. SMITH, RICHMOND,	1857.
†REV. J. M. STEVENSON, D. D., NEW YORK CITY,	1857.
‡REV. E. W. WRIGHT, DELPHI,	1857.
‡HON. S. HANNA, FORT WAYNE,	1857.
*REV. H. H. CAMBERN, RUSHVILLE,	1858.
*REV. T. E. THOMAS, D. D., NEW ALBANY,	1858.
*HON. C. E. WALKER, MADISON,	1858.
*COL. JAMES BLAKE, INDIANAPOLIS,	1858.
‡REV. C. K. THOMPSON, DARLINGTON,	1858.
‡REV. S. C. LOGAN, CINCINNATI, O.,	1858.
†REV. D. D. McKEE, MARION, IOWA,	1858.
†JAMES M. RAY, INDIANAPOLIS,	1858.
*JOHN KING, MADISON,	1859.
*REV. WM. SICKELS, INDIANAPOLIS,	1859.
*W. M. DUNN, MADISON,	1859.
*W. A. BULLOCK, VERNON,	1859.
†REV. JOSEPH WARREN, D. D., GREENSBURG,	1859.
†REV. T. S. CROWE, HANOVER,	1859.
‡REV. I. N. SHANNON, MT. VERNON, O.,	1859.
‡REV. J. C. BROWN, VALPARAISO,	1859.
*DR. P. S. SHIELDS, NEW ALBANY,	1860.
*R. S. McKEE, MADISON,	1860.
*REV. J. G. SYMMES, CRANBERRY, N. J.,	1860.
*REV. J. EDWARDS, D. D., HANOVER,	1860.
†REV. JAS. A. McKEE, FRANKLIN,	1860.
†REV. J. W. BLYTHE, VINCENNES,	1860.
‡REV. F. P. CUMMINS, LA PORTE,	1860.
‡REV. ROBERT IRWIN, SEN'R, MONTICELLO,	1860.

*Appointed by the Board.
†Appointed by the Synod of Indiana.
‡Appointed by the Synod of Northern Indiana.

Officers of the Board.

REV. J. F. CROWE, D. D., President.
REV. J. EDWARDS, D. D., Secretary.
S. McKEE, Madison, Treasurer.

Executive Committee.

REV. J. EDWARDS, REV. J. F. CROWE,
REV. T. S. CROWE, W. M. DUNN,
JOHN KING.

FACULTY.

REV. JONATHAN EDWARDS, D. D., PRESIDENT,
PROFESSOR OF BIBLICAL INSTRUCTION, PSYCHOLOGY AND ETHICS.

REV. JOHN FINLEY CROWE, D. D.
PROFESSOR OF RHETORIC, LOGIC, HISTORY AND POLITICAL ECONOMY.

REV. S. HARRISON THOMSON, A. M.
PROFESSOR OF MATHEMATICS AND MECHANICAL PHILOSOPHY.

REV. WILLIAM BISHOP, A. M.
PROFESSOR OF GREEK LANGUAGE AND LITERATURE.

REV. JOSHUA B. GARRITT, A. M.
PROFESSOR OF LATIN LANGUAGE AND LITERATURE.

AUGUSTUS W. KING,
PROFESSOR OF NATURAL SCIENCE.

WILLIAM COCHRAN, } TUTORS.
JOHN McMURRAY,

REV. J. FINLEY CROWE, D. D.
LIBRARIAN.

UNDERGRADUATES.

SENIOR CLASS.

Leonard Fisk Andrews,..................................Quiver, Ill.
William Cochrane,..Cincinnati, O.
William Means Crozier,..................................Iowa City, Iowa.
John McMurray,..New Concord, O.
David McKnight Williamson,..............................Logansport.
   Seniors,..............................5.

JUNIOR CLASS.

William Peter Baker,....................................Fort Wayne.
Alexander Miller Crawford,..............................Graysville.
Jacob Reasoner Geyer,...................................Norwich, O.
Samuel Telford Hanna,...................................Fort Wayne.
Horace Hovey Hanna,.....................................Fort Wayne.
John David McClintock,..................................Millersburg, Ky.
James Baird McClure,....................................Vincennes.
Robert Campbell McKinney,...............................Sullivan.
David William Moffat,...................................Vernon.
James Barnes Patterson,.................................Dayton, O.
James Alexander Piper,..................................La Porte.
Robert Gaines Ross,.....................................Twenty-mile Stand O.
Isaac Coe Sickels,......................................Indianapolis.
Augustus Taylor,..Fort Madison, Iowa.
James Harvey Vannuys,...................................Franklin.
Cornelius Pleasant Voris,...............................Bennington.
William Bates Warren,...................................Louisville, Ky.
Edward Peet Williams,...................................Fort Wayne.
   Juniors,...............................18.

SOPHOMORE CLASS.

Albert Long Adams,......................................Pleasant.
Thomas Leander Adams,...................................Hanover.
Jacob Armstrong Bruner,.................................Hanover.
Samuel Montgomery Cambern,..............................Rushville.
Henry Ellet Crawford,...................................Bedford.
Thomas Cleland Cunningham,..............................Madison.
James William Edie,.....................................Stewartstown, Pa.
John Fox,...Bruceville.
Sylvester Franklin Gilmore,.............................Manhattan.
Columbus De Witt Huston,................................New Philadelphia.
William Beattie Laughlin,...............................Rushville.
Robert Lenington,.......................................Kokomo.
Henry Partlo Montgomery,................................Ghent, Ky.
Madison Hall Rose,......................................North Salem.
Thomas Norwood Sickels,.................................Indianapolis.
Benjamin F. Stearns,....................................Lovell, Maine.
William George Thomas,..................................Indian Creek, Va.

Samuel Finley Thompson,..................................Darlington.
John Bacon Vawter,..Franklin.
Francis George Wilson,····································Austin.
          Sophomores,...........................20.

FRESHMAN CLASS.

John Newton Abernathy,..................................Knightstown.
John McKnight Bloss,....................................New Philadelphia
William S. Coulter,......................................N. Manchester, V
William Robert Davidson,.................................Madison.
George Monfort Gilchrist,...............................Vinton, Iowa.
Samuel Henry Howe,......................................Flemingsburg, K
Robert Calvin Irwin,....................................Hanover.
Reuben Franklin Middleton,..............................Frankfort, Ky.
Ebenezer Muse,..Milton, Ky.
Ezra Fitch Peabody, Jr.,................................Vernon.
John Steele Paxton,.....................................Grand View, Ill.
James Hervey Robinson, Jr.,.............................Fort Wayne.
Eli Symmes Shorter,.....................................Columbus, Ga.
Benjamin Simpson,.......................................Vernon.
Edward Livingston Taylor,...............................Columbus, O.
William Colclough Thompson,.............................Massillon, O.
Samuel Demaree Voris,...................................Bennington.
Meade Creighton Williams,...............................Fort Wayne.
Joseph McCroskey Wilson,................................Clifton, O.
James Wilson,...Hanover.
Joseph Putnam Wood,.....................................Bardstown, Ky.
          Freshmen,............................21.

SCIENTIFIC DEPARTMENT.

THIRD YEAR.

Hiram Francis Braxtan,..................................Paoli.
James William Raine,....................................Nolin, Ky.
David Taylor, Jr.,......................................Columbus, O.
John Newton Voris,......................................Pleasant.

SECOND YEAR.

Preston Loughborough Bland,.............................Louisville, Ky.
William Schenck Evans,..................................Franklin, O.
James Leander Furgason,.................................Knightstown.
James Riley Paddock,....................................Terre Haute.
Jonathan Clinton Wood,..................................Bardstown, Ky.

FIRST YEAR.

Daniel Ellis Conner,....................................Bardstown, Ky.
William Hays,...Louisville, Ky.
James Innis,..Cross Plains.
Charles Harrison Johnson,...............................Fort Wayne.
Oliver Bright McIntire,.................................Madison.
John Snyder McPheeters,.................................Livonia.

HANOVER COLLEGE.

Jacob Fullinwider Mount, ...Shannondale.
Oliver Mulvey, ...Madison.
Samuel Davies Redus, ...Livonia.
John Woodburn Shrewsbury, ...Madison.
Solon McCollough Tilford, ...Kent.
George Martin Whiteley, ...New York City.
    Scientific Department.....................21.

PREPARATORY DEPARTMENT.

SENIOR CLASS.

Thompson Kenton Allen, ...Louisville, Ky.
Walter Alexander Blake, ...Indianapolis.
Ashley Brown, ...Dayton, O.
John Robinson Carmichael, ...Rushville.
George Washington Cummings, ...Logansport.
Solomon Frederick Denton, ...Cincinnati, O.
Samuel Patterson Dillon, ...Cincinnati, O.
Charles Garritt, ...Delphi.
Joseph Henry Innis, ...Cross Plains.
John Arel Johnson, ...Evansville.
Stephen Paul Lee, ...Hanover.
Henry Venable Martin, ...Livonia.
Albert A. C. Martyn, ...Vincennes.
William Crawford Pogue, ...Mace.
Howard Erskine Stansbury, ...Cleveland, O.
Edmund Lynch Sturgis, ...Fort Wayne.
Raphael Shorter Ward, ...Columbus, Ga.
John Terry Warner, ...Jamesport, L. I.
Barton R. Zantzinger, ...San Antonio, Texas
    Sen. Prep., ...19.

JUNIOR CLASS.

Lois Octavus Bachman, ...Madison.
George Bollman Boomer, ...New Philadelphia.
Felix Jennerette Brandt, ...Hanover.
Gson Britton, ...Milton, Ky.
Francis Marion Broady, ...Vienna.
Simeon Buchanan, ...Bellville.
William James Carter, ...Plainfield.
James William Cochran, ...Hanover.
Andrew Jackson Crum, ...Pigeon Roost.
George Washington Ewing, Jr., ...Fort Wayne.
Isaac Newton Forman, ...High Grove, Ky.
Ebenezer Gelpin, ...Hanover.
Richard Andrew Graham, ...Washington, Daviess Co.
Jotus Hall, Jr., ...Cattaraugus Co N.Y
James Barclay Henley, ...San Francisco, Cal.
Charles Louis Holstein, ...Madison.
William Dunn Hynes, ...Greenville, Ill.
Augustus Adolph Joss, ...Constantine, Mich.

CATALOGUE OF

James Woods Kyle,..Hanover.
Charles Philo Leavitt, ...Hanover.
William Dorson Lewis,..Vincennes.
George Merriwether McCampbell,...........................Jeffersonville.
Anson Wellington Merwin, ...Hanover.
Thornburn Charters Merwin,..................................Hanover.
Thomas Norris Peoples,..Bean Blossom.
James Smith Pritchett,...Vincennes.
Lewis Reasoner,..Wheeling.
Franklin Shannon,..Hanover.
Elwood Paxton Sine,...Logansport.
James Wilson Spear,...Hanover.
George Mason Warmoth, ...New Frankfort.
Jesse Brown Wilson,..Lexington.
Thomas Hart Woodward,......................................Hanover.
   Jun. Prep.,...................................33.

SUMMARY.

Seniors,.. 5
Juniors,..18
Sophomores,..20
Freshmen,..21
Scientific Department,..21
Preparatory Department, ...52

 Total,..137

RECAPITULATION.

Indiana,..91
Kentucky,..15
Ohio,..14
Illinois,.. 3
Iowa,.. 3
Virginia, New York and Georgia, two each,................ 6
California, Michigan, Pennsylvania Maine and Texas, one each,..... 5

 Total,..137

CALENDAR.

1857.

SEPT. 21, 22.	Examination of candidates for admission	Monday and Tuesday.
SEPT. 23.	First term begins	Wednesday.
DEC. 24.	First term ends	Thursday.

WINTER VACATION OF TWO WEEKS.

1858.

JAN. 6.	Second term begins	Wednesday.
APRIL 7.	Exhibition of the Philalethian Society	Wednesday.
APRIL 8.	Exhibition of the Union Literary Society	Thursday.
APRIL 8.	Second term ends	Thursday.

SPRING VACATION OF FOUR WEEKS.

MAY 5.	Third term begins	Wednesday.
JULY 5.	Biennial examination, Senior Class, begins	Monday.
JULY 28.	General examination begins	Wednesday.
AUG. 1.	Baccalaureate Sermon,	Sabbath.
AUG. 3.	General examination ends	Tuesday.
AUG. 3.	Annual meeting of the Board of Trustees	Tuesday.
AUG. 4.	Anniversary of the Literary Societies,	Wednesday.
AUG. 4.	Anniversary of the Society of Religious Inquiry	Wednesday.
AUG. 5.	COMMENCEMENT DAY	Thursday,

SUMMER VACATION OF SEVEN WEEKS.

SEPT. 20, 21.	Examination of candidates for admission	Monday and Tuesday.
SEPT. 22.	First term begins	Wednesday.

ADMISSION.

CANDIDATES for admission into the Freshman Class are examined in Arithmetic, and Algebra Ancient and Modern Geography; the English, Latin and Greek Grammars; Cæsar's Commentaries; four Orations of Cicero; the first three books of Virgil's Æneid; Arnold's Prose Composition; Bullion's Greek Reader, and the Anabasis of Xenophon, or what is equivalent to these attainments. They must furnish testimonials of good character; and, if from another College, must bring certificates of honorable dismission. Candidates for a higher standing, are examined upon that part of the course already studied by the class which they propose to enter.

No one can be admitted to the Freshman Class until he has completed his fourteenth year; nor to an advanced standing, without a proportional increase of age.

"Before a student shall be admitted to actual standing in any class, he shall present to the President a receipt from the Treasurer, showing that he has complied with the statutes relating to College Charges and Scholarships."

N. B, The regular examination for admission into College, commences on the Monday preceding the beginning of each term.

COURSE OF INSTRUCTION.

Preparatory Department.

Latin and Greek Grammars, with praxis; Latin and Greek Readers; Cæsar Virgil; Latin Prose Composition, first XII chapters; Xenophon's Anabasis Classical and Biblical Geography; Higher Arithmetic; Algebra; English Bible New Testaments and Pentateuch.

Scientific Department.

FIRST YEAR.

Algebra, completed; Plane Geometry; Plane Trigonometry; Surveying and Navigation; History; English Bible, historical books.
Linear Drawing (extra.)

SECOND YEAR.

Solid Geometry; Spherical Trigonometry, and its applications; Analytic Geometry; Natural Philosophy, and Astronomy; Rhetoric, Logic, and Political Economy; English Bible, Poetical books.

THIRD YEAR.

Zoology; Anatomy and Physiology; Botany; Physical Geography; Chemistry Geology; Natural Theology and Butler's Analogy; Psychology, and Ethics English Bible, Mine Explored.

Academic Department.

FRESHMAN CLASS.

FIRST SESSION.

Greek Harmony of the Gospels.
Biblical Antiquities.
Virgil, with Prosody.
Roman Antiquities.
Heroditus.
Plane Geometry.

SECOND SESSION.

Greek Harmony, continued.
Virgil and Sallust.
Thucydides.
Grecian History.
Grecian Antiquities.
Plane Trigonometry.

THIRD SESSION.

Greek Harmony, completed.
Sallust, with Review of Latin.
Thucydides.
Grecian History, completed.
Grecian Antiquities, completed.
Surveying and Navigation.
English Bible, Historical books; Latin and Greek Prose Composition; Vocal Music throughout the year.

SOPHOMORE CLASS.

FIRST SESSION.

Greek Testament, (Acts.)
Livy.
Iliad.
Solid Geometry.
Roman History.

SECOND SESSION.

Greek Testament, (Epistles.)
Horace, with study of the Horatian metres.
Iliad.
Plane Trigonometry, reviewed.
Spherical Trigonometry, with its applications.
English History.

THIRD SESSION.

Greek Testament, Epistles.
Horace, continued, with review of Latin.
Æschylus.
Analytical Geometry.
American History.
English Bible, Poetical books; Latin and Greek Prose Composition, throughout the year.

JUNIOR CLASS.

FIRST SESSION.

Hebrew Grammar.
Genesis.
Tacitus.
Æchines against Cteiphon.
Natural Philosophy.
Rhetoric.

SECOND SESSION.

Hebrew, (Genesis.)
Cicero de Oratore.
Æschines, completed.
Demosthenes de Corona.
Natural Philosophy.
Logic.

THIRD SESSION.

Hebrew, (Psalms.)
Cicero's Tusculan Disputations.
Demosthenes de Corona, completed.
Astronomy.
Pilitical Economy.
English Bible, Prophetical books, throughout the year.

SENIOR CLASS.

FIRST SESSION.

Select portions of the Hebrew Bible, with Lectures.
Psychology, with Lectures.
Latin reviewed, with Lectures on Latin Literature.
Exercises in Latin Composition.
Chemistry, with Lectures.
Anatomy and Physiology, with Lectures.
Botany, with Lectures.

SECOND SESSION.

Select Hebrew.
Psychology.
Chemistry.
Natural Theology.
Greek reviewed, with Lectures on Grecian Art, Literature, &c.

THIRD SESSION.

Hebrew reviewed.
Butler's Analogy.
Ethics, with Lectures.
Geology.
Mineralogy.
English Bible reviewed, Mine Explored, throughout the year.

N. B. The text books needed for any part of the College course, may be procure at the Hanover Book Store, at Cincinnati and Louisville prices.

TEXT BOOKS.

DEPARTMENT OF LANGUAGES.

LATIN.—Bullions' Grammar and Reader, Andrews' or Leverett's Lexicon, Bullon's Cæsar, Cooper's Virgil, Arnold's Latin Prose Composition, Bojesen's Roman Antiquities, Butler & Sturgus' Sallust, Lincoln's Livy, Lincoln's Horace, Tyler's Tacitus, Dillaway's De Oratore, Chase's Tusculan Disputations.

GREEK.—Bullion's Grammar and Reader, Liddell & Scott's or Pickering's Lexicon, Owen's Anabasis, Mitchell's Classical Geography, Bojesen's Grecian Antiquities, Johnson's Herodotus, Owen's Thucydides, Owen's Iliad, Woolsey's Æschylus, Champlin's Æschines, Champlin's Demosthenes.

HEBREW.—Stuart's Rœdiger's Grammar, Gesenius' Lexicon, Biblia Hebraica.

DEPARTMENT OF BELLES-LETTRES.

Blair's Rhetoric, (University edition,) Whately's Logic, Wayland's Political Economy, Smith's Grecian History, Pinnock's Goldsmith's Roman History, Clark's English History, American History.

DEPARTMENT OF MATHEMATICS.

Robinson's Algebra, (University edition,) Davies' Legendre, Davies' Surveying, Davies' Analytical Geometry, Olmsted's Natural Philosophy, do. Astronomy.

DEPARTMENT OF NATURAL SCIENCE.

Silliman's Chemistry, Cutter's Physiology, Gray's Botany, Paley's Natural Theology, Lyell's Geology, Butler's Analogy, Dana's Mineralogy, Agassiz & Gould's Zoology, Sommerville's Physical Geography.

DEPARTMENT OF METAPHYSICS.

Walker's Reid on the Intellectual Powers, Sir William Hamilton's Philosophy, (Wight's edition,) Stewart's Active and Moral Powers, Alexander's Moral Science.

DEPARTMENT OF RELIGIOUS INSTRUCTION.

General Assembly's Hymn Book, Jacobus' Notes and Questions, English Bible, Robinson's Greek Harmony, Owen on Acts, Greek Testament, Mine Explored.

REFERENCE BOOKS.

The following works are recommended for more extended consultation by the student in private: Zumpt's Latin Grammar, Kuhner's and Crosby's Greek Grammars, Crusius' Homeric Lexicon, Munk's Greek and Latin Metres, Eschenburg's Classical Manual, Nordheimer's Hebrew Grammar, Lowth's Hebrew Poetry, Roget's English Thesaurus, Ramshorn's Latin Synonymes, Donaldson's New Cratylus, De Vere's Comparative Philology.

DISTRIBUTION OF RECITATIONS, &c.

	Department of Bibl. Instruction & Phil	Department of Rhetoric, Hist., Logic	Department of Natural Science.	Department of Mathemat. & Mech Phil	Department of Gr. Lang. & Literature	Department of Lat. Lang. & Literature
	I.	I.	I.	I.	I.	I.
J.P.		Bible			Greek Grammar	Latin Grammar
S.P.		Bible		Plane Geom	Analysis	Bullion's Cæsar
F	½ Harmon of Gospels			Algebra, finished	Herodotus	Virgil, continued
So.	½ Acts	Ancient History	Zoology	Solid Geometry	½ Iliad	Livy
J.	Hebrew	½ Rhetoric	Anatomy and Physiol	Nat. Philosophy	½ Æschines	½ Tacit Germ. & Agric
S.	½ Hebrew, Psychol		Chemistry			
	II.	II.	II.	II.	II.	II.
J.P.		Bible			Greek Reader	Gram. and Cæsar
S.P.		Bible			Anabasis	Cicero's Orations
F	½ Harmon of Gospels			Plane Trigonom	Thucydides	Virgil and Sallust
So.	½ Epistles	Modern History	Phys. Geography	Spher. Trig. & Applic.	½ Iliad and Gorgias	½ Horace
J.	Hebrew	½ Logic	Light and Heat	Nat. Philosophy	½ Æsch. & Demosth.	½ Cicero de Oratore
S.	½ Hebrew, Psychol		Chem. and Mineral		½ Greek Tragedies	
	III.	III.	III.	III.	III.	III.
J.P.		Bible			Greek Reader	Cæsar and Gram
S.P.		Bible	Algebra		Anabasis	Virgil
F	½ Harmon, Gospels			Surveying	Thucydides	Livy
So.	½ Epistles	Eccles. History	Botany	Analyt. Geometry	Æschylus	½ Horace
J.	Hebrew	½ Pol. Economy	Electricity	Astronomy	½ Demosthenes	Cic. Tus. Dis.
S.	½ Hebrew, Mor. Phil.		Geol. & Nat. Theol.			

PERMANENT RECITATION HOURS IN ALL DEPARTMENTS.

A.M.						
8	½ Seniors	Sophomores	½ Seniors	Juniors	Sen. Prep.	Freshmen
9	Juniors		Seniors	Sophomores	Freshmen	Sen. Prep.
10	Seniors	Sen. and Jun. Prep.		Freshmen	½ Sophs. and Juniors	Sophs and Juniors

PERMANENT RECITATION HOURS---SCIENTIFIC DEPARTMENT.

M.	FIRST CLASS.	SECOND CLASS.	THIRD CLASS.
8	History	Nat. Philos. and Astron	Nat. Sci. and Nat. Theol.
9		Mathematics	Chem. and Butl. Anal.
10	Mathematics		Psychol. and Mor. Phil.
11		½ Rhet., Log., Pol. Econ	

The preceding course is so arranged, in all departments, as to require from every class, except the Senior, an average of THREE HOURS AND A HALF in recitation daily, excepting Saturday. These recitations are attended without loss of time, between the hours of 8 and 12, A. M., leaving the remainder of the day for study and recreation.

SCIENTIFIC DEPARTMENT.

The three years' course of English, Mathematical and Scientific instruction pursued in this department, embraces all that is included in the college scheme, except the Classical Languages. Such as desire it, however, may pursue the study of Latin or French, in connection with a Scientific Course. We do not recommend it as in any sense an equivalent for a thorough Classical course; nor is it intended for mere boys, since the subjects which it includes are entirely above their capacity; but to young men, who have obtained a respectable common school education, including the elements of Algebra, and who have not time nor means to prosecute a Classical course, this system of studies will, it is hoped, commend itself as solid, comprehensive, and practical. Those who shall complete the prescribed Scientific course, will receive a Diploma, certifying the extent of their attainments.

COLLEGE YEAR—EXAMINATIONS.

THE COLLEGIATE YEAR is divided into three Terms of thirteen weeks each, and three Vacations. The First Term begins on the Fourth Wednesday in September; the Second, on the First Wednesday in January; and the Third, on the First Wednesday in May, closing with the First Thursday in August, which is commencement day.

IT IS OF GREAT IMPORTANCE that Students attend from the very beginning of the term; especially since so considerable a portion of time is allotted to vacations. In most cases, the loss of a few weeks, or even days, seriously affects the future standing of the pupil. Absence during term time, without special leave, is prohibited.*

PUBLIC EXAMINATIONS will be held, hereafter, only at the close of the college year, when the Freshman and Junior Classes will be examined on the studies of the preceding year, and the Sophomore and Senior Classes, upon those of the two preceding years. These last examinations will be FINAL, for the studies pursued in those years. All the examinations will be THOROUGH and RIGID; and will be con-

---

* Parents are respectfully advised to give their sons no such permission to be absent, except in cases of NECESSITY.

ducted, chiefly, by the use of written questions, prepared by the Faculty and t]
Examining Committee, covering the whole field of study prosecuted during a give
period, and entirely unknown to the Student until the moment of examinatio
These questions must be answered in writing before the Committee; and corre
answers to a definite portion of them will be the passport of admission to a high
standing. Similar examinations, of a briefer and less decisive character, howeve
and by way of preparation for the final trial, may be conducted privately, at t,
pleasure of the Faculty,

RELIGIOUS INSTRUCTION AND SERVICES.

The attention of a Christian community is respectfully invited to the system
Biblical Instruction which forms a characteristic feature of our course of Stud
The Grammar School Classes recite statedly in the English Bible; and eve
College Class has a daily or triweekly recitation in the Greek Testament, or t
Hebrew. Proficiency in these, as in other studies, is tested by the usual examin
tions. In addition to this, Biblical Geography and Antiquities, Ecclesiastic
History, Natural Theology, and the Analogy of Religion, Natural and Revealed,
the constitution and course of nature, are carefully and faithfully studied. The
is also a Bible or Catechetical exercise on Sabbath mornings; a public service
Sabbath afternoons, appropriated to the Students; and daily morning praye
The Students are expected to attend the Sabbath morning service of the congreg
tion worshipping in the chapel, or of some other congregation in the vicinity,
their parents prefer any of the latter. The Methodist, Associate, and Associa
Reformed Churches, have regular services in or near the village.

An experiment of several years in this Institution, has established the fact th
the daily study of God's word by no means interferes with, but rather promote
sound and comprehensive attainments in other branches of knowledge. Som
indeed, have questioned the expediency of adding Hebrew to an already overbu
dened curriculum; especially since Theological Students may acquire it in t
Seminary, and non-theologians are unlikely to make any particular use of such
acquisition. Our confident answer is,—FIRST, that Theological Students ne
more acquaintance with Hebrew than with Greek, when they enter t
Seminary, since familiarity with the Old Testament is more rare, and m
difficult of attainment, than familiarity with the New.—SECONDLY, that the mor
discipline secured by this study is fully equal to that obtained from any other:
THIRDLY, that a knowledge of Hebrew, as connected with the Indo-Europea
tongues, greatly contributes to the Student's mastery of the latter:—FOURTHL
that non-theogical students are as likely to cultivate the Hebrew, when on
acquired, as the higher Mathematics and the Classics:—FIFTHLY, that the Hebre
Scriptures contain more valuable, practicable truth, than all the pagan classics p
together:—and LASTLY, that the day is to be dreaded when ability to peruse t]
Sacred Volume, in the originals, shall be the exclusive property of the Clergy.

HANOVER COLLEGE.

EXPENSES.

The entire annual expenditures of a Student need not much exceed $150, viz:

Tuition and contingent fee, $10 per term,	$30 00
Boarding with private families, and a furnished room, at $2 50 per week,	97 50
Fuel, light, washing, &c.,	15 00
Books, &c.,	$5 to 10 00

Boarding in clubs will cost from seventy-five cents to one dollar twenty-five cents a week; and some board themselves even at a lower rate. The cost of clothing, and the amount spent as pocket-money, will vary with the taste and habits of the Student, and with the wishes of parents. As a general rule, the more money allowed to a young man beyond what is strictly necessary, the less likely is he to reflect honor upon his parents and instructors. Although Hanover presents comparatively few temptations to extravagance, yet parents are earnestly advised to require of their sons a detailed account of their expenditures, and peremptorily to refuse the payment of any debt incurred by them without a written permission. It is also recommended that the funds of young pupils be deposited with some one of the Faculty, and expended under his direction. The younger Students are required to board where the Faculty may direct, and where they may exercise a more careful and frequent supervision.

N. B. Students placed upon Scholarships by the Faculty, are relieved in part, or wholly, as the case may require, from the payment of tuition fees.

DISCIPLINE.

A record is kept by the Faculty, in which is entered weekly, the grade of scholarship of the Student, his absence from the exercises of the Institution, and such other facts as are worthy of notice with respect to his General Deportment. From this record, a report is made out at the end of each session and sent to the Parent or Guardian of each Student. In case of deficiency in scholarship, negligence in study, irregularity in attendance upon the exercises of the Institution or improper conduct, the Student will be privately admonished, and the Parent or Guardian will be promptly informed of the fact.

It is the object of this arrangement to keep Parents and Guardians accurately informed with regard to their sons and wards in this Institution, and thus to secure their co-operation with the Faculty in a mild system of discipline. Whenever it is ascertained that a Student is deriving no advantage from his connection with the Institution, or is pursuing courses injurious to himself or fellow-students, the Faculty will take decisive action, and his Parent or Guardian will be promptly addressed on the subject, and requested to remove him from the Institution.

SCHOLARSHIPS.

The endowment of this Institution, is in the form of Scholarships; of which the Board has established several sorts. The sum of $400 paid, or secured to the Corporation by note payable within five years, and bearing six per cent. interest in advance upon principal remaining unpaid—purchases for the owner, his heirs and assigns, a perpetual right to the tuition of one scholar, in Hanover College. The sum of $200 paid, or subscribed under similar conditions, secures the right to twenty years' tuition; after which time, the scholarship is subject to the disposal of the Board for the gratuitous education of candidates for the Gospel Ministry. A church scholarship of $200 secures to the church so contributing, a perpetual right to the tuition of one student, who shall be a member of that church, and appointed by the session. A Presbyterial scholarship of $200 secures a similar right to a Presbytery in behalf of pupils who shall be candidates for the Ministry under its care. The PRINCIPAL paid on these scholarships is invested by the Corporation in some safe and productive stock; and the INTEREST ONLY can be expended for the support of the College.

The sum of $100, paid within two years at fartherest with interest in advance on unpaid principal, purchases a right to ten years' tuition within twenty year from the date of subscription. Both principal and interest of this scholarship may be employed for contingent purposes, and the scholarship expires with the owners right to its use.

The sum of $100 paid into the building fund; or the sum of $50 paid in like manner, secures the right to ten, or five years' tuition of one student.

Every person applying for admission as a beneficiary of a scholarship under the control of the donors, shall present to the Treasurer, at the beginning of each term A WRITTEN CERTIFICATE from those controling the scholarship, of his right to such benefit; when, after paying whatever interest may be due on said scholarship, he shall receive an acknowledgment of his right, which he shall lodge with the President.

"The scholarships subject to the disposal of the Corporation, may be occupied by such applicants as the Faculty may select, after inquiry into their circumstance character and attainments; the preference being, (cœteria paribus,) to those who give the best evidence of scholarship.

"There shall at no time be more than one student upon each scholarship."

ACCOMMODATIONS.

The community system of Boarding in Commons, or of rooming in large Lodging Halls, is not adopted in Hanover. Arrangements are made to accommodate the students with Board and Rooms in respectable private families, where the number together can never be large; and where all shall be brought under domestic influence.

SETTLEMENT OF ACCOUNTS.

No Diploma nor Honorable Dismission shall be granted until the student shall exhibit a Receipt of Settlement of all his Bills for Boarding, Room and Washing.

DEGREES.

No Degrees are conferred in course. Candidates for Literary Honors are reported to the Board upon their ascertained or acknowledged merits.

SOCIETIES, LIBRARIES, &c.

There are two Societies connected with the College, the UNION LITERARY and the PHILALETHEAN, whose Libraries number each about twelve hundred volumes.

There is also a SOCIETY OF RELIGIOUS INQUIRY, which has begun to collect a Library, Maps, &c., and which in connection with another association formed for the purpose, sustains a valuable Reading Room.

The College Library contains near three thousand well selected volumes, and is accessible to the Students.

The Cabinet contains several thousand specimens in Mineralogy and Geology.

The friends of the College are advised that contributions to the Library, to the Cabinet, or to or for the Laboratory are much needed, and will be thankfully received.

PROHIBITED SECRET SOCIETIES.

The following order was passed by the Board of Trustees in July 1855, viz:
"RESOLVED, That this Board disapprove of the existence among the Students of Hanover College of any Society or Association of which the Faculty are not ex-officio members; and will not permit the public exhibition of any such Society."

LOCATION, BUILDINGS, &c.,

The villiage of Hanover is situated upon an elevated bluff of the Ohio river, six miles below Madison, Indiana, in a region of remarkable salubrity and natural beauty. The village and neighborhood are characterized by morality, and the absence of all ordinary temptations to vice and idleness. The Ohio river, and the railways from Madison, New Albany, and Cincinnati, place Hanover within twenty-four hours of all the principal points in Indiana, Kentucky, Western Ohio, and Eastern Illinois. A Plank Road from Madison to Hanover, renders the village easy of access at all seasons of the year.

Hanover College is controlled by a Board of Trustees; one half of whom are appointed by the Board itself, and the other half by the Synods of Indiana and Northern Indiana.

The Board purchased, some years ago, a farm of two hundred acres, lying between the villiage and the Ohio river, upon a beautiful point of which overlooking the river from an elevation of four hundred feet, they have erected a commodious College edifice, now nearly completed. The new College consits of a center building, nearly eighty feet square, with lateral and transverse wings. The whole length is about two hundred feet. It contains no dormitories for Students; (an undesirable provision;) but affords ample and convenient halls, library, cabinet, lecture and recitation rooms, and a spacious chapel.

The building commands an exceedingly diversified view of the river, for six miles up and ten miles down it course.

THE

TWENTY-SIXTH ANNUAL

Catalogue and Circular

OF

HANOVER COLLEGE,

AUGUST, 1858.

CINCINNATI:
ROBERT CLARKE & CO.
BOOKSELLERS, STATIONERS & IMPORTERS,
1858.

THE
TWENTY-SIXTH ANNUAL
Catalogue and Circular
OF
HANOVER COLLEGE,
AUGUST, 1858.

CINCINNATI:
ROBERT CLARKE & CO.
BOOKSELLERS, STATIONERS & IMPORTERS,
1858.

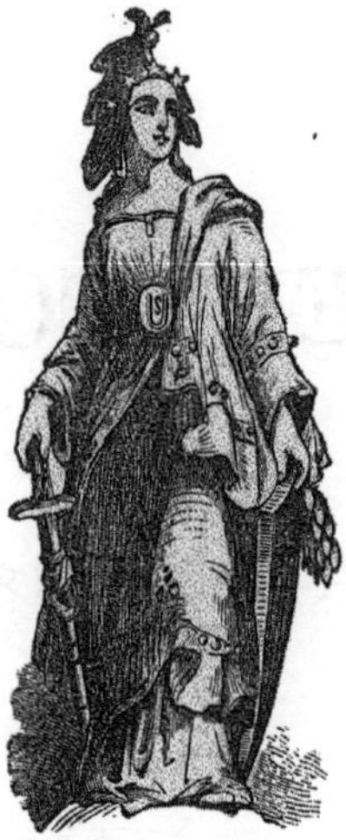

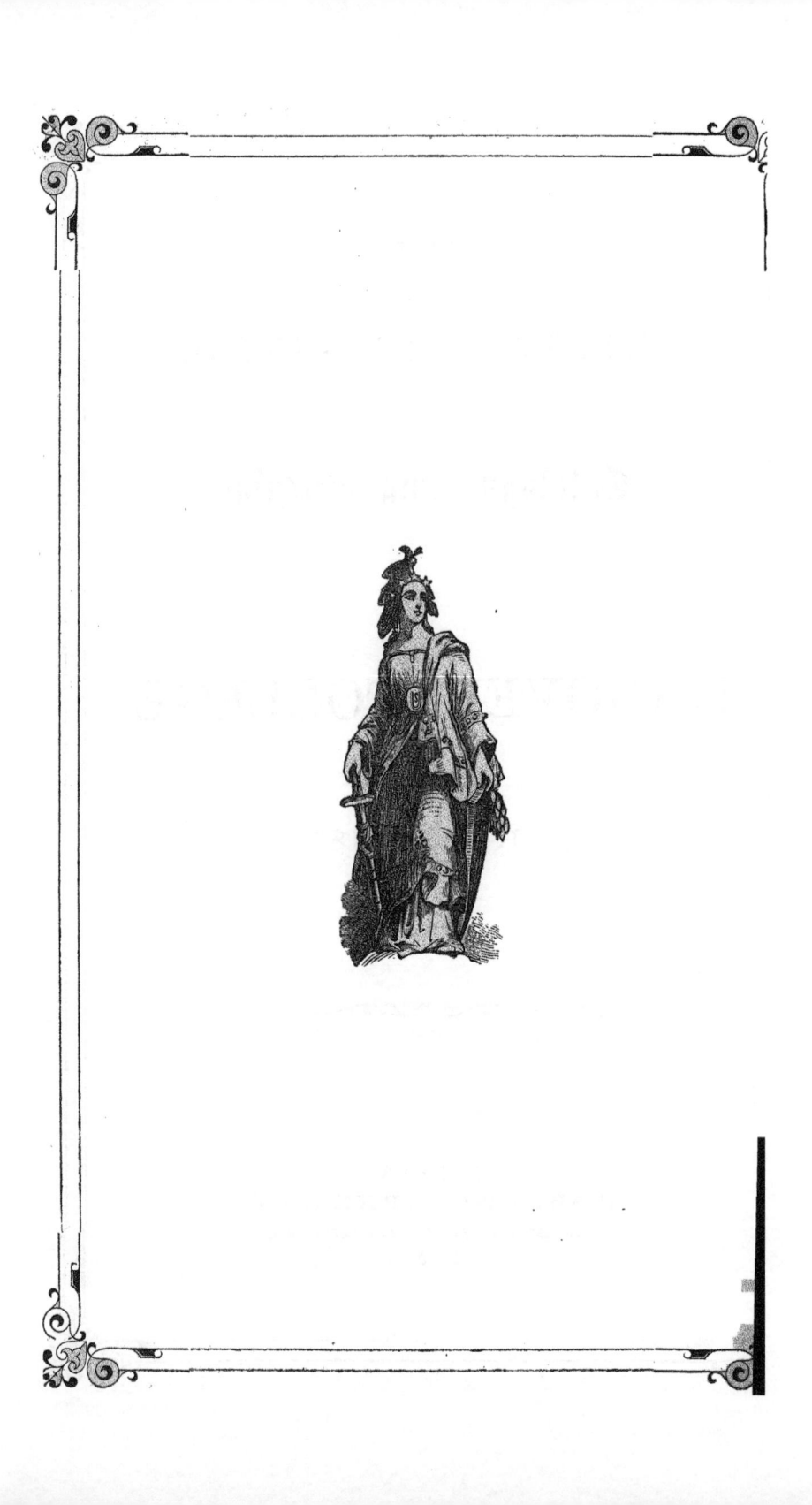

BOARD OF TRUSTEES.

* REV. H. H. CAMBERN, Rushville,..1858.
* REV. T. E. THOMAS, D. D., Dayton, O.,....................................1858.
* HON. C. E. WALKER, Madison,...1858.
* COL. JAMES BLAKE, Indianapolis,..1858.
‡ REV. C. K. THOMPSON, Darlington,...1858.
‡ REV. S. C. LOGAN, Cincinnati, O.,...1858.
† REV. D. D. McKEE, Marion, Iowa,..1858.
† JAMES M. RAY, Esq.,..1858.
* JOHN KING, ESQ., Madison,..1859.
* REV. WM. SICKELS, Indianapolis,..1859.
* W. M. DUNN, ESQ., Madison,...1859.
* W. A. BULLOCK, ESQ., Vernon,..1859.
† REV JOSEPH WARREN, D. D., Quincy, Ills...............................1859.
* REV. T. S. CROWE, Hanover,..1859.
‡ REV. J. N. SHANNON (deceased), Mt. Vernon, O........................1859.
‡ REV. J. C. BROWN, Valparaiso,..1859.
* DR. P. S. SHIELDS, New Albany,..1860.
* R. S. McKEE, ESQ., Madison,...1860.
* DR. ANDREW SPEAR, Hanover,...1860.
* REV. J. EDWARDS, D. D., Philadelphia, Pa.,................................1860.
† REV. JAMES A. McKEE, Franklin,..1860.
† REV. J. W. BLYTHE, Hanover,...1860.
‡ REV. F. P. CUMMINS, La Porte,...1860.
‡ REV. ROBERT IRWIN, SEN, Monticello,.....................................1860.
* REV. JOHN F. CROWE, D. D., Hanover,......................................1861.
* REV. SAMUEL NEWELL, Paris, Ill.,..1861.
* A. R. FORSYTH, ESQ., Greensburg,...1861.
* JESSE L. WILLIAMS, ESQ., Ft. Wayne,.......................................1861.
† REV. JOHN F. SMITH, Richmond,...1861.
† REV. JOHN CROZIER, Olney, Ill.,...1861.
‡ REV. E. W. WRIGHT, Delphi,...1861.
‡ REV. W. M. DONALDSON, Bluffton,...1861.

* Appointed by the Board.
† Appointed by the Synod of Indiana.
‡ Appointed by the Synod of Northern Indiana.

Officers of the Board.

COL. JAMES BLAKE, President.   REV. T. S. CROWE, Secretary.
T. P. MATTHEWS, ESQ., Madison, Treasurer.

Executive Committee.

W. M. DUNN, ESQ.,   REV. T. S. CROWE,   JOHN KING, ESQ.,
R. S. McKEE, ESQ.,   HON. C. E. WALKER,   DR. A. SPEAR,
REV. J. W. BLYHTE.

Auditing Committee.

W. M. DUNN, ESQ.   HON. C. E. WALKER.

General Agent.

REV. J. W. BLYTHE, Hanover.

FACULTY.

———— ———— PRESIDENT,
Professor of Biblical Instruction, Psychology and Ethics.

REV. JOHN FINLEY CROWE, D. D.
Emeritus Professor of Rhetoric, Logic, Political Economy and History.

REV. S. HARRISON THOMPSON, A. M.,
Professor of Mathematics and Mechanical Philosophy.

MINARD STURGUS, A. M.,
Professor of Greek Language and Literature.

REV. JOSHUA B. GARRITT, A. M.,
Professor of Latin Language and Literature.

AUGUSTUS W. KING, A. M.,
Professor of Natural Science.

OLIVER MULVEY,   J. M. BLOSS,   W. K. PERRINE,
Tutors.

REV. J. F. CROWE, D. D.,
Librarian.

M. J. J. N. PIEDFOURCK,
Teacher of French and Drawing.

WILLIAM BROWN,
Janitor.

UNDERGRADUATES.

SENIOR CLASS.

William Peter Baker	Fort Wayne.
Jacob Reasoner Geyer	Norwich, O.
Horace Hovey Hanna	Fort Wayne.
John David McClintock	Hanover.
James Baird McClure	Vincennes.
Thomas Johnson McElrath	Cincinnati, O.
David William Moffat	Vernon.
James Alexander Piper	La Porte.
Robert Gains Ross	Twenty-mile Stand, O.
Augustus Taylor	Fort Madison, Iowa.
James Harvey Vannuys	Franklin.
Cornelius Pleasant Voris	Bennington.

JUNIOR CLASS.

Robert Long Adams	Pleasant.
John Jefferson Abernathy	Dunlapsville.
Samuel Montgomery Cambern	Rushville.
Samuel Ellet Crawford	Bedford.
James William Edie	Stewartstown, Pa.
John Fox	Bruceville.
Columbus De Witt Huston	New Philadelphia.
Robert Lenington	Kokomo.
John Anthony Middleton	Shelbyville, Ky.
Madison Hall Rose	North Salem.
Isaac Coe Sickels	Indianapolis.
Benjamin Franklin Stearns	Lovell, Me.
William George Thomas	Indian Creek, Va.
Samuel Findley Thompson	Darlington.
John Bacon Vawter	Franklin.

SOPHOMORE CLASS.

John Newton Abernathy	Knightstown.
John McKnight Bloss	New Philadelphia.
William S. Coulter	New Manchester, Va.
John Wevly Crawford	Bedford.
John Harvey Hendricks	Jamestown.
Samuel Henry Howe	Flemingsburgh, Ky.

Reuben Franklin Middleton..............................Frankfort, Ky.
Ebenezer Muse..Milton, Ky.
Henry Augustus Newell..................................Paris, Ill.
Ezra Fitch Peabody..Vernon.
Reuben T. Patterson.......................................Sardinia.
William King Perrine......................................Monroe, O.
Henry C Pitcher...Mt. Vernon.
Benjamin Simpson...Vernon.
Lewellyn Oliver Snoddy..................................Dayton.
Samuel Demaree Voris....................................Bennington.
Samuel Eldbridge Vance.................................Paris, Ill.
James Wilson..Hanover.
Joseph Putnam Wood......................................Bardstown, Ky.
Williamson Swift Wright................................Delphi.

FRESHMAN CLASS.

Thompson Kenton Allen..................................Louisville, Ky.
Walter Alexander Blake..................................Indianapolis.
John Robinson Carmichael..............................Rushville.
George Washington Cummins.........................Logansport.
Solomon Fredrick Denton...............................Cinncinati, O.
Samuel Patterson Dillon.................................Cincinnati, O.
James Brown Forman....................................St. Matthews, Ky.
Samuel Kendall Hough..................................Charlestown.
Joseph Henry Innis..Cross Plains.
Stephen Paul Lee..Saluda.
Henry Venable Martin...................................Levonia.
Edward T. McCrea..Shelbyville.
John T. Mclintock...Cynthiana, Ky.
Robert Anderson Reid Sturgus........................Hanover.
John Terry Warner..Jamesport, N. Y.
Barton R. Zantzinger.....................................San Antonio Texas.

SCIENTIFIC DEPARTMENT.

SECOND YEAR.

Silas Dole Abbott..Churchville, N. Y.
John P. Brown..Rising Sun.
Daniel Ellis Conner..Bardstown, Ky.
Marshall P. Hayden.......................................Rising Sun.

Charles Harrison Johnson..............................Fort Wayne.
John Arel Johnson..Quindaro, Kansas.
Oliver Mulvey..Madison.
John Woodburn Shrewsbury........................Madison.
Solon McCollough Tillford...........................Kent.
George Martin Whitely................................San Antonio, Texas.

FIRST YEAR.

John Clinton Barnes....................................Saluda.
Quinton Bennett..Fairfield, Ky.
Francis Marion Broady................................Vienna.
William Hamilton Clark..............................Monroe, O.
William Andrew Collins..............................Edinburgh.
Samuel Crothers..Hanover.
Pollock G. Ewing...Port Royal, Ky.
Nathaniel Field, Jr.,....................................Jeffersonville.
Ezekiel S. Forman.......................................Middletown, Ky.
Robert D. Froman.......................................Vevay.
Lysander Froman..
Richard F. Graham......................................Washington.
Justus Marshall Hall...................................Kent.
James Barkley Henley.................................San Francisco, Cal.
George Hughes..Volga.
Thomas Volney Huston..............................New Philadelphia.
Walter Mackay..Bardstown, Ky.
Hyner McMeekin..Bardstown, Ky.
Luther Tilford Matheny..............................Salirsa, Ky.
Charles Henry Mead..................................Carrolton, Ky.
Joseph Alexander Moore............................Madison
Thomas Norris Peoples..............................Parker, P. O.
William Fleming Rogers............................Lower Blue Lick, Ky.
George Mathias Scifers..............................Vienna.
Franklin Shannon.......................................Hanover.
William O. Speed.......................................Bardstown, Ky.
Thomas A. Stewart.....................................Vevay.
John R. Stratford.......................................Jefferson co.
Robert K. Tichnor......................................Rensselar.
William Ferdinand Thompson..................Washington.
Andrew Vannuys.......................................Bennington.

PREPARATORY DEPARTMENT.

SENIOR CLASS.

Alois Octavus Backman	Madison.
George Bollman Boomer	New Philadelphia.
Orson Britton	Milton, Ky.
William Emery Brown	Valparaiso.
Leonidas W. S. Downs	Jeffersonville.
Charles Garrett	Delphi.
Augustus Chester Hirst	Cincinnati, O.
Charles Louis Holstein	Madison.
Augustus Adolph Joss	Constantine, Mich.
George Merriweather McCampbell	Jeffersonville.
William Crawford Pogue	Mace.
William Hind Roberts	Verona, Ky.
Thomas H. Rucker	Rushville.
Walter Sullivan	Mt. Vernon.
Jesse Brown Wilson	New Lexington.

JUNIOR CLASS.

Felix Jennerette Brandt	Hanover.
Robert Grace	Cincinnati, O.
Charles B. Harris	Goshen.
William Dunn Hynes	Pocahontas, Ill.
Hugh Jameson	Rising Sun.
James Woods Kyle	Hanover.
David R. P. McDermett	Dallas, Texas.
Edward J. McDermett	Dallas, Texas.
Anson Wellington Merwin	Hanover.
James A. Smith	Rochester.
James Wilson Spear	Hanover.
Thomas Hart Woodward	Hanover.

SUMMARY.

Seniors	12
Juniors	15
Sophomores	21
Freshmen	16
Scientifics, 2nd, Year	10
" 1st, Year	31
Senior Preparatory	15
Junior	12
Total	132

STATES.

Indiana	86
Kentucky	20
Ohio	9
Texas	4
Illinois	3
New York	2
Virginia	2
Maine	1
Iowa	1
Kansas	1
California	1
Pennsylvania	1
Michigan	1
Total	132

CALENDAR.

1858.
SEPT. 20, 21.—Exam. of candidates for admission, Monday & Tuesday.
SEPT. 22.—First term begins..Wednesday.
DEC. 23.—First terms ends..Thursday.

WINTER VACATION OF TWO WEEKS.

1859.
JAN. 5.—Second term begins..Wednesday.
APRIL 6.—Exhibition of the Union Literary Society........Wednesday.
APRIL 7.—Exhibition of the Philalethian Society..............Thursday.
APRIL 7.—Second term ends..Thursday.

SPRING VACATION OF FOUR WEEKS.

MAY 4.—Third term begins...Wednesday.
JULY 5.—Biennial examination, of Senior Class begins......Tuesday.
JULY 27.—General examination begins.................................Wednesday.
JULY 31.—Baccalaureate Sermon...Sabbath.
AUG. 2.—General examinations ends....................................Tuesday.
AUG. 2.—Annual meeting of Board of Trustees...................Tuesday.
AUG. 3.—Anniversary of the Alumni Society.....................Wednesday.
AUG. 3.—Anniversary of the Literary Societies................Wednesday.
AUG. 3.—Anniversary of the Society of Religious Inquiry..Wednesday.
AUG. 4.—COMMENCEMENT DAY...Thursday.

SUMMER VACATION OF SEVEN WEEKS.

SEPT. 19, 20.—Exam. of candidates for admission, Monday & Tuesday.
SEPT. 22.—First terms begins...Wednesday.

ADMISSION.

CANDIDATES for admission into the Freshman Class are examined in Arithmetic, and Algebra; Ancient and Modern Geography; the English, Latin and Greek Grammars; Cæsar's Commentaries; Arnold's Prose Composition; Greek Reader, and the Anabasis of Xenophon, or what is equivalent to these attainments. They must furnish testimonials of good character; and, if from another College, must bring certificates of honorable dismission. Candidates for higher standing, are examined upon that part of the course already studied by the class which they propose to enter.

No one can be admitted to the Freshman Class until he has completed his fourteenth year; nor to an advanced standing, without a proportional increase of age.

"Before a student shall be admitted to actual standing in any class, he shall present to the President a receipt from the Treasurer, showing that he has complied with the statutes relating to College Charges and Scholarships."

N. B. The regular examination for admission into College, commences on the Monday preceding the beginning of each term.

COURSE OF INSTRUCTION.

Preparatory Department.

Andrew's Latin Lessons, Grammar, Reader and Exercises; Andrew's Cæsar; Butler and Sturgus Sallust; McClintock and Crook's I and II Greek books; Classical and Biblical Geography; Arithmetic; Robinson's Algebra; (University edition,) English Bible.

Scientific Department.

FIRST YEAR.

Algebra, completed; Plane Geometry; Plane Trigonometry; Surveying and Navigation; History; English Bible, historical books.
Linear Drawing (extra.)

SECOND YEAR.

Solid Geometry; Spherical Trigonometry, and its Applications; Analytical Geometry; Natural Philosophy, and Astronomy; Rhetoric, Logic, and Political Economy; English Bible, Poetical books.

THIRD YEAR.

Zoology; Anatomy and Physiology; Botany; Physical Geography; Chemistry; Geology; Natural Theology and Butler's Analogy; Psychology, and Ethics; English Bible, Mine Explored.

Collegiate Department.

FRESHMAN CLASS.

FIRST CLASS.

Greek Harmony, of the Gospel...................................Robinson.
Biblical Antiquities..Nevin.
Virgil..Cooper.
Roman Antiquites..Bojesin.
Xenophon's Anabasis..Boise.
Plane Geometry..Davies' Legendre.

SECOND SESSION.

Greek Harmony, continued..............................
Virgil, continued..
Anabasis, continued....................................
Grecian Antiquites............................Bojesin.
Plane Trigonometry.....................Davies' Legendre.

THIRD SESSION.

Greek Harmony, completed.............................
Livy...
Xenophon's Memorabilia........................Robbins.
Grecian Antiquities....................................
Latin and Greek Exercises..............................
Surveying and Navigation......................Davies'.

SOPHOMORE CLASS.

FIRST SESSION.

Greek Testament, (Acts.)........................Owen.
Livy, continued..
Homer's Odyssey.................................Owen.
Greek History...................................Smith.
Solid Geometry.........................Davies' Legendre.
Zoology..............................Agassiz & Gould.

SECOND SESSION.

Greek Testament, (Epistles.)...........................
Horace..Lincoln.
Homer's Odyssey, continued............................
Roman History.................................Liddell.
Plane Trigonometry, reviewed..........................
Spherical Trigonometry, with its Applications.........Davies' Legendre.
Physical Geography.........................Sommerville.

THIRD SESSION.

Greek Testament, (Epistles.)..........................
Horace..
Plato's Gorgias...............................Woolsey.
English History.......................Clark and Moffat.
Analytical Geometry...........................Davies'.
Botany..Wood.
Latin and Greek Exercises, throughout the year........

JUNIOR CLASS.

FIRST SESSION.

Hebrew Grammar and Hebrew; Genesis, (Optional.)
Tacitus' Histories, continued.................Tyler.
Plato's Gorgias, continued............................

Natural Philosophy..Olmsted.
Rhetoric..Blair.
Anatomy and Physiology...................................Cutter.

SECOND SESSION.

Hebrew, (Genesis continued.)..............................
Tacitus' continued..
Demosthenes De Corona....................................Champlin.
Natural Philosophy, continued.............................
Logic...Whately.
Light and Heat..Bird.

THIRD SESSION.

Hebrew, (Psalms.)...
Cicero's Tusculan Disputation...........................Anthon.
Demosthenes De Corona, completed..........................
Astronomy...Olmsted.
Political Economy.......................................Wayland.
Electricity...Bird.

SENIOR CLASS.

FIRST SESSION.

Select portions of the Hebrew Bible.......................
Intellectual Philosophy.................................Walker's Reid.
Cicero's Tuscalan Disputations continued................
Greek Tragedies...Woolsey.
Chemistry...Silliman.
Mathematics reviewed......................................

SECOND SESSION.

Select Hebrew, continued..................................
Intellectual Philosophy.................................Hamilton.
Chemistry, and Mineralogy...............................Dana.
Natural Theology..Paley.
Juvenal Greek Tragedies.................................Woolsey.

THIRD SESSION.

Hebrew, continued...
Butler's Analogy..Wilson's Edition.
Moral Science...Wayland.
Geology,..Lyell's Elements.
Juvenal, continued..
Æschylus' Prometheus Vintus.............................Woolsey.
Mathematics reviewed......................................

N. B. The text-books needed for any part of the College course, may be procured at the Hanover Book Store.

SCIENTIFIC DEPARTMENT.

The three years' course of English, Mathematical and Scientific instruction pursued in this department, embraces all that is included in the college scheme, except the Classical Languages. Such as desire it, however, may pursue the study of Latin or French, in connection with a Scientific Course. We do not recommend it as in any sense an equivalent for a thorough Classical course; nor is it intended for mere boys, since the subjects which it includes are entirely above their capacity; but to young men, who have obtained a respectable common school education, including the elements of Algebra, and who have not time or means to prosecute a Classical course, this system of studies will, it is hoped, commend itself as solid, comprehensive, and practical. Those who complete the prescribed Scientific course, will receive a Diploma, certifying the extent of their attainments.

COLLEGE YEAR—EXAMINATIONS.

THE COLLEGIATE YEAR is divided into three Terms of thirteen weeks each, and three Vacations. The First Term begins on the Fourth Wednesday in September; the Second, on the First Wednesday in January; and the Third, on the First Wednesday in May, closing with the First Thursday in August, which is commencement day.

IT IS OF GREAT IMPORTANCE that Students attend from the very beginning of the term; especially since so considerable portion of time is allotted to vacations. In most cases, the loss of a few weeks, or even days, seriously affects the future standing of the pupil. Absence during term time, without special leave, is prohibited.*

PUBLIC EXAMINATIONS will be held, hereafter, only at the close of the college year, when the Freshman and Junior Classes will be examined on the studies of the preceding year, and the Sophomore and Senior Classes, upon those of the two preceding years. These last examinations will be FINAL, for the studies pursued in those years. All the examinations will be THOROUGH and RIGID; and will be conducted, chiefly, by the use of written questions, prepared by the Faculty and the Examining Committee, covering the whole field of study prosecuted during a given period, and entirely unknown to the Student until the moment of examination. These questions must be answered in writing before the Committee; and correct answers to a definite portion of them will be the passport of admission to a higher standing. Similar examinations, of a briefer and and less decisive character, however, and by way of preparation for the final trial, may be conducted privately, at the pleasure of the Faculty.

RELIGIOUS INSTRUCTION AND SERVICES.

The attention of a Christian community is respectfully invited to the system of Biblical Instruction which forms a characteristic feature of our course of Study. The Grammar School Classes recite statedly in the English Bible; and every College Class has a daily or triweekly recitation in the Greek Testament, or the Hebrew. Proficiency in these, as in other studies, is tested by the usual

---

* Parents are respectfully advised to give their sons no such permission to be absent except in cases of necessity.

examinations. In addition to this, Biblical Geography and Antiquities, Ecclesiastical History; Natural Theology, and the Analogy of Religion, Natural and Revealed, to the constitution and course of nature, are carefully and faithfully studied. There is also a Bible or Catechetical exercise on Sabbath mornings ; a public service on Sabbath afternoon, appropriated to the Students; and daily morning prayers. The Students are expected to attend the Sabbath morning service of the congregation worshipping in the chapel, or of some other congregation in the vicinity, if their parents perfer any of the latter. The Methodist and United Presbyterian Churches, have regular services in or near the village.

An experiment of several years in this Institution, has established the fact that the daily study of God's word by no means interferes with, but rather promotes, sound and comprehensive attainments in other branches of knowledge.

EXPENSES.

The entire annual expenditures of a Student need not much exceed $150, viz:

Tuition and contingent fee, $10 per term,- - - - - - - - - $30 00
Boarding with private families, and a furnished room, at $1 75 to $2 50 per week, - - - - - - - - - - - - - - 70 00 to 97 50
Fuel, light, washing, &c., - - - - - - - - - - - - 15 00
Books, &c., - - - - - - - - - - - - - - $5 to 10 00

Boarding in clubs will cost from seventy-five cents to one dollar twenty-five cents a week; and some board themselves even at a lower rate. The cost of clothing, and the amount spent as pocket-money, will vary with the taste and habits of the Student, and with the wishes of parents. As a general rule, the more money allowed to a young man beyond what is strictly necessary, the less likely is he to reflect honor upon his parents and instructors. Although Hanover presents comparatively few temptations to extravagance, yet parents are earnestly advised to require of their sons a detailed account of their expenditures, and peremptorily to refuse the payment of any debt incurred by them without a written permission. It is also recommended that the funds of young pupils be deposited with some one of the Faculty, and expended under his direction. The younger Students are required to board where the Faculty may direct. and where they may exercise a more careful and frequent supervision.

N. B. Students placed upon Scholarships by the Faculty, are relieved in part, or wholly, as the case may require, from the payment of tuition fees.

DISCIPLINE.

A record is kept by the Faculty, in which is entered weekly, the grade of scholarship of the Student, his absence from the exercises of the Institution, and such other facts as are worthy of notice with respect to his General Deportment. From this record, a report is made out at the end of each session and sent to the Parent or Guardian of each Student. In case of deficiency in scholarship, negligence in study, irregularity in attendance upon the exercises of the institution or improper conduct, the Student will be privately admonished, and the Parent or Guardian will be promptly informed of the fact.

It is the object of this arrangement to keep Parents and Guardians accurately informed with regard to their sons and wards in this Institution, and thus to secure their co-operation with the Faculty in a mild system of discipline. Whenever it is ascertained that a Student is deriving no advantage from his connection with the Institution, or is pursuing a course injurious to himself or fellow-students, the Faculty will take decisive action, and his Parent or Guardian will be promptly addressed on the subject, and requested to remove him from the Institution.

SCHOLARSHIPS.

The endowment of this Institution is in the form of Scholarships, of which the Board has established several sorts. The sum of $400 paid, or secured to the Corporation by note payable within five years, and bearing six per cent. interest in advance upon principal remaining unpaid—purchases for the owner, his heirs and assigns, a perpetual right to the tuition of one scholar, in Hanover College. The sum of $200 paid, or subscribed under similiar conditions, secures the right to twenty years' tuition; after which time, the scholarship is subject to the disposal of the Board for the gratuitous education of candidates for the Gospel Ministry. A church scholarship of $200 secures to the church so contributing, a perpetual right to the tuition of one student, who shall be a member of that church, and appointed by the session. A Presbyterial scholarship of $200 secures a similiar right to a Presbytery in behalf of pupils who shall be candidates for the ministry under its care. The PRINCIPAL paid on these scholarships is invested by the Corporation in some safe and productive stock; and the INTEREST ONLY can be expended for the support of the College.

The sum of $100, paid within two years at the farthest with interest in advance on unpaid principal, purchases a right to ten years' tuition within twenty years from the date of subscription. Both principal and interest of this scholarship may be employed for contingent purposes, and the scholarship expires with the owners' right to its use.

The sum of $100 paid into the building fund; or the sum of $50 paid in like manner, secures the right to ten, or five years' tuition of one student.

Every person applying for admission as a beneficiary of a scholarship under the control of the donors, shall present to the Treasurer, at the beginning of each term, A WRITTEN CERTIFICATE from those controling the scholarship, of his right to such benefit: when, after paying whatever interest may be due on said scholarship, he shall receive an acknowledgment of his right, which he shall lodge with the President.

"The scholarships subject to the disposal of the Corporation, may be occupied by such applicants as the Faculty may select, after inquiry into their circumstances, character and attainments; the preference being, (ceteris paribus,) to those who give the best evidence of scholarship.

"There shall at no time be more than one student upon each scholarship."

ACCOMMODATIONS.

The community system of Boarding in Commons, or of rooming in large Lodging Halls, is not adopted in Hanover. Arrangements are made to accommodate the students with Board and Rooms in respectable private families, where the number together can never be large; and where all shall be brought under domestic influence.

SETTLEMENT OF ACCOUNTS.

No Diploma nor honorable dismission shall be granted until the student shall exhibit a Receipt of Settlement of all his Bills for Boarding, Room and Washing.

DEGREES.

No Degrees are conferred in course. Candidates for Literary Honors are reported to the Board upon their ascertained or acknowledged merits.

SOCIETIES, LIBRARIES, &c.

There are two societies connected with the College, the UNION LITERARY, and the PHILALATHEAN, whose Libraries number each about twelve hundred volumes.

There is also a SOCIETY OF RELIGIOUS INQUIRY, which has begun to collect a Library, Maps, &c., and which in connection with another association formed for the purpose, sustains a valuable Reading Room.

The College Library contains near three thousand well selected volumes, and is accessible to the Students.

The Cabinet contains several thousand specimens in Mineralogy and Geology.

The friends of the College are advised that contributions to the Library, to the Cabinet, or to the Laboratory are much needed, and will be thankfully received.

PROHIBITED SECRET SOCIETIES.

The following order was passed by the Board of Trustees in July, 1855, viz:
"RESOLVED, That this Board disapprove of the existence among the Students of Hanover College of any Society or Association of which the Faculty are not ex-officio members; and will not permit the public exhibition of any such Society."

LOCATION, BUILDINGS, &c.

The village of Hanover is situated upon an elevated bluff of the Ohio river, six miles below Madison, Indiana, in a region of remarkable salubrity and natural beauty. The village and neighborhood are characterized by morality, and the absence of all ordinary temptations to vice and idleness. The Ohio river, and the Railways from Madison, New Albany, and Cincinnati, place Hanover within twenty-four hours, of all the principal points in Indiana, Kentucky, Western Ohio, and Eastern Illinois. A Plank Road from Madison to Hanover, renders the village easy of access at all seasons of the year.

Hanover College is controlled by a Board of Trustees; one half of whom are appointed by the Board itself, and the other half by the Synods of Indiana and Northern Indiana.

The Board purchased, some years ago, a farm of two hundred acres, lying between the village and the Ohio river, upon a beautiful point of which, overlooking the river from an elevation of four hundred feet, they have erected a commodious College edifice, now completed and occupied. The new College consists of a center building, nearly eighty feet square, with lateral and transverse wings. The whole length is about two hundred feet. It contains no dormitories for Students; (an undesirable provision;) but affords ample and convenient halls, library, cabinet, lecture and recitation rooms, and a spacious chapel.

The building commands an exceedingly diversified view of the river, for six miles up, and ten miles down it course.

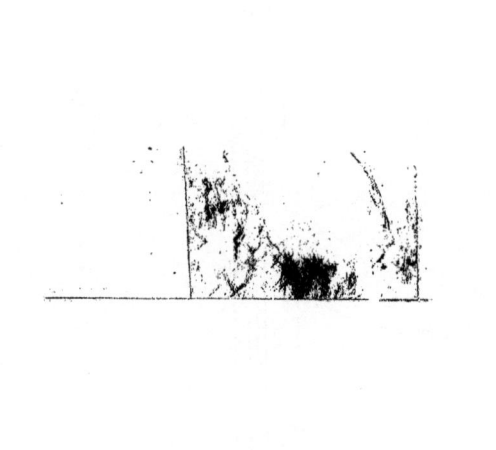

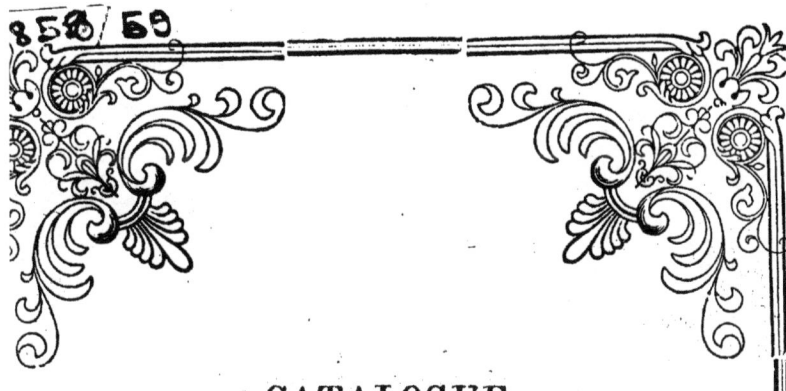

CATALOGUE

OF

HANOVER COLLEGE,

INDIANA.

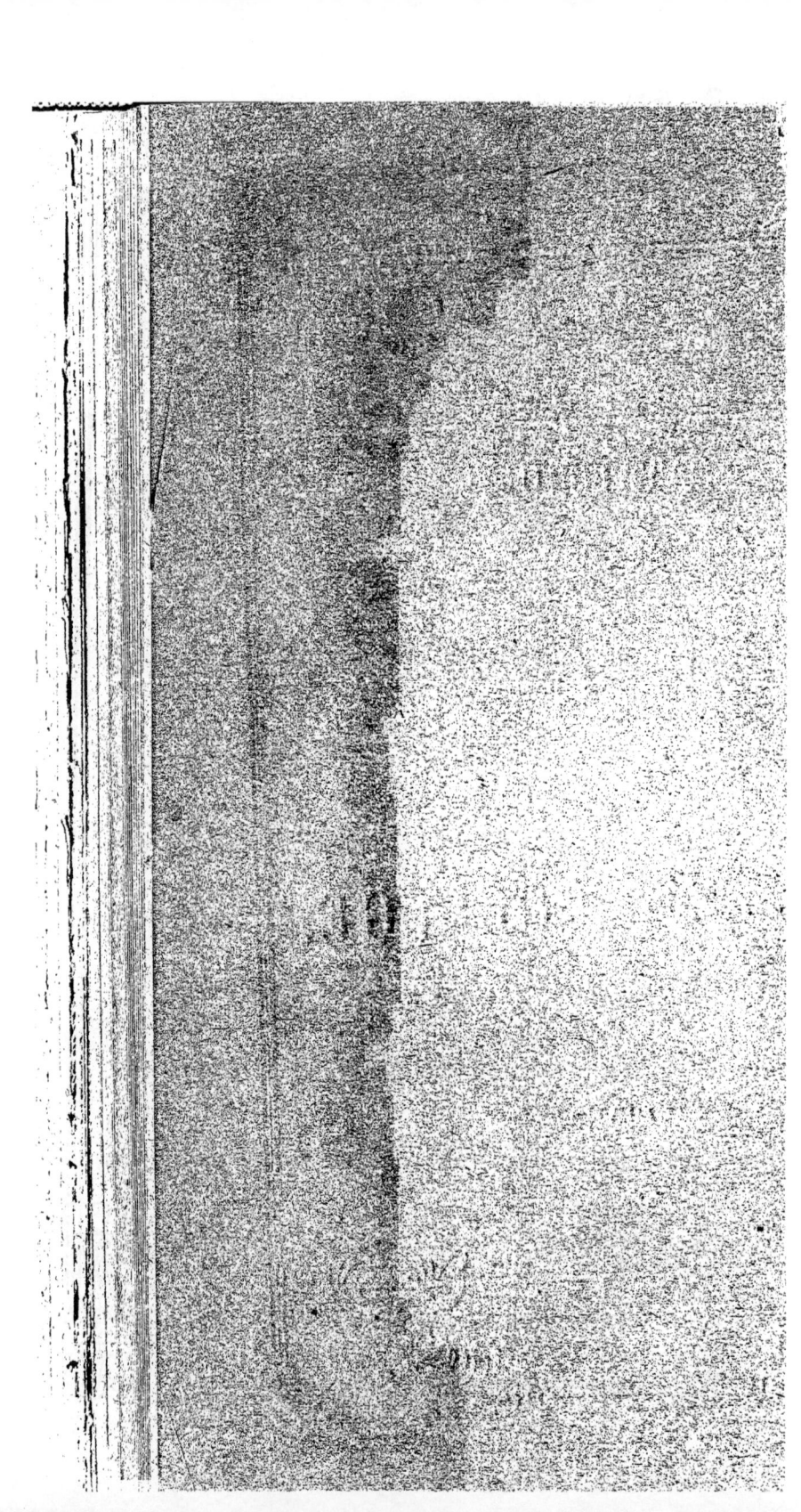

THE TWENTY-SEVENTH
Annual Catalogue & Circular,

OF

HANOVER COLLEGE,

AND

NINTH TRIENNIAL

Catalogue of the Alumni.

AUGUST, 1859.

MADISON, IND.
COURIER STEAM JOB PRINTING ESTABLISHMENT.
1859.

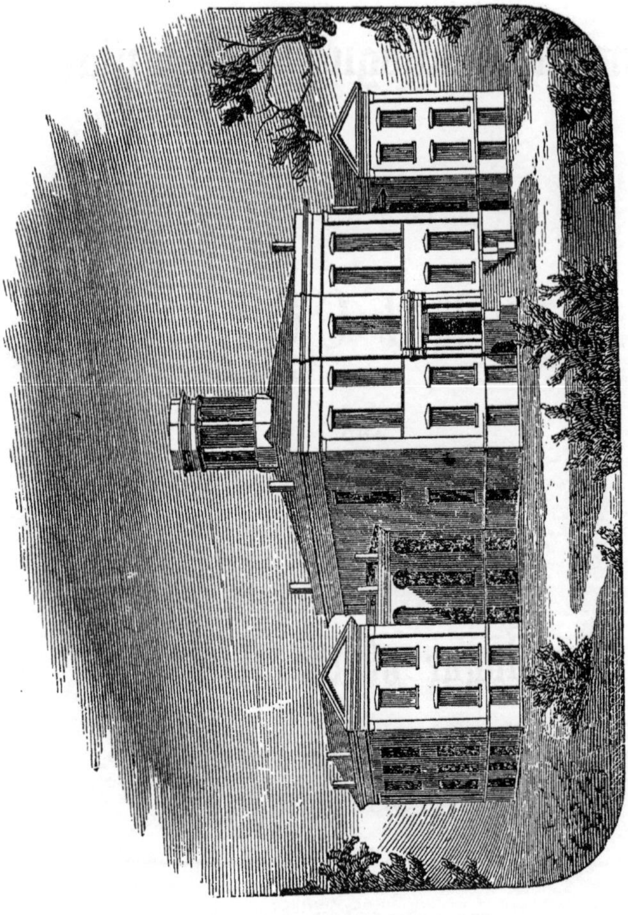

TRIENNIAL CATALOGUE.

☞ Those deceased are marked with a *

Officers of the College.

PRESIDENTS.

1832—1836.	*Rev. James Blythe, D. D.
1836—1838.	*Rev. John Matthews, D. D. (pro. tem.)
1838—1838.	Rev. Duncan Macaulay, D. D.
1838—1843.	Rev. Erasmus D. McMaster, D. D.
1846—1849.	*Rev. Sylvester Scovel, D. D.
1849—1854.	Rev. Thomas E. Thomas, D. D.
1854—1855.	Rev. Jared M. Stone, (pro. tem.)
1855—1857.	Rev. Jonathan Edwards, D. D.
1857—1859.	Rev. S. Harrison Thomson, (pro. tem.)
1859.	Rev. James Wood, D. D.

VICE PRESIDENTS.

1832—1857.	Rev. John Finley Crowe, D. D.

PROFESSORS.

1832—1837.	Rev. John Finley Crowe, D. D., Rhet. Logic. Pol. Econ. and History.
1832—1836.	*Rev. Mark A. H. Niles, A. M., Prof. of Ancient Languages.
1832—1838.	John H. Harney, A. M., Prof. of Mathematics.
1833—1835.	Wm. McKee Dunn, A. B. Principal of Prep. Department.
1835—1888.	Charles K. Thompson, A. B., Principal of Prep. Department.
1835—1837.	Wm. McKee Dunn, A. M., Prof. of Nat. Science.
1836—1889.	Noble Butler, A. B., Prof. of Ancient Languages.
1888—1843.	Thomas W. Hynes, A. M., Prof. of Math. and Nat. Science.
1839—1840.	Samuel Galloway, A. M., Prof. of Ancient Languages.
1840—1841.	Minard Sturgus, A. M., Principal of Prep. Dep. and Acting Prof. of Ancient Languages.
1841—1852.	Minard Sturgus, A. M., Prof. of Ancient Languages.
1841—1843.	Zebulon B. Sturgus, A. B. Principal of Prep. Department.
1843—1843.	Rev. Wm. C. Anderson, A. M., Prof. of Rhet. Logic, Pol. Econ. and History.
1844—1850.	S. Harrison Thomson, A. M., Prof. of Math. and Nat. Science.
1844—1852.	Absalom C. Knox, A. M., Adj. Prof. of Ancient Lang. and Principal of Prep. Department.
1850—1856.	Rev. Jared M. Stone, A. M., Prof. of Nat. Science.
1856.	S. Harrison Thomson, Prof. of Math. and Mech. Phil.
1852—1857.	Rev. William Bishop, A. M., Prof. of Greek.
1852—1854.	Rev. William Hamilton, A. M., Prof. of Latin.
1854—1855.	Henry R. Lott, M. D., Prof. of Latin.
1857.	Rev. John Finley Crowe, D. D., Emeritus Prof. of Rhet. Logic, Pol. Economy and History.
1856—1859.	Rev. Joshua B. Garritt, A. M., Prof. of Latin.
1857.	Augustus W. King, A. M., Prof. of Nat. Science.
1858—1859.	Minard Sturgus, A. M., Prof. of Greek.
1843—1844.	Frederick Eckstein, Teacher of French and German.
1845—1846.	Rev. F. Augustus Willard, A. M., Lecturer on Chemistry.
1851.	Mons. J. J. Piedfourck, Univ. of Paris., Teacher of French, Drawing, and Civil Engineering.

Board of Trustees.

TERM EXPIRES.

Bd. JOHN KING, ESQ., Madison,......................1863.
Bd. REV. WM. SICKLES, Indianapolis, Ind................1863.
Bd. HON. WM. McKEE DUNN, M. C., Madison,............1863.
Bd. W. A. BULLOCK, ESQ., Vernon, Ind...................1863.
S. S.
S. S. REV. THOMAS S. CROWE, Hanover,
N. S.
N. S. REV. JAMES C. BROWN, D.D., Valparaiso,...........1859.
Bd. DR. P. S. SHIELDS, New Albany,......................1860.
Bd. R. S. McKEE ESQ., Madison,............................1860.
Bd; DR. ANDREW SPEAR, Hanover,.........................1860.
Bd. REV. JONATHAN EDWARDS D. D. Philadelphia, Pa...1860.
S. S. REV. JAMES A. McKEE, Franklin,......................1860.
S. S. REV. J. W. BLYTHE, Hanover,..........................1860.
N. S. REV. F. P. CUMMINS, La Porte,........................1860.
N. S. REV. ROBERT IRWIN, SEN. Monticello,...............1860.
Bd. REV. J. F. CROWE, D. D. Hanover,......................1861.
Bd. REV. SAMUEL NEWELL, Paris, Ill.......................1861.
Bd. A. R. FORSYTH ESQ., Greensburg.......................1861.
Bd. JESSE L. WILLIAMS ESQ., Ft. Wayne,..................1861.
S. S. REV. L. HAWES, Madison..............................1861.
S. S. REV. JOHN CROZIER, Olney, Ill......................1861.
N. S. REV. E. W. WRIGHT, Delphi,..........................1861.
N. S. REV. W. M. DONALDSON, Bluffton,...................1861.
Bd. REV. H. H. CAMBERN, Rushville,......................1862.
Bd. ROBERT DEAN, ESQ., Hanover..........................1862.
Bd. HON. C. E. WALKER, Madison..........................1862.
Bd. COL. JAMES BLAKE, Indianapolis,.....................1862.
S. S. REV. A. C. ALLEN, Indianapolis.......................1862
S. S. REV. S. E. BARR, Livonia..............................1862.
N. S. REV. C. K. THOMPSON, Thorntown,..................1862.
N. S. REV. T. L. CUNNINGHAM, Indianapolis, Ind.........1862.

OFFICERS OF THE BOARD.

COL. JAMES BLAKE, PRESIDENT.   REV. T. S. CROWE, SECRETARY.
ROBERT DEAN, TREASURER.

EXECUTIVE COMMITTEE.

HON. W. M. DUNN,   REV. T. S. CROWE,   JOHN KING, ESQ.,
R. S. McKEE, ESQ.,   HON. C. E. WALKER,   DR. A. SPEAR,
REV. J. W. BLYTHE.   ROBERT DEAN.

AUDITING COMMITTEE.

HON. W. M. DUNN.   HON. C. E. WALKER.

GENERAL AGENT.

REV. J. W. BLYTHE, South Hanover, Indiana.

Faculty.

REV. JAMES WOOD, D. D., President.
Professor of Biblical Instruction, Psychology and Ethics.

REV. JOHN FINLEY CROWE, D. D.
Emeritus Professor of Logic, Rhetoric, Political Economy and History.

REV. S. HARRISON THOMSON, A. M.
Professor of Mathematics, Mechanical Philosophy and Astronomy.

MINARD STURGUS, A. M.
Professor of the Latin Language and Literature.

REV. JOSHUA B. GARRITT, A. M.
Professor of the Greek Language and Literature.

AUGUSTUS W. KING, A. M.
Professor of Natural Science.

HENRY E. CRAWFORD, JAMES WILSON, JOHN M. BLOSS, AND OLIVER MULVEY.
Tutors.

[No Tutors will be employed the ensuing year.]

REV. JOHN FINLEY CROWE, D. D.
Librarian.

WILLIAM BROWN,
Janitor.

HONORARY DEGREES.

L. L. D.

1834. Hon. Isaac Blackford, Judge of the Supreme Court of Indiana.
1838. John Delafield, *Cincinnati, Ohio.*
1840. Hon. Charles Dewey, } Judges of the Supreme Court of Ind'a.
" Hon. Jeremiah Sullivan·

D. D.

1837. Rev. David McDill, *Hamilton, O.*
" Rev. Elihu W. Baldwin, *President of Wabash University, Indiana.*
1839. Rev. Stewart Bates, *Glasgow, Scotland.*
1841. Rev. James Murphy, *Herkimer, New York.*
1843. Rev. William L. Breckinridge, *Louisville, Ky.*
" Rev. Thomas C. Reed, *Prof. of Int. Philos. Union College, New York.*
1845. Rev. David Monfort, *Franklin, Ind.*
1846. Rev. Sylvester Scovel, *New Albany, Ind.*
1847. Rev. Edward P. Humphrey, *Louisville, Ky.*
" Rev. Robert C. Grundy, *Maysville, Ky.*
1848. Rev. J. L. Yantis, *Missouri.*
" Rev. John. C. Backus, *Baltimore, Md.*
1853. Rev. Leroy J. Halsey, *Louisville, Ky.*
" Rev. Elias Riggs, *Missionary at Smyrna, Asia Minor.*
" Rev. I. N. Candee, *Lafayette, Ind.*
1854. Rev. John M. Stevenson, *New Albany, Ind.*
" Rev. Thornton A. Mills, *Indianapolis, Ind.*
1858. Rev. Josiah D. Smith, *Columbus, Ohio.*
1859. Rev. James Brown, *Keokuk, Iowa.*
" Rev. J. C. Brown, *Valparaiso, Ind.*

A. M.

1833. Rev. John Finley Crowe, *Vice President of Hanover College, Ind.*
" Rev. M. A. H. Niles, *Professor of Languages, Hanover College, Ind.*
1834. Rev. John W. Cunningham, *Tennessee.*
1839. Rev. David Monfort, *Franklin, Ind.*
1840. Samuel Reid, M. D., *Salem, Ind.*
" Leonard Bliss, jr., *Louisville, Ky.*
1843. Rev. Monroe T. Allen, *Raleigh, Tenn.*
" Samuel M. Elliott, M. D., *New York City.*
1845. John L. Scott, Esq., *Cincinnati, Ohio.*
" James P. Holcombe, Esq., *Cincinnati, Ohio.*
" Rev. Daniel Lattimore, *Vernon, Ind.*

1845. Rev. David V. Smock, *Franklin, Ind.*
" Rev. James Brownlee, *Livonia, Ind.*
1846. Rev. James C. Burt, M. D., *Vernon, Ind.*
1847. Rev. George J. Reed, *Charlestown, Ind.*
" Rev. Mason D. P. Williams, *Louisville, Ky.*
" Rev. Robert C. McComb, *London, Ohio.*
" Rev. John C. Eastman, *Crawfordsville, Ind.*
1948. Rev. Thomas Brown, *Xenia, Ohio.*
" John W. Shields, Esq., *Cincinnati, Ohio.*
" Thomas H. Shreve, Esq., *Louisville, Ky.*
" Ben. Casseday, Esq., *Louisville, Ky.*
1849. Bland Ballard, Esq., *Louisville, Ky.*
1850. Dr. E. S. Cooper, *Knox County, Illinois.*
" Charles Axtell, Esq., *Indianapolis, Ind.*
" John Orr, jr., Esq., *Macon, Tenn.*
1852. Robert S. Knox, Esq., *Livonia, Ind.*
1853. William A. Churchman, Esq., *Indianapolis, Ind.*
1856. C. W. Kimball, Esq., *Lebanon, Ohio.*
" Dr. James M. Logan, *Palestine, Ill.*
1857. Philip A. Emery, Esq., *Indianapolis, Ind.*
1858. John H. Tate, M. D., *Cincinnati, Ohio.*
1859. Ashley Peirce, Esq., *Valparaiso, Ind.*

A. B.

1846. Dr. John S. Burt, *Washington, Arkansas.*
1854. Hickerson B. Wayland, Esq., *Mt. Washington, Ky.*

ALUMNI.

1834.

NAMES.	PROFESSION.	RESIDENCE.
*William Hamilton Bruner, A. M.	Minister	
*Selby Harney	Teacher	
John Lyle Martin	Minister	Waveland, Ind.
John Mason McChord, A. M.	Minister	Bruceville, Ind,
Isaac McCoy, A. M.	Farmer	Marion, Ill.
Isaac Newton Shepherd, A. M.	Minister	Marion, Ohio.
-Charles Kilgore Thompson, A. M.	Minister	Thorntown, Ind.

1835.

Robert Sherrard Bell, A. M.	Minister	Washington, Va.
James Brown. A. M., D. D.,	Minister	Keokuk, Iowa.
†Jonathan Edwards, A. M. D. D	Minister	Philadelphia, Pa.
Robert Simpson, A. M.	Minister	Newton, Ill.
‡Middleton Goldsmith, A. M. M. D.	Physician	Louisville, Ky.
*James Allen Watson	Teacher	

1836.

S. J. P. Anderson, A. M. D. D.	Minister	St. Louis, Mo.
§Noble Butler, A. M.	Teacher	Louisville, Ky.
*Andrew Fulton, M. D.	Physician	
‖Thomas Woodruff Hynes, A. M.	Minister	Pocahontas, Ill.
*Nathaniel T. Schillinger	Minister	
*David Edward Young Rice, A. M.	Minister	
*William Wylie McLain, A. M.	Minister	

-Principal of Prep. Dep. 1834–8.
†President of Hanover College, 1855–57.
‡Prof. in Vermont Medical College, and Ky. Med. Coll.
§Prof. in Han. Coll. 1836–39.
‖Prof. in Han. Coll. 1838–43.
¶Prof. in Han. Coll. 1840–52, 2858.

ALUMNI.

NAMES.	PROFESSION.	RESIDENCE.
Amos Hynes Rogers, A. M.	Minister	Atlanta, Ill.
Samuel Frame Morrow, A. M.	Minister	Albany, N. Y.
Samuel Newell, A. M.	Minister	Paris, Ill.
Josiah Crawford, A. M.	Minister	Polk Run, Ind.
David Hays Cummins, A. M.	Minister	Mountain, Tenn.
¶Minard Sturgus, A. M.	Teacher	S. Hanover, Ind.
S. Ramsay Wilson, A. M. D. D.	Minister	Cincinnati, Ohio.

1837.

Thomas H. Alderdice,	Minister	Scaffold Prairie Ind
Franklin Berryhill,	Minister	Bellbrook, Ohio.
James Black,	Minister	Cincinnati, Ohio.
*Samuel N. Evans, A. M.	Minister	
Edmund Waller Hawkins, A. M.	Lawyer	Covington, Ky.
John Macartney Hoge	Minister	Beech Bluff, Ark.
Braxton D. Hunter	Minister	
Sylvanus Jewett	Minister	Roscoe, Ill.
*John Wright McCormick, A. M.	Minister	
James A. McKee, A. M.	Minister	Franklin, Ind.
Asahel Munson, A. M.	Minister	Jackson, Mo.
*William Cowper Scott, A. M.	Minister	
Josiah D. Smith, A. M. D. D.	Minister	Columbus, Ohio.
†Samuel Harrison Thomson, A. M.	Minister	S. Hanover, Ind.
James F. Wood.	Physician	Greensburg, Penn.

1838.

George B. Armstrong	Minister	Crittenden, Ky.
*William Blair	Minister	
‡James E. Blythe, A. M.	Lawyer	Evansville, Ind.
William Kirkpatrick Brice, A. M.	Minister	Pleasant, Ohio.
Alex. Montgomery Brown A. M.	Lawyer	Paris, Ky.
William M. Cheever, A. M.	Minister	Troy, Ohio.
James Blythe Crowe, A. M.	Minister	Crawfordsville, Ind
Thomas Searle Crowe, A. M.	Minister	S. Hanover, Ind.
Joseph F. Fenton, A. M.	Minister	Washington, Mo.
James J. Gardiner, A. M.	Teacher	Cape Girardeau, Mo
Robert A. Gibson, A. M.	Farmer	Monmouth, Ill.
Abram T. Hendricks, A. M.	Minister	Petersburg, Ind.
John Jones		
James W. Matthews, A. M.	Teacher	Macomb, Ill.
George Frederick Whitworth, A. M.	Minister	Olympia, W. T.

1839.

Samuel Stanhope Crowe, A. M.	Lawyer	Nebraska City, N. T
David M. Dunn	Lawyer	Logansport, Ind.

¶Prof. in Han. Coll. 1840-52, 2858.
†Prof. in Han. Coll. 1844.
‡Member Ind. Const. Conv. and Ind. H. Rep.

ALUMNI.

NAMES.	PROFESSION.	RESIDENCE.
William W. Gilliland, A. M.	Lawyer	Charlestown, Ind.
*Philander Hamilton	Lawyer	
Ephraim K. Lynn, A. M.	Minister	Aledo, Ill.
Fielding G. Strahan, A. M.	Minister	Danville, Ky.

1840.

Harleigh Blackwell, A. M.	Minister	Snow Hill, Mo.
Samuel G. Haas	Business	Valparaiso, Ind.
†Absalom C. Knox, A. M.	Teacher	———— Cal.
Robert C. Matthews, A. M.	Minister	Monmouth, Ill.
Robert S. Symington, A. M.	Minister	Kansas City, Mo.

1841.

Charles M. Hays	Lawyer	Pittsburg, Penn.
John Lyle King	Lawyer	Chicago, Ill.
*George C. Lyon	Physician	

1842.

Alexander M. Johnston, A. M. M. D.	Physician	Cincinnati, Ohio.
*Thomas C. McCutchen, A. M.	Farmer	
Alexander McHatton, A. M.	Minister	Marion, Ind.
*George McMillan, A. M	Minister	
James Newton Saunders, A. M.	Minister	Bloomfield, Ky.
*William W. Simonson, A. M	Minister	
†Zebulon Barton Sturgus, A. M.	Teacher.	Charlestown, Ind.

1843.

Daniel Lambert Fouts,	Farmer	N. Washington, Ind
*James G. Hopkins, A. M	Minister	
George A. Irwin, A. M	Minister	Ft. Wayne, Ind.
Samuel Barr Keys, A. M.	Lawyer	Cincinnati, Ohio.
Joseph Chambers McKibbin, M. C.	Lawyer	————Cal.
Francis Peterson Monfort, A. M.	Minister	Auburn, Kan.
John F. Read	Lawyer	Jeffersonville, Ind.
J. Franklin Trenchard, A. M. M. D.	Druggist	Philadelphia, Pa.

1844.

John C. Greer	Planter	————Tenn.

1845.

William T. Robinson, A. M.	Lawyer	————Miss.
David R. Thompson,	Lawyer	————Miss.

1846.

*William H. G. Butler, A. M.	Teacher	
John A. Frazer, A. M.	Teacher	————Oregon.
Samuel Crothers Logan, A. M.	Minister	Cincinnati, Ohio.

†Prof. in Han. Coll. 1844–52.
‡Principal of Prep. Department in Hanover College, 1841–43.

ALUMNI.

NAMES.	PROFESSION.	RESIDENCE.

1847.

Samuel Emmett Barr, A. M........Minister................Livonia, Ind.
Fauntleroy Senour, A. M..........Minister................Louisville, Ky.

1848.

Addison W. Bare, A. M.............Physician .... Bryantsville, Ind.
John Wesley Blake, A. M..........Lawyer................Frankfort, Ind.
John C. Caldwell, A. M............Minister................Stillwater, Minn.
*†Moses S. Coulter, A. M..........Minister................
*Robert G. Jackson, A. M..........Teacher................
Robert S. Shannon, A. M. M. D....Physician..............Lagrange, Tex.
Samuel C. Taggart, A. M.M. D.....Physician . ...Charlestown, Ind.
James Harvey L. Vannuys, A.-M...Minister................Goshen, Ind.

1849.

Samuel C. Baldridge, A. M...........Minister................Friendsville, Ill.
*Jesse Y. Higbee, A. M. M. D.......Physician ....
Nathan S. Palmer, A. M............Minister................Brazil, Ind.
Xenophon Boone Sanders, A. M....Lawyer .... Memphis, Tenn.
Williamson Dunn Symington, A. M.Minister................Savannah, Mo.
John White Taylor, A. M...........Lawyer................Palestine, Tex.
Henry E. Thomas, A. M............Minister................Charlestown, Ind.

1850.

William Maxwell Blackburn, A. M.Minister................Erie, Penn.
Joshua Selby Brengle ....Physician ....Carlisle, Ind.
*Avery Williams Bullock, A. M....Lawyer................Hampshire.
John Simpson Frierson,............Minister................———Tenn.
*Samuel David Hawthorn,.........
John Alexander Kimmons..........Minister................Saltilo, Miss.
Claudius. B. H. Martin, A. M......Minister................Corydon, Ind.
Samuel Clarke Mercer,. ....Editor.............. ....Hopkinsville, Ky.
Robert Symington Reese, A. M....Minister................Pleasant Hill, Mo.
William Harvey Rice,..............Minister .. ..Palestine, Texas
William Walton Sickels, A. M......Minister.................Kingstown, Ind.
Alexander Stuart Walker,.........Lawyer................Georgetown, Tex.
Austin Warner,....................Minister...............N. Bloomfield, Mo.
Benjamin Rush Whitney,..........Engineer ....———Mo.
William Alexander Martin Young..Lawyer................Salem, Ind.

1851.

James Madison Alexander,........Minister................Palestine, Ill.
Henry Martyn Bayless,............Business................Chicago, Ill.
Joseph Boon,......................Minister................Lagrange, Tex.
James Bruce, A. M................Minister................Mercersburgh, Pa.
James Huston Burns, A. M........Minister................Monroe, Ohio.
Theophilus Wilson Guy, A. M......Farmer ....Oxford, Ohio.
*James Simpson Jones............Lawyer................
James McEwen Kimmons A. M.....   Miss.

*Missionary to China.

ALUMNI.

NAMES.	PROFESSION.	RESIDENCE.
Cornelius McKain, A. M.	Minister	Iowa Point, Kan.
Hugh McHatton, A. M.	Minister	Cedarville, Ohio.
Archibald V. McKee, A. M.	Lawyer	Troy, Mo.
†William James McKnight, A. M.	Minister	Danville, Ky.
Alexander Mayne, A. M.		
Edward Ethel Porter, A. M.	Minister	Memphis, Tenn.
Benjamin Niles Sawtelle, A. M.	Minister	Batesville, Ark.
Joseph Gaston Symmes, A. M.	Minister	Cranberry, N. J.
Robert Francis Taylor, A. M.	Minister	Vernon, Ind.
Joseph Greene Wells, A. M.	Minister	Jackson, Mo.

1852.

Joseph Mayo Bachelder, A. M.	Minister	Albia, Iowa.
Shephen James Bovell,	Minister	Palestine, Ill.
Jonathan Turner Carthel, A. M.	Lawyer	Trenton, Tenn.
John McCutchen Coyner, A. M.	Teacher	Waveland, Ind.
Benjamin Parke Dewey,	Lawyer	Charlestown, Ind.
Henry Michael Giltner, A. M	Minister	Nebraska City, N T
Thomas Maise Hopkins, A. M.	Minister	Bloomington, Ind.
Alexander Martin, A. M.	Teacher	New Albany, Ind.
Robert Langdon Neely, A. M.	Minister	Denmark, Tenn.
James Matlack Scovel, A. M.	Lawyer	Camden, N. J.
Francis Marion Symmes, A. M.	Minister	Pleasant, Ind.
Daniel Price Young, A. M.	Minister	Georgetown, Ky.

1853.

Lyman Beecher Andrews, A. M.	Teacher	Cape Girardean, Mo.
James Andrew Cunningham,	Business	Madison, Ind.
Lewis Isaac Drake, A. M.	Minister	West Liberty, Ohio
Jeremiah Mead Drake, A. M.	Minister	West Reshville, O.
‡Joshua Bolles Garritt, A. M.	Minister	S. Hanover, Ind.
Edward John Hamilton, A. M.	Minister	Oyster Bay, N. Y.
Henry Seymour Kritz, A. M.	Teacher	Waveland, Ind.
Charles Lee, A. M.	Minister	Scipio, Ind.
William Pope Lemaster, A. M.	Minister	Memphis, Tenn.
Gideon Blackburn McLeary, A. M.	Lawyer	
James Alexander McRee, A. M.	Minister	Rolling Prairie, Ind
Joseph Warren Mahan, A. M.	Teacher	Clermont Co. O.
Henry Thomas Morton, A. M.	Minister	Newton, Ill.
*Henry Spencer Scovel,	Student of Theology	
Sylvester Fithian Scovel, A. M.	Minister	Jeffersonville, Ind.
Jackson Jay Smith, A. M.	Lawyer	Louisville, Ky.
*William Wheat,	Minister	

1854.

Stephen Cromwell Adair,	Lawyer	Morganfield, Ky.
David Gilkerson Herron,	Teacher	Canton, Miss.
Robert Irwin Jr.	Minister	Logansport.

†Prof. of Languages in Austin College, Texas.
‡Prof. in Han. Coll. 1856.

ALUMNI.

NAMES.	PROFESSION.	RESIDENCE.
Robert Alexander Johnston,	Lawyer	Batavia, Ohio.
Isaac Brown Moore,	Minister	Gillman, Ill.
Edwin Hubbard Rutherford,	Minister	Vicksburg, Miss.
Edward Cooke Sickels,	Minister	St. Louis, Mo.
William Rondeau Sim,	Minister	Jordan's Grove, Ill.
Thomas Wallace, A. M.	Teacher	Monroe, Ohio.
James Edward Wilson,		Concord, Tenn.
Jared Ryker Woodfill,	Teacher	

1855.

James Robinson Evans,	Teacher	
†Michael Montgomery Fisher, A. M.	Minister	Fulton, Mo.
James H. Hunter,	Teacher	Prescott, Wis.
William Hall Huston,	Farmer	Hamilton, Ohio.
Robert J. L. Matthews, A. M.	Teacher	Minerva, Ky.
Robert Clarke McGee,	Student of Theology.	Danville, Ky.
John Quincy McKeehan,	Minister	Franklin, Ind.
Charles H. Park,	Minister	Danville, Penn.
William A. Sample,	Minister	
William Bloomer Truax,	Student of Theology	Princeton, N. J.
Thomas Marion Tucker,	Physician	N. Philadelphia, Ia
Archibald Cameron Voris,	Lawyer	Bedford, Ind.

1856.

James Baillie Adams	Minister	Bantam, O.
James William Allison	Minister	Arcola, Ill.
Robert Brown Herron	Teacher	
Henry Keigwin	Minister	Jeffersonville, Ind.
Harvey Lamb	Teacher	
*James Kennedy Patterson, A. M.,	Teacher	Clarksville, Tenn.
James Sanderson Rankin	Teacher	Madison, Ind.
Richmond Kelly Smoot	Teacher	Bowling Green, Ky.
James Harvey Tedford	Minister	Michigan.
Benjamin Dubois Wykoff	Minister	Carlisle Station, O.

BACHELOR OF SCIENCE.

Cyrus Alexander Johnson		Memphis, Tenn,
James Edwin Rankin		Henderson, Ky.

1857.

Leonard Fisk Andrews	Teacher	Cape Girardeau, Mo
William Cochrane	Minister	Jersey City, N. J.
William Means Crozier	Student of Theology	Princeton, N. J.
John McMurray	Student of Theology	Princeton, N. J.
David McKnight Williamson	Minister	Olney, Ill.

BACHELOR OF SCIENCE.

Hiram Francis Braxton		Paoli.
David Taylor, Jr.		Columbus, O.
John Newton Voris		Bennington.

†Prof. in Westminister Coll. Mo. 1855.
*Prof. in Stewart College.

ALUMNI.

NAMES.	PROFESSION.	RESIDENCE.

1858.

William Peter Baker..............Teacher.....................——— Ky.
Jacob Reasoner Geyer.............Student of Theology....Princeton, N. J.
Horace Hovey Hanna..............Student of Law........Ft. Wayne, Ind.
John David McClintock...S. Hanover, Ind.
James Baird McClure............Student of Theology....Princeton, N. J.
Thomas Johnston McIlrath.........Student of Law.........Cincinnati, O.
David William Moffatt............Student of Theology....Princeton, N. J.
James Alexander Piper............Student of Theology....Princeton, N. J.
Robert Gaines Ross..............Student of Theology....Princeton, N. J.
Augustus Taylor..................Student of Theology....Alleghany City, Pa.
James Harvey Vannuys............Student of Theology....Princeton, N. J.
Cornelius Pleasant Voris..........Student of Theology....Princeton, N. J.

1859.

Robert Long Adams...............Student of Theology....Princeton, N. J.
Henry Ellet Crawford............Student of Theology....Princeton, N. J.
John Fox.........................Student of Theology....Alleghany City, Pa.
Columbus DeWitt Huston..........Student of Theology...Alleghany City, Pa.
Samuel Finley Thompson...Thorntown, Ind.
John Bacon Vawter...............Student of Theology...Alleghany City, Pa.

BACHELOR OF SCIENCE.

Charles Henry Johnson...Ft. Wayne.
Oliver Mulvey...Madison.
George Martin Whitely...San Antonio, Texas.

Total number of Bachelors of Arts....22
" " Bachelors of Science. 8

UNDERGRADUATES.

SENIORS.

Robert Long Adams...Pleasant,
Henry Ellet Crawford......................................Lawrenceport.
John Fox..Bruceville.
Columbus DeWitt Huston....................................New Philadelphia.
Samuel Finley Thompson....................................Thorntown.
John Bacon Vawter...Franklin.

JUNIORS.

John McKnight Bloss.......................................New Philadelphia.
John Wesley Crawford......................................Lawrenceport.
William S. Coulter..Dayton.
Samuel Henry Howe...Flemingsburg, Ky.
Reuben Franklin Middleton.................................Frankfort, Ky.
Ezra Fitch Pabody...Vernon.
William King Perrine......................................Monroe, Ohio.
Benjamin Simpson..Vernon.
William George Thomas.....................................Indian Creek, Va.
Samuel Demaree Voris......................................Benningtan.
James Wilson..Hanover.

SOPHOMORES.

George Washington Cummins.................................Logansport.
Samuel Paterson Dillon....................................Cincinnati, Ohio.
Samuel Kendall Hough......................................Charlestown.
Joseph Henry Innis..Cross Plains.
Adam J. Johnson...Spades.
Stephen Paul Lee..Saluda.
Edward T. McCrea..Shelbyville.
John W. Paxton..Princeton.
Thomas Speed..Bardstown, Ky.

FRESHMEN.

Henry Beecher Alvord......................................Indianapolis.
William Emery Brown.......................................Valparaiso.
Leonidas Winfield Scott Downs.............................Jeffersonville.

CATALOGUE OF

Moses Fell Dunn	Bedford.
Augustine Chester Hirst	Cincinnati, O.
George Proffitt Huckeby	Rome.
Augustus Adolph Joss	Constantine, Mich.
Albert Newton Keigwin	Louisville, Ky.
Howard Campbell Laforce	Bedford.
George McCampbell	Jeffersonville.
William Crawford Pogue	Mace.
William Hind Roberts	Crittenden, Ky.
Henry Clifton Thomson	Hanover.
Jesse Brown Wilson	New Lexington.

SCIENTIFIC DEPARTMENT.

THIRD YEAR.

Charles Henry Johnson	Ft. Wayne.
Oliver Mulvey	Madison.
Solon McCullough Tilford	Kent.
George Martin Whitely	San Antonio, Texas.

SECOND YEAR.

John Pinckney Brown	Rising Sun.
Francis Marion Broady	Vienna.
William Andrew Collins	Edinburgh.
Marshall Pratby Hayden	Rising Sun.
Walter Mackay	Bardstown, Ky.
William Oliver Speed	Bardstown, Ky.

FIRST YEAR.

John Andrew Bailey	Cincinnati, O.
Oliver Boyd	Allensville.
Churchill Crittenden	San Francisco, Cal.
Samuel Pratt Dale	Bedford.
Jacob Wittmer Dritt	Logansport.
Alexander Campbell Dunn	Emerson, Mo.
George Pollock Ewing	Port Royal, Ky.
Robert Denwelton Froman	Vevay.
Samuel J. Gelpin	Hanover.
William Jackson Hays	Water Proof, La.
George W. Hughes	Volga.
Winfield Scott McDaneld	Jeffersonville.
Robert D. Porter McDermett	Dallas, Texas.
Joseph McLain	Austin.
William Barkley McKinney	Memphis, Tenn.
Robert E. Officer	Smyrna.
Franklin Shannon	Hanover.

Thomas A. Stewart............Vevay.
Aaron Vawter............Franklin.
Lorenzo Wallace............Hamburg.
James B. Walden............Mount Sterling.

PREPARATORY DEPARTMENT.

SENIORS.

Samuel Edgar Adams............Pleasant.
*Drowned May 21st, 1859.
Felix Jennerette Brandt............Hanover.
Henry Clay Donnell............Greenville, Ill.
Hugh Jameson............Rising Sun.
Thomas Alexander Jeffery............Franklin.
James Woods Kyle............Hanover.
Jesse Link............Cannelton.
Robert Symington McChord............Bruceville.
Andrew McFarland Patterson............North Madison.
Amos William Patterson............Hanover.
William Henry Sawtelle............Binghamton, N. Y.
Benjamin W. Tucker............New Philadelphia.
James Wilson Spear............Hanover.
Thomas Hart Woodward............Hanover.

JUNIORS.

John Finley Crowe............New Lexington.
Robert Sharon Dean............Hanover.
James Albert Dean............Hanover.
James Benjamin Finnell............Crittenden, Ky.
Reben Nelson Gelpin............Hanover.
Robert A. Grace............Cincinnati, O.
Nicholas Henry Hobbs............Mt. Washington, Ky
Robert Thomson Jeffery............Franklin.
John Kerns............Hanover.
Thorburn Charters Merwin............Hanover.
Richard Wasson Sipe............Swanville.
William Wallace Speirs............Austin.
Martin VanBuren VanArsdale............Washington.

SUMMARY.

Seniors............6.	2d Scientific............6.
Juniors............10.	1st Scientific............21.
Sophomores............9.	Senior Preparatory............14.
Freshmen............14.	Junior Preparatory............13.
Scientific............4.	Total............97.

TEXT BOOKS.

DEPARTMENT OF LANGUAGES.

LATIN.—Andrews' Grammar and Reader, Andrews' or Leverett's Lexicon, Crooks & Schem's, or Andrews' Cæsar, Cooper's Virgil, Bojesen's Roman Antiquities, Butler & Sturgus' Sallust, Lincoln's Livy, Lincoln's Horace, Tyler's Tacitus, Chase's Tusculan Disputations.

GREEK.—Crosby's Grammar and Lessons, Liddell & Scott's or Pickering's Lexicon, Owen's or Boise's, Anabasis, Bojesen's Grecian Antiquities, Owen's Homer, Woolsey's Greek Plays, Champlin's Demosthenes.

HEBREW.—Stuart's Rœdiger's Grammar, Gesenius' Lexicon, Biblia Hebraica.

DEPARTMENT OF BELLES-LETTERS.

Blair' Rhetoric, (University edition,) Whately's Logic, Wayland's Political Economy, Smith's Grecian History, Liddell's Rome, Clark's English History, American History.

DEPARTMENT OF MATHEMATICS.

Robinson's Algebra, (University edition,) Davies' Legendre, Davies' Surveying, Davies' Analytical Geometry, Olmsted's Natural Philosophy, do. Astronomy.

DEPARTMENT OF NATURAL SCIENCE.

Silliman's Chemistry, Cutter's Physiology, Wood's Botany, Lyell's Geology, Butler's Analogy, Dana's Mineralogy, Agassiz & Gould's Zoology, Somerville's Physical Geography.

DEPARTMENT OF METAPHYSICS.

Walker's Reid on the Intellectual Powers, Sir William Hamilton's Philosophy, (Wight's edition,) Stewart's Active and Moral Powers, Alexander's Moral Science.

DEPARTMENT OF RELIGIOUS INSTRUCTION.

English Bible, Hodge's, Alexander's or Jacobus' Notes, Greek Testament, Robin-son's Greek Harmony, Old Testament Hebrew, Septuagint, Westminister Catechism, General Assembly's Psalm and Hymn Book, Paley's Natural Theology.

PERMANENT RECITATION HOURS.

A.M.	The President.	Prof. Thomson.	Prof. Sturgus.	Prof. Garritt.	Prof. King.
8	½ Senior & 3d Scientific	Sophomore & 2d Scientific	Junior Preparatory	½ Senior Prep. and ½ Senior and Junior	Freshman & 1st. Scientific
9	½ Freshman and ½ Senior and 3d Scien.	Senior Prep & 1st Scientific	½ Sen. and Junior and ½ Sophomore	Junior Preparatory	½ Soph. & 2d Scientific & ½ Junior and 2d Scien.
10	Junior & 2d Scientific	Seniors and 3d Scientific	Sophomore & 1st Scientific	Freshman	Senior Preparatory
11	½ Sophomore	Junior and 3d Scientific	Freshmen	½ Sophomore and ½ Sen. Prep.	Senior and 2d Scientific

DISTRIBUTION OF RECITATIONS.

FIRST TERM.

Junior Prepar.			Lat. Less. & Class. Geog.	Greek Grammar	Caesar
Senior Prepar.		Algebra	Virgil	Greek Reader	Plane Geometry
Freshmen	½ Harmony of Gospels	Solid Geometry	History and ½ Livy	Anabasis	½ Zoology
Sophomores	½ Acts	Natural Philosophy	½ Tacitus	½ Odyssey	½ Anat. and Physiology
Juniors	Rhetoric—Hebrew	Logic	½ Tusc. Disp.	½ Gorgias	Chemistry
Seniors	Psychology—Hebrew			½ Greek Tragedies	

SECOND TERM.

Junior Prepar.			Lat. Less. & Class. Geog	Greek Grammar	Sallust
Senior Prepar.		Algebra	Virgil	Greek Reader	Plane Trigonometry
Freshmen	½ Harmony	Spher. Trig. and Applic.	History and ½ Horace	Xen. Memorabilia	½ Phys. Geography
Sophomores	½ Epistles	Natural Philosophy	½ Tacitus	½ Odyssey	½ Light and Heat
Juniors	Nat. Theology—Hebrew	Butler's Analogy	½ Juvenal	½ Demosthenes	Chemistry
Seniors	Psychology—Hebrew			½ Greek Tragedies	

THIRD TERM.

Junior Prepar.			Lat. Read. & Class. Geog.	Greek Grammar	Sallust
Senior Prepar.		Algebra	Livy	Greek Reader	Surveying
Freshmen	½ Harmony	Analyt. Geometry	History and ½ Horace	Xen. Memorabilia	½ Botany
Sophomores	½ Epistles	Astronomy	½ Tusc. Disputations	½ Gorgias	½ Electricity
Juniors	Pol. Economy—Hebrew	Review	½ Review of Latin	½ Demosthenes	Chemistry and Geology
Seniors	Moral Science—Hebrew			½ Greek Tragedies	

SCIENTIFIC DEPARTMENT.

The three years' course of English, Mathematical and Scientific instruction pursued in this department, embraces all that is included in the college scheme, except the Classical Languages. Such as desire it, however, may pursue the study of Latin or French, in connection with a Scientific Course. We do not recommend it as in any sense an equivalent for a thorough Classical course; nor is it intended for mere boys, since the subjects which it includes are entirely above their capacity; but to young men, who have obtained a respectable common school education, including the elements of Algebra, and who have not time nor means to prosecute a Classical course, this system of studies will, it is hoped, commend itself as solid, comprehensive, and practical. Those who shall complete the prescribed Scientific course, will receive a Diploma, certifying the extent of their attainments.

COLLEGE YEAR---EXAMINATIONS.

THE COLLEGE YEAR is divided into three Terms of thirteen weeks each, and three Vacations. The First Term begins on the Fourth Wednesday in September; the Second, on the First Wednesday in January; and the Third, on the First Wednesday in May, closing with the First Thursday in August, which is commencement day.

IT IS OF GREAT IMPORTANCE that Students attend from the very beginning of the term; especially since so considerable portion of time is allotted to vacations. In most cases, the loss of a few weeks, or even days, seriously affects the future standing of the pupil. Absence during term time, without special leave, is prohibited.*

PUBLIC EXAMINATIONS will be held, hereafter, only at the close of the college year, when the Freshmen and Junior Classes will be examined on the studies of the preceding year, and the Sophomore and Senior Classes, upon those of the two preceding years. These last examinations will be FINAL, for the studies pursued in those years. All the examinations will be THOROUGH and RIGID; and will be conducted, chiefly, by the use of written questions, prepared by the Faculty and the Examining Committee, covering the whole field of study prosecuted during a given period, and entirely unknown to the Student until the moment of examination. These questions must be answered in writing before the Committee; and correct answers to a definite portion of them will be the passport of admission to a higher standing. Similar examinations, of a briefer and less decisive character, however, and by way of preparation for the final trial, may be conducted privately, at the pleasure of the Faculty.

---

*Parents are respectfully advised to give their sons no such permission to be absent, except in cases of NECESSITY.

RELIGIOUS INSTRUCTION AND SERVICES.

The attention of a Christian community is respectfully invited to the system of Biblical Instruction which forms a characteristic feature of our course of Study. The Grammar School Classes recite statedly in the English Bible; and every College Class has a daily or tri-weekly recitation in the Greek Testament, or the Hebrew. Proficiency in these, as in other studies, is tested by the usual examinations. In addition to this, Biblical Geography and Antiquities, Ecclesiastical History, Natural Theology, and the Analogy of Religion, Natural and Revealed, to the constitution and course of nature, are carefully and faithfully studied. There is also a Bible or Catechetical exercise on Sabbath mornings; a public service on Sabbath afternoons, appropriated to the Students; and daily morning prayers. The Students are expected to attend the Sabbath morning service of the congregation worshiping in the chapel, or of some other congregation in the vicinity, if their parents prefer any of the latter. The Methodist, and United Presbyterian Churches, have regular services in or near the village.

An experiment of several years in this Institution, has established the fact that the daily study of God's word by no means interferes with, but rather promotes, sound and comprehensive attainments in other branches of knowledge.

ADMISSION.

CANDIDATES for admission into the Freshman Class are examined in Arithmetic, and Algebra; Ancient and Modern Geography; the English, Latin and Greek Grammars; Cæsar's Commentaries; and Greek Reader, or what is equivalent to these attainments. They must furnish testimonials of good character; and, if from another College, must bring certificates of honorable dismission. Candidates for high standing, are examined upon that part of the course already studied by the class which they propose to enter.

No one can be admitted to the Freshman Class until he has completed his fourteenth year; nor to an advanced standing, without a proportional increase of age.

"Before a student shall be admitted to actual standing in any class, he shall present to the President a receipt from the Treasurer, showing that he has complied with the statutes relating to College Charges and Scholarships."

N. B. The regular examination for admission into College, commences on the Monday preceding the beginning of each term.

COURSE OF INSTRUCTION.

PREPARATORY DEPARTMENT.

Andrew's Latin Lessons, Grammar, Reader and Exercises; Andrew's Cæsar; Butler and Sturgus' Sallust; Crosby's Greek Grammar and Lessons; Classical and Biblical Geography; Arithmetic; Robinson's Algebra; (University edition,) English Bible.

SCIENTIFIC DEPARTMENT.

FIRST YEAR.

Algebra, completed; Plane Geometry; Plane Trigonometry; Surveying and Navigation; History; English Bible, historical books.
Linear Drawing (extra.)

SECOND YEAR.

Solid Geometry; Spherical Trigonometry, and its Applications; Analytical Geometry; Natural Philosophy, and Astronomy; Rhetoric, Logic, and Political Economy; English Bible, Poetical books.

THIRD YEAR.

Zoology; Anatomy and Physiology; Botany; Physical Geography; Chemistry; Geology; Natural Theology and Butler's Analogy; Psychology, and Ethics; English Bible; Mind Explored.

COLLEGIATE DEPARTMENT.

FRESHMEN CLASS.
FIRST CLASS.

Greek Harmony, of the Gospel............................Robinson.
Biblical Antiquities......................................Nevin.
Virgil...Cooper.
Roman Antiquites..Bojesin.

Xenophons's Anabasis ....Boise.
Plane Geometry...Davies' Legendre.

SECOND SESSION.

Greek Harmony, continued.................................
Virgil, continued...
Anabasis, continued...
Grecian Antiquites...Bojesen.
Plane Trigonometry.......................................Davies' Legendre.

THIRD SESSION.

Greek Harmony, completed..............................
Livy..
Xenophon's Memorabilia...............................Robbins.
Grecian Antiquites..
Latin and Greek Exercises..............................
Surveying and Navigation...............................Davies'

SOPHOMORE CLASS.

FIRST SESSION.

Greek Testament, (Acts.)................................Owen.
Livy, continued..
Homer's Odyssey..Owen.
Greek History..Smith.
Solid Geometry..Davies' Legendre.
Zoology..Agassiz & Gould.

SECOND SESSION.

Greek Testament, (Epistles,).............................
Horace...Lincoln.
Homer's Odyssey, continued............................
Roman History...Liddell.
Plane Trigonometry, reviewed..........................
Spherical Trigonometry, with its Applications.......Davies' Legendre.
Physical Geography......................................Sommerville.

THIRD SESSION.

Greek Testament, (Epistles,).............................
Horace...
Plato's Gorgias..Woolsey.
English History..Clark and Moffat.
Analytical Geometry......................................Davies'
Botany...Wood.
Latin and Greek Exercises, throughout the year...........

JUNIOR CLASS.

FIRST SESSION.

Hebrew Grammar and Hebrew; Genesis, (Optional.)......
Tacitus' Histories..Tyler.
Plato's Gorgias, continued...............................
Natural Philosophy.......................................Olmsted.
Rhetoric..Blair.
Anatomy and Physiology................................Cutter.

SECOND SESSION.

Hebrew, (Genesis continued.)..............................
Tacitus continued..
Demosthenes De Corona ....Champlin.
Natural Philosophy, continued.............................
Logic...Whately.
Light and Heat..Bird.

THIRD SESSION.

Hebrew, (Psalms,)..
Cicero's Tusculan Disputations.................Anthon.
Demosthenes De Corona, completed..........................
Astronomy.......................................Olmsted.
Political Economy...............................Wayland.
Electricity..Bird.

SENIOR CLASS.
FIRST SESSION.

Select portions of the Hebrew Bible. ....
Intellectual Philosophy.....................Walker's Reid.
Cicero's Tusculan Disputations, continued.................
Greek Tragedies..............................Woolsey.
Chemistry....................................Silliman.
Mrthematics reviewed......................................

SECOND SESSION.

Select Hebrew, continued..................................
Intellectual Philosophy.....................Hamilton.
Chemistry, and Mineralogy ....Dana.
Natural Theology............................Paley.
Greek Tragedies.............................Woolsey.
Juvenal.....................................Anthon.

THIRD SESSION.

Hebrew, continued...
Butler's Analogy.........................Wilson's Edition.
Moral Science.............................Wayland.
Geology..................................Lyell's Elements.
Review of Latin...
Æschylus' Prometheus Vintus...............Woolsey.
Mathematics reviewed......................................

N. B. The text-books needed for any part of the College course, may be procured at the Hanover Book Store.

EXPENSES.

The entire expenditures of a Student need not much exceed $150, viz:
  Tuition and contingent fee, $10 per term..........................$30 00
  Boarding with private families, and a furnished room, at $2 00
    to $2 50 per week,...................................$78 00 to $97 50
  Fuel, light, washing, &c.,..15 00
  Books, &c.,...$5 to 10 00

Boarding in clubs will cost from seventy-five cents to one dollar twenty-five cents a week; and some board themselves even at a lower rate. The cost of clothing, and the amount spent as pocket money will vary with the taste and habits of the Student, and with the wishes of parents. As a general rule, the more money allowed to a young man beyond what is strictly necessary, the less likely is he to reflect honor upon his parents and instructors. Although Hanover presents comparatively few temptations to extravagance, yet parents are earnestly advised to require of their sons a detailed account of their expenditures, and peremptorily to refuse the payment of any debt incurred by them without a written permission. It is also recommended that the funds of young pupils be deposited with some one of the Faculty, and expended under his direction. The younger Students are required to board where the Faculty may direct, and where they may exercise a more careful and frequent supervision.

N. B. Students placed upon Scholarships by the Faculty, are relieved in part, or wholly, as the case may require, from the payment of tuition fees.

DISCIPLINE.

A record is kept by the Faculty, in which is entered weekly, the grade of scholarship of the Student, his absence from the exercises of the Institution, and such other facts as are worthy of notice with respect to his general deportment. From this record, a report is made out at the end of each session and sent to the Parent or Guardian of each Student. In case of deficiency in scholarship, negligence in study, irregularity in attendance upon the exercises of the institution or improper conduct, the Student will be privately admonished, and the Parent or Guardian will be promptly informed of the fact.

It is the object of this arrangement to keep Parents and Guardians accurately informed with regard to their sons and wards in this Institution, and thus to secure their co-operation with the Faculty in a mild system of discipline. Whenever it is ascertained that a Student is deriving no advantage from his connection with the Institution, or is pursuing a course injurious to himself or fellow-students the Faculty will take decisive action, and his Parent or Guardian will be promptly addressed on the subject, and requested to remove him from the Institution.

SCHOLARSHIP.

The endowment of this Institution is in the form of Scholarships, of which the Board has established several sorts. The sum of $400 paid, or secured to the Corporation by note payable within five years, and bearing six per cent. interest in advance upon principal remaining unpaid—purchases for the owner, his heirs and assigns, a perpetual right to the tuition of one scholar, in Hanover College. The sum of $200 paid, or subscribed under similiar conditions, secures the right to twenty years' tuition; after which time, the scholarship is subject to the disposal of the Board for the gratuitious education of candidates for the Gospel Ministry. A church schorarship of $200 secures to the church so contributing, a perpetual right to the tuition of one student, who shall be a member of that church, and appointed by the session. A Presbyterial scholarship of $200 secures a similiar right to a Presbytery in behalf of pupils who shall be candidates for the ministry under its care. PRINCIPAL paid on these scholarships is invested by the Corporation in some safe and productive stock; and the INTEREST ONLY can be expended for the support of the College.

The sum of $100, paid within two years at the farthest with interest in advance on unpaid principal, purchases a right to ten years' tuition within twenty years from the date of subscription. Both principal and interest of this scholarship may be employed for contingent purposes, and the scholarship expires with the owners' right to its use.

The sum of $100 paid into the building fund; or the sum of $50 paid in like manner, secures the right to ten, or five years' tuition of one student.

Every person applying for admission as a beneficiary of a scholarship under the control of the donors, shall present to the Treasurer, at the beginning of each term, A WRITTEN CERTIFICATE from those controling the scholarship, of his right to such benefit: when, after paying whatever interest may be due on said scholarship, he shall receive an acknowledgment of his right, which he shall lodge with the President.

"The scholarships subject to the disposal of the Corporation, may be occupied by such applicants as the Faculty may select, after inquiry into their circumstances, character and attainments; the preference being, (ceteris paribus,) to those who give the best evidence of scholarship.

"There shall at no time be more than one student upon each scholarship."

ACCOMMODATIONS.

The community system of Boarding in Commons, or of rooming in large Lodging Halls, is not adopted in Hanover. Arrangements are made to accommodate the students with Board and Rooms in respectable private families, where the number together can never be large; and where all shall be brought under domestic influence.

SETTLEMENT OF ACCOUNTS.

No Diploma nor honorable dismission shall be granted until the student shall exhibit a Receipt of Settlement of all his Bills for Boarding, Room and Washing.

DEGREES.

No Degrees are conferred in course. Candidates for Literary Honors are reported to the Board upon their ascertained or acknowledged merits.

SOCIETIES, LIBRARIES, &c.

There are two societies connected with the College, the UNION LITERARY and the PHILALETHEAN, whose Libraries number each about twelve hundred volumes.

There is also a SOCIETY OF RELIGIOUS INQUIRY, which has begun to collect a Library, Maps, &c., and which in connection with another association formed for the purpose, sustains a valuable Reading Room.

The College Library contains near three thousand well selected volumes, and is accessible to the Students.

The Cabinet contains several thousand specimens in Mineralogy and Geology.

The friends of the College are advised that contributions to the Library, to the Cabinet, or to the Laboratory are much needed, and will be thankfully received.

PROHIBITED SECRET SOCIETIES.

The following order was passed by the Board of Trustees in July, 1858, viz:

"RESOLVED, That this Board disapprove of the existence among the Students of Hanover College of any Society or Association of which the Faculty are not ex-officio members; and will not permit the public exhibition of any such Society."

LOCATION, BUILDINGS, &c.

The village of Hanover is situated upon an elevated bluff of the Ohio river, six miles below Madison, Indiana, in a region of remarkable salubrity and natural beauty. The village and neighborhood are characterized by morality, and the absence of all ordinary temptation to vice and idleness. The Ohio river, and the Railways from Madison, N. Albany, and Cincinnati, place Hanover within twenty-four hours, of all the principal points in Indiana, Kentucky, Western Ohio, and Eastern Illinois. A Turnpike from Madison to Hanover, renders the village easy of access at all seasons of the year.

Hanover College is controlled by a Board of Trustees; one half of whom are appointed by the Board itself, and the other half by the Synods of Indiana and Northern Indiana.

The Board purchased, some years ago, a farm of two hundred acres, lying between the village and the Ohio river, upon a beautiful point of which, overlooking the river from an elevation of four hundred feet, they have erected a commodious College edifice, now completed and occupied. The new College consists of a center building, nearly eighty feet square, with lateral and transverse wings. The whole length is about two hundred feet. It contains no dormitories for Students; (an undesirable provision;) but affords ample and convenient halls, library, cabinet, lecture and recitation rooms, and a spacious chapel.

The building commands an exceedingly diversified view of the river, for six miles up, and ten miles down its course.

NOTICE.

OFFICERS FOR THE ENSUING YEAR.

While the Catalogue was passing through the press, the annual meeting of the Board was held, and the following changes were made.

Rev. J. G. Monfort, D. D. and Rev. James Wood, D. D., were elected Trustees in place of Rev. Wm. Sickles and W. A. Bullock, Esq., resigned. James Ray, Esq., was elected President, and James Wood, Treasurer.

EXECUTIVE COMMITTE.—Messrs. James Wood, T. S. Crowe, J. W. Blythe, W. M. Dunn, and R. S. McKee.

AUDITORS.—R. S. McKee and John King.

Remittances of money, and letters pertaining to funds may be addressed to Rev. James Wood, Treasurer, or Rev. J. W. Blythe, General Agent, South Hanover, Ind.

By an inadvertance the names of James M. Ray, Esq., and Rev. Thos. McIntyre, have been omitted from the list of Trustees on the sixth page. Mr. Ray was re-elected by the Synod of Indiana at its last meeting; and Mr. McIntyre was elected by the Synod of Northern Indiana in the place of Rev. I. N. Shannon, deceased.

THE TWENTY-EIGHTH

ANNUAL CATALOGUE AND CIRCULAR,

OF

HANOVER COLLEGE,

HANOVER, IND.

JUNE, 1860.

MADISON, INDIANA:
WM. P. LEVY & CO'S. PRINTING AND BINDING ESTABLISHMENT.
1860.

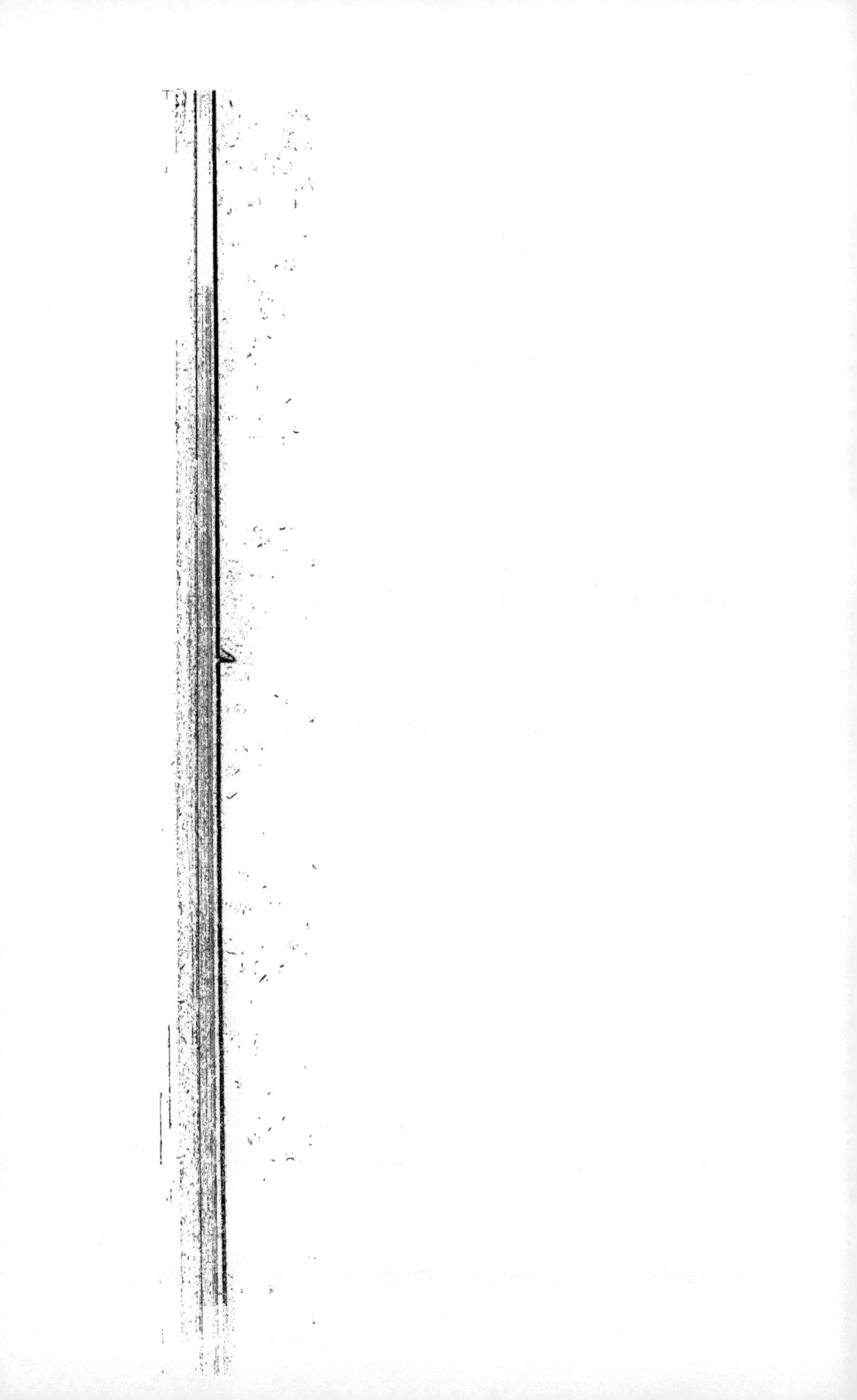

THE TWENTY-EIGHTH

ANNUAL CATALOGUE AND CIRCULAR,

OF

Hanover College,

HANOVER, IND.

JUNE, 1860.

MADISON, INDIANA:
WM. P. LEVY & CO'S. PRINTING AND BINDING ESTABLISHMENT.
1860.

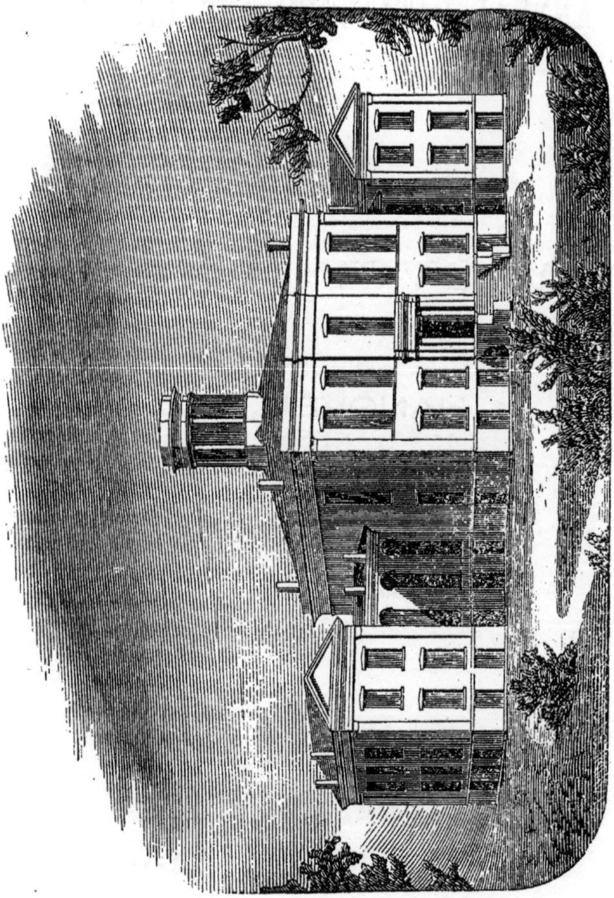

CATALOGUE.

BOARD OF TRUSTEES.

	TERM EXPIRES.
Bd. DR. P. S. SHIELDS, New Albany,	1864.
Bd. ASHLEY PIERCE, ESQ., Valparaiso,	1864.
Bd. DR. ANDREW SPEAR, Hanover,	1864.
Bd. REV. WILLIAM Y. ALLEN, Rockville,	1864.
S. S. REV. JAMES A. McKEE, Minneapolis, Minn.,	1860.
S. S. REV. J. W. BLYTHE, Hanover,	1860.
N. S. REV. F. P. CUMMINS, La Porte	1860.
N. S. REV. ROBERT IRWIN, SEN., Monticello,	1860.
Bd. REV. D. D. McKEE, Hanover,	1861.
Bd. REV. SAMUEL NEWELL, Paris, Ill.,	1861.
Bd. A. R. FORSYTH, ESQ., Greensburg,	1861.
Bd. JESSE L. WILLIAMS, ESQ., Fort Wayne,	1861.
S. S. REV. JOHN CROZIER, Olney, Ill.,	1861.
S. S. REV. LOWMAN HAWES, Madison,	1861.
N. S. REV. E. W. WRIGHT, Delphi,	1861.
N. S. REV. W. M. DONALDSON, Bluffton,	1861.
Bd. REV. H. H. CAMBERN, Rushville,	1862.
Bd. ROBERT DEAN, ESQ., Hanover,	1862.
Bd. HON. C. E. WALKER, Madison,	1862.
Bd. COL. JAMES BLAKE, Indianapolis,	1862.
S. S. REV. A. C. ALLEN, Indianapolis,	1862.
S. S. REV. S. E. BARR, Livonia,	1862.
N. S. REV. C. K. THOMPSON, Thorntown,	1862.
N. S. REV. T. M. CUNNINGHAM, Chicago,	1862.
Bd. JOHN KING, ESQ., Madison,	1863.
Bd. J. G. MONFORT, D. D., Cincinnati, O.,	1863.
Bd. HON. W. McKEE DUNN, Madison,	1863.
Bd. REV. JAMES WOOD, D.D., Hanover,	1863.
S. S. REV. ROBERT L. BRECK, New Albany,	1863.
S. S. JOHN H. VANNUYS, ESQ., Franklin,	1863.
N. S. JAMES M. RAY, ESQ., Indianapolis,	1863.
N. S. REV. THOMAS McINTYRE, Indianapolis,	1863.

OFFICERS OF THE BOARD.

JAMES M. RAY, ESQ., *President.* REV. D. D. McKEE, *Secretary.*
REV. JAMES WOOD, D. D., *Treasurer.*

EXECUTIVE COMMITTEE.

HON. W. McKEE DUNN,   JOHN KING, ESQ.,
REV. JAMES WOOD, D. D.,   REV. J. W. BLYTHE,
REV. D. D. McKEE.

AUDITING COMMITTEE.

HON. W. McKEE DUNN,   HON. C. E. WALKER.

GENERAL AGENT.

REV. J. W. BLYTHE, Hanover, Ind.

FACULTY.

REV. JAMES WOOD, D. D., PRESIDENT,
    Professor of Biblical Instruction, Psychology, and Ethics.

REV. S. HARRISON THOMSON, A. M.,
    Professor of Mathematics, Mechanical Philosophy, and Astronomy.

MINARD STURGUS, A. M.,
    Professor of the Latin Languages and Literature.

REV. JOSHUA B. GARRITT, A. M.,
    Professor of the Greek Languages and Literature.

THEOPHILUS PARVIN, A. M., M. D.,
    Professor Elect of Natural Science.

REV. JOSHUA B. GARRITT, A. M.,
    Librarian.

WILLIAM BROWN,
    Janitor.

UNDERGRADUATES.

SENIORS.

John McKnight Bloss,..................................New Philadelphia
John Wesley Crawford,...............................Lawrenceport.
William Stanley Coulter,.............................Hanover.
Reuben Franklin Middleton,........................Frankfort, Ky.
William George Thomas,..............................Indian Creek, Va.
Samuel Demaree Voris,...............................Bennington.
James Wilson,..Hanover.

JUNIORS.

Thomas Leander Adams,.............................Hanover.
Solomon Frederick Denton,..........................Cincinnati, O.
Samuel Patterson Dillon,.............................Cincinnati, O.
Hugh Stuart Fullerton,................................South Salem, O.
Samuel Kendall Hough,...............................Charlestown.
S. M. Irwin,...South Salem, O.
Adam J. Johnson,......................................Spades.
Stephen Paul Lee,......................................Saluda.
William Henry Smith,.................................Vincennes.

SOPHOMORES.

Irwin L. Caton,.., O.
Samuel T. Danner,......................................Rushville.
Moses Fell Dunn,.......................................Bedford.
George Monfort Gilchrist,............................Vinton, Iowa.
George Proffitt Huckeby,.............................Rome.
Albert Newton Keigwin,..............................Louisville, Ky.
Howard Campbell Laforce,..........................Bedford.
George Meriwether McCampbell,.................Jeffersonville.
Elias Riggs Monfort,...................................Glendale, O.
William Henry Sawtelle,..............................Binghamton, N.Y.
William Crawford Pogue,............................Mace.
Robert Anderson Sturgus,............................Hanover.

Henry Clifton Thomson,......................Hanover.
Eugene C. Warren,..........................Louisville, Ky.
John C. Youngken,..........................Friendsville, Ill.

FRESHMEN.

Henry Clay Donnell,........................Greenville, Ill.
Theodore C. Fitch,.........................Glendale, O.
*Charles Garritt,..........................Delphi.
Samuel Burke Hynes,........................Greenville, Ill.
Hugh Jamieson,.............................Rising Sun.
Thomas A. Jeffery,.........................Franklin.
Augustus Adolphus Joss,....................Constantine, Mich
James Woods Kyle,..........................Hanover.
Robert Symington McChord,..................Hanover.
Francis C. Monfort,........................Glendale, O.
Ames William Patterson,....................Hanover.
James Wilson Spear,........................Hanover.
Benjamin W. Tucker,........................New Philadelphia
John Weston,...............................Galena, Ill.

SCIENTIFIC DEPARTMENT.

THIRD YEAR.

William Andrew Collins,....................Madison.
George Washington Cummins,.................Logansport.
Joseph Marshall Story,.....................Vernon.

SECOND YEAR.

Churchill Crittenden,......................San Francisco, Cal
Samuel J. Gelpin,..........................Hanover.
Marshall P. Hayden,........................Rising Sun.
Franklin Shannon,..........................Hanover.

* Deceased.

FIRST YEAR.

William A. Adams, ... Beanblossom.
Willis Barnes, ... Saluda.
Felix Jennerette Brandt, ... Hanover.
Orson Britton, ... Hamilton, O.
Samuel W. Crothers, ... Hanover.
William Eastman, ... Hanover.
Thomas Handy, ... Boonville.
William Jackson Hays, ... Water Proof, La.
John C. Hunter, ... Symmes' Cor., O.
Robert D. P. McDermett, ... Dallas, Texas.
Simon Myers, ... Bruce's Lake.
Ephraim J Reel, ... Vincennes.
B. F. Scott, ... Clear Spring.
Thomas Sering, ... Madison.
Richard Q. Sleet, ... Verona, Ky.
Thomas Hart Woodward, ... Hanover.
*John C. Watson, ... Clarke Co.

PREPARATORY DEPARTMENT.

SENIORS.

John A. Blair, ... Rushville.
John Finley Crowe, ... New Lexington.
Robert Sharon Dean, ... Hanover.
James Albert Dean, ... Hanover.
James Benjamin Finnell, ... Crittenden, Ky.
Eben Nelson Gelpin, ... Hanover.
William Henderson Hillis, ... Madison.
Isaac A. Helm, ... Rushville.
John Kerns, ... Hanover.
Thorburn Charters Merwin, ... Hanover.
John Donald Miller, ... Clarksburg.

* Deceased.

Peter Hathaway Kemper McComb,.....................Hanover.
Kearsly Greer McComb,.............................Hanover.
Arthur Rose,......................................Hanover.
Richard Wasson Sipe,..............................Swanville.
Martin VanBuren Vanarsdale,.......................Washington.
Robert M. Webster,................................Tallahoma, Iowa.
Isaac N. Winston,.................................Liberty.

JUNIORS.

Paul J. D. Caton,.................................Symmes, O.
William Chamberlain,..............................Hanover.
Myron Dudley Fabrique,............................Corydon.
John Hunt,..Columbus.
Calvin S. Hunter,.................................Symmes' Cor., O.
Thomas Jordan,....................................Kent.
Henry H. Kalb,....................................Canal Winchester, O.
Joseph K. McIlhenny,..............................Beanblossom.
Alfred McKeehan,..................................Pierceton.
Preston McKinney,.................................Livonia.
William Lindley Lee,..............................Saluda.
Jeremiah Long,....................................Bardolph, Ill.
David L. McCampbell,..............................Covington.
Robert E. Officer,................................Volga.
William P. Sharp,.................................Canal Winchester, O.
John P. Sharp,....................................Canal Winchester, O.
L. Howell Vinnedge,...............................Jones' Station, O.

SUMMARY.

Seniors,..................	7	Scientific, second Year,........	4
Juniors,..................	9	Scientific, first Year,.........	17
Sophomores,..............	15	Senior Preparatory,.............	18
Freshmen,................	14	Junior Preparatory,.............	17
Scientific, third Year,....	3	Total,...........................	104

TEXT BOOKS.

DEPARTMENT OF LANGUAGES.

LATIN.—Andrews' Grammar and Reader; Andrews' or Leverett's Lexicon; Crooks & Schem's, or Andrews', Cæsar; Cooper's Virgil; Bojesen's Roman Antiquities; Butler & Sturgus' Sallust; Lincoln's Livy; Lincoln's Horace; Tyler's Tacitus; Chase's Tusculan Disputations.

GREEK.—Crosby's Grammar and Lessons; Liddell & Scott's, or Pickering's Lexicon; Owen's, or Boise's Anabasis; Bojesen's Grecian Antiquities; Owen's Homer; Woolsey's Greek Plays; Champlin's Demosthenes.

HEBREW.—Stuart's Rœdiger's Grammar; Gesenius' Lexicon; Biblia Hebraica.

DEPARTMENT OF BELLES-LETTRES.

Blair's Rhetoric, (University Edition); Whately's Logic; Wayland's Political Economy; Smith's Grecian History; Liddell's Rome; Clark's English History; American History.

DEPARTMENT OF MATHEMATICS.

Robinson's Algebra, (University Edition); Davies' Legendre; Davies' Surveying; Davies' Analytical Geometry; Olmstead's Natural Philosophy; Olmstead's Astronomy.

DEPARTMENT OF NATURAL SCIENCE.

Silliman's Chemistry; Cutter's Physiology; Wood's Botany; Lyell's Geology; Butler's Analogy; Dana's Mineralogy; Agassiz & Gould's Zoology; Somerville's Physical Geography.

DEPARTMENT OF METAPHYSICS.

Walker's Reid on the Intellectual Powers; Sir William Hamilton's Philosophy, (Wight's Edition); Stewart's Active and Moral Powers; Alexander's Moral Science; Haven's Mental Philosophy.

DEPARTMENT OF RELIGIOUS INSTRUCTION.

English Bible; Hodge's, Alexander's, or Jacobus' Notes; Greek Testament; Robinson's Greek Harmony; Old Testament Hebrew; Septuagint; Westminster Catechism; General Assembly's Psalm and Hymn Book; Paley's Natural Theology; Coleman's Sacred Geography.

SCIENTIFIC DEPARTMENT.

The three years' course of English, Mathematical and Scientific instruction pursued in this Department, embraces all that is included in the College Scheme, except the Classical Languages. Such as desire it, however, may pursue the study of Latin or French, in connection with a Scientific Course. We do not recommend it in any sense an equivalent for a thorough Classical Course; nor is it intended for mere boys, since the subjects which it includes are entirely above their capacity; but to young men who have obtained a respectable Common School education, including the elements of Algebra, and who have not time nor means to prosecute a Classical Course, this system of Studies will, it is hoped, commend itself as solid, comprehensive, and practical. Those who shall complete the Scientific Course, will receive a Diploma certifying the extent of their attainments.

COLLEGE YEAR.—EXAMINATIONS.

The *College Year* is divided into two Terms. The First Term begins on the last Wednesday of August, and continues 16 weeks. The Second Term begins on the first Wednesday of January, and continues 24 weeks. The Annual Commencement occurs on Thursday before the 25th of June.

It is of great importance that Students attend from the very beginning of the Term. In most cases, the loss of a few weeks, or even days, seriously affects the future standing of the Pupil. Absence during Term time, without special leave, is prohibited.*

Public Examinations will be held, hereafter, only at the close of the College Year, when the Freshmen and the Junior Classes will be examined on the studies of the preceding year, and the Sophomore and Senior Classes upon those of the two preceding years. These last examinations will be *final* for the studies pursued in those years. All the examinations will be *thorough* and *rigid*; and will be conducted, chiefly, by the use of

---

*Parents are respectfully advised to give their sons no such permisson to be absent, except in case of NECESSITY.

written questions, prepared by the Faculty and the Examining Committee, covering the whole field of study prosecuted during a given period, and entirely unknown to the Student until the moment of examination. These questions must be answered in writing before the Committee, and correct answers to a definite portion of them will be the passport of admission to a higher standing. Similar examinations, of a briefer and less decisive character, however, and by way of preparation for the final trial, may be conducted privately, at the pleasure of the Faculty.

RELIGIOUS INSTRUCTION AND SERVICES.

The attention of a Christian community is respectfully invited to the system of Biblical Instruction which forms a characteristic feature of our course of study. The Grammar School Classes recite statedly in the English Bible; and every College Class has a daily or tri-weekly recitation in the Greek Testament, or the Hebrew. Proficiency in these, as in other studies, is tested by the usual examinations. In addition to this, Biblical Geography and Antiquities, Ecclesiastical History, Natural Theology, and the Analogy of Religion, Natural and Revealed, to the constitution and course of Nature, are carefully and faithfully studied. There is also a Bible or Catechetical exercise on Sabbath mornings; a public service on Sabbath afternoons, appropriated to the Students; and daily morning prayers. The Students are expected to attend the Sabbath morning services of the congregation worshiping in the Chapel, or of some other congregation in the vicinity, if their parents prefer any of the latter. The Methodist and United Presbyterian Churches have regular services in or near the village.

An experiment of several years in this Institution, has established the fact that the daily study of God's Word by no means interferes with, but rather promotes, sound and comprehensive attainments in other branches of knowledge.

ADMISSION.

Candidates for admission into the Freshmen Class, are examined in Arithmetic and Algebra; Ancient and Modern Geography; the English, Latin, and Greek Grammars; Cæsar's Commentaries, and Greek Reader; or what is equivalent to these attainments. They must furnish testimonials of good character, and, if from another College, must bring certificates of honorable dismission. Candidates for high standing are examined upon that part of the course already studied by the Class which they propose to enter.

No one can be admitted to the Freshmen Class until he has completed his fourteenth year; nor to an advanced standing without a proportional increase of age.

"Before a Student shall be admitted to actual standing in any Class, he shall present to the President a receipt from the Treasurer, showing that he has complied with the Statutes relating to College Charges and Scholarships.

N.B. The regular Examination for admission into College, commences on the Monday preceding the beginning of each Term.

COURSE OF INSTRUCTION.

PREPARATORY DEPARTMENT.

Andrew's Latin Lessons, Grammar, Reader, and Exercises; Andrew's Cæsar; Butler and Sturgus' Sallust; Crosby's Greek Grammar and Lessons; Classical and Biblical Geography; Arithmetic; Robinson's Algebra, (University Edition); English Bible.

SCIENTIFIC DEPARTMENT.

FIRST YEAR.

Algebra, completed; Plane Geometry; Plane Trigonometry; Surveying and Navigation; History; English Bible; Historical Books; Sacred Geography. Linear Drawing, Extra.

SECOND YEAR.

Solid Geometry; Spherical Trigonometry, and its Applications; Analytical Geometry; Natural Philosophy, and Astronomy; Rhetoric, Logic, and Political Economy; English Bible; Poetical Books.

THIRD YEAR.

Zoology; Anatomy and Physiology; Botany; Physical Geography; Chemistry; Geology; Natural Theology, and Butler's Analogy; Psychology, and Ethics; English Bible.

COLLEGIATE DEPARTMENT.

FRESHMEN CLASS.

FIRST SESSION.

Greek Harmony of the Gospels,.....................Robinson.
Biblical Antiquities,.............................Nevin.
Virgil, ...Cooper.
Roman Antiquities,................................Bojesin.
Xenophon's Anabasis,..............................Boise.
Plane Geometry,...................................Davies' Legendre.

SECOND SESSION.

Greek Harmony, (continued),.......................
Virgil, (continued),..............................
Anabasis, (continued),............................
Grecian Antiquities,..............................Bojesen.
Plane Trigonometry,...............................Davies' Legendre.

THIRD SESSION.

Greek Harmony, (completed),.......................
Livy, ...
Xenophon's Memorabilia,...........................Robbins.
Grecian Antiquities,..............................
Latin and Greek Exercises,........................
Surveying and Navigation,.........................Davies.

SOPHOMORE CLASS.

FIRST SESSION.

Greek Testament, (Acts),..........................Owen.
Livy, (continued),................................
Homer's Odyssey,..................................Owen.
Greek History,....................................Smith.
Solid Geometry,...................................Davies' Legendre.
Zoology, ...Agassiz & Gould.

SECOND SESSION.

Greek Testament, (Epistles),......................
Horace,...Lincoln.
Homer's Odyssey, (continued),.....................
Roman History,....................................Liddell.
Plane Trigonometry, (reviewed),...................
Spherical Trigonometry, with its Applications,....Davies' Legendre.
Physical Geography,...............................Sommerville.

THIRD SESSION.

Greek Testament, (Epistles),........................
Horace,..
Plato's Gorgias,................................Woolsey.
English History,............................Clark and Moffat.
Analytical Geometry,...........................Davies.
Botany,.......................................Wood.
Latin and Greek Exercises throughout the year,........

JUNIOR CLASS.

FIRST SESSION.

Hebrew Grammar and Hebrew—Genesis, (optional),....
Tacitus' Histories,............................Tyler.
Plato's Gorgias, (continued),....................
Natural Philosophy,...........................Olmsted.
Rhetoric,.....................................Blair.
Anatomy and Physiology,......................Cutter.

SECOND SESSION.

Hebrew, (Genesis continued,).....................
Tacitus, (continued),............................
Demosthenes De Corona,.......................Champlin.
Natural Philosophy, (continued),................
Logic,.......................................Whately.
Light and Heat,..............................Bird.

THIRD SESSION.

Hebrew, (Psalms),...............................
Cicero's Tusculan Disputations................Anthon.
Demosthenes De Corona, (completed),.............
Astronomy,...................................Olmsted.
Political Economy,...........................Wayland.
Electricity,.................................Bird.

SENIOR CLASS.

FIRST SESSION.

Select Portions of the Hebrew Bible,..............
Intellectual Philosophy,......................Walker's Reid.
Cicero's Tusculan Disputations, (continued).......
Greek Tragedies,..............................Woolsey.
Chemistry,....................................Silliman.
Mathematics reviewed,............................

SECOND SESSION.

Select Hebrew, (continued),..........................
Intellectual Philosophy,............................Hamilton.
Chemistry and Mineralogy,..........................Dana.
Natural Theology,..................................Paley.
Greek Tragedies,...................................Woolsey.
Juvenal,...Anthon.

THIRD SESSION.

Hebrew, (continued),................................
Butler's Analogy,..................................Wilson's Edition.
Moral Science,.....................................Wayland.
Geology,...Lyell's Elements.
Review of Latin,...................................
Æschylus' Prometheus Vintus,.......................Woolsey.
Mathematics Reviewed,..............................

N.B. The Text-Books needed for any part of the College Course, may be procured at the Hanover Book-Store.

EXPENSES.

The entire Expenditures of a Student need not much exceed $150, viz:

Tuition, (Contingent Fee, per Year, $5,) $30 00
Boarding with private families, and furnished room, at $2 00 to
    $2 50 per week, ... : . . . . 78 00 to 97 50
Fuel, Lights, Washing, &c., ... 15 00
Books, &c., ... 5 00 to 10 00

Boarding in Clubs will cost from seventy-five cents to one dollar and twenty-five cents per week; and some board themselves even at a lower rate. The cost of clothing, and the amount spent as pocket money, will vary with the taste and habits of the Student, and with the wishes of his parents. As a general rule, the more money allowed to a young man, beyond what is strictly necessary, the less likely is he to reflect honor upon his Parents and Instructors. Although Hanover presents comparatively few temptations to extravagance; yet parents are earnestly advised to require of their sons a detailed account of their expenditures, and peremptorily refuse the payment of any debt incurred by them without a written permission. It is also recommended that the funds of young pupils be deposited with some one of the Faculty, and expended as he may direct. The younger Students are required to board where the Faculty may direct, and where they may exercise a more careful and frequent supervision.

N. B. Students placed upon Scholarships by the Faculty, are relieved in part, or wholly, as the case may be, from the payment of Tuition Fees. The Contingent Fee is required of those on Scholarships the same as others. This is now $2 00 for the first Term, and $3 00 for the second.

DISCIPLINE.

A record is kept by the Faculty, in which is entered weekly, the grade of scholarship of the Student, his absence from the exercises of the Institution, and such other facts as are worthy of notice with respect to his general deportment. From this record a report is made out at the end of each Session, and sent to the Parent or Guardian of each Student. In case of deficiency in scholarship, negligence in study, irregularity in attendance upon the exercises of the Institution, or improper conduct, the Student will be privately admonished, and the Parent or Guardian will be promptly informed of the fact.

The object of this arrangement is to keep Parents and Guardians accurately informed with regard to their sons and wards in this Institution, and thus to secure their co-operation with the Faculty in a mild system of discipline. Whenever it is ascertained that a Student is deriving no advantage from his connection with the Institution, or is pursuing a course injurious to himself or fellow-students, the Faculty will take decisive action, and his Parent or Guardian will be promptly addressed on the subject, and requested to remove him from the Institution.

SCHOLARSHIPS.

The endowment of this Institution is in the form of Scholarships, of which the Board has established several sorts. The sum of $400 paid, or secured to the Corporation by note payable within five years, and bearing six per cent. interest in advance upon principal remaining unpaid, purchases for the owner, his heirs and assigns, a perpetual right to the tuition of one Scholar, in Hanover College. The sum of $200 paid, or subscribed under similar conditions secures the right to twenty years' tuition; after which time the Scholarship is subject to the disposal of the Board for the gratuitous education of candidates for the Gospel Ministry. A Church Scholarship of $200, secures to the Church so contributing, a perpetual right to the tuition of one Student, who shall be a member of that Church, and appointed by the Session. A Presbyterial Scholarship of $200 secures a similar right to a Presbytery, in behalf of pupils who shall be candidates for the Ministry under its care. *Principal* paid on these Scholarships is invested by the Corporation in some safe and productive Stock, and the *Interest only* can be expended for the support of the College.

Every person applying for admission as a beneficiary of a Scholarship under the control of the donors, shall present to the Treasurer, at the beginning of each Term, *a written Certificate* from those controlling the Scholarship, of his right to such benefit; — when, after paying whatever interest may be due on said Scholarship, he shall receive an acknowledgment of his right, which he shall lodge with the President.

"The Scholarships subject to the disposal of the Corporation, may be occupied by such applicants as the Faculty may select, after inquiry into their circumstances, character, and attainments; the preference being, *ceteris paribus*, to those who give the best evidence of scholarship.

"There shall at no time be more than one Student upon each Scholarship."

ACCOMMODATIONS.

The community system of Boarding in Commons, or of rooming in large Lodging Halls, is not adopted in Hanover. Arrangements are made to accommodate the Students with board and rooms in respectable private families, where the number together can never be large; and where all shall be brought under domestic influence.

SETTLEMENT OF ACCOUNTS.

No Diploma nor honorable dismission shall be granted until the Student shall exhibit a Receipt of Settlement of all his bills for boarding, room, and washing.

DEGREES.

No Degrees are conferred in Course. Candidates for Literary Honors are reported to the Board upon their ascertained or acknowledged merits.

SOCIETIES, LIBRARIES, &c.

There are two Societies connected with the College, the UNION LITERARY and the PHILALETHEAN, whose Libraries number each about twelve hundred volumes.

There is also a SOCIETY OF RELIGIOUS INQUIRY, which has begun to collect a Library, Maps, &c., and which, in connection with another Association formed for the purpose, sustains a valuable Reading Room.

The College Library contains near three thousand well selected volumes and is accessible to the Students.

The Cabinet contains several thousand specimens in Mineralogy and and Geology.

The friends of the College are advised that contributions to the Library, to the Cabinet, or to the Laboratory, are much needed and will be thankfully received.

PROHIBITED SECRET SOCIETIES.

The following order was passed by the Board of Trustees, in July, 1858, viz:

"*Resolved*, That this Board disapprove of the existence among the Students of Hanover College, of any Society or Association of which the Faculty are not *ex-officio* Members, and will not permit the public exhibition of any such Society."

LOCATION, BUILDINGS, &c.

The Village of Hanover is situated upon an elevated bluff of the Ohio River, six miles below Madison, Indiana, in a region of remarkable salubrity and natural beauty. The village and neighborhood are characterized by morality, and the absence of all the ordinary temptations to vice and idleness. The Ohio River, and the Railways from Madison, New Albany, and Cincinnati, place Hanover within twenty-four hours of all the principal points in Indiana, Kentucky, Western Ohio, and Eastern Illinois. A turnpike from Madison to Hanover, renders the village easy of access at all seasons of the year.

Hanover College is controlled by a Board of Trustees;—one-half of whom are appointed by the Board itself, and the other half by the Synods of Indiana and Northern Indiana.

The Board purchased, some years ago, a farm of two hundred acres, lying between the Village and the Ohio River, upon a beautiful point of which,—overlooking the River from an elevation of four hundred feet,—they have erected a commodious College edifice, now completed and occupied. The new College consists of a center building nearly eighty feet square, with lateral and transverse wings. The whole length is about two hundred feet. It contains no dormitories for Students,—an undesirable provision,—but affords ample and convenient Halls, Library, Cabinet, Lecture, and Recitation Rooms, and a spacious Chapel.

The building commands an exceedingly diversified view of the River, for six miles up and ten miles down its course.

THE TWENTY-NINTH

ANNUAL CATALOGUE AND CIRCULAR

OF

HANOVER COLLEGE,

HANOVER, IND.

JUNE, 1861.

MADISON, INDIANA:
WM. P. LEVY & CO'S PRINTING AND BINDING ESTABLISHMENT.
1861.

THE TWENTY-NINTH

ANNUAL CATALOGUE AND CIRCULAR

OF

HANOVER COLLEGE,

HANOVER, IND.

JUNE 1861.

MADISON, INDIANA:
WM. P. LEVY & CO'S PRINTING AND BINDING ESTABLISHMENT.
1861.

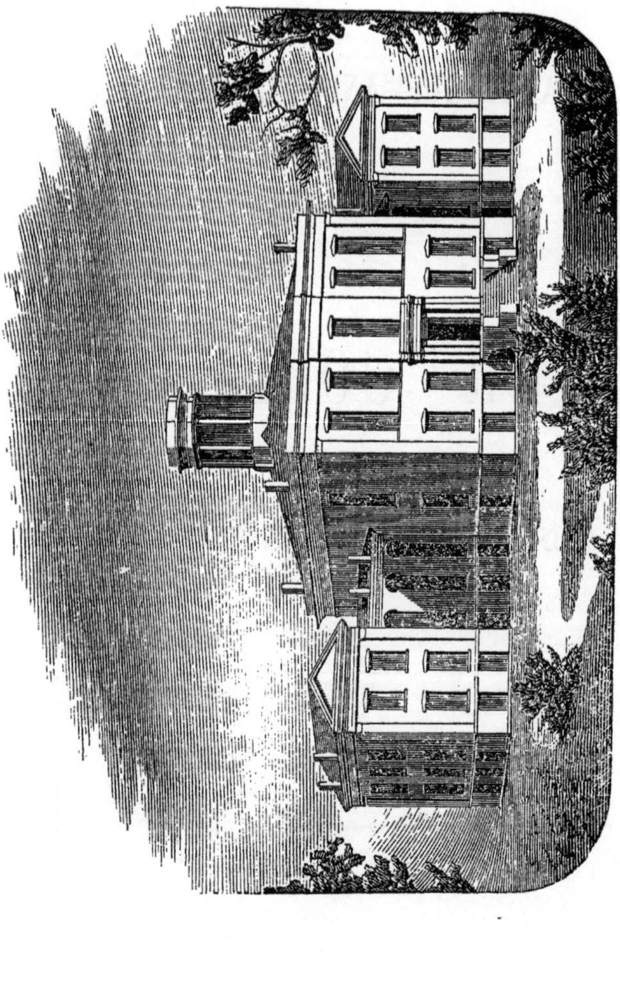

CATALOGUE.

BOARD OF TRUSTEES.

                                                                                           TERM EXPIRES.

Bd. DR. P. S. SHIELDS, New Albany..................................1864.
Bd. JOSEPH PIERCE ESQ., Valparaiso,.............................1864.
Bd. DR, ANDREW SPEAR, Hanover,..................,,................1864.
Bd. REV. WILLIAM Y. ALLEN, Rockville,........................1864.
S. S. REV ISAAC W. MONFORT. Pleasant Ridge,O............1864.
S. S. REV. J. W. BLYTHE. Hanover,.................................1864.
N. S. THOMAS P. GORDON, D. D. Terrehaute,......................1864.
N. S. REV. ROBERT IRWIN, Sen., Monticello,.....................1864.
Bd. REV. D. D McKEE, Hanover,..1861
Bd. REV. SAMUEL NEWELL, Paris, Ill.,...............................1861.
Bd. A. R. FORSYTH, ESQ., Greensburg,.................................1861.
Bd. JESSE L. WILLIAMS, ESQ., Fort Wayne.........................1861.
S. S. JAMES H, McCAMBELL, ESQ.. Jeffersonville...............1861.
S. S. REV, LOWMAN HAWES. Madison,..................................1861,
N. S. REV. E. W. WRIGHT, Delphi,.....................................1861.
N. S. REV. W. M. DONALDSON. Ossian,..............................1861.
Bd. JAMES M. RAY, ESQ Indianapolis..................................1862.
Bd. ROBERT DEAN, Hanover,..1862.
Bd. HON. C. E. WALKER, Madison,......................................1862.
Bd. COL. JAMES BLAKE. Indianapolis,.................................1862.
S. S. SILAS C. DAY, ESQ. New Albany,..............................1862.
S. S. REV. S. E. BARR, Livonia,..1862.
N. S. REV. C K. THOMPSON, Thorntown,.............................1862.
N. S. REV. T. M, CUNNINGHAM, Chicago, Ill.....................1862.
Bd. JOHN KING. ESQ., Madison,..1863.
Bd. REV. J. G. MONFORT, D. D., Cincinnatt O.,...................1863.
Bd   HON. W. McKEE, DUNN, Madison,..................................1863.
S. S. REV. JAMES WOOD, D. D.. Hanover............................1863.
S. S. REV. F. P. MORTON, Vincenns,..................................1863.
S. S. JOHN H. VAN VANNUYS; ESQ., Franklin....................1863.
N. S. REV. J. C. BROWN, Valparaiso, D D.........................1863.
N. S. REV. THOMAS McINTYRE, Indianapolis,.....................1863.

OFFICERS OF THE BOARD.

JAMES M. RAY, ESQ., *President.* REV. D. D. McKEE, *Secetary.*
REV. JAMES WOOD, D. D., *Treasurer.*

EXECUTIVE COMMITTEE.

HON. W. McKEE DUNN, JOHN KING, ESQ.,
REV. JAMES WOOD, D. D., REV. J. W. BLYTHE,
REV. D. D. McKEE.

AUDITING COMMITTEE.

HON. W. McKEE DUNN. HON. C. E. WALKER.

FACULTY.

REV. JAMES WOOD, D. D., President,
  Professor of Biblical Instruction, Pyschology, Logic, and Ethics.

REV. S. HARRISON THOMSON, A. M.,
  Professor of Mathematics, Mechanical Philosophy, and Astronomy.

MINARD STURGUS, A. M.,
  Professor of the Latin Languages and Literature.

REV. JOSHUA B. GARRITT, A. M.
  Professor of the Greek Languages and Literature.

REV. J. W. SCOTT, D. D.
  Professor of Natural Science.

REV. JOSHUA B. GARRITT, A. M.,
  Librarian.

WILLIAM BROWN
  Janitor.

UNDERGRADUATES.

SENIORS.
Solomon Frederick Denton..........................Cincinnati, O.
Samuel Henry Howe....................................Flemingsburg, Ky.
S. M. Irwin..South Salem, O.
Adam J. Johnson..Spades.
Stephen Paul Lee...Saluda.
Edward Fortesene Reid...............................Kinross, Scotland.
Benjamin F. Simpson..................................Vernon.
William Henry Smith,..................................Vincennes.

JUNIORS.
Robert Coyner...South Salem, O.
Moses Fell Dunn,...Bedford.
George Monfort Gilchrist,...........................Vinton, Iowa.
George Proffitt Huckeby..............................Rome.
Howard Campbell Laforce..........................Bedford.
George Meriwether McCampbell................Jeffersonville.
Samuel T. McClure......................................Vincennes.
Elias Riggs Monfort....................................Glendale, O.
James Trimble Patterson............................Delphi.
William Crawford Pogue.............................Mace.
William Henry Sawtelle...............................Binghamton, N.Y.
Levi M. Schofield..Newport, Ky.
Henry Clifton Thomson...............................Hanover.
Eugene C. Warren.......................................Louisville Ky
John C. Youngken.......................................Friendsville, Ill.

SOPHOMORES.
. W. Alexander...Vincennes.
William E. Brown...Valparaiso.
Henry Clay Donnell.....................................Greenville, Ill.
Theodore C. Fitch.......................................Glendale, O.

W. H. Fullenwider..Waveland.
Augustus Adolphus Joss,.....................................Constantine, M.
James Woods Kyle,...Hanover.
John D. Miller..Hanover.
Francis C. Monfort..Glendale, O.
Amos W Patterson..Hanover.
Emanuel N. Pires...Jacksonville, Ill.
Eberle Thompson..Greensburg.
Benjamin W. Tucker..N. Philadelphia.
John Weston...Galena. Ill

FRESHMEN.

William Chamberlain..Hanover.
Robert Sharon Dean...Hanover.
James Albert Dean...Hanover.
Josiah Daugherty..Ladoga.
Ebenezer Nelson Gelpin..Hanover.
Isaac A. Helm...Rushville.
William Henderson Hillis......................................Madison.
Charles Lewis Holstein..Madison.
William Dunn Hynes...Greenville, Ill.
James Burke Hynes...Greenville, Ill.
John Kerns..Hanover.
Peter H. Kemper McComb.....................................Hanover.
Kearsly Greer McComb..Hanover.
William A. Patton..Spruce Hill Pa.
Arthur Rose...Hanover.
Richard Wasson Sipe...Swanville.
Willis P. Storms...Pleasant Hill, Mo.
Martin Van Buren Vanarsdale...............................Washington.
Robert M. Webster..Tallahoma, Iowa.

SCIENTIFIC DEPARTMENT.

THIRD YEAR.

Samuel J. Gelpin..Hanover.
John B. Richardson..Shelbyville, Ky.
John W. Shrewsbury..Madison.
Solon McCollough Tilford......................................Kent.

SECOND YEAR.

Felix Jennerette Brandt..............................Hanover.
Samuel W. Crothers....................................Hanover.
Alexander Hamilton...................................Morganfield, Ky.
Robt. D. P. McDermett................................Dallas, Texas.
Wallace Estill McHenry...............................Owensboro, Ky.
J. F. Scott..Clear Spring.
James Wilson Spear,..................................Hanover.
Albert Verhoeff......................................Grandview.
Thomas Hart Woodward.................................Hanover.

FIRST YEAR.

John R. Armstrong ....Jeffersonville.
Robert J. Brackenridge...............................Texana, Texas.
Charles H. Bruce.....................................Ladoga.
William McGuffy Casterline...........................Liberty.
John P. Cravens......................................Madison.
George Washington Fitch..............................Hanover.
John Thomas Fitch....................................Hanover.
Robert Jamieson......................................Rising Sun.
John W. Jones..Indianapolis.
William L. McKnight..................................N. Philadelphia.
James H. McMillen....................................Logansport.
Willis H. Ryker......................................Manville.
Burtney Oscar Ruley..................................Oregon, Mo.
Homer Sering...Madison.
William H. Simmons...................................Texana, Texas.
William Butler Sturgus...............................Hanover.
William B. Wilson....................................Elizabethtown.

PREPARATORY DEPARTMENT.

SENIORS.

Robert C. Hamilton...................................Greensburg.
John Hunt..Columbus.
Calvin S. Hunter ....Symmes Cor., O.
V. L. Lee..Saluda.
Jeremiah Long..Bardolph, Ill.
Daniel Newton McKee..................................Vincennes.

Alfred McKeeham..Pierceton.
Preston McKinney..Livonia.
Robert M. Miller..Hanover.
Edward Quinche..Galena, Ill.
Samuel E. Smock..Acton.
Isaac F. Winston..PleasantRidge,O

JUNIORS.

J. Calvin Eastman..Hanover.
John Calvin Fontts..Scott, O,
William Armstrong Gilchrist...................................Worthsville.
Ebenezer Gordon..New Lexington.
Samuel W. E. McLean..North Liberty O.
John Perry Seawright..Thornton.
Isaac P. Spining..Highland, Ka.
Andrew Stevenson..Greenville, Ill.
Jesse Warren Tilford..Kent.
James Walker..Washington.
John C. Woods..Franklin.
James Monfort Woods..Franklin.

SUMMARY.

Seniors....................	8.	Scientific, 2 year....................	9.
Juniors....................	15.	Scientific, 1 year....................	17.
Sophmores................	14.	Senior Preparatory................	12.
Freshmen................	19.	Junior Preparatory................	12.
Scientific 3 year........	4.	Total..........................	110.

TEXT BOOKS.

DEPARTMENT OF LANGUAGES.

LATIN,—Andrews' Grammar and Reader; Andrews' or Leverett,s Lexicon; Cooks & Schem's or Andrews' Cæsar; Cooper's Virgil; Bojesen's Roman Antiquities; Butlers & Sturgus, Sallust; Lincoln,s Livy; Lincoln's Horace; Tyler's Tacitus; Chase's Tusculan Disputations.

GREEK—Crosby's Grammar and Lessons; Liddell & Scott's, or Pickering's Lexicon; Owen's, or Boise's Anabasis; Bojesen's Grecian Antiquities; Owen's Homer; Woolsey's Greek Plays; Champlin's Demosthenes.

HEBREW—Stuart's Rœdiger's Grammar; Gesenius' Lexicon; Biblia Hebraica.

DEPARTMENT OF BELLES-LETTERS.

Blair's Rhetoric, (University Edition); Whately's Logic; Wayland's Political Economy; Smith's Grecian History; Liddell's Rome; Clark's English History; American History and the Constitution of the U. S. A.

DEPARTMENT OF MATHEMATICS.

Robinson's Algebra, (University Edition); Davies' Legendre, Davies' Surveying, Davies' Analytical Geometry, Olmstead's Natural Philosophy; Olmstead's Astronomy

DEPARTMENT OF NATURAL SCIENCE.

Silliman's Chemistry; Cutter,s Physiology; Wood's Botany; Lyell's Geology; Butler's Analogy; Dana's Mineralogy; Agassiz & Gould's Zoology, Somerville's Physical Geography.

DEPARTMENT OF METAPHYSICS.

Walker's Reid on the Intellectual Powers; Sir William Hamilton's Philosophy, (Wiget's Edition); Stewart's Active and Moral Powers; Alexander's Moral Science; Haven's Mental Philosophy.

DEPARTMENT OF RELIGIOUS INSTRUCTION.

English Bible, Hodge's, Alexander's or Jacobus' Notes; Greek Testament, Robinson's Greek Harmony; Old Testament Hebrew; Septuagint; Westminister Catechism; General Assembly's Psalm and Hymn Book; Paley's Natural Theology; Coleman's Sacred Geography; Alexander's Evidences of Christianity.

SCIENTIFIC DEPARTMENT.

The three years' course of English, Mathematical and Scientific instruction pursued in this Department, embraces all that is included in the College Scheme, except the Classical Languages. Such as desire it, however, may pursue the study of Latin or French, in connection with a Scientific Course. We do not recommend it in any sense an equivalent for a thorough Classical Course; nor is it intended for mere boys, since the subjects which it includes are entirely above their capacity; but to young men who have obtained a respectable Common School education, including the elements of Algebra, and who have not time nor means to prosecute a Classical Course, this system of Studies will, it is hoped, commend itself as solid, comprehensive, and practical. Those who shall complete the Scientific Course, will receive a Diploma certifying the extent of their attainments.

COLLEGE YEAR.—EXAMINATIONS.

The *College Year* is divided into 2 Terms. The First Term begins on the Wednesday before the 25th of August, and continues 16 weeks. The Second Term begins on the first Wednesday of January, and continues 24 weeks. The Annual Commencement occurs on Thursday before the 25th of June.

It is *of great importance* that Students attend from the very beginning of the Term. In most cases, the loss of a few weeks, or even days, seriously affects the future standing of the Pupil. Absence during Term time, without special leave, is prohibited.*

Public Examinations will be held, hereafter, only at the close of the College Year, when the Freshmen and the Junior Classes will be examined on the studies of the preceding year, and the Sophomore and Senior Classes upon those of the two preceding years. These last examinations will be *final* for the studies pursued in those years. All the examinations will be *thorough* and *rigid*; and will be conducted, chiefly, by the use of written questions, prepared by the Faculty and the Examining Commit-

---

*Parents are respectfully advised to give their sons no such permisson to be absent, except in case of NECESSITY.

tee, covering the whole field of study prosecuted during a given period, and entirely unknown to the Student until the moment of examination. These questions must be answered in writing before the Committee, and correct answers to a definite portion of them will be the passport of admission to a higher standing. Similar examinations, of a briefer and less decisive character, however, and by way of preparation for the final trial, may be conducted privately, at the pleasure of the Faculty.

RELIGIOUS INSTRUCTION AND SERVICES.

The attention of a Christian community is respectfully invited to the system of Biblical Instruction which forms a characteristic feature of our course of study. The Grammar School Classes recite steadily in the English Bible; and every College Class has a daily or tri-weekly recitation in the Greek Testament, or the Hebrew. Proficiency in these, as in other studies, is tested by the usual examinations. In addition to this, Biblical Geography and Antiquities, Ecclesiastical History, Natural Theology, and the Analogy of Religion, Natural and Revealed, to the constitution and course of Nature, are carefully and faithfully studied. There is also a Bible or Catechetical exercise on Sabbath mornings; a public service on Sabbath afternoons, appropriated to the Students; and daily morning prayers. The Students are expected to attend the Sabbath morning services of the congregation worshiping in the Chapel, or of some other congregation in the vicinity, if their parents prefer any of the latter. The Methodist, Associate, and United Presbyterian Churches have regular services in or near the village.

An experiment of several years in this Institution, has established the fact that the daily study of God's Word by no means interferes with, but rather promotes, sound and comprehensive attainments in other branches of knowledge.

ADMISSION.

Candidates for admission into the Freshmen Class, are examined in Arithmetic and Algebra; Ancient and Modern Geography; the English, Latin, and Greek Grammars; Cæsar's Commentaries, and Greek Reader; or what is equivalent to these attainments. They must furnish testimonials of good character, and, if from another College, must bring certificates of honorable dismission. Candidates for higher standing are examined upon that part of the course already studied by the Class which they propose to enter.

No one can be admitted to the Freshmen Class until he has completed his fourteenth year; nor to an advanced standing without a proportional increase of age.

Before a student shall be admitted to actual standing in any Class, he shall present to the President a receipt from the Treasurer, showing that he has complied with the Statutes relating to College Charges and Scholarships.

N. B. The regular examination for admission into College, commences on the Monday preceding the beginning of each Term.

COURSE OF INSTRUCTION.

PREPARATORY DEPARTMENT.

Andrew's Latin Lessons, Grammar, Reader, and Exercises; Andrew's Cæsar; Butler and Sturgus' Sallust; Crosby's Greek Grammar and Lessons; Classical and Biblical Geography; Arithmetic; Robinson's Algebra (University Edition); English Bible.

SCIENTIFIC DEPARTMENT.

FIRST YEAR.

Algebra, completed; Plane Geometry; Plane Trigonometry, Surveying and Navigation; History; English Bible; Historical Books, Sacred Geography. Linear Drawing, Extra.

SECOND YEAR.

Solid Geometry; Spherical Trigonometry, and its Applications; Analytical Geometry; Natural Philosophy Astronomy, Rhetoric, Logic, and Political Economy, English Bible; Poetical Books; Chemistry, Light, Heat, Electricity.

THIRD YEAR.

Anatomy and Physiology; Botany. Chemistry, Mineralogy, Geology; Natural Theology, Evidence of Christianity Butler's Analogy Psychology, and Ethics; English Bible, Constitution of the U. S. A.

COLLEGIATE DEPARTMENT.

FRESHMEN CLASS.
FIRST SESSION.
Greek Harmony of the Gospels............................Robinson.
Biblical Antiquities...Nevin.
Virg l ....Cooper;
Roman Antiquities..Bojesin.
Xenophon's Anabasis,..Boise.
Plane Geometry,..Davies' Legendre.

SECOND SESSION.
Greek Harmony, (continued),.................................
Virgil (continued)..
Anabasis, (continued),..
Grecian Antiquities,..Bojesen.
Plane Trigonometry...Davies' Legendre.

THIRD SESSION.
Greek Harmony, (completed)..................................
Livy..
Xenophon's Memorabilia..Robbins.
Grecian Antiquities..
Latin and Greek Exercises.....................................
Surveying and Navigation......................................Davies.

SOPHOMORE CLASS.
FIRST SESSION.
Greek Testament, (Acts),......................................Owen.
Livy; (continued)..
Homer's Odyssey..Owen.
Greek History..Smith.
Solid Geometry..Davies' Legendre.

SECOND SESSION.
Greek Testament, (Epistles)....................................
Horace..Lincoln.
Homer's Odyssey; (continued)................................
Roman History,...Liddell.
Plane Trigonometry' (reviewed)..............................
Spherical Trigonometry, with its Applications............Davies' Legendre.

THIRD SESSION.
Greek Testament, (Epistles)....................................
Horace..

Plato's Gorgias..Woolsey.
English History..Clark and Moffat.
Analytical Geometry..Davies.
Latin and Greek exercises throughout the year.......

JUNIOR CLASS.
FIRST SESSION.
Hebrew Grammar and Hebrew—Genesis, (optional)...
Tacitus' Histories..Tyler.
Plato's Gorgias, (continued)..............................
Natural Philosophy..Olmsted.
Rhetoric..Blair.
Chemistry...Silliman.

SECOND SESSION.
Hebrew (Genesis continued)..............................
Tacitus, (continued)..
Demosthenes De Corona...................................Champlin.
Natural Philosophy (continued)........................
Logic..Whately.
Chemistry (continued).....................................Bird.

THIRD SESSION.
Hebrew, (Psalms)...
Cicero's Tusculan Disputations.........................Anthon.
Demosthenes De Corona, (completed)..............
Astronomy..Olmsted.
Political Economy..Wayland.
Electricity...Bird.
Light..

SENIOR CLASS
FIRST SESSION.
Anatomy and Physiology..................................Cutter.
Select Portions of the Hebrew Bible.................
Intellectual Philosophy....................................Walker's Reid.
Cicero's Tusculan Disputations, (continued).........
Greek Tragedies...Woolsey.
Chemistry, Lectures...
Mathematics reviewed....................................

SECOND SESSION.
Select Hebrew, (continued)..............................
Intellectual Philosophy....................................Hamilton.
Chemistry, Lectures...
Minerology..Dana.

Botany...Wood.
Natural Theology..............................Paley.
Moral Science...................................Wayland.
Greek Tragedies................................Woolsey.
Juvenal...Anthon.

THIRD SESSION.

Hebrew, (continued).............................
Butler's Analogy..............................Wilson's Edition.
Botany, (continued).............................
Geology..Lyell's Elements.
Review of Latin..................................
Æschylus' Prometheus Vintus................Woolsey.
Mathematics Reviewed...........................
Constitution of the U. S. A.,...................

N. B. The Text-Books needed for any part of the College Course, may be procured at the Hanover Book Store.

EXPENSES.

The entire Expenditures of a Student need not much exceed $150, viz:
Tuition, per year...$20 00
Contingent fee... 5 00
These are required in advance by the session.—1st session $.4 second session $2'.
Boarding with private families, and furnished room, at $2 00 to
$2 50 per week,.....................................78 00 to 97 50
Fuel, Light, Washing &c.....................................15 00
Books, &c.,.....................................5 00 to 10 00

Boarding in Clubs will cost from seventy-five cents to one dollar and twenty-five cents per week; and some board themselves even at a lower rate. The cost of clothing, and the amount spent as pocket money, will vary with the taste and habit of the Student, and with the wishes of his parents. As a general rule the more money allowed to a young man, beyond what is strictly necessary, the less likely he is to reflect honor opon his Parents and Instructors. Although Hanover presents comparativaly few temptations to extravagance, yet parents are earnestly advised to require of their sons a detailed account of their expenditures, and peremptorily refuse the payment of any debt incurred by them without a written permission. It is also recommended that the funds of young pupils be deposited with some one of the Faculty, and expended as he may direct. The younger Students are required to board where the Faculty may direct, and where they may exercise a more careful and frequent supervision.

N. B. Students placed upon Scholarships by the Faculty, are relieved in part, or wholly, as the case may be, from the payment of Tuition Fees. The Contingent Fee is required of those on Scholarships the same as others. This is now $2 00 for the first Term, and $3 00 for the second.

DISCIPLINE.

A record is kept by the Faculty, in which is entered weekly, the grade of scholarship of the Student, his absence from the exercises of the Institution, and such other facts as are worthy of notice with respect to his general deportment. From this record a report is made out at the end of each Session, and sent to the Parent or Guardian of each Student. In case of deficiency in scholarship, negligence in study, irregularity in attendance upon the exercises of the Institution, or improper conduct, the Student will be privately admonished, and the Parent or Guardian will be promptly informed of the fact.

The object of this arrangement is to keep Parents and Guardians accurately informed with regard to their sons and wards in this Institution, and thus to secure their co-operation with the Faculty in a mild system of discipline. Whenever it is ascertained that a Student is deriving no advantage from his connection with the Institution, or is pursuing a course injurious to himself or fellow-students, the Faculty will take decisive action, and his Parent or Guardian will be promptly addressed on the subject, and requested to remove him from the Institution.

SCHOLARSHIPS.

The endowment of this Institution is in the form of Scholarships, of which the Board has established several sorts. The sum of $400 paid, or secured to the Corporation by note payable within five years; and bearing six per cent. interest in advance upon principal remaining unpaid, purchases for the owner, his heirs and assigns, a perpetual right to the tuition of one Scholar, in Hanover College. The sum of $200 paid, or subscribed under similar conditions secures the right to twenty years' tuition; after which time the Scholarship is subject to the disposal of the Board for the gratuitous education of candidates for the Gospel Ministry. A Church Scholarship of $200, secures to the Church so contributing, a perpetual right to the tuition of one Student, who shall be a member of that Church; and appointed by the Session. A Presbyterial Scholarship of $200 secures a similar right to a Presbytery, in behalf of pupils who shall be candidates for the Ministry under its care. Principal paid on these Scholarship is invested by the Corporation in some safe and productive Stock, and the Interest only can be expended for the support of the College.

Every person applying for admission as a beneficiary of a Scholarship under the controll of the donors, shall present to the Treasurer, at the beginning of each Term, a written Certificate from those controlling the Scholarship, of his right to such benefit;—when, after paying whatever interest may be due on said Scholarship, he shall receive an acknowledgment of his right, which he shall lodge with the President.

"The Scholarships subject to the disposal of the Corporation, may be occupied by such applicants as the Faculty may select, after inquiry into their circumstances, character, and attainments, the preference being, ceteris paribus, to those who give the best evidence of Scholarship.

"There shall at no time be more than one Student upon each Scholarship."

ACCOMMODATIONS.

The community system of Boarding in Commons, or of rooming in large Lodging Halls; is not adopted in Hanover. Arrangements are made to accommodate the Students with board and rooms in respectable private families, where the number together can never be large; and where all shall be brought under domestic influence.

SETTLEMENT OF ACCOUNTS.

No Diploma nor honorable dismission shall be granted until the Student shall exhibit a Receipt of Settlement of all his bills for boarding, room, and washing.

DEGREES.

No Degrees are conferred in Course. Candidates for Literary Honors are reported to the Board upon their ascertained or acknowledged merits.

SOCIETIES, LIBRARIES, &c.

There are two Societies connected with the College, the UNION LITERARY and the PHILALETHEAN, whose Libraries number each about twelve hundred volumes.

There is also a SOCIETY OF RELIGIOUS INQUIRY, which has begun to collect a Library, Maps, &c., and which, in connection with another Association formed for the purpose, sustains a valuable Reading Room.

The College Library contains near three thousand well selected volumes and is accessible to the Students.

The Cabinet contains several thousand specimens in Mineralogy and Geology.

The friends of the College are advised that contributions to the Library; to the Cabinet, or to the Laboratory, are much needed and will be thankfully received

PROHIBITED SECRET SOCIETIES.

The following order was passed by the Board of Trustees, in July 1858, viz:

"*Resolved*, That this Board disapprove of the existence among the Students of Hanover College, of any Society or Association of which the Faculty are not *ex officio* Members, and will not permit the public exhibition of any such Society."

LOCATION, BUILDINGS, &c.

The Village of Hanover is situated upon an elevated bluff of the Ohio River, six miles below Madison, Indiana, in a region of remarkable salubrity and natural beauty. The village and neighborhood are characterized by morality, and the absence of all the ordinary temptations to vice, and idleness. The Ohio River, and the Railways from Madison, New Albany, and Cincinnati, place Hanover within twenty-four hours of all the principal points in Indiana, Kentucky, Western Ohio, and Eastern Illinois. A turnpike from Madison to Hanover, renders the village easy of access at all seasons of the year.

Hanover College is controlled by a Board of Trustees; one-half of whom are appointed by the Board itself, and the other half by the Synods of Indiana and Northern Indiana.

The Board purchased, some years ago, a farm of two hundred acres, lying between the Village and the Ohio River, upon a beautiful point of which,—overlooking the River from an elevation of four hundred feet,—they have erected a commodious College edifice, now completed and occupied. The new College consists of a center building nearly eighty feet square, with lateral and transverse wings. The whole length is about two hundred feet. It contains no dormitories for Students,—an undesirable provision,—but affords ample and convenient Halls, Library, Cabinet, Lecture, and Recitation Rooms, and a spacious Chapel.

The building commands an exceedingly diversified view of the River, for six miles up and ten miles down its course. A visitor of large acquaintance with our Country asserts that a more delightful prospect cannot be found in America

FORM OF CONVEYANCES AND BEQUESTS.

The corporate name of this institution is "THE TRUSTEES OF HANOVER COLLEGE."

Donors residing in other States should also designate the place in which the college is located, thus: "*The Trustees of Hanover College, located at Hanover, in the State of Indiana.*"

The friends of Education in Indiana and elsewhere are respectfully solicited to make donations and legacies to this Institution. Since the College was chartered in 1832, about 3,000 have received all or part of their education here, and not less than 800 of these were candidates for the Gospel Ministry. The College has enjoyed 23 revivals of Religion. Over one half of the students in the present catalogue, are members of the Church, and one fourth or more have in view the sacred office.

*

THE

THIRTIETH

Annual Catalogue and Circular

OF

HANOVER COLLEGE,

AND

TENTH TRIENNIAL

CATALOGUE OF THE ALUMNI.

JUNE 1862.

MADISON, INDIANA:
WM. P. LEVY & CO'S. PRINTING AND BINDING ESTABLISHMENT.
1862.

THE

THIRTIETH

Annual Catalogue and Circular

OF

HANOVER COLLEGE,

AND

TENTH TRIENNIAL

CATALOGUE OF THE ALUMNI.

JUNE, 1862.

MADISON, INDIANA:
WM. P. LEVY & CO'S. PRINTING AND BINDING ESTABLISHMENT.
1862.

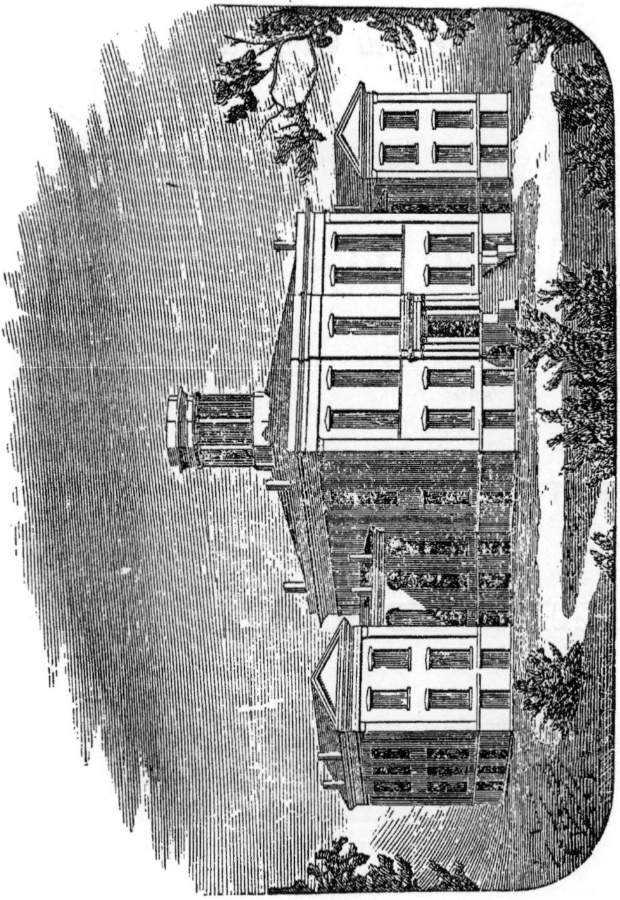

TRIENNIAL CATALOGUE.

OFFICERS OF THE COLLEGE.

PRESIDENTS.

1832—1836.	*Rev. James Blythe, D. D.
1836—1838.	*Rev. John Matthews, D. D. (pro. tem.)
1838—1838.	Rev. Duncan Macaulay, D. D.
1838—1843.	Rev. Erasmus D. McMaster, D. D.
1846—1849.	*Rev. Sylvester Scovel, D. D.
1849—1854.	Rev. Thomas E. Thomas, D. D.
1854—1855.	Rev. Jared M. Stone, (pro. tem.)
1855—1857.	Rev. Jonathan Edwards, D. D.
1857—1859.	Rev. S. Harrison Thomson, (pro. tem.)
1859.	Rev. James Wood, D. D.

VICE PRESIDENTS.

1832—1857. *Rev. John Finley Crowe, D. D.

PROFESSORS.

1832—1837.	*Rev. John Finley Crowe, D. D., Rhet. Logic, Pol. Econ. and History.
1832—1836.	*Rev. Mark A. H. Niles, A. M., Prof. of Ancient Languages.
1832—1838.	John H. Harney, A. M., Prof. of Mathematics.
1833—1835.	Wm. McKee Dunn A. B. Principal of Prep. Department.
1835—1838.	Charles K. Thompson, A. B., Principal of Prep. Department.
1835—1837.	Wm. McKee Dunn, A. M., Prof. Natural Science.
1836—1839.	Noble Butler, A. B. Prof. of Ancient Languages.
1838—1843.	Thomas W. Hynes, A. M., Prof. Math. and Nat. Science.
1839—1840.	Samuel Galloway, A. M., Prof. of Ancient Languages.
1840—1841.	*Minard Sturgus, A. M., Principal of Prep. Dep. and Acting Prof. of Ancient Languages.
1841—1852.	*Minard Sturgus, A. M. Prof. of Ancient Languages.
1841—1843.	Zebulon B. Sturgus, A. B., Principal of Prep. Department.
1843—1843.	Rev. Wm. C. Anderson, A. M., Prof. of Rhet. Logic, Political Economy and History.
1844—1850.	S. Harrison Thomson, A M., Prof. of Math. and Nat. Science.
1844—1852.	Absalom C. Knox, A. M., Adj. Prof. of Ancient Lang. and Principal of Prep. Department.
1850—1856.	Rev. Jared M. Stone, A. M. Prof. of Nat. Science.
1850.	S. Harrison Thomson, Prof. of Math. and Mech. Phil.
1852—1857.	Rev. Wm. Bishop, A. M., Prof. of Greek.
1852—1854.	Rev. William Hamilton, A. M., Prof of Latin.
1854—1855.	Henry R. Lott, M. D., Prof. of Latin,
1857.	Rev. John Finley Crowe, D. D. Emeritus Prof. of Rhet. Logic, Pol. Economy and History,
1856.	Rev. Joshua B. Garritt, A. M., Prof. of Latin.
1857—1859.	Augustus W. King, A. M., Prof. of Natural Science.
1858—1862.	*Minard Sturgus, A. M., Prof. of Greek.
1843—1844.	Frederick Eckstein, Teacher of French and German.
1845—1846.	Rev. F. Augustus Willard, A. M., Lecturer on Chemistry.
1851.	Mons. J. J. Piedfourck, Univ. of Paris, Teacher of French, Drawing ond Civil Engineering.
1860.	Rev. J. W. Scott, D. D., Prof. of Natural Science.

---

*Deceased.

BOARD OF TRUSTEES

Bd.	DR. P. S. SHIELDS, New Albany	1864.
Bd.	JOSEPH PIERCE, Esq., Valparaiso	1864.
Bd.	DR. ANDREW SPEAR. Hanover	1864,
Bd.	REV. WILLIAM Y. ALLEN, Waveland	1864.
S. S.	REV. ISAAC W. MONFORT, Chaplain U. S. A	1864.
S. S.	REV. J. W. BLYTHE, Hanover	1864.
N. S.	THOMAS P. GORDON, D. D., Terre Haute	1864.
N. S.	REV. ROBERT IRWIN, Sen., Muncie	1864.
Bd.	REV. D. D. McKEE, Hanover	1865.
Bd.	JOHN W. BLACKBURN, Esq., Paris, Ill	1865.
Bd.	REV. W. A. HOLLIDAY, Indianapolis	1865.
Bd.	JESSE L. WILLIAMS, Esq., Fort Wayne	1865.
S. S.	JAMES H. McCAMBELL, Esq., Jeffersonville	1865.
S. S.	REV. DAVID MONFORT, Greensburg	1865.
N. S.	REV. E. W WRIGHT, D. D., Delphi	1865.
N. S.	REV. W. M. DONALDSON, Ossian	1865.
Bd.	JAMES M. RAY, Esq., Indianapolis	1865.
Bd.	ROBERT DEAN, Esq., Hanover	1865.
Bd.	HON. C. E. WALKER, Madison	1865.
Bd.	COL. JAMES BLAKE, Indianapolis	1865.
S. S.	SILAS C. DAY, Esq., New Albany	1862.
S. S.	REV. S. E. BARR, Livonia	1862.
N. S.	REV. C. K. THOMPSON, Lebanon	1862.
N. S.	REV. JAMES B. CROWE, Crawfordsville	1862.
Bd.	JOHN KING, Esq , Madison	1863.
Bd.	REV. J. G. MONFORT, D .D., Cincinnati, Ohio	1863.
Bd.	HON. W. McKEE DUNN, Madison	1863.
S. S.	REV. JAMES WOOD, D. D., Hanover	1863.
S. S.	REV. P. MORTON, Vincennes	1863.
S. S.	JOHN H. VAN VANNUYS, Esq., Franklin	1863.
N. S.	REV. J. C. BROWN, Chaplain U. S. A	1863.
N. S.	REV. THOMAS McINTIRE, Indianapolis	1863.

OFFICERS OF THE BOARD

JAMES M. RAY, ESQ., *President.*   REV. D. D. McKEE, *Secretary.*

REV, JAMES WOOD, D. D.. *Treasurer.*

EXECUTIVE COMMITTEE.

HON. W. McKEE DUNN,   JOHN KING. ESQ..

REV. JAMES WOOD, D.D.,   ROBERT DEAN, Esq.

REV. D. D. McKEE.

AUDITING COMMITTEE.

HON. W. McKEE DUNN.   HON. C. E. WALKER.

FACULTY.

REV. JAMES WOOD, D. D., President,
Professor of Biblical Instruction, Psychology, Logic, and Ethics.

REV. S. HARRISON THOMSON, A. M.
Professor of Mathematics, Mechanical Philosophy, and Astronomy.

*MINARD STURGUS, A. M.,
Professor of the Latin Language and Literature.

REV. JOSHUA B. GARRITT, A. M.
Professor of the Greek Language and Literature.

REV. J. W. SCOTT, D. D.,
Professor of Natural Science.

REV. JOSHUA GARRITT, A. M.,
Librarian.

WILLIAM BROWN,
Janitor.

HONORARY DEGREES.

L. L, D.

1834. Hon. Isaac Blackford, Judge of the Supreme Court of Indiana.
1838. John Delafield, *Cincinnati, Ohio.*
1840. *Hon. Charles Dewey,
" Hon. Jeremiah Sullivan, } Judges of the Supreme Court of Ind.

D. D.

1857. Rev. David McDill, *Hamilton, Ohio*
" *Rev. Elihu W. Baldwin, *President of Wabash University, Indiana.*
1839. Rev. Stewart Bates, *Glasgow, Scotland.*
1841. Rev. James Murphy, *Herkimer, New York.*
1843. Rev. William L. Breckinridge, *Louisville, Ky.*
" Rev. Thomas C. Reed, *Prof. of Int. Philos. Union College, N. Y.*
1845. Rev. David Monfort, *Franklin, Ind.*
1846. *Rev. Sylvester Scovel, *New Albany, Ind.*
1847. Rev. Edward P. Humphrey, *Louisville, Ky.*
" Rev. Robert C Grundy, *Memphis, Tenn.*
1848. Rev. J. L. Yantis, *Missouri.*
" Rev. John C. Backus, *Baltimore, Md.*
1853. Rev. Leroy J. Halsey, *Chicago, Ill.*
" Rev. Elias Riggs, *Missionary at Smyrna, Asia Minor.*
" Rev. I. N. Candee, *Galesburg, Ill.*
1854. Rev. John M. Stevenson, *New York.*
" Rev. Thornton A. Mills, *New York.*
1858. Rev. Josiah D. Smith, *Columbus, Ohio.*
1859. Rev. James Brown, *Keokuk, Iowa.*
" Rev. J. C. Brown, *Valparaiso, Ind., Chaplain U. S. A.*
1861. Rev. N. C. Burt, *Cincinnati, Ohio.*
" Rev. J. W. Lowrie, *Fort Wayne, Ind.*
1862. Rev. E. W. Wright, *Delphi, Ind.*

A. M.

1833. *Rev. John Finley Crowe, *Vice Prest. of Hanover College Indiana.*
" *Rev. M. A. H. Niles, *Professor of Languages, Hanover College, Ind.*
1834. Rev. John W. Cunningham, *Tennessee.*
1839. *Rev. David Monfort, *Franklin, Ind.*
1840. Samuel Reid, M. D., *Salem, Ind.*

"	Leonard Bliss, jr., *Louisville, Ky.*
1843.	Rev. Monroe T. Allen, *Raleigh, Tenn.*
"	Samuel M. Elliott, M. D., *New York City.*
1845.	*John L. Scott, Esq., *Cincinnati, Ohio.*
"	James P. Holcombe, Esq., *Cincinnati, Ohio.*
"	*Rev. Daniel Lattimore, *Vernon, Ind.*
1845.	Rev. David V. Smock, *Sigourney, Iowa.*
"	Rev. James Brownlee, *Livonia, Ind.*
1846.	Rev. James C. Burt, M. D., *Vernon, Ind.*
1847.	Rev. George J. Reed, *Chaplain U. S. A.*
"	*Rev. Mason D. P. Williams, *Louisville, Ky.*
"	Rev. Robert C. McComb, *London, Ohio.*
"	*Rev. John C. Eastman, *Crawfordsville, Ind.*
1848.	Rev. Thomas Brown, *Xenia, Ohio.*
"	John W. Shields, Esq., *Cincinnati, Ohio.*
"	Thomas H. Shreve, Esq., *Louisville, Ky.*
"	*Ben Casseday, Esq., *Louisville, Ky.*
1849.	Bland Ballard, Esq., *Louisville, Ky.*
1850.	Dr. E. S. Cooper, *Knox Co., Ills.*
"	Rev. Charles Axtell, *Knightstown, Ind.*
"	John Orr, Esq., *Macon, Tenn.*
1852.	Robert S. Knox, Esq. *Livonia, Ind.*
1853.	William A. Churchman, Esq., *Indianapolis, Ind.*
1856.	C. W. Kimball, Esq., *Lebanon, Ohio.*
"	Dr. James M. Logan, *Hanover, Ind.*
1857.	Philip A. Emery, Esq., *Indianapolis, Ind.*
1858.	John H. Tate, M. D., *Cincinnati, Ohio.*
1859.	Ashley Pierce, Esq., *Valparaiso, Ind.*
1862.	Ebenezer Neal, M. D., *Philadelphia, Pa.*
"	Rev. Geo. W. Hays, *McComb, Ill.*

A. B.

1846.	Dr. John S. Burt, *Washington, Arkansas.*
1854.	Dickerson B. Wayland, Esq., *Mt. Washington, Ky.*

ALUMNI.

1834.

| NAMES. | PROFESSION. | RESIDENCE. |

*William Hamilton Bruner, A. M...Minister ....
*Selby Harney........................Teacher................
John Lyle Martin.....................Minister ....Crawfordsville, Ind.
John Mason McChord, A. M..........Minister ....Texas.
Isaac McCoy, A. M....................Farmer ....Marion, Ill.
Isaac Newton Shepherd, A. M.......Minister ....Marion, Ohio.
–Charles Kilgore Thompson, A. M...Minister ....Lebanon, Ind.

1835.

Robert Sherrard Bell, A. M..........Minister ....Washington, Va.
James Brown, A. M., D. D...........Minister ....Keokuk, Iowa.
†Jonathan Edwards, A. M., D. D....Minister ....Philadelphia, Pa.
Robert Simpson, A. M................Minister ....Newton, Ill.
‡Middleton Goldsmith, A. M.,M. D..Physician ....Louisville, Ky.
*James Allen Watson..................Teacher ....

1836.

S. J. P. Anderson, A. M., D. D.......Minister ....St. Louis, Mo.
§Noble Butler, A. M...................Teacher...............Louisville, Ky.
*Andrew Fulton, M. D................Physician ....
‖Thomas Woodruff Hynes, A. M.....Minister ....Pocahontas, Ill.
*Nathaniel T. Schillinger............Minister ....
*David Edward Young Rice, A. M..Minister ....
*William Wylie McLain, A. M.......Minister ....

*Deceased.

–Principal of Prep. Dep. 1834–8.
†President of Hanover College, 1855–57.
‡Prof. of Vermont Medical College, and Ky. Med. Coll.
§Prof. in Hanover College, 1836–39.
‖Prof. in Hanover College, 1838–43.

NAMES,	PROFESSION.	RESIDENCE.
Amos Hynes Rogers, A. M.	Minister	Atlanta, Ill.
Samuel Frame Morrow, A. M.	Minister	Albany, N. Y.
Samuel Newell, A. M.	Minister	Paris, Ill.
Josiah Crawford, A. M.	Minister	Polk Run, Ind.
David Hays Cummins, A. M.	Minister	Mountain, Tenn.
¶Minard Sturgus, A. M.*	Teacher	S. Hanover. Ind.
S. Ramsay Wilson, A. M., D. D.	Minister	New York.

1837,

Thomas H. Alderdice	Minister	Scaffold Prairie, Ind.
Franklin Berryhill	Minister	Bellbrook, Ohio
James Black	Minister	Cincinnati, Ohio.
*Samuel N. Evans, A. M.	Minister	
Edmund Waller Hawkins, A. M.	Lawyer	Covington, Ky.
John Macartney Hoge	Minister	Beech Bluff, Ark.
Braxton D. Hunter	Minister	
Sylvanus Jewett	Minister	Roscoe, Ill.
*John Wright McCormick, A. M.	Minister	
James A. McKee, A. M.	Minister	Minneapolis, Min.
Asahel Munson, A. M.	Minister	Jackson, Mo.
*William Cooper Scott, A. M.	Minister	
Josiah D. Smith, A. M., D. D.	Minister	Columbus, Ohio.
†Samuel Harrison Thomson, A. M.	Minister	S. Hanover, Ind.
James F. Wood	Lawyer	Greensburg, Penn.

1838.

George B. Armstrong	Minister	Crittenden, Ky.
*William Blair	Minister	
‡James E. Blythe, A. M.	Lawyer	Evansville, Ind.
William Kirkpatrick Brice, A. M.	Minister	Pleasant, Ohio.
Alex. Montgomery Brown, A. M.	Lawyer	Mound City, Ind.
William M. Cheever, A. M.	Minister	Troy, Ohio.
James Blythe Crowe, A. M.	Minister	Crawfordsville, Ind.
Thomas Searle Crowe, A. M.	Minister	Jeffersonville, Ind.
Joseph F. Fenton, A. M.	Minister	Washington, Mo.
James J. Gardiner, A. M.	Teacher	Cape Girardeau, Mo.
Robert A. Gibson, A. M.	Farmer	Monmouth, Ill.
Abram T. Hendricks, A., M.	Minister	Petersburg, Ind.
John Jones		
James W. Matthews, A. M.	Teacher	Macomb, Ill.
George Frederick Whitworth, A. M.	Minister	Whitby Island. W. T.

1839.

Samuel Stanhope Crowe, A. M.	Lawyer	New Lexington, Ind.
David M. Dunn	Lawyer	Logansport, Ind.

¶Prof. in Hanover College, 1840–52, 1858.
†Prof. in Hanover College, 1844.
‡Member Indiana Const. Cony. and Ind. H. Rep.

ALUMNI.

NAMES.	PROFESSION.	RESIDENCE.
William W. Gilliland, A M	Lawyer	Charlestown, Ind.
*Philander Hamilton	Lawyer	
Ephriam K. Lynn, A. M	Minister	Carlisle, Kansas.
Fielding G. Strahan, A. M	Minister	Danville, Ky.

1840.

Harleigh Blackwell, A. M	Minister	Snow Hill, Mo.
*Samuel G. Hass	Business	Valparaiso, Ind.
†Absalom C. Knox, A. M	Teacher	Vacaville, Cal.
Robert C. Matthews, A. M	Minister	Monmouth, Ill.
Robert S. Symington, A. M	Minister	Kansas City, Mo.

1841.

Charles M. Hays,	Lawyer	Pittsburg, Penn.
John Lyle King	Lawyer	Chicago, Ill.
*George C. Lyon	Physician	

1842.

Alexander M. Johnston, A. M. M.D.	Physician	Cincinnati, Ohio.
*Thomas C. McCutchen, A. M	Farmer	
Alexander McHatton, A. M	Minister	Marion, Ind.
*George McMillan, A. M	Minister	
James Newton Saunders, A. M	Minister	Bloomfield, Ky.
*William W. Simonson, A. M	Minister	
‡Zebulon Barton Sturgus, A. M	Teacher	Charlestown, Ind.

1843.

Daniel Lambert Fouts	Farmer	N. Washington, Ind.
*James G. Hopkins, A. M	Minister	
George A. Irwin, A. M	Minister	Ft. Wayne, Ind.
Samuel Barr Keys, A. A	Lawyer	Cincinnati, Ohio.
Joseph Chambers McKibbin, M. C.	Lawyer	————, Cal.
Francis Peterson Monfort, A. M	Minister	Auburn, Kan.
John F. Read	Lawyer	Jeffersonville, Ind.
J. Franklin Trenchard, A. M. M. D.	Druggist	Philadelphia, Pa.

1844.

John C. Greer	Planter	Jackson, Tenn.

1845.

William T. Robinson, A. M	Lawyer	———— Miss.
David R. Thompson	Lawyer	———— Miss.

1846.

*William H. G. Butler, A. M	Teacher	
John A. Frazer, A. M	Teacher	———— Oregon.
Samuel Crothers Logan, A. M	Minister	Valparaiso, Ind.

†Prof. in Hanover College, 1844–52.
‡Principal of Prep. Department in Hanover College, 1841–43.

ALUMNI.

NAMES.	PROFESSION.	RESIDENCE.

1847.
Samuel Emmett Barr, A. M..........Minister............Livonia, Ind.
Fauntleroy Senour, A. M.............Minister............Indianapolis, Ind.

1848.
Addison W. Bare, A. M...............Physician...........Bryantsville, Ind.
John Wesley Blake, A. M.............Lawyer.............Lafayette, Ind.
John C. Caldwell, A. M...............Minister............Stillwater, Minn.
*†Moses S. Coulter, A. M.............Minister.............
*Robert G. Jackson, A. M............Teacher............
Robert S. Shannon, A. M. M. D.....Physician..........Lagrange, Texas.
Samuel C. Taggart, A. M. M. D......Physician..........Charlestown, Ind.
James Harvey L. Vannuys, A. M...Minister............Goshen, Ind.

1849.
Samuel C. Baldridge, A. M..........Minister............Friendsville, Ill.
*Jesse Y. Higbee, A. M. M. D........Physician...........
Nathan S. Palmer, A. M..............Minister............Brazil, Ind.
Xenophon Boone Sanders, A. M....Lawyer.............Memphis, Tenn.
Williamson D. Symington, A. M...Minister............Danville, Ky.
John White Taylor, A. M.............Lawyer.............Palestine, Texas.
Henry E. Thomas, A. M...............Minister............Augusta, Ky.

1850.
Wm. Maxwell Blackburn, A. M....Minister............Erie, Penn.
Joshua Selby Brengle.................Physician..........Carlisle, Ind.
*Avery Williams Bullock, A. M...Lawyer.............Hampshire.
John Simpson Frierson...............Minister............Ashwood, Tenn.
*Samuel David Hawthorn.............
John Alexander Kimmons............Minister............Saltilo, Miss.
Claudius B. H. Martin, A. M........Minister............Bedford, Ind.
Samuel Clarke Mercer, A. M.........Editor................Nashville, Tenn.
Robert Symington Reese, A. M......Minister............Pleasant Hill, Mo.
William Harvey Rice..................Minister............Palestine, Texas.
William Walton Sickles, A. M......Minister............Shelbyville, Ind.
Alexander Stuart Walker............Lawyer.............Georgetown, Texas.
Austin Warner.........................Minister............Moneka, Kansas.
Benjamin Rush Whitney............Engineer............———— Mo.
William Alexander Martin Young..Lawyer.............Salem, Ind.

1851.
James Madison Alexander............Minister ....Palestine, Ill.
Henry Martyn Bayless................Business............Chicago, Ill.
Joseph Boon...........................Minister............Lagrange, Texas.
James Bruce, A. M....................Minister............Mercersburgh, Pa.
James Huston Burns, A. M..........Minister............Monroe, Ohio.
Theophilus Wilson Guy, A. M.......Farmer.............Oxford, Ohio.
*James Simpson Jones.................Lawyer.............
James McEwen Kimmons, A. M....   Miss.

†Missionary to China.

ALUMNI.

NAMES.	PROFESSION.	RESIDENCE.
Cornelius McKain, A. M.	Minister	Iowa Point, Kan.
Hugh McHatton, A. M.	Minister	Cedarville, Ohio.
Archibald V. McKee, A. M.	Lawyer	Troy, Mo.
†William James McKnight, A. M.	Minister	Danville, Ky.
Alexander Mayne, A. M.		
Edward Ethel Porter, A. M.	Minister	Memphis, Tenn.
Benjamin Niles Sawtelle, A. M.	Minister	Batesville, Ark.
Joseph Gaston Symmes, A. M.	Minister	Cranberry, N. J.
Robert Francis Taylor, A. M.	Minister	Vernon, Ind.
Joseph Greene Wells, A. M.	Minister	Jackson, Mo.

1852.

Joseph Mayo Bachelder, A. M.	Minister	Albia, Iowa.
Stephen James Bovell, A. M.	Minister	Palestine, Ill.
Jonathan Turner Carthel, A. M.	Lawyer	Trenton, Tenn.
John McCutchen Coyner, A. M.	Teacher	Lebanon, Ind.
Benjamin Parke Dewey	Lawyer	
Henry Michael Giltner, A. M.	Minister	Nebraska City, N. T.
Thomas Maise Hopkins, A. M.	Minister	Bloomington, Ind.
Alexander Martin, A. M.	Teacher	U. S. A.
Robert Langdon Neely, A. M.	Minister	Denmark, Tenn.
James Matlack Scovel, A. M.	Lawyer	Camden, N. J.
Francis Marion Symmes, A. M.	Minister	Vernon, Ind.
Daniel Price Young, A. M.	Minister	Georgetown, Ky.

1853.

*Lyman Beecher Andrews, A. M.	Teacher	Cape Girardeau, Mo.
James Andrew Cunningham	Business	Madison, Ind.
Lewis Isaac Drake, A. M.	Minister	West Liberty, Ohio.
Jeremiah Mead Drake, A. M.	Minister	West Rushville, O.
‡Joshua Bolles Garritt, A. M.	Minister	S. Hanover, Ind.
Edward John Hamilton, A. M.	Minister	Oyster Bay, N. Y.
Henry Seymour Kritz, A. M.	Teacher	Waveland, Ind.
Charles Lee, A. M.	Minister	Hanover, Ind.
William Pope Lemaster, A. M.	Farmer	Memphis, Tenn.
Gideon Blackburn McLeary, A. M.	Lawyer	
James Alexander McRee, A. M.	Minister	Vernon, Ind.
Joseph Warren Mahan, A. M.	Teacher	Clermont Co., O.
Henry Thomas Morton, A. M.	Minister	
*Henry Spencer Scovel	Student Theology.	
Sylvester Fithian Scovel, A. M.	Minister	Springfield, O.
*Jackson Jay Smith, A. M.	Lawyer	Louisville, Ky.
*William Wheat	Minister	

1854.

Stephen Cromwell Adair	Lawyer	Morganfield, Ky.
David Gilkerson Hecron	Teacher	Canton, Miss.
Robert Irwin, jr., A. M.	Minister	Logansport.

†Prof. of Languages in Austin College, Texas.
‡Prof. in Han. College, 1856.
*Deceased.

ALUMNI.

NAMES.	PROFESSION.	RESIDENCE.
Robert Alexander Johnson,	Lawyer	Cincinnati, Ohio.
Isaac Brown Moore,	Minister	Waveland, Ind.
Edwin Hubbard Rutherford,	Minister	Vicksburg, Miss.
Edward Coles Sickles.	Minister	St. Louis, Mo.
William Rondeau Sim,	Minister	Jordon's Grove, Ill.
Thomas Wallace, A. M.	Teacher	
James Edward Wilson		Concord, Tenn.
Jared Ryker Woodfil,	Teacher	Near Madison.

1855.

James Robinson Evans	Teacher.	Near Memphis, Tenn
†Michael Montgomery Fisher, A. M.	Minister	Fulton, Mo.
James H. Hunter,	Student of Theol	Allegheny City.
William Hall Huston,	Farmer.	Hamilton, Ohio.
Robert J. L. Matthews, A. M.	Minister	Charlestown, Ind.
Robert Clarke McGee,	Minister	
John Quincy McKeehan, A. M.	Minister	Queensville, Ind.
Charles H. Park,	Minister	Potts' Grove, Penn.
William A. Sample,	Minister	Arkansas.
William Bloomer Truax,	Minister	Keosaqua, Wis.
Thomas Marion Tucker,	Physician	N. Philadelphia, Ind.
Archibald Cameron Voris, A. M.	Lawyer	Bedford, Ind.

1856.

James Baillie Adams,	Minister	Princeton, N. J.
James William Allison, A. M.	Minister	Arcola, Ill.
Robert Brown Herron.	Minister	Hillsborough, Ohio.
Henry Keigwin,	Minister	Louisville, Ky.
Harvey Lamb	Teacher	Texas.
‡James Kennedy Patterson, A. M.	Teacher	Lexington, Ky.
James Sanderson Rankin,	Teacher	Madison, Ind.
Richmond Kelly Smoot,	Minister	Bowling Green, Ky.
James Harvey Tedford,	Minister	Michigan.
¿Benjamin Dubois Wykoff	Minister	Allahabad, India.

BACHELOR OF SCIENCE.

Cyrus Alexander Johnson	Business	Memphis, Tenn.
James Edwin Rankin		

1857.

Leonard Fisk Andrews,	Teacher	Cape Girardeau, Mo.
William Cochrane,	Minister	Jersey City, N. J.
William Means Crozier,		
John McMurray,	Minister	Chapel Hill, Texas.
David McKnight Williamson,	Minister	Olney, Ill.

BACHELOR OF SCIENCE.

Hiram Francis Braxton.		Paoli.
David Taylor, Jr		Columbus, Ohio.
John Newton Voris		Washington, D. C.

†Prof. in Westminster College, Mo., 1855.
‡Prof. in Stewart College.
¿Missionary in India.

ALUMNI.

NAMES.	PROFESSION.	RESIDENCE.

1858.

William Peter Baker	Teacher	
Jacob Reasoner Geyer	Minister	Peru, Ind.
Horace Hovey Hanna	Business	Ft. Wayne, Ind.
John David McClintock	Student of Theol.	Princeton, N. J.
James Baird McClure	Minister	Fulton, Ill.
Thomas Johnson McIlrath	Lawyer	
David William Moffit	Minister	Vernon, Ind.
James Alexander Piper	Minister	Quincy, Ill.
Robert Gaines Ross	Minister	Princeton, N. J.
Augustus Taylor	Minister	Amanda, Ohio.
James Harvey Vannuys	Minister	Franklin, Ind.
Cornelius Pleasant Voris	Minister	N. Lexington, Ind.

1859.

Robert Long Adams	Minister	Pleasant.
Henry Ellet Crawford	Minister	Pleasant
John Fox	Minister	
Columbus De Witt Huston	Minister	
Samuel Finley Thompson	U. S. A	
John Bacon Vawter	Minister	Franklin, Ind.

BACHELOR OF SCIENCE.

Charles Henry Johnson	Business	Franklln, Ind.
Oliver Mulvey	Artist	Madison.
George Martin Whitely		San Antonio, Texas

1860.

John McKnight Bloss		U. S. Army.
John W. Crawford	Minister	
W. S. Coulter	Teacher	Friendsville, Ill.
R. F. Middleton,	Minister	Franfort, Ky.
W. G. Thomas	Minister	
*Samuel D. Voris	Student of Theol.	Benington, Ind.
James Wilson,		Hanover, Ind.

BACHELOR OF SCIENCE.

W. A. Collins	Student of Med.	Madison, Ind.
George W. Cummins	Student of Law	Logansport, Ind.
J. Marshall Story,		U. S. Army.

1861.

S. F. Denton	Student of Theol.	Chicago, Ill.
S. H. Howe	Student of Theol.	Princeton, N. J.
T. M. Irwin	Teacher	Hanover, Ind.
Stephen S. Lee		U. S. Army.
Edward F. Reid		U. S. Army.
B. F. Simpson		Vernon, Ind.
W. H. Smith	Student of Theol.	Allegheny, Penn.

BACHELOR OF SCIENCE.

J. B. Richardson,		Shelbyville, Ky.
J. W. Shrewsberry		
S. M. Tilford		Kent, Ind.

*Deceased.

UNDERGRADUATES.

Seniors.

|Robert Coyner..South Salem, Ohio.
Moses Fell Dunn...................................Bedford.
George Proffitt Huckeby.........................Rome.
George M. McCampbell..........................Jeffersonville.
Samuel T. McClure................................Vincennes.
James T. Patterson................................Delphi.
Wm. H. Sawtelle...................................Binghampton, N. Y.
Levi M. Schofield..................................Newport, Ky.
Henry C. Thomson.................................Hanover.
John C. Youngken..................................Friendsville, Ill.

Juniors.

Josiah Dougherty..................................Ladoga.
J. Addison Day....................................New Albany.
Henry C. Donnell..................................Greenville, Ill.
George Hippard....................................Logansport.
Augustus A. Joss..................................Constantine, Mich.
Francis C. Monfort ....Glendale, O.
J. D. Miller..Hanover.
Amos W. Patterson...............................Hanover.
Emanuel N. Pires ....Jacksonville, Ill.
William C. Smock.................................Sigourney, Iowa.
Eberle Thomson...................................Greensburg.
William Torrence..................................Terre Haute.
Robert A. Sturgus................................Hanover.
Benjamin W. Tucker..............................N. Philadelphia.

|In the army.

Sophomores.

Philip M. Adams..................................Rockville, Pa.
W. F. Andrus......................................Fairland.
Noble C. Butler...................................Salem.
John Canan..Vincennes.
William Chamberlain..........................Hanover.
Robert S. Dean...................................Hanover.
James A. Dean....................................Hanover.
Francis M. Elliott................................Blue Grass.
John H. Harbolt..................................Charlestown.
John Kerns..Hanover.
Robert McConnell..............................Fairland.
Peter H. R. McComb..........................Hanover.
*Kearsly G. McComb..........................Hanover.
R. A. Mathes......................................Altonburg, Mo.
William A. Patton...............................Spruce Hill, Pa.
Arthur Rose.......................................Cincinnati, O.
Richard W. Sipe.................................Swanville.
William R. Smyth...............................Shelbyville.
Albert Taggart....................................Charlestown.
Martin B. V. Van Arsdale....................Washington.
Robert M. Webster.............................Tallahoma, Iowa.
John Weston......................................Galena, Ill.

Freshmen.

Silas D. Abbot....................................Taylorsville, Ky.
John R. Armstrong.............................Jeffersonville.
James G. Blythe.................................Shelbyville.
J. C. Eastman....................................Hanover.
George W. Fitch.................................Hanover.
Francis M. Gilchrist............................Fairland.
Ebenezer N. Gelpin............................Hanover.
Robert C. Hamilton............................Greensburg.
‖W. L. Lee..Hanover.
Jeremiah Long...................................Bardolph, Ill.
John H. McConnell.............................Fairland.
Preston McKinney..............................Livonia.
Robert R. Miller..................................Hanover.
Edward Quinche................................Galena, Ill.
William W. Ross.................................Peru.
Robert A. Scovel................................Springfield, O.
Isaac P. Spinning...............................Highland, Kansas.
Minard S. Smith.................................Vincennes.
Thomas Tracy....................................Louisville, Ky.
Leonidas V. Winston..........................Richmond.

*Deceased.
‖In the army.

SCIENTIFIC DEPARTMENT.

Third Year.
Felix J. Brandt..Hanover.

Second Year.
Robert Jamieson..Rising Sun.
‖Robert E. P. McDermett................................Dallas, Texas.
Franklin Shannon..Hanover.
John Shelby...Charlestown.

First Year.
William C. Aikman..Washington.
Henry B. Aikman..Washington.
Thomas J. Jordan..Kent.
Wm. J. Meredith..Lafayette.
George Meriweather..Louisville, Ky.
James T. Ramsey...Hanover.
George Scoggan...Bedford.
Thomas C. Vannuys..Morefield.

PREPARATORY DEPARTMENT.

Seniors.
Charles B. Chamberlin....................................Hanover.
John C. Foutts...Scott, O.
Ebenezer Gordon...New Lexington.
William A. Graham...New Washington.
George M. Lodge...Springfield, Ill.
William M. Malcom..Pittsburgh.
James H. McMillan...Logansport.
John P. Seawright..Frankfort.
Andrew Stevenson..Greenville, Ill.
*James Walker..Washington.

Juniors.
Alfred Barngrover...Fairland.
¶Nathan R. Griggs..Jefferson.

‖Left soon after the beginning of the year.
*Deceased.
¶Left on account of ill health.

John T. Fitch..Hanover.
John A. Kellar..North Vernon.
Daniel J. Lattimore..Vernon.
Henry R. Lee...Hanover.
‡Joseph K. McIlhenny..Bean Blossom.
Alexander S. Peck..Omaha City, N. T.
David W. Rogers..Hanover.
A. T. Ross..Madison.
William B. Sturgus..Hanover.
James H. Thomson..Hanover.

SUMMARY.

Seniors	10	Scientific, 2d year	4
Juniors	14	Scientific, 1st year	8
Sophomores	22	Senior Preparatory	10
Freshmen	20	Junior Preparatory	12
Scientific, 3d year	1		
Total			101

‡Left to attend an Academy:

TEXT BOOKS.

DEPARTMENT OF LANGUAGES

LATIN,—Andrews' Grammar and Reader; Andrews' or Leverett's Lexicon; Crooks & Schem's or Andrews' Cæsar; Cooper's Virgil; Bojsen's Roman Antiquities; Butler & Sturgus' Sallust; Lincoln's Livy; Lincoln's Horace; Tyler's Tacitus; Chase's Tusculan Disputations.

GREEK—Crosby's Grammar and Lessons; Liddell & Scott's, or Pickering's Lexicon; Owen's, or Boise's Anabasis; Bojesen's Grecian Antiquities; Owen's Homer; Woolsey's Greek Plays; Champlin's Demosthenes.

HEBREW—Stuart's Rœdiger's Grammar; Gesenius' Lexicon; Biblia Hebraica.

DEPARTMENT OF BELLES-LETTERS.

Blair's Rhetoric, (University Edition); Whately's or Coupee's Logic; Wayland's Political Economy; Smith's Grecian History: Liddell's Rome; Clarks' English History; American History and the Constitution of the U. S. A.

DEPARTMENT OF MATHEMATICS.

Rays' Algebra, 2nd part; Davies' Legendre; Davies' Surveying, Coffin's Conic Sections and Analytical Geometry, Olmstead's Natural Philosophy; Olmstead's Astronomy.

DEPARTMENT OF NATURAL SCIENCE.

Silliman's Chemistry; Cutter,s Physiology; Wood's Botany; Lyell's Geology; Butler's Analogy; Dana's Mineralogy; Agassiz & Gould's Zoology, Somerville's Physical Geography.

DEPARTMENT OF METAPHYSICS.

Walker's Reid on the Intellectual Powers; Sir William Hamilton's Philosophy, (Wight's Edition); Stewart's Active and Moral Powers; Wayland's Moral Science; Haven's Mental Philosophy.

DEPARTMENT OF RELIGIOUS INSTRUCTION.

English Bible, Hodge's, Alexander's or Jacobus' Notes; Greek Testament, Robinsen's Greek Harmony; Old Testament Hebrew; Septuagint, Westminister Catechism; General Assembly's Psalm and Hymn Books; Paley's Natural Theology; Coleman's Sacred Geography; Alexander's Evidences of Christianity.

ORDER OF RECITATIONS AND COURSE OF STUDY FOR 1862-3.

FIRST TERM.

Dr. Wood.	Prof. Thomson.	Prof. Garritt.	Dr. Scott.	Tutor.
Executive............	Freshman and 1st Sci... Plane Geometry....... Davies' Legendre......	Junior................ ½ Demosth. Sel. Orat... ½ Tacitus History, Tyler...	Sophomore............ Livy, Lincoln.........	Senior Preparatory.... Latin Reader and Grammar... Andrews'...........
½ Sen. Hebrew.........				
Sophomore and 1st Sci... History of Greece......	Junior and 3d Scientific... Natural Phil., Olmsted. Mathematical Part.....	Senior Preparatory.... Greek, McClintock & Crooks. First and Second Books...	Freshman............. Sallust, Butler & Sturgus. Latin Exercises.......	
Junior and 2d Sci...... Rhetoric, Blair........ ½ Hebrew.............	Senior Preparatory and 1st Sci. Algebra............... Ray, Second Part......	Sophomore............ Homer's Odyssey...... Owen................	Senior and 3rd Sci..... Anatomy and Phys., Cutter. Zoology, Agassiz......	Junior Preparatory.... Greek, McClintock & Crook's. First Part...........
Senior and 3d Sci...... Psychology............	Sophomore and 2nd Sci... Solid Geometry........ Davies' Legendre......	Freshman............. Anabasis............. Greek Prose Composition.		Junior Preparatory.... Latin Lessons......... Andrews'............
½ Freshman, Harmony... ½ Sophomore, Acts..... Greek.................		Senior................ ½ Cicero, Tusc Disput.. ½ Greek Tragedies, Woolsey.	Junior and 2nd Sci..... Chemistry............ Silliman.............	

SECOND TERM.

SESSION FIRST.

Executive............	Freshman and 1st Sci... Practical Plane Trigonometry. and Mens. Surf. Davies Leg...	Junior................ ½ Demosth. Sel. Orat... ½ Tacitus...........	Sophomore............ Livy, Lincoln......... Roman Antiquities.....	Senior Preparatory.... Latin Reader and Grammar... Andrews'...........
½ Senior Hebrew.......				
Sophomore and 1st Sci... History of Rome.......	Junior and 3d Sci...... Natural Philosophy.... Applications..........	Senior Preparatory.... Greek, McClintock & Crooks. Second Book..........	Freshman............. Sallust.............. Latin Exercises.......	

Order of Recitations and Course of Study for 1862-3.—Continued.

Junior and 2nd Sci.........	Senior Preparatory and 1st Sci Sophomore	Senior and 3rd Sci.........
Logic......................	Algebra...................	Odyssey	½ Natural Theology, Paley..	Greek, McClintock & Crook's.
½ Hebrew..................		Apology and Crito.........	½ Mineralogy...............	First Book ....
Senior and 3d Sci..........	Sophomore and 2nd Sci.....	Freshman..................		Junior Preparatory.........
Butler's Analogy...........	Analytical Plane Trig. Spher.	Anabasis..................		Latin Lessons..............
Moral Science, Wayland....	Trig. and Mens. Solids, Appl.	Greek Prose Composition...		Andrews'.
½ Fresh. Harmony..........		Senior.....................	Junior and Second Sci	
½ Soph. Epistles............		½ Latin, Juvenal...........	Chemistry and Botany......	
(Greek Test)		½ Greek Tragedies..........	(Wood's).	

SECOND TERM.

SESSION SECOND.

Executive.................	Freshman and 1st Sci.......	Junior.....................	Sophomore.................	Senior Preparatory.........
½ Senior Hebrew...........	Surveying and Navigation...	½ Alcestis of Eurip.........	Horace, Lincoln............	Cæsar and Grammar--
	Davies'.	½ Cicero, Tusc. Disp.......		Andrews'.
Sophomore and Second Sci..	Junior and 3rd Sci..........	Senior Preparatory.........	Freshman..................	
Modern History............	Astronomy.................	Greek, Second Book.......	Virgil, Cooper..............	
	Olmsted...................	McClintock & Crooks.......	Latin Exercises............	
Junior and 2nd Sci.........	Senior Prep. and 1st Sci.....	Sophomore.................	Senior and 3rd Sci.........	Junior Preparatory.........
Political Economy, Wayland.	Algebra, Ray, Second Part...	Apol. and Orito. Tyler.....	Geology.	Greek, First Book..........
½ Hebrew..................		Greek Antiquities, Bojesen		McClintock & Crook's......
Senior and 3d Scientific...	Sophomore and 2nd Sci.....	Freshman..................		Junior Preparatory.........
½ Constitution U. S. Story..	Conic Sections, Coffin.....	Memorabilia................		Latin Reader and Grammar.
½ Moral Science............		Greek Prose Composition...		Andrews'.
½ Fresh— Greek Harmony..		Senior.....................	Junior and 2nd Sci.........	
½ Soph. Epistles............		½ Latin Review............	½ Optics and Electricity...	
		½ Greek Tragedy..........	½ Botany..................	

SCIENTIFIC DEPARTMENT.

The three years' course of English, Mathematical and Scientific instruction pursued in this department, embraces all that is included in the College scheme, except the Classical Languages. Such as desire it, however, may pursue the study of Latin and French, in connection with a Scientific Course. We do not recommend it as in any sense an equivalent for a thorough Classical Course; nor is it intended for mere boys, since the subjects which it includes are entirely above their capacity; but to young men, who have attained a respectable common school education, including the elements of Algebra, and who have not time nor means to prosecute a Classical course, this system of studies will, it is hoped, commend itself as solid, comprehensive and practical. Those who shall complete the prescribed Scientific course, will receive a Diploma, certifying the extent of their attainments.

COLLEGE YEAR--EXAMINATIONS.

The College Year is divided into two Terms. The First Term begins on the Wednesday after the 25th day of August, and continues 16 weeks.— The Second Term begins on the first Wednesday in January and continues 24 weeks. The Annual Commencement occurs on Thursday before the 25th of June.

It is of great importance that students attend from the very beginning of the Term;e specially since so considerable a portion of time is allotted to vacations. In most cases, the loss of a few weeks, or even days, seriously affects the future standing of the pupil. Absence during term time, without special leave, is prohibited.*

Public Examinations will be held, hereafter, only at the close of the College year, when the Freshmen and Junior Classes will be examined on the studies of the preceding year, and the Sophomore and Senior Classes upon those of the two preceding years. These last examinations will be FINAL, for the studies pursued in those years. All the examinations will be THOROUGH and RIGID; and will be conducted, in part by the use of written questions, prepared by the Faculty and the Examining Committee, covering the whole field of study prosecuted during a given period, and entirely unknown to the Student until the moment of examination.— These questions must be answered in writing before the Committee; and correct answers to a definite portion of them will be the passport of admission to a higher standing. Similar examinations of a briefer and less decisive character, however, and by way of preparation for the final trial, may be conducted privately, at the pleasure of the Faculty.

*Parents are respectfully advised to give their sons no such permission to be absent, except in cases of NECESSITY.

Religious Instruction and Services.

The attention of a Christian community is respectfully invited to the system of Biblical Instruction which forms a characteristic feature of our course of Study. The Grammar School Classes recite statedly in the English Bible; and every College Class has a daily or tri-weekly recitation in the Greek Testament, or the Hebrew. Proficiency in these, as in other studies, is tested by the usual examinations. In addition to this, Biblical Geography and Antiquities, Ecclesiastical History, Natural Theology, and the Analogy of Religion, Natural and Revealed, to the constitution and course of nature, are carefully and faithfully studied. There is also a Bible or Catechetical exercise on Sabbath mornings; a public service on Sabbath afternoon, appropriated to the Students; and daily morning prayers. The Students are expected to attend the Sabbath morning services of the congregation worshiping in the chapel, or of some other congregation in the vicinity, if their parents prefer any of the latter. The Methodist and United and Associate Presbyterian Churches have regular services in or near the Village.

ADMISSION.

Candidates for admission into the Freshmen Class, are examined in Arithmetic and Algebra; Ancient and Modern Geography; History of the U. S. A.; the English, Latin, and Greek Grammars; Cæsar's Commentaries, and Greek Reader, or what is equivalent to these attainments. They must furnish testimonials of good character, and, if from another College, must bring certificates of honorable dismission. Candidates for higher standing are examined upon that part of the course already studied by the Class which they propose to enter.

No one can be admitted to the Freshman Class until he has completed his fourteenth year, nor to an advanced standing without a proportional increase of age.

Before a student shall be admitted to actual standing in any Class, he shall present to the President a receipt from the Treasurer, showing that he has complied with the Statutes relating to College Charges and Scholarships.

N. B. The regular examination for admission into College, commences on the Monday preceding the beginning of each Term.

COURSE OF INSTRUCTION.

Preparatory Department.

Andrew's Latin Lessons, Grammar, Reader, and Exercises; Andrew's Cæsar; Butler and Sturgus' Sallust; Crosby's Greek Grammar and Lessons; Classical and Biblical Geography; Arithmetic; Ray's Algebra, 2nd part, English Bible.

Scientific Department.

FIRST YEAR.

Algebra, Rays', 2nd part; Plane Geometry; Plane Trigonometry, Mensuration of Surfaces, Surveying and Navigation; History; English Bible; Historical Books, and Sacred Geography.

SECOND YEAR.

Solid Geometry; Analytical Plane Trigonometry; Mensuration of Solids; and Application of Algebra to Geometry; Spherical Trigonometry; Analytical Geometry; Conic Sections; Rhetoric, Logic; Political Economy, English Bible; Poetical Books; Chemistry, Light, Heat, Electricity, and Botany.

THIRD YEAR.

Natural Philosophy, Astronomy, Anatomy, Zoology and Physiology; Mineralogy; Geology, Natural Theology, Butler's Analogy, Psychology, Moral Science, English Bible, Constitution of the U. S. A.

COLLEGIATE DEPARTMENT.

FRESHMEN CLASS.

FIRST TERM.

Greek Harmony of the Gospels...................................Robinson.
Biblical Antiquities ....Nevin.
Sallust...Butler & Sturgus.
Latin Exercises—Greek Prose Composition.....................
Xenophon's Anabasis ....Boise.
Plane Geometry...Davies' Legendre.

SECOND TERM—SESSION FIRST.

Greek Harmony, continued...Robinson
Sallust, continued...Butler & Sturgus.
Latin Exercises and Greek Composition, continued..........
Practical Plane Trig. and Mensuration of Surfaces..........Davies' Legendre.
This Session closes with the Spring Exhibitions, the last week in March.

SECOND TERM—SESSION SECOND.

Greek Harmony, completed...
Virgil ....Cooper.
Xenophon's Memorabilia..Robins,
Latin and Greek Exercises..
Surveying and Navigation..Davies.

SOPHOMORE CLASS.

FIRST TERM.

Greek Testament, Acts..Owen.
Livy ....Lincoln.
Homer's Odyssey...Owen.
Greek History..Smith.
Solid Geometry ....Davies' Legendre.

SECOND TERM—SESSION FIRST.

Greek Testament, Epistles..
Livy, continued...
Homer's Odyssey, continued.................... ....Apology & Crito.
Roman History ....Liddell.
Roman Antiquities ....Bojesen.
Analytical Plane Trigonometry......................................
Spherical Trigonometry, Mensuration of Solids and Application of Algebra to Geometry...

SECOND TERM—SESSION SECOND.

Greek Testament (Epistles)..
Horace ....Lincoln.
Greek Antiquities...Bojesen.
Apology and Crito..Tyler.
Plato's Gorgias..Woolsey.
Modern History..Lord.
Analytical Geometry and Conic Sections.................Coffin.

JUNIOR CLASS.

FIRST TERM.

Hebrew Grammar and Hebrew—Genesis (optional)......
Tacitus' Histories..Tyler.
Demosthenes' Select Orations....................................
Natural Philosophy, Mathematical part....................Olmsted.
Rhetoric..Blair.
Chemistry..Silliman.

SECOND TERM—SESSION FIRST.

Hebrew (Genesis continued).......................................
Tacitus (continued)..
Demosthenes' Select Orations (continued)................
Natural Philosophy—Applications............................
Logic ....Coupee.
Chemistry (continued)..
Botany ....Wood.

SECOND TERM—SESSION SECOND.

Hebrew (Psalms)...
Cicero's Tusculan Disputations.................................Anthon.
Alcestis of Euripides...
Astronomy..Olmsted.
Political Economy...Wayland.
Optics and Electricity...Olmsted.
Botany (continued)..Wood.

SENIOR CLASS.

FIRST TERM.

Anatomy and Physiology..........................Cutter.
Zoology ....Agassiz.
Selections of the Hebrew Bible...................
Psychology...Haven.
Cicero's Tusculan Disputations (continued).............
Greek Tragedies......................................Woolsey.

SECOND TERM—SESSION FIRST.

Select Hebrew (continued)..........................
Mineralogy and Geology............................Dana and Lyell.
Butler's Analogy.....................................Wilson's Edition.
Natural Theology....................................Paley.
Moral Science..Wayland.
Greek Tragedies (continued)........................
Juvenal ....Anthon.

SECOND TERM—SESSION SECOND.

Hebrew (continued)..................................
Geology (continued).................................
Moral Science (continued)..........................
Review of Latin......................................
Review of Greek Tragedies..........................
Constitution of the U. S. A.........................Story.

Department of English Literature and Philology.

The studies and exercises belonging to this Department are attended to by the Faculty. The Alumni Professorship, which was commenced some years ago, had in view the support of a separate Professor, who should devote his entire labors to this Department. The object contemplated is highly important, and the attention of the Alumni and other friends of the College is respectfully solicited to the endowment of this Professorship.

N. B. The Text Books needed for any part of the College Course may be procured at the Hanover Book Store.

EXPENSES &C.

The entire Expenditures of a Student need not much exceed $150, viz:

Tuition, per year..$30 00
Contingent fee.. 5 00
These are required in advance by the Term—first Term $14
second Term, $21.
Boarding with private families, and furnished room, at $2 00 to
$2 50 per week,..78 00 to 97 50
Fuel, Light, Washing &c,...15 00
Books, &c.,..5 00 to 10 00

Boarding in Clubs will cost from seventy-five cents to one dollar and twenty-five cents per week; and some board themselves even at a lower rate. The cost of clothing, and the amount spent as pocket money, will vary with the taste and habit of the Student, and with the wishes of his parents. As a general rule the more money allowed to a young man, beyond what is strictly necessary, the less likely he is to reflect honor upon his Parents and Instructors. Although Hanover presents comparatively few temptations to extravagance, yet parents are earnestly advised to require of their sons a detailed account of their expenditures, and to refuse the payment of any debt incurred by them, except for ordinary current expenses, without a written permission. It is also recommended that the funds of young pupils be deposited with some one of the Faculty, and expended under his direction. The younger Students are required to board where the Faculty may direct, and where they may exercise a more careful and frequent supervision.

N. B. Students placed upon Scholarships by the Faculty, are relieved in part, or wholly, as the case may be, from the payment of Tuition Fees. The Contingent Fee is required of those on Scholarships the same as others. This is now $2 00 for the first Term, and $3 00 for the second.

DISCIPLINE.

A record is kept by the Faculty, in which is entered weekly, the grade of scholarship of the Student, his absence from the exercises of the Institution, and such other facts as are worthy of notice with respect to his general deportment. From this record a report is made out at the end of each Session, and sent to the Parent or Guardian of each Student. In case of deficiency in scholarship, negligence in study, irregularity of attendance upon the exercises of the Institution, or improper conduct, the

Student will be privately admonished, and the Parent or Guardian will be promptly informed of the fact.

The object of this arrangement is to keep Parents and Guardians accurately informed with regard to their sons and wards in this Institution, and thus to secure their co-operation with the Faculty in a mild system of discipline. Whenever it is ascertained that a Student is deriving no advantage from his connection with the Institution, or is pursuing a course injurious to himself or fellow-students, the Faculty will take decisive action, and his Parent or Guardian will be promptly addressed on the subject, and requested to remove him from the Institution.

SCHOLARSHIPS.

The endowment of this Institution is in the form of Scholarships, of which the Board has established several sorts. The sum of $400 paid, or secured to the Corporation by note payable within five years; and bearing six per cent. interest in advance upon principal remaining unpaid, purchases for the owner, his heirs and assigns, a perpetual right to the tuition of one Scholar, in Hanover College. The sum of $200 paid, or subscribed under similar conditions, secures the right to twenty years' tuition; after which time the Scholarship is subject to the disposal of the Board for the gratuitous education of candidates for the Gospel Ministry. A Church Scholarship of $200, secures to the Church so contributing, a perpetual right to the tuition of one Student, who shall be a member of that Church; and appointed by the Session. A Presbyterial Scholarship of $200 secures a similar right to a Presbytery, in behalf of pupils who shall be candidates for the Ministry under its care. Principal paid on these Scholarships is invested by the Corporation in some safe and productive Stock, and the Interest only can be expended for the support of the College.

Every person applying for admission as a beneficiary of a Scholarship under the control of the donors, shall present to the Treasurer, at the beginning of each Term, a written Certificate from those controlling the Scholarship, of his right to such benefit;—when, after paying whatever interest may be due on said Scholarship, he shall receive an acknowledgment of his right, which he shall lodge with the President.

"The Scholarships subject to the disposal of the Corporation, may be occupied by such applicants as the Faculty may select, after inquiry into their circumstances, character, and attainments, the preference being ceteris paribus, to those who give the best evidence of Scholarship.

"There shall at no time be more than one Student upon each Scholarship."

ACCOMMODATIONS.

The community system of Boarding in Commons, or of rooming in large Lodging Halls; is not adopted in Hanover. Arrangements are made to accommodate the Students with board and rooms in respectable private families, where the number together can never be large; and where all shall be brought under domestic influence.

SETTLEMENT OF ACCOUNTS.

No Diploma nor honorable dismission shall be granted until the Student shall exhibit a Receipt of Settlement of all his bills for boarding, room and washing.

DEGREES.

No Degrees are conferred in Course. Candidates for Literary Honors are reported to the Board upon their ascertained or acknowledged merits.

SOCIETIES, LIBRARIES &C.

There are two Societies connected with the College, the UNION LITERARY, and the PHILALETHEAN, whose Libraries number each about twelve hundred volumes.

There is also a SOCIETY OF RELIGIOUS INQUIRY, which has begun to collect a Library, Maps, &c., and which receives regularly several valuable religious papers and periodicals.

The College Library contains near three thousand well selected volumes and is accessible to the Students.

The Cabinet contains several thousand specimens in Mineralogy and Geology.

The friends of the College are advised that contributions to the Library, to the Cabinet, or to the Laboratory, are much needed and will be thankfully received.

Public Literary Exercises and Annual Commencement.

Ample opportunity is offered to the Students, once a week, to improve themselves in Composition and Elocution, and several times a year Literary entertainments are given in public, which furnish occasions for honorable competition among the Students, and an interesting and profitable repast to their friends. Three of these entertainments occur annually, viz: on the evening of Washington's birth-day; on Tuesday and Wednesday evening, of the last week in March, and on the week of Commencement, when the two Literary Societies and the Society of Inquiry have addresses by gentlemen from abroad, and the Senior Class deliver their Graduating Orations,—altogether occupying over two days.

THE COMMENCEMENT DAY IS ON THE THURSDAY PRECEDING THE 25TH OF JUNE, after which there is a vacation till the last Wednesday of August.

PROHIBITED SECRET SOCIETIES.

The following order was passed by the Board of Trustees, in July, 1858, viz:

"*Resolved*, That this Board disapprove of the existence among the Students of Hanover College, of any Society or Association of which the Faculty are not *ex officio* Members, and will not permit the public exhibition of any such Society."

LOCATION, BUILDINGS &C.

The Village of Hanover is situated upon an elevated bluff of the Ohio River, six miles below Madison, Indiana, in a region of remarkable salubrity and natural beauty. The village and neighborhood are characterized by morality, and the absence of all the ordinary temptations to vice and idleness. The Ohio River, and the Railways from Madison, New Albany, and Cincinnati, place Hanover within twenty-four hours of all the principal points in Indiana, Kentucky, Western Ohio, and Eastern Illinois. A turnpike from Madison to Hanover, renders the village easy of access at all seasons of the year.

Hanover College is controlled by a Board of Trustees; one-half of whom are appointed by the Board itself, and the other half by the Synods of Indiana and Northern Indiana.

The Board purchased, some years ago, a farm of two hundred acres, lying between the Village and the Ohio River, upon a beautiful point of which,—overlooking the River from an elevation of four hundred feet,—they have erected a commodious College edifice, now completed and occupied. The new College consists of a center building nearly eighty feet square, with lateral and transverse wings. The whole length is about two hundred feet. It contains no dormitories for Students,—an undesirable provision,—but affords ample and convenient Halls, Library, Cabinet, Lecture, and Recitation Rooms, and a spacious Chapel.

The building commands an exceedingly diversified view of the River, for six miles up and ten miles down its course. A visitor of large acquaintance with our Country and the world, asserts that a more delightful prospect can not be found in America or Europe.

FORM OF CONVEYANCES AND BEQUESTS.

The corporate name of this institution is "THE TRUSTEES OF HANOVER COLLEGE."

Donors residing in other States should also designate the place in which the college is located, thus: "*The Trustees of Hanover College, located at Hanover, in the State of Indiana.*"

The friends of Education in Indiana and elsewhere are respectfully solicited to make donations and legacies to this Institution. Since the College was chartered in 1832, about 3,000 have received all or part of their education here, and not less than 800 of these were candidates for the Gospel Ministry. The College has enjoyed 23 revivals of Religion. Over one half of the students in the present catalogue, are members of the Church, and one fourth or more have in view the sacred office.

HANOVER COLLEGE.

Thursday, June 19, 1862.

Commencement Exercises.

Music, and Destribution of Orders.

PRAYER—MUSIC.

ORATION—Independence............................M. F. DUNN, Bedford, Ind.

MUSIC.

ORATION—Honor, the Reward of Virtue........G. P. HUCKEBY, Rome, Ind.

MUSIC.

ORATION—"By this Conquer" (the Cross)......
G. M. MCCAMPBELL, Jeffersonville, Ind.

MUSIC.

ORATION—Dignity of Condescension......S. T. MCCLURE, Vincennes, Ind

MUSIC.

ORATION—Life's Problem...........................J. T. PATTERSON, Delphi, Ind.

MUSIC.

ORATION—Immaturity.................W. H. SAWTELLE, Binghampton, N. Y.

MUSIC.

ORATION—"Fenelon"..............................L. M. SCOFIELD, Newport, Ky.

MUSIC.

ORATION—Mental Philosophers...............H. C. THOMSON, Hanover, Ind.

MUSIC.

ORATION—"Think of Living"............J. C. YOUNGKEN, Friendsville, Ill.

MUSIC.

Delivery of Diplomas, etc.

MUSIC.

PRAYER AND BENEDICTION.

MUSIC.

THE

THIRTY-FIRST

Annual Catalogue and Circular

OF

HANOVER COLLEGE,

AT

HANOVER, INDIANA.

JUNE, 1863.

MADISON, IND.:
WM. P. LEVY'S PRINTING AND BINDING ESTABLISHMENT.
1863.

THE

THIRTY-FIRST

Annual Catalogue and Circular

OF

HANOVER COLLEGE,

AT

HANOVER, INDIANA.

JUNE, 1863.

MADISON, IND.:
WM. P. LEVY'S PRINTING AND BINDING ESTABLISHMENT.
1863.

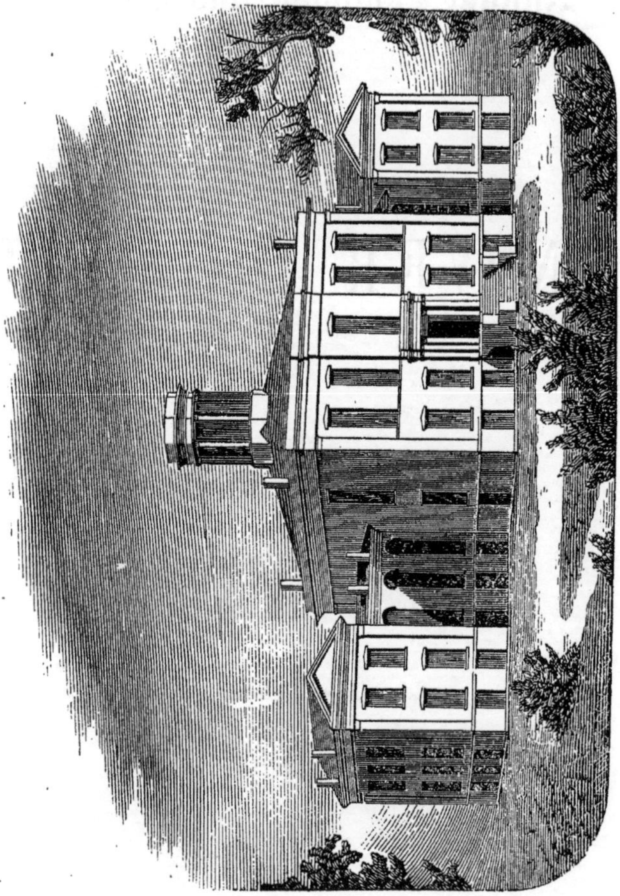

BOARD OF TRUSTEES.

Bd. DR. P. S. SHIELDS, New Albany,......................................1864.
Bd. JOSEPH PIERCE, Esq., Valparaiso,...............................1864.
Bd. DR. ANDREW SPEAR, Hanover...................................1864.
Bd. REV. WILLIAM Y. ALLEN, Waveland.............................1864.
S. S. REV. ISAAC W. MONFORT, Chaplain U. S A..................1864.
S. S. REV. J. W. BLYTHE, Hanover..1864.
N. S. THOMAS P. GORDON, D. D., Terre Haute......................1864.
N. S. REV ROBERT IRWIN, Sen., Muncie................................1864.
Bd. REV. D. D. McKEE, Hanover..1865.
Bd. JOHN W. BLACKBURN, Esq., Paris, Ill............................1865.
Bd. REV. W. A. HOLLIDAY, Indianapolis...............................1865.
Bd. JESSE L. WILLIAMS, Esq., Fort Wayne............................1865.
S. S. JAMES H. McCAMPBELL, Esq., Jeffersonville................1865.
S. S. REV. DAVID MONFORT, Greensburg.............................1865.
N. S. REV. E. W. WRIGHT, D. D., Delphi................................1865.
N. S. REV. W. M. DONALDSON, Ossian.................................1865.
Bd. JAMES M. RAY, Esq., Indianapolis...................................1866.
Bd. ROBERT DEAN, Esq., Hanover...1866.
Bd. HON. C. E. WALKER, Madison..1866.
Bd. COL. JAMES BLAKE, Indianapolis....................................1866.
S. S. SILAS C. DAY, Esq., New Albany...................................1866.
S. S. REV. THOMAS S. CROWE, Jeffersonville........................1866.
N. S. REV. C. K. THOMPSON, Lebanon..................................1866.
N. S. REV. JAMES B. CROWE, Crawfordsville........................1866.
Bd. JOHN KING, Esq., Madison..1863.
Bd. REV. J. G. MONFORT, D. D., Cincinnati, Ohio.................1863.
Bd. HON. W. McKEE DUNN, Madison....................................1863.
Bd. REV. JAMES WOOD, D. D., Hanover................................1863.
S. S. REV. P. MORTON, Vincennes...1863.
S. S. JOHN H. VANNUYS, Esq., Franklin................................1863.
N. S. REV. JOHN M. LOWRIE, D. D., Fort Wayne...................1863.
N. S. REV. THOMAS McINTIRE, Indianapolis.........................1863.

Officers of the Board.

JAMES M. RAY, Esq., *President.*   REV. D. D. McKEE, *Secretary.*
REV. JAMES WOOD, D. D., *Treasurer.*

Executive Committee.

HON. W. McKEE DUNN,   JOHN KING, Esq.,
REV. JAMES WOOD, D. D.,   ROBERT DEAN, Esq.,
REV. D. D. McKEE.

Auditing Committee.

HON. W. McKEE DUNN.   HON. C. E. WALKER.

FACULTY.

REV. JAMES WOOD, D. D., President,
Professor of Biblical Instruction, Psychology, Logic and Ethics.

REV. S. HARRISON THOMSON, A. M.,
Professor of Mathematics, Mechanical Philosophy, and Astronomy.

....
Professor of the Latin Language and Literature.

REV. JOSHUA B. GARRITT, A. M.,
Professor of the Greek Language and Literature.

REV. J. W. SCOTT, D. D.,
Professor of Natural Science.

HENRY C. THOMSON, A. B.,
Tutor.

REV. JOSHUA B. GARRITT, A. M.,
Librarian.

WILLIAM BROWN,
Janitor.

UNDERGRADUATES.

SENIORS.

Josiah Daugherty	Ladoga.
J. Addison Day	New Albany.
Henry C. Donnell	Greenville, Ill.
George Hippard	Indianapolis.
Adam J. Johnson	Spades.
Augustus A. Joss	Constantine, Mich.
Hugh W. McKee	Harrodsburg, Ky.
Amos W. Patterson	Hanover.
Emanuel N. Pires	Jacksonville, Ill.
William C. Smock	Sigourney, Iowa.
Eberle Thomson	Greensburg.
William Torrance	Terre Haute.
Benjamin W. Tucker	N. Philadelphia.

JUNIORS.

Samuel Brown	Shelbyville, Ky.
William W. Brown	Shelbyville, Ky.
Noble C. Butler	Salem.
William B. Chamberlin	Hanover.
James A. Dean	Hanover.
John H. Harbolt	Charlestown.
J. D. Harrington	Shelbyville, Ky.
John H. Holliday	Indianapolis.
John Kerns	Hanover.
Robert McConnel	Fairland.
Peter H. K. McComb	Hanover.
R. A. Mathes	Altonburg, Mo.
J. Graham Moore	Louisville Ky.

William A. Patton..Spruce Hill, Pa.
Arthur Rose...Cincinnati, O.
Martin V. Van Arsdale..Washington.
Robert M. Webster..Tallahoma, Iowa.
John Weston..Galena, Ill.

SOPHOMORES.

John G. Blake..Indianapolis.
J. C. Eastman..Hanover.
George W. Fitch...Hanover.
W. H. Fullenwider..Waveland.
Francis M. Gilchrist..Fairland.
John H. McConnell...Fairland.
Preston McKinney..Livonia.
Robert M. Miller..Hanover.
U. W. Miller..Louisville, Ky.
Edward Quinche...Galena, Ill.
Richard W. Sipe...Swanville.
Thomas Tracy..Louisville, Ky.
Leonidas V. Winston...Richmond.

FRESHMEN.

Nathan Hall Downing..Virginia, Ill.
John C. Foutts...Scott, O.
James M. Justice..Logansport.
John A. Kellar...North Vernon.
George M. Lodge..Springfield, Ill.
James A. Miller..Louisville, Ky.
Thaddeus S. Rollins..Logansport.
Augustus T. Stone...Princeville, Ill.
William Wilson Thomson.......................................Delphi.

SCIENTIFIC DEPARTMENT.

THIRD YEAR.
Felix J. Brandt..Hanover.

SECOND YEAR.
John R. Armstrong......................................Jeffersonville.
Robert S. Dean...Hanover.
Wm. J. Meredith...Lafayette.
George Merriwether...................................Louisville, Ky.
James T. Ramsay......................................Hanover.
George Scoggan..Bedford.
Samuel M. Strader....................................Madison.

FIRST YEAR.
Albert L. Dean..Urbana, Ill.
William Henry Gilliland..............................Charlestown.
Erskine G. Hammond................................Troy, Mo.
William B. Kennedy...................................Louisville, Ky.
John D. Lester...Eddyville, Ky.
Abraham T. McCurry.................................Kent.
John W. O'Bannon....................................Pleasureville, Ky.
James R. Parker.......................................Grandview.
Absalom Augustus Steagald....................Decaturville, Tenn.
B. B. Summers..Bardstown, Ky.
James L. Swan...Saluda.
William A. Terrell......................................Bloomfield, Ky.
Finley White...Kent.
Harvey W. Wiley..Kent.
Andrew D. Wilson.....................................Hanover.

PREPARATORY DEPARTMENT.

SENIORS.

Samuel Wilson Elliott	Dayton.
Henry R. Lee	Hanover.
Charles W. Moore	Louisville, Ky.
Alexander S. Peck	Omaha City, N. T.
William B. Sturgus	Hanover.
James H. Thomson	Hanover.

JUNIORS.

George Cowan Blythe	Evansville.
Jesse Caldwell	Jeffersonville.
Thomas Brown Dean	Hanover.
*David V. Demaree	Canaan.
Edward Gelpin	Hanover.
James Hardin	Bardstown, Ky.
William Keiry	Nashville, Ill.
Amos G. McCampbell	Louisville, Ky.
James W. Pearson	Madison.
George C. Reed	Hanover.
Henry M. Robb	Hanover.
David W. Rogers	Hanover.
William Wilder Taylor	Louisville, Ky.

SUMMARY.

Seniors	13	Scientific, 2d year	7
Juniors	18	Scientific, 1st year	15
Sophomores	13	Senior Preparatory	6
Freshmen	9	Junior Preparatory	13
Scientific, 3d year	1		
Total			95

*Drowned May 30, 1863.

TEXT BOOKS.

DEPARTMENT OF LANGUAGES

LATIN.—Andrews' Grammar and Reader; Andrews' or Leverett's or Crooks & Schem's Lexicon; Andrews' Cæsar; Cooper's Virgil; Bojesen's Roman Antiquities; Butler & Sturgus' Sallust; Lincoln's Livy; Lincoln's Horace; Tyler's Tacitus; Chase's or Anthon's Tusculan Disputations.

GREEK—Hadley's Grammar; Liddell & Scott's, or Pickering's Lexicon; Owen's, or Boise's Anabasis; Bojesen's Grecian Antiquities; Owen's Homer; Woolsey's Greek Plays; Champlin's Demosthenes; Plutarch.

HEBREW—Stuart's Rœdiger's Grammar; Gesenius' Lexicon; Biblia Hebraica.

DEPARTMENT OF BELLES-LETTERS.

Blair's Rhetoric, (University Edition); Whately's or Coppee's Logic; Wayland's Political Economy; Smith's Grecian History: Liddell's Rome; Lord's Modern History; American History and the Constitution of the U. S. A.

DEPARTMENT OF MATHEMATICS.

Rays' Algebra, 2nd part; Davies' Legendre; Davies' Surveying, Coffin's Conic Sections; Loomis' Analytical Geometry and Calculus, Olmsted's Natural Philosophy; Olmsted's Astronomy.

DEPARTMENT OF NATURAL SCIENCE.

Silliman's Chemistry; Cutter's Physiology; Wood's Botany; Lyell's Geology; Dana's Mineralogy; Agassiz & Gould's Zoology, Somerville's Physical Geography.

DEPARTMENT OF METAPHYSICS.

Walker's Reid on the Intellectual Powers; Sir William Hamilton's Philosophy, (Wight's Edition); Stewart's Active and Moral Powers; Wayland's Moral Science; Haven's Mental Philosophy.

DEPARTMENT OF RELIGIOUS INSTRUCTION.

English Bible, Hodge's, Alexander's or Jacobus' Notes; Greek Testament, Robinson's Greek Harmony; Old Testament Hebrew; Septuagint; Westminister Catechism; General Assembly's Psalm and Hymn Books; Butler's Analogy; Paley's Natural Theology; Coleman's Sacred Geography; Alexander's Evidences of Christianity.

Scientific Department.

The three years' course of English, Mathematical and Scientific instruction pursued in this department, embraces all that is included in the College scheme, except the Classical Languages. Such as desire it, however, may pursue the study of Latin and French, in connection with a Scientific Course. We do not recommend it as in any sense an equivalent for a thorough Classical Course; nor is it intended for mere boys, since the subjects which it includes are entirely above their capacity; but to young men, who have attained a respectable common school education, including the elements of Algebra, and who have not time nor means to prosecute a Classical course, this system of studies will, it is hoped, commend itself as solid, comprehensive and practical. Those who shall complete the prescribed Scientific course, will receive a Diploma, certifying the extent of their attainments.

COLLEGE YEAR--EXAMINATIONS.

The College Year is divided into two Terms. The First Term begins on the Wednesday after the 25th day of August, and continues 16 weeks.— The Second Term begins on the first Wednesday in January and continues 24 weeks. The Annual Commencement occurs on Thursday before the 25th of June.

It is of great importance that students attend from the very beginning of the Term; especially since so considerable a portion of time is allotted to vacations. In most cases, the loss of a few weeks, or even days, seriously affects the future standing of the pupil. Absence during term time without special leave, is prohibited.*

Public Examinations will be held, hereafter, only at the close of the College year, when the Freshman and Junior Classes will be examined on the studies of the preceding year, and the Sophomore and Senior Classes upon those of the two preceding years. These last examinations will be FINAL, for the studies pursued in those years. All the examinations will be THOROUGH and RIGID; and will be conducted, in part by the use of written questions, prepared by the Faculty and the Examining Committee, covering the whole field of study prosecuted during a given period, and entirely unknown to the Student until the moment of examination.— These questions must be answered in writing before the Committee; and correct answers to a definite portion of them will be the passport of admission to a higher standing. Similar examinations of a briefer and less decisive character, however, and by way of preparation for the final trial, may be conducted privately, at the pleasure of the Faculty.

---

*Parents are respectfully advised to give their sons no such permission to be absent, except in cases of NECESSITY.

Religious Instruction and Services.

The attention of a Christian community is respectfully invited to the system of Biblical Instruction which forms a characteristic feature of our course of Study. The Grammar School Classes recite statedly in the English Bible; and every College Class has a daily or tri-weekly recitation in the Greek Testament, or the Hebrew. Proficiency in these, as in other studies, is tested by the usual examinations. In addition to this, Biblical Geography and Antiquities, Ecclesiastical History, Natural Theology, and the Analogy of Religion, Natural and Revealed, to the constitution and course of nature, are carefully and faithfully studied. There is also a Bible or Catechetical exercise on Sabbath mornings; a public service on Sabbath afternoon, appropriated to the Students; and daily morning prayers. The Students are expected to attend the Sabbath morning services of the congregation worshiping in the chapel, or of some other congregation in the vicinity, if their parents prefer any of the latter. The Methodist and United and Associate Presbyterian Churches have regular services in or near the Village.

ADMISSION.

Candidates for admission into the Freshman Class, are required to be proficient in Arithmetic and Algebra; Ancient and Modern Geography; History of the U. S. A.; the English, Latin, and Greek Grammars; Cæsar's Commentaries, and Greek Reader, or what is equivalent to these attainments. They must furnish testimonials of good character, and, if from another College, must bring certificates of honorable dismission.— Candidates for higher standing are examined upon that part of the course already studied by the Class which they propose to enter.

No one can be admitted to the Freshman Class until he has completed his fourteenth year, nor to an advanced standing without a proportional increase of age.

Before a student shall be admitted to actual standing in any Class, he shall present to the President a receipt from the Treasurer, showing that he has complied with the Statutes relating to College Charges and Scholarships.

N. B. The regular examination for admission into College, commences on the Monday preceding the beginning of each Term.

COURSE OF INSTRUCTION.

Preparatory Department.

Andrew's Latin Lessons, Grammar, Reader, and Exercises; Andrew's Cæsar; Butler and Sturgus' Sallust; McClintock & Crook's 1st and 2d Greek Books; Classical and Biblical Geography; Ray's Algebra, 2nd part, English Bible.

Scientific Department.

FIRST YEAR.

Algebra, Rays', 2nd part; Plane Geometry; Plane Trigonometry, Mensuration of Surfaces, Surveying and Navigation; History; English Bible; Historical Books, and Sacred Geography.

SECOND YEAR.

Solid Geometry; Analytical Plane Trigonometry; Mensuration of Solids; and Application of Algebra to Geometry; Spherical Trigonometry; Conic Sections; Rhetoric, Logic; Political Economy, English Bible, Poetical Books; Chemistry, Light, Heat, Electriciy, and Botany.

THIRD YEAR.

Analytical Geometry and Calculus; Natural Philosophy, Astronomy, Anatomy, Zoology and Physiology; Mineralogy; Geology, Natural Theology, Butler's Analogy, Psychology, Moral Science, English Bible, Constitution of the U. S. A.

COLLEGIATE DEPARTMENT.

Freshman Class.

FIRST TERM.

Greek Harmony of the Gospels	Robinson.
Biblical Antiquities	Nevin.
Sallust	Butler & Sturgus.
Latin Exercises	Andrews.
Greek Prose Composition	Boise.
Xenophon's Anabasis	Boise.
Plane Geometry	Davies' Legendre.

SECOND TERM—SESSION FIRST.

Greek Harmony, continued	Robinson
Sallust, continued	Butler & Sturgus.
Latin Exercises and Greek Composition, continued	
Practical Plane Trig. and Mensuration of Surfaces	Davies' Legendre.

This Session closes with the Spring Exhibitions, the last week in March.

SECOND TERM—SESSION SECOND.

Greek Harmony, completed	
Virgil	Cooper.
Xenophon's Memorabilia	Robbins.
Latin and Greek Exercises	
Surveying and Navigation	Davies.

SOPHOMORE CLASS.

FIRST TERM.

Greek Testament, Acts	Owen.
Livy	Lincoln.
Homer's Odyssey	Owen.
Greek History	Smith.
Solid Geometry	Davies' Legendre.

SECOND TERM—SESSION FIRST.

Greek Testament, Epistles..
Livy, continued...
Homer's Odyssey, continued.......................................
Plato's Apology & Crito.....................................Tyler.
Roman History ....Liddell.
Roman Antiquities ....Bojesen.
Analytical Plane Trigonometry...................................
Spherical Trigonometry, Mensuration of Solids and Application of Algebra to Geometry...........................

SECOND TERM—SESSION SECOND.

Greek Testament (Epistles)..
Horace ....Lincoln.
Greek Antiquities ....Bojesen.
Apology and Crito, continued.........................Tyler.
Modern History..Lord.
Conic Sections...Coffin.

JUNIOR CLASS.

FIRST TERM.

Hebrew Grammar and Hebrew—Genesis (optional)......
Tacitus' Germania and Agricola.......................Tyler.
Demosthenes' Select Orations.......................Champlin
Analytical Geometry and Calculus................Loomis.
Rhetoric..Blair.
Chemistry...Silliman.

SECOND TERM—SESSION FIRST.

Hebrew (Genesis continued)...
Tacitus (continued)..
Demosthenes' Select Orations (continued).................
Natural Philosophy, Mathematical part............Olmsted.
Logic ....Coppee.
Chemistry (continued)...
Botany ....Wood.

SECOND TERM—SESSION SECOND.

Hebrew (Psalms)...
Cicero's Tusculan Disputations......................Anthon.
Alcestis of Euripides......................................Woolsey.
Natural Philosophy—Applications.................Olmsted.
Political Economy..Wayland.
Optics and Electricity....................................Olmsted.
Botany (continued)...Wood.

SENIOR CLASS.
FIRST TERM.

Anatomy and Physiology..................................Cutter.
Zoology ....Agassiz.
Selections of the Hebrew Bible............................
Psychology...Haven.
Cicero's Tusculan Disputations (continued)..............
Greek Tragedies..Woolsey.
Astronomy and Review....................................Olmsted.

SECOND TERM—SESSION FIRST.

Select Hebrew (continued)..................................
Mineralogy and Geology...................................Dana and Lyell.
Butler's Analogy...
Natural Theology..Paley.
Moral Science...Wayland.
Greek Tragedies (continued)...............................
Juvenal ....Anthon.
Ouranography and Review.................................

SECOND TERM—SESSION SECOND.

Hebrew (continued)..
Geology (continued)...
Moral Science (continued)..................................
Juvenal...
Plutarch ....Hackett.
Constitution of the U. S. A................................Story.
Astronomy and Ouranography and Review...............

Department of English Literature and Philology.

The studies and exercises belonging to this Department are attended to by the Faculty. The Alumni Professorship, which was commenced some years ago, had in view the support of a separate Professor, who should devote his entire labors to this Department. The object contemplated is highly important, and the attention of the Alumni and other friends of the College is respectfully solicited to the endowment of this Professorship.

N. B. The Text Books needed for any part of the College Course will be furnished by one of the Professors, at Cincinnati prices.

EXPENSES &C.

The entire Expenditures of a Student need not much exceed $150, viz:

Tuition, per year..$30 00
Contingent fee.. 5 00
These are required in advance by the Term—first Term $14 second Term, $21.
Boarding with private families, and furnished room, at $2 00 to
$2 50 per week,...78 00 to 97 50
Fuel, Light, Washing &c,..15 00
Books, &c.,..5 00 to 10 00

Boarding in Clubs will cost from seventy-five cents to one dollar and twenty-five cents per week; and some board themselves even at a lower rate. The cost of clothing, and the amount spent as pocket money, will vary with the taste and habit of the Student, and with the wishes of his parents. As a general rule the more money allowed to a young man beyond what is strictly necessary, the less likely he is to reflect honor upon his Parents and Instructors. Although Hanover presents comparatively few temptations to extravagance, yet parents are earnestly advised to require of their sons a detailed account of their expenditures, and to refuse the payment of any debt incurred by them, except for ordinary current expenses, without a written permission. It is also recommended that the funds of young pupils be deposited with some one of the Faculty, and expended under his direction. The younger Students are required to board where the Faculty may direct, and where they may exercise a more careful and frequent supervision.

N. B. Students placed upon Scholarships by the Faculty, are relieved in part, or wholly, as the case may be, from the payment of Tuition Fees. The Contingent Fee is required of those on Scholarships the same as others. This is now $2 00 for the first Term, and $3 00 for the second.

DISCIPLINE.

A record is kept by the Faculty, in which is entered weekly, the grades of scholarship of the Student, his absence from the exercises of the Institution, and such other facts as are worthy of notice with respect to his general deportment. From this record a report is made out at the end of each Session, and sent to the Parent or Guardian of each Student. In case of deficiency in scholarship, negligence in study, irregularity of attendance upon the exercises of the Institution, or improper conduct, the

Student will be privately admonished, and the Parent or Guardian will be promptly informed of the fact.

The object of this arrangement is to keep Parents and Guardians accurately informed with regard to their sons and wards in this Institution, and thus to secure their co-operation with the Faculty in a mild system of discipline. Whenever it is ascertained that a Student is deriving no advantage from his connection with the Institution, or is pursuing a course injurious to himself or fellow-students, the Faculty will take decisive action, and his Parent or Guardian will be promptly addressed on the subject, and requested to remove him from the Institution.

Resolutions of the Faculty Adopted Dec. 20, 1862.

An absence during the latter part of the College Term greatly injures the Scholarship of Students, impairs their habits of study, breaks the integrity of Classes, discourages study among students that remain, and thus lowers the literary standard of the Institute, therefore,

RESOLVED, 1st. That after this date, Dec. 20, 1862, all such absences (not made unavoidable by the Providence of God,) shall be recorded as unexcused, and each recitation thus lost, registered as Zero.

RESOLVED, 2d. That this Resolution be published in the Catalogue and Quarterly Review.

SCHOLARSHIPS.

The endowment of this Institution is in the form of Scholarships, of which the Board has established several sorts. The sum of $400 paid, or secured to the Corporation by note payable within five years; and bearing six per cent. interest in advance upon principal remaining unpaid, purchases for the owner, his heirs and assigns, a perpetual right to the tuition of one Scholar, in Hanover College. The sum of $200 paid, or subscribed under similar conditions, secures the right to twenty years' tuition; after which time the Scholarship is subject to the disposal of the Board for the gratuitous education of candidates for the Gospel Ministry. A Church Scholarship of $200, secures to the Church so contributing, a perpetual right to the tuition of one Student, who shall be a member of that Church; and appointed by the Session. A Presbyterial Scholarship of $200 secures a similar right to a Presbytery, in behalf of pupils who shall be candidates for the Ministry under its care. Principal paid on these Scholarships is invested by the Corporation in some safe and productive Stock, and the Interest only can be expended for the support of the College.

Every person applying for admission as a beneficiary of a Scholarship under the control of the donors, shall present to the Treasurer, at the beginning of each Term, a written Certificate from those controling the Scholarship, of his right to such benefit;—when, after paying whatever interest may be due on said Scholarship, he shall receive an acknowledgment of his right, which he shall lodge with the President.

"The Scholarships subject to the disposal of the Corporation, may be occupied by such applicants as the Faculty may select, after inquiry into their circumstances, character, and attainments, the preference being ceteris paribus, to those who give the best evidence of Scholarship.

"There shall at no time be more than one Student upon each Scholarship."

ACCOMMODATIONS.

The community system of Boarding in Commons, or of rooming in large Lodging Halls, is not adopted in Hanover. Arrangements are made to accommodate the Students with board and rooms in respectable private families, where the number together can never be large; and where all shall be brought under domestic influence.

SETTLEMENT OF ACCOUNTS.

No Diploma nor honorable dismission shall be granted until the Student shall exhibit a Receipt of Settlement of all his bills for boarding, room and washing.

DEGREES.

No Degrees are conferred in Course. Candidates for Literary Honors are reported to the Board upon their ascertained or acknowledged merits.

Student will be privately admonished, and the Parent or Guardian will be promptly informed of the fact.

The object of this arrangement is to keep Parents and Guardians accurately informed with regard to their sons and wards in this Institution, and thus to secure their co-operation with the Faculty in a mild system of discipline. Whenever it is ascertained that a Student is deriving no advantage from his connection with the Institution, or is pursuing a course injurious to himself or fellow-students, the Faculty will take decisive action, and his Parent or Guardian will be promptly addressed on the subject, and requested to remove him from the Institution.

Resolutions of the Faculty Adopted Dec. 20, 1862.

An absence during the latter part of the College Term greatly injures the Scholarship of Students, impairs their habits of study, breaks the integrity of Classes, discourages study among students that remain, and thus lowers the literary standard of the Institute, therefore,

RESOLVED, 1st. That after this date, Dec. 20, 1862, all such absences (not made unavoidable by the Providence of God,) shall be recorded as unexcused, and each recitation thus lost, registered as Zero.

RESOLVED, 2d. That this Resolution be published in the Catalogue and Quarterly Review.

SCHOLARSHIPS.

The endowment of this Institution is in the form of Scholarships, of which the Board has established several sorts. The sum of $400 paid, or secured to the Corporation by note payable within five years; and bearing six per cent. interest in advance upon principal remaining unpaid, purchases for the owner, his heirs and assigns, a perpetual right to the tuition of one Scholar, in Hanover College. The sum of $200 paid, or subscribed under similar conditions, secures the right to twenty years' tuition; after which time the Scholarship is subject to the disposal of the Board for the gratuitous education of candidates for the Gospel Ministry. A Church Scholarship of $200, secures to the Church so contributing, a perpetual right to the tuition of one Student, who shall be a member of that Church; and appointed by the Session. A Presbyterial Scholarship of $200 secures a similar right to a Presbytery, in behalf of pupils who shall be candidates for the Ministry under its care. Principal paid on these Scholarships is invested by the Corporation in some safe and productive Stock, and the Interest only can be expended for the support of the College.

Every person applying for admission as a beneficiary of a Scholarship under the control of the donors, shall present to the Treasurer, at the beginning of each Term, a written Certificate from those controling the Scholarship, of his right to such benefit;—when, after paying whatever interest may be due on said Scholarship, he shall receive an acknowledgment of his right, which he shall lodge with the President.

"The Scholarships subject to the disposal of the Corporation, may be occupied by such applicants as the Faculty may select, after inquiry into their circumstances, character, and attainments, the preference being ceteris paribus, to those who give the best evidence of Scholarship.

"There shall at no time be more than one Student upon each Scholarship."

ACCOMMODATIONS.

The community system of Boarding in Commons, or of rooming in large Lodging Halls, is not adopted in Hanover. Arrangements are made to accommodate the Students with board and rooms in respectable private families, where the number together can never be large; and where all shall be brought under domestic influence.

SETTLEMENT OF ACCOUNTS.

No Diploma nor honorable dismission shall be granted until the Student shall exhibit a Receipt of Settlement of all his bills for boarding, room and washing.

DEGREES.

No Degrees are conferred in Course. Candidates for Literary Honors are reported to the Board upon their ascertained or acknowledged merits.

SOCIETIES, LIBRARIES &C.

There are two Societies connected with the College, the UNION LITERARY and the PHILALETHEAN, whose Libraries number each about twelve hundred volumes.

There is also a SOCIETY OF RELIGIOUS INQUIRY, which has begun to collect a Library, Maps, &c., and which receives regularly several valuable religious papers and periodicals.

The College Library contains near three thousand well selected volumes and is accessible to the Students.

The Cabinet contains several thousand specimens in Mineralogy and Geology.

The friends of the College are advised that contributions to the Library to the Cabinet, or to the Laboratory, are much needed and will be thankfully received.

Public Literary Exercises and Annual Commencement.

Ample opportuntiy is offered to the Students, once a week, to improve themselves in Composition and Elocution, and several times a year Literary entertainments are given in public, which furnish occasions for honorable competition among the Students, and an interesting and profitable repast to their friends. Three of these entertainments occur annually, viz: on the evening of Washington's birth-day; on Tuesday and Wednesday evening, of the last week in March, and on the week of Commencement, when the two Literary Societies and the Society of Inquiry have addresses by gentlemen from abroad, and the Senior Class deliver their Graduating Orations,—altogether occupying over two days.

THE COMMENCEMENT DAY IS ON THE THURSDAY PRECEDING THE 25TH OF JUNE, after which there is a vacation till the last Wednesday of August.

Prohibited Secret Societies.

The following order was passed by the Board of Trustees, in July, 1858, viz:

"*Resolved*, That this Board disapprove of the existence among the Students of Hanover College, of any Society or Association of which the Faculty are not *ex officio* Members, and will not permit the public exhibition of any such Society."

LOCATION, BUILDINGS &C.

The Village of Hanover is situated upon an elevated bluff of the Ohio River, six miles below Madison, Indiana, in a region of remarkable salubrity and natural beauty. The village and neighborhood are characterized by morality, and the absence of all the ordinary temptations to vice and idleness. The Ohio River, and the Railways from Madison, New Albany, and Cincinnati, place Hanover within twenty-four hours of all the principal points in Indiana, Kentucky, Western Ohio, and Eastern Illinois. A turnpike from Madison to Hanover, renders the village easy of access at all seasons of the year.

Hanover College is controlled by a Board of Trustees; one-half of whom are appointed by the Board itself, and the other half by the Synods of Indiana and Northern Indiana.

The Board purchased, some years ago, a farm of two hundred acres, lying between the Village and the Ohio River, upon a beautiful point of which,—overlooking the River from an elevation of four hundred feet,—they have erected a commodious College edifice, now completed and occupied. The new College consists of a center building nearly eighty feet square, with lateral and transverse wings. The whole length is about two hundred feet. It contains no dormitories for Students,—an undesirable provision,—but affords ample and convenient Halls, Library, Cabinet, Lecture, and Recitation Rooms, and a spacious Chapel.

The building commands an exceedingly diversified view of the River, for six miles up and ten miles down its course. A visitor of large acquaintance with our Country and the world, asserts that a more delightful prospect can not be found in America or Europe.

FORM OF CONVEYANCES AND BEQUESTS.

The corporate name of this institution is "THE TRUSTEES OF HANOVER COLLEGE."

Donors residing in other States should also designate the place in which the college is located, thus: "*The Trustees of Hanover College, located at Hanover, in the State of Indiana.*"

The friends of Education in Indiana and elsewhere are respectfully solicited to make donations and legacies to this Institution. Since the College was chartered in 1832, about 3,000 have received all or part of their education here, and not less than 800 of these were candidates for the Gospel Ministry. The College has enjoyed 23 revivals of Religion. Over one half of the students in the present catalogue, are members of the Church, and one fourth or more have in view the sacred office.

SOCIETIES, LIBRARIES &C.

There are two Societies connected with the College, the UNION LITERARY and the PHILALETHEAN, whose Libraries number each about twelve hundred volumes.

There is also a SOCIETY OF RELIGIOUS INQUIRY, which has begun to collect a Library, Maps, &c., and which receives regularly several valuable religious papers and periodicals.

The College Library contains near three thousand well selected volumes and is accessible to the Students.

The Cabinet contains several thousand specimens in Mineralogy and Geology.

The friends of the College are advised that contributions to the Library to the Cabinet, or to the Laboratory, are much needed and will be thankfully received.

Public Literary Exercises and Annual Commencement.

Ample opportuntiy is offered to the Students, once a week, to improve themselves in Composition and Elocution, and several times a year Literary entertainments are given in public, which furnish occasions for honorable competition among the Students, and an interesting and profitable repast to their friends. Three of these entertainments occur annually, viz: on the evening of Washington's birth-day; on Tuesday and Wednesday evening, of the last week in March, and on the week of Commencement, when the two Literary Societies and the Society of Inquiry have addresses by gentlemen from abroad, and the Senior Class deliver their Graduating Orations,—altogether occupying over two days.

THE COMMENCEMENT DAY IS ON THE THURSDAY PRECEDING THE 25TH OF

Prohibited Secret Societies.

The following order was passed by the Board of Trustees, in July, 1858, viz:

"*Resolved*, That this Board disapprove of the existence among the Students of Hanover College, of any Society or Association of which the Faculty are not *ex-officio* Members, and will not permit the public exhibition of any such Society."

LOCATION, BUILDINGS &C.

The Village of Hanover is situated upon an elevated bluff of the Ohio River, six miles below Madison, Indiana, in a region of remarkable salubrity and natural beauty. The village and neighborhood are characterized by morality, and the absence of all the ordinary temptations to vice and idleness. The Ohio River, and the Railways from Madison, New Albany, and Cincinnati, place Hanover within twenty-four hours of all the principal points in Indiana, Kentucky, Western Ohio, and Eastern Illinois. A turnpike from Madison to Hanover, renders the village easy of access at all seasons of the year.

Hanover College is controlled by a Board of Trustees; one-half of whom are appointed by the Board itself, and the other half by the Synods of Indiana and Northern Indiana.

The Board purchased, some years ago, a farm of two hundred acres, lying between the Village and the Ohio River, upon a beautiful point of which,—overlooking the River from an elevation of four hundred feet,—they have erected a commodious College edifice, now completed and occupied. The new College consists of a center building nearly eighty feet square, with lateral and transverse wings. The whole length is about two hundred feet. It contains no dormitories for Students,—an undesirable provision,—but affords ample and convenient Halls, Library, Cabinet, Lecture, and Recitation Rooms, and a spacious Chapel.

The building commands an exceedingly diversified view of the River, for six miles up and ten miles down its course. A visitor of large acquaintance with our Country and the world, asserts that a more delightful prospect can not be found in America or Europe.

FORM OF CONVEYANCES AND BEQUESTS.

The corporate name of this institution is "THE TRUSTEES OF HANOVER COLLEGE."

Donors residing in other States should also designate the place in which the college is located, thus: "*The Trustees of Hanover College, located at Hanover, in the State of Indiana.*"

The friends of Education in Indiana and elsewhere are respectfully solicited to make donations and legacies to this Institution. Since the College was chartered in 1832, about 3,000 have received all or part of their education here, and not less than 800 of these were candidates for the Gospel Ministry. The College has enjoyed 23 revivals of Religion. Over one half of the students in the present catalogue, are members of the Church, and one fourth or more have in view the sacred office.

THE

THIRTY-SECOND

𝔄nnual 𝔈atalogue and 𝔈ircular

OF

HANOVER COLLEGE,

AT

HANOVER, INDIANA,

JUNE, 1864.

MADISON, IND.:
W. P. LEVY'S PRINTING AND BINDING ESTABLISHMENT.
1864.

THE

THIRTY-SECOND

Annual Catalogue and Circular

OF

HANOVER COLLEGE,

AT

HANOVER INDIANA,

JUNE, 1864.

MADISON. IND.:
W. P. LEVY'S PRINTING AND BINDING ESTABLISHMENT.
1864.

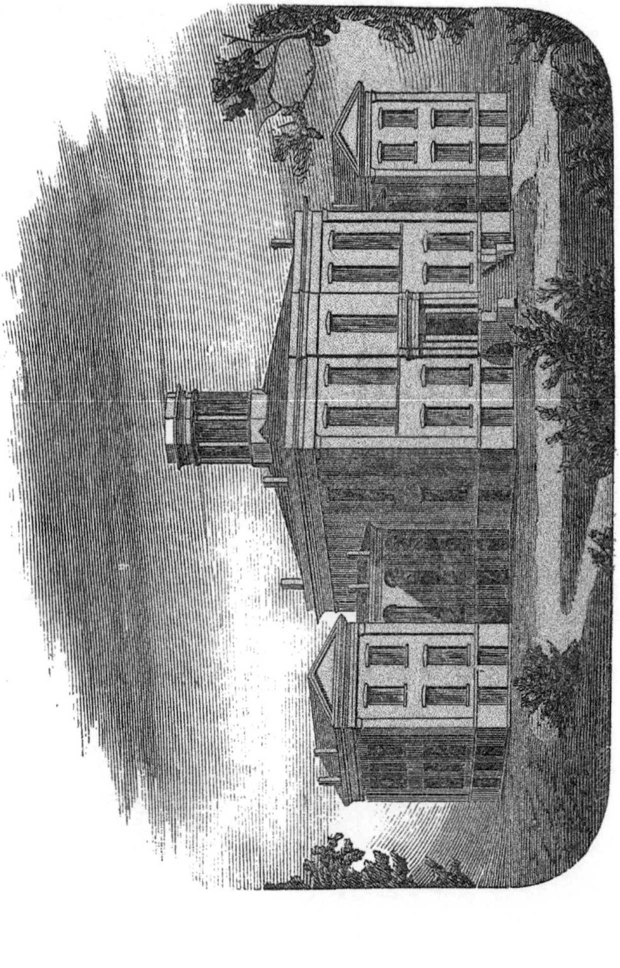

BOARD OF TRUSTEES.

Bd. REV. G. D. ARCHIBALD, Madison,...1868.
Bd. DR. ANDREW SPEAR, Hanover..1868.
Bd. WILLIAM P. INSKEEP, Esq., Madison..1868.
Bd. CHARLES N. TODD, Esq., Indianapolis.......................................1868.
S. S. REV. ISAAC W. MONFORT, Chaplain U. S. A................................1864.
S. S. REV. J. W. BLYTHE, Hanover..1864.
N. S. THOMAS P. GORDON, D. D., Terre Haute..................................1864.
N. S. REV. ROBERT IRWIN, Sen., Muncie...1864.
Bd. REV. D. D. McKEE, Hanover..1865.
Bd. JOHN W. BLACKBURN, Esq., Paris, Ill..1865.
Bd. REV. W. A. HOLLIDAY, Indianapolis..1865.
Bd. JESSE L. WILLIAMS, Esq., Fort Wayne......................................1865.
S. S. JAMES H. McCAMPBELL, Esq., Jeffersonville.............................1865.
S. S. REV. DAVID MONFORT, Greensburg..1865.
N. S. REV. E. W. WRIGHT, D. D., Delphi...1865.
N. S. REV. W. M. DONALDSON, Ossian..1865.
Bd. JAMES M. RAY, Esq., Indianapolis..1866.
Bd. ROBERT DEAN, Esq., Hanover...1866.
Bd. HON. C. E. WALKER, Madison..1866.
Bd. COL. JAMES BLAKE, Indianapolis...1866.
S. S. SILAS C. DAY, Esq., New Albany..1866.
S. S. REV. THOMAS S. CROWE, Jeffersonville...................................1866.
N. S. REV. C. K. THOMPSON, Lebanon...1866.
N. S. REV. JAMES B. CROWE, Crawfordsville ....1866.
Bd. JOHN KING, Esq., Madison..1867.
Bd. REV. J. G. MONFORT, D. D., Cincinnati, Ohio..............................1867.
Bd. HON. W. McKEE DUNN, Madison...1867.
Bd. REV. JAMES WOOD, D. D., Hanover...1867.
S. S. REV. E. S. WILSON, Vincennes..1867.
S. S. JOHN H. VANNUYS, Esq., Franklin..1867.
N. S. REV. JOHN M. LOWRIE, D. D., Fort Wayne...............................1867.
N. S. REV. ISAAC N. SHEPHERD, Muncie...1867.

Officers of the Board.

JAMES M. RAY, Esq., *President.*   REV. G. D. ARCHIBALD, *Sec'y.*
REV. JAMES WOOD, D. D., *Treasurer.*

Executive Committee.

REV. JAMES WOOD, D. D.,   HON. C. E. WALKER.
JOHN KING, Esq.,   ROBERT DEAN, Esq.,
REV. W. A. HOLLIDAY,   REV. G. D. ARCHIBALD,
             JAMES M. RAY, Esq.

FACULTY.

REV. JAMES WOOD, D. D., President,

Professor of Biblical Instruction, Psychology, Logic and Ethics.

REV. S. HARRISON THOMSON, A. M.,

Professor of Mathematics, Mechanical Philosophy, and Astronomy.

REV. JOSHUA B. GARRITT, A. M.,

Professor of the Greek Language and Literature.

REV. J. W. SCOTT, D. D.,

Professor of Natural Science.

REV. W. A. HOLLIDAY, A. M.,

Professor of the Latin and Modern Languages.

HENRY C. THOMSON, A. B.,

Tutor.

REV. JOSHUA B. GARRITT, A. M.,

Librarian.

WILLIAM BROWN,

Janitor.

UNDERGRADUATES.

SENIORS.

Samuel Brown..Shelbyville, Ky.
*William W. Brown..Shelbyville, Ky.
William B. Chamberlin......................................Hanover.
James A. Dean..Hanover.
John H. Harbolt...Charleston.
J. D. Harrington..Shelbyville, Ky.
John H. Holliday..Indianapolis.
Robert McConnell...Fairland.
Peter H. K. McComb..Hanover.
R. A. Mathes...Altonburg, Mo.
William A. Patton..Spruce Hill, Pa.
Arthur Rose...Cincinnati, Ohio.
Robert A. Sturgus...Hanover.
Robert M. Webster..Tullahoma, Iowa.
John Weston...Galena, Ill.

JUNIORS.

John G. Blake..Indianapolis.
Robert S. Dean..Hanover.
J. C. Eastman...Hanover.
George W. Fitch..Hanover.
W. H. Fullenwider..Waveland.
Charles L. Holstein..Madison.

*Deceased.

Robert M. Miller............Hanover.
Elias R. Monfort............Glendale, Ohio.
Edward Quinche............Galena, Ill.
William R. Smythe............Shelbyville.
Thomas Tracy............Louisville, Ky.

SOPHOMORES.

Samuel P. Dale............Bedford.
Nathan H. Downing............Virginia, Ill.
John A. Kellar............North Vernon.
John M. Lodge............Springfield, Ill.
Augustus T. Stone............Princeville, Ill.

FRESHMEN.

John Boyle............Hanover.
George G. Dunn............Bedford.
Samuel W. Elliott............Dayton.
William A. Graham............New Washington.
Alexander S. Peck............Omaha City, N. T.
Joseph L. Potter............New Albany.
O. S. Thomson............Camden.
Harvey W. Wiley............Kent.
J. M. C. Wilson............Clifton, Ohio.

SCIENTIFIC DEPARTMENT.

THIRD YEAR.

John R. Armstrong............Jeffersonville.
George Scoggan............Bedford.
Samuel M. Strader............Madison.

SECOND YEAR.

James M. Carson............Greensburg.
James L. Hall............Shelbyville, Ky.
James M. Justice............Logansport.
Thaddeus S. Rollins............Logansport.

Franklin Shannon..................Hanover.
James Swan.......................Saluda.
Andrew D. Wilson.................Hanover.

FIRST YEAR.

John M. Abbott...................Milton, Ky.
Albert Bare......................New Philadelphia.
James H. Blythe..................Evansville.
James G. Boyle...................Hanover.
Wallace Cable....................Ft. Donaldson, Tenn.
Thomas J. Charlton...............Pleasant.
Emanuel M. Donelson..............Waldron.
William C. Gardiner..............La Crescent Minn.
Erskine G. Hammond...............Troy, Mo.
Thomas J. Heady..................Bennington.
John E. Henry....................Pleasant.
Charles F. Howes.................Utica.
Andrew Hughes....................Frankfort, Ky.
William W. Jones.................Hanover.
George Kester....................Rockford.
Daniel Lattimore.................Vernon.
B. Lawrence......................Milton, Ky.
J. Lawrence......................Milton, Ky.
John D. Lester...................Eddyville, Ky.
George W. McGee..................Polk Run.
Justin M. Nicholson..............Jeffersonville.
Floyd Ogden......................Utica.
L. N. O'Neal.....................Louisville, Ky.
James R. Parker..................Grandview.
James W. Radcliffe...............Pleasuresville, Ky.
J. A. Ramsey.....................Kent.
Joseph Roberts...................Bagdad, Ky.
Walter Roberts...................Madison.
Oscar W. Shryer..................Bloomfield.
Charles Sturdevant...............Indianapolis.
William A. Terrill...............Bloomfield, Ky.
John L. Walker...................Salines, W. Va.
William H. Williams..............Louisville, Ky.
Finley White.....................Kent.

PREPARATORY DEPARTMENT.

SENIORS.

Jesse Caldwell	Jeffersonville.
T. B. Dean	Hanover.
Edward Gelpin	Hanover.
William Keiry	Nashville, Ill.
A. J. McCampbell	Louisville, Ky.
George G. Reed	Hanover.
Henry M. Robb	Shelbyville, Ky.
William B. Sturgus	Hanover.
W. W. Taylor	Louisville, Ky.
James H. Thomson	Hanover.
Frank Trigg	Freeborn, Minn.
Arthur P. Twineham	Lacrescent, Minn.

JUNIORS.

M. Amick	Scipio.
W. N. Amick	Missouri.
J. B. Anderson	Hanover.
W. S. Anderson	Hrnover.
George C. Blythe	Evansville.
William Boyle	Hanover.
Joseph Light	Austin.
Charles R. Logan	Hanover.
Abraham T. McCurry	Kent.
James E. Newkirk	Mt. Prospect.
Richard B. Robinson	Franklin, Ky.
D. Rogers	Hanover.
Robert Taylor	Madison.
T. A. Wilson	Austin.
Jacob Zulauf	New Albany.

SUMMARY.

Seniors	15	Scientific, 2nd year	7
Juniors	11	Scientific, 1st year	34
Sophomores	5	Senior Preparatory	12
Freshmen	9	Junior Preparatory	15
Scientific, 3d year	3		
Total			111

TEXT BOOKS.

DEPARTMENT OF LANGUAGES

LATIN.—Andrews' Grammar and Reader; Andrews' or Leverett's or Crooks & Schem's Lexicon; Andrews' Cæsar; Cooper's Virgil; Bojesen's Roman Antiquities; Butler & Sturgus' Sallust; Lincoln's Livy; Lincoln's Horace; Tyler's Tacitus; Chase's or Anthon's Tusculan Disputations.

GREEK—Hadley's Grammar; Liddell & Scott's, or Pickering's Lexicon; Owen's, or Boise's Anabasis; Bojesen's Grecian Antiquities; Owen's Homer; Woolsey's Greek Plays; Champlin's Demosthenes; Plutarch.

HEBREW—Stuart's Rœdiger's Grammar; Gesenius' Lexicon; Biblia Hebraica.

DEPARTMENT OF BELLES-LETTERS.

Blair's Rhetoric, (University Edition); Coppee's Logic; also for reference, Whately and Hamilton's Logic—the latter as reduced by Day; Wayland's Political Economy; Smith's Grecian History; Liddell's Rome; Lord's Modern History; American History and the Constitution of the U. S. A. For reference Day's Rhetorical Praxis.

DEPARTMENT OF MATHEMATICS.

Rays' Algebra, 2nd part; Davies' Legendre; Davies' Surveying, Coffin's Conic Sections; Loomis' Analytical Geometry and Calculus, Olmsted's Natural Philosophy; Olmsted's Astronomy.

DEPARTMENT OF NATURAL SCIENCE.

Silliman's Chemistry; Cutter's Physiology; Wood's Botany; Lyell's Geology; Dana's Mineralogy; Agassiz & Gould's Zoology, Somerville's Physical Geography.

DEPARTMENT OF METAPHYSICS.

Walker's Reid on the Intellectual Powers; Sir William Hamilton's Philosophy, (Wight's Edition); Stewart's Active and Moral Powers; Wayland's Moral Science; Haven's Mental Philosophy.

DEPARTMENT OF RELIGIOUS INSTRUCTION.

English Bible, Hodge's, Alexander's or Jacobus' Notes; Greek Testament, Robinson's Greek Harmony; Old Testament Hebrew; Septuagint; Westminister Catechism; General Assembly's Psalm and Hymn Books; Butler's Analogy; Paley's Natural Theology; Coleman's Sacred Geography; Alexander's Evidences of Christianity.

Scientific Department.

The three years' course of English, Mathematical and Scientific instruction pursued in this department, embraces all that is included in the College scheme, except the Classical Languages. Such as desire it, however, may pursue the study of Latin and French, in connection with a Scientific Course. We do not recommend it as in any sense an equivalent for a thorough Classical Course; nor is it intended for mere boys, since the subjects which it includes are entirely above their capacity; but to young men, who have attained a respectable common school education, including the elements of Algebra, and who have not time nor means to prosecute a Classical course, this system of studies will, it is hoped, commend itself as solid, comprehensive and practical. Those who shall complete the prescribed Scientific course, will receive a Diploma, certifying the extent of their attainments.

COLLEGE YEAR--EXAMINATIONS.

The College Year is divided into two Terms. The First Term begins on the Wednesday after the 25th day of August, and continues 16 weeks.—The Second Term begins on the first Wednesday in January and continues 24 weeks. The Annual Commencement occurs on Thursday before the 25th of June.

It is of great importance that students attend from the very beginning of the Term; especially since so considerable a portion of time is allotted to vacations. In most cases, the loss of a few weeks, or even days, seriously affects the future standing of the pupil. Absence during term time without special leave, is prohibited.*

Public Examinations will be held, hereafter, only at the close of the College year, when the Freshman and Junior Classes will be examined on the studies of the preceding year, and the Sophomore and Senior Classes upon those of the two preceding years. These last examinations will be FINAL, for the studies pursued in those years. All the examinations will be THOROUGH and RIGID; and will be conducted, in part by the use of written questions, prepared by the Faculty and the Examining Committee, covering the whole field of study prosecuted during a given period, and entirely unknown to the Student until the moment of examination.—These questions must be answered in writing before the Committee; and correct answers to a definite portion of them will be the passport of admission to a higher standing. Similar examinations of a briefer and less decisive character, however, and by way of preparation for the final trial, may be conducted privately, at the pleasure of the Faculty.

*Parents are respectfully advised to give their sons no such permission to be absent, except in cases of NECESSITY.

Religious Instruction and Services.

The attention of a Christian community is respectfully invited to the system of Biblical Instruction which forms a characteristic feature of our course of Study. The Grammar School Classes recite statedly in the English Bible; and every College Class has a daily or tri-weekly recitation in the Greek Testament, or the Hebrew. Proficiency in these, as in other studies, is tested by the usual examinations. In addition to this, Biblical Geography and Antiquities, Ecclesiastical History, Natural Theology, and the Analogy of Religion, Natural and Revealed, to the constitution and course of nature, are carefully and faithfully studied. There is also a Bible or Catechetical exercise on Sabbath mornings; a public service on Sabbath afternoon, appropriated to the Students; and daily morning prayers. The Students are expected to attend the Sabbath morning services of the congregation worshiping in the chapel, or of some other congregation in the vicinity, if their parents prefer any of the latter. The Methodist and United and Associate Presbyterian Churches have regular services in or near the Village.

Admission.

Candidates for admission into the Freshman Class, are required to be proficient in Arithmetic and Algebra; Ancient and Modern Geography; History of the U. S. A.; the English, Latin, and Greek Grammars; Cæsar's Commentaries, and Greek Reader, or what is equivalent to these attainments. They must furnish testimonials of good character, and, if from another College, must bring certificates of honorable dismission.—Candidates for higher standing are examined upon that part of the course already studied by the Class which they propose to enter.

No one can be admitted to the Freshman Class until he has completed his fourteenth year, nor to an advanced standing without a proportional increase of age.

Before a student shall be admitted to actual standing in any Class, he shall present to the President a receipt from the Treasurer, showing that he has complied with the Statutes relating to College Charges and Scholarships.

N. B. The regular examination for admission into College, commences on the Monday preceding the beginning of each Term.

Course of Instruction.

Preparatory Department.

Andrew's Latin Lessons, Grammar, Reader, and Exercises; Andrew's Cæsar; Butler and Sturgus' Sallust; McClintock & Crook's 1st and 2d Greek Books; Classical and Biblical Geography; Ray's Algebra, 2nd part, English Bible.

Scientific Department.

FIRST YEAR.

Algebra, Rays', 2nd part; Plane Geometry; Plane Trigonometry, Mensuration of Surfaces, Surveying and Navigation; History; English Bible; Historical Books, and Sacred Geography.

SECOND YEAR.

Solid Geometry; Analytical Plane Trigonometry; Mensuration of Solids; and Application of Algebra to Geometry; Spherical Trigonometry; Conic Sections; Rhetoric, Logic; Political Economy, English Bible, Poetical Books; Chemistry, Light, Heat, Electricity, and Botany.

THIRD YEAR.

Analytical Geometry and Calculus; Natural Philosophy, Astronomy, Anatomy, Zoology and Physiology; Mineralogy; Geology, Natural Theology, Butler's Analogy, Psychology, Moral Science, English Bible, Constitution of the U. S. A.

Collegiate Department.

Freshman Class.

FIRST TERM.

Greek Harmony of the Gospels......................Robinson.
Biblical Antiquities...............................Nevin.
Sallust...Butler & Sturgus.
Latin Exercises...................................Andrews.
Greek Prose Composition...........................Boise.
Plane Geometry....................................Plane Geometry.

SECOND TERM—SESSION FIRST.

Greek Harmony, continued..........................Robinson.
Sallust, continued................................Butler & Sturgus.
Latin Exercises and Greek Composition, continued...
Practical Plane Trig, and Mensuration of Surfaces...Davie's Legendre.
  This Session closes with the Spring Exhibitions, the last week in March.

SECOND TERM—SESSION SECOND.

Greek Harmony, completed..........................
Virgil..Cooper.
Xenophon's Memorabilia............................Robbins.
Latin and Greek Exercises.........................
Surveying and Navigation..........................Davies.

SOPHOMORE CLASS.

FIRST TERM.

Greek Testament, Acts.............................Owen.
Livy..Lincoln.
Homer's Odyssey...................................Owen.
Greek History.....................................Smith.
Solid Geometry....................................Davies' Legendre.

SECOND TERM—SESSION FIRST.

Greek Testament, Epistles..................................
Livy, continued...
Homer's Odyssey, continued..............................
Plato's Apology and Crito.........................Tyler.
Roman History....................................Liddell.
Roman Antiquities................................Bojesen.
Analytical Plane Trigonometry..........................
Spherical Trigonometry, Mensuration of Solids, and
   Application of Algebra to Geometry................

SECOND TERM—SESSION SECOND.

Greek Testament (Epistles)..............................
Horace ....Lincoln.
Greek Antiquities................................Bojesen.
Apology and Crito, continued.......................Tyler.
Modern History.....................................Lord.
Conic Sections....................................Coffin.

JUNIOR CLASS.

FIRST TERM.

Hebrew Grammar and Hebrew—Genesis (optional)
Tacitus' Germania and Agricola....................Tyler.
Demosthenes' Select Orations...................Champlin.
Analytical Geometry and Calculus.................Loomis.
Rhetoric..Blair.
Chemistry......................................Silliman.

SECOND TERM—SESSION FIRST.

Hebrew (Genesis continued)..............................
Tacitus (continued).....................................
Demosthenes' Select Orations (continued)...............
Natural Philosophy, Mathematical part............Olmsted.
Logic..Coppee.
Chemistry (continued)...................................
Botany..Wood.

SECOND TERM—SESSION SECOND.

Hebrew (Psalms)...
Cicero's Tusculan Disputations...................Anthon.
Alcestis of Euripides...........................Woolsey.
Natural Philosophy—Applications..................Olmsted.
Political Economy................................Wayland.
Optics and Electricity...........................Olmsted.
Botany (continued).................................Wood.

SENIOR CLASS.
FIRST TERM.

Anatomy and Physiology..........................Cutter.
Zoology...Agassiz.
Selections of the Hebrew Bible....................
Psychology..Haven.
Cicero's Tusculan Disputations (continued)..........
Greek Tragedies.....................................Woolsey.
Astronomy and Review..............................Olmsted.

SECOND TERM—SESSION FIRST.

Select Hebrew (continued)..........................
Mineralogy and Geology............................Dana and Lyell.
Butler's Analogy....................................
Natural Theology....................................Paley.
Moral Science.......................................Wayland.
Greek Tragedies (continued).........................
Juvenal..Anthon.
Ouranography and Review............................

SECOND TERM—SESSION SECOND.

Hebrew (continued)..................................
Geology (continued).................................
Moral Science (continued)...........................
Juvenal..
Plutarch...Hackett.
Constitution of the U. S. A........................Story.
Astronomy and Ouranography and Review..............

Department of English Literature and Philology.

The studies and exercises belonging to this Department are attended to by the Faculty. The Alumni Professorship, which was commenced some years ago, had in view the support of a separate Professor, who should devote his entire labors to this Department. The object contemplated is highly important, and the attention of the Alumni and other friends of the College is respectfully solicited to the endowment of this Professorship.

N. B. The Text Books needed for any part of the College Course will be furnished by one of the Professors, at Cincinnati prices.

EXPENSES &C.

The entire Expenditures of a Student need not much exceed $200, viz

Tuition, per year..$30 00
Contingent fee... 5 00
These are required in advance by the Term—first Term $14
    second Term, $21.
Boarding with private families, and furnished room, at $3 00 to
    $4 00 per week,..$117 00 to 156 00
Fuel, Light, Washing &c,..15 00
Books, &c.,...5 00 to 10 00

Boarding in Clubs will cost from one dollar and twenty-five cents to two dollars per week; and some board themselves even at a lower rate. The cost of clothing, and the amount spent as pocket money, will vary with the taste and habit of the Student, and with the wishes of his parents. As a general rule the more money allowed to a young man beyond what is strictly necessary, the less likely he is to reflect honor upon his Parents and Instructors. Although Hanover presents comparatively few temptations to extravagance, yet parents are earnestly advised to require of their sons a detailed account of their expenditures, and to refuse the payment of any debt incurred by them, except for ordinary current expenses, without a written permission. It is also recommended that the funds of young pupils be deposited with some one of the Faculty, and expended under his direction. The younger Students are required to board where the Faculty may direct, and where they may exercise a more careful and frequent supervision.

N. B. Students placed upon Scholarships by the Faculty, are relieved in part, or wholly, as the case may be, from the payment of Tuition Fees. The Contingent Fee is required of those on Scholarships the same as others. This is now $2 00 for the first Term, and $3 00 for the second.

DISCIPLINE.

A record is kept by the Faculty, in which is entered weekly, the grades of scholarship of the Student, his absence from the exercises of the Institution, and such other facts as are worthy of notice with respect to his general deportment. From this record a report is made out at the end of each Session, and sent to the Parent or Guardian of each Student. In case of deficiency in scholarship, negligence in study, irregularity of attendance upon the exercises of the Institution, or improper conduct, the Student will be privately admonished, and the Parent or Guardian will be promptly informed of the fact.

The object of this arrangement is to keep Parents and Guardians accurately informed with regard to their sons and wards in this Institution, and thus to secure their co-operation with the Faculty in a mild system of discipline. Whenever it is ascertained that a Student is deriving no advantage from his connection with the Institution, or is pursuing a course injurious to himself or fellow-students, the Faculty will take decisive action, and his Parent or Guardian will be promptly addressed on the subject, and requested to remove him from the Institution.

Resolutions of the Faculty, Adopted Dec. 20, 1862.

As absence during the latter part of the College Term greatly injures the Scholarship of Students, impairs their habits of study, breaks the integrity of Classes, discourages study among students that remain, and thus lowers the literary standard of the Institute, therefore,

RESOLVED, 1st. That after this date, Dec. 20, 1862, all such absences (not made unavoidable by the Providence of God,) shall be recorded as unexcused, and each recitation thus lost registered as Zero.

RESOLVED, 2d. That this Resolution be published in the Catalogue and Quarterly Report.

SCHOLARSHIPS.

The endowment of this Institution is in the form of Scholarships, of which the Board has established several sorts. The sum of $400 paid, or secured to the Corporation by note payable within five years; and bearing six per cent. interest in advance upon principal remaining unpaid, purchases for the owner, his heirs and assigns, a perpetual right to the tuition of one Scholar in Hanover College. The sum of $200 paid, or subscribed under similar conditions, secures the right to twenty years' tuition; after which time the Scholarship is subject to the disposal of the Board for the gratuitous education of candidates for the Gospel Ministry. A Church Scholarship of $200, secures to the Church so contributing, a perpetual right to the tuition of one Student, who shall be a member of that Church; and appointed by the Session. A Presbyterial Scholarship of $200 secures a similar right to a Presbytery, in behalf of pupils who shall be candidates for the Ministry under its care. Principal paid on these Scholarships is invested by the corporation in some safe and productive Stock, and the Interest only can be expended for the support of the College.

Every person applying for admission as a beneficiary of a Scholarship under the control of the donors, shall present to the Treasurer, at the beginning of each Term, a written Certificate from those controlling the

Scholarship, of his right to such benefit;—when, after paying whatever interest may be due on said Scholarship, he shall receive an acknowledgment of his right, which he shall lodge with the President.

"The Scholorships subject to the disposal of the Corporation, may be occupied by such applicants as the Faculty may select, after, inquiry into their circumstances, character, and attainments, the preference being ceteris paribus, to those who give the best evidence of Scholarship.

"There shall at no time be more than one Student upon each Scholarship."

ACCOMMODATIONS.

The community system of Boarding in Commons, or of rooming in large Lodging Halls, is not adopted in Hanover. Arrangements are made to accommodate the Students with board and rooms in respectable private families, where the number together can never be large; and where all shall be brought under domestic influence.

Settlement of Accounts.

No Diploma nor honorable dismission shall be granted until the Student shall exhibit a Receipt of Settlement of all his bills for boarding, room and washing.

Degrees.

No Degrees are conferred in Course. Candidates for Literary Honors are reported to the Board upon their ascertained or acknowledged merits.

Societies, Libraries &c.

There are two Societies connected with the College, the UNION LITERARY and the PHILALETHEAN, whose Libraries number each about twelve hundred volumes.

There is also a SOCIETY OF RELIGIOUS INQUIRY, which has begun to collect a Library, Maps, &c., and which receives regularly several valuable religious papers and periodicals.

The College Library contains near three thousand well selected volumes and is accessible to the Students.

The Cabinet contains several thousand specimens in Mineralogy and Geology.

The friends of the College are advised that contributions to the Library to the Cabinet, or to the Laboratory, are much needed and will be thankfully received.

Public Literary Societies and Annual Commencement.

Ample opportuntiy is offered to the Students, once a week, to improve themselves in Composition and Elocution, and several times a year Literary entertainments are given in public, which furnish occasions for honorable competition among the Students, and an interesting and profitable repast to their friends. Three of these entertainments occur annually, viz :on the evening of Washington's birth-day ; on Tuesday and Wednesday evening, of the last week in March, and on the week of Commencement, when the two Literary Societies and the Society of Inquiry have addresses by gentlemen from abroad, and the Senior Class deliver their Graduating Orations,—altogether occupying over two days.

THE COMMENCEMENT DAY IS ON THE THURSDAY PRECEDING THE 25TH OF JUNE, after which there is a vacation till the last Wednesday of August.

Prohibited Secret Societies.

The following order was passed by the Board of Trustees, in July, 1858, viz:

"*Resolved*, That this Board disapprove of the existence among the Students of Hanover College, of any Society or Association of which the Faculty are not *ex officio* Members, and will not permit the public exhibition of any such Society."

The following Resolution was adopted June, 1864.

"*Resolved*, By the Board of Trustees of Hanover College, that the Students of this Institution are prohibited from organizing and becoming members of secret, political or literary Societies of which the Faculty of the College are not honorary members; and, further, that a violation of this Resolution by any Student shall be disciplined by the Faculty in such manner as to them shall seem to be right.

Location, Buildings &c.

The Village of Hanover is situated upon an elevated bluff of the Ohio River, six miles below Madison, Indiana, in a region of remarkable salubrity and natural beauty. The village and neighborhood are characterized by morality, and the absence of all the ordinary temptations to vice and idleness. The Ohio River, and the Railways from Madison, New Albany, and Cincinnati, place Hanover within twenty-four hours of all the principal points in Indiana, Kentucky, Western Ohio, and Eastern Illinois. A turnpike from Madison to Hanover, renders the village easy of access at all seasons of the year.

Hanover College is controlled by a Board of Trustees; one-half of whom are appointed by the Board itself, and the other half by the Synods of Indiana and Northern Indiana.

The Board purchased, some years ago, a farm of two hundred acres, lying between the Village and the Ohio River, upon a beautiful point of which,—overlooking the River from an elevation of four hundred feet,—they have erected a commodious College edifice, now completed and occupied. The new College consists of a center building nearly eighty feet square, with lateral and transverse wings. The whole length is about two hundred feet. It contains no dormitories for Students,—an undesirable provision,—but affords ample and convenient Halls, Library, Cabinet, Lecture, and Recitation Rooms, and a spacious Chapel.

The building commands an exceedingly diversified view of the River, for six miles up and ten miles down its course. A visitor of large acquaintance with our Country and the world, asserts that a more delightful prospect can not be found in America or Europe.

Form of Conveyances and Bequests.

The corporate name of this institution is "THE TRUSTEES OF HANOVER COLLEGE."

Donors residing in other States should also designate the place in which the college is located, thus: "*The Trustees of Hanover College, located at Hanover, in the State of Indiana.*"

The friends of Education in Indiana and elsewhere are respectfully solicited to make donations and legacies to this Institution. Since the College was chartered in 1832, about 3,000 have received all or part of their education here, and not less than 800 of these were candidates for the Gospel Ministry. The College has enjoyed 24 revivals of Religion. Over one half of the students in the present catalogue, are members of the Church, and one fourth or more have in view the sacred office.

HANOVER COLLEGE.

Thursday, June 23, 1864.

Commencement Exercises.

Music and Distribution of Orders.

PRAYER—MUSIC.

ORATION—Victory: then the Crown..........John R. Armstrong, Jeffersonville, Ind.
MUSIC.
ORATION—Energy of the Will..........Samuel Brown, Shelbyville, Ky.
MUSIC.
ORATION—Mirage..........Wm. B. Chamberlin, Hanover, Ind.
MUSIC.
ORATION—Nothing Impossible to a Willing Mind..........Jas. A. Dean, Hanover, Ind.
MUSIC.
ORATION—Our Government..........John H. Harbolt, Charleston, Ind.
MUSIC.
ORATION—Go where Glory awaits Thee..........J. D. Harrington, Shelbyville, Ky.
MUSIC.
ORATION—Patent Medicines..........John H. Holliday, Indianapolis, Ind.
MUSIC.
ORATION—The People don't Think..........Peter H. K. McComb, Hanover, Ind.
MUSIC.
ORATION—Christian Philanthropy..........R. A. Mathes, Altonburg, Mo.
MUSIC.
ORATION—The American Flag..........Wm. A. Patton, Spruce Hill, Pa.
MUSIC.
ORATION—Iconoclasm and Christian Art..........Arthur Rose, Cincinnati, Ohio.
MUSIC.
ORATION—Loyalty to the Federal Government..........George Scoggan, Bedford, Ind.
MUSIC.
ORATION—Heroes of the Past..........Samuel M. Strader, Madison, Ind.
MUSIC.
ORATION—The Right of Revolution..........Robert A. Sturgus, Hanover, Ind.
MUSIC.
ORATION—The Freedmen..........Robt. M. Webster, Fairfield, Iowa.
MUSIC.
ORATION—Truth, Our Guiding Star..........John Weston, Galena, Ill.
MUSIC.

Delivery of Diplomas.
MUSIC.
Prayer and Benediction.
MUSIC.

BEAVER COLLEGE.

Thursday, June 23, 1864.

Commencement Exercises.

Distribution of Orations.

PRAYER—MUSIC.

1ST.—*The Orator*............John R. Anderson, Jeffersonville, Ind.
MUSIC.

2ND—*Sr.*...................Sarah Parry, Philipsville, Ky.
MUSIC.

3RD—*Mrs.* ....Wm. H. Carpenter, Hanover, Ind.
MUSIC.

4TH—*Memory, Isle to a Willing Mind*....Ira A. Dean, Hanover, Ind.
MUSIC.

5TH—*I would*..........................Jas. C. Hoover, Sparland, Ind.
MUSIC.

6TH—*Are there Holy Lands Thus*....J. B. Hazzard, Sandyville, Ky.
MUSIC.

7TH—*..of Mythology*................Jos. C. Johnson, Indianapolis, Ind.
MUSIC.

8TH.—*People that Think*......Prof. H. K. Holsman Brown, Ind.
MUSIC.

9TH—*Latin Philosophy*.......R. A. Martus, Zanesville, O.
MUSIC.

10TH.—*The....*...
MUSIC.

11TH—*Learning and Christian Art*....Frank Goss, Madison, O.
MUSIC.

12TH.—*..of our Federal Government*....James Hooker, Bedford, Ind.
MUSIC.

13TH.—*Heroes of The Past*............Samuel M. Sturgeon, Bigford, Ind.
MUSIC.

14TH.—*The B...of Revolution*.......Bessie A. Gooding, Hanover, Ind.
MUSIC.

15TH.—*The Teacher*...................Rev. M. Wesson, Fairfield, Iowa.
MUSIC.

16TH.—*Our Guiding Star*..............John Wasson, Galena, Ill.
MUSIC.

Delivery of Diplomas.

MUSIC.

Prayer and Benediction.

MUSIC.

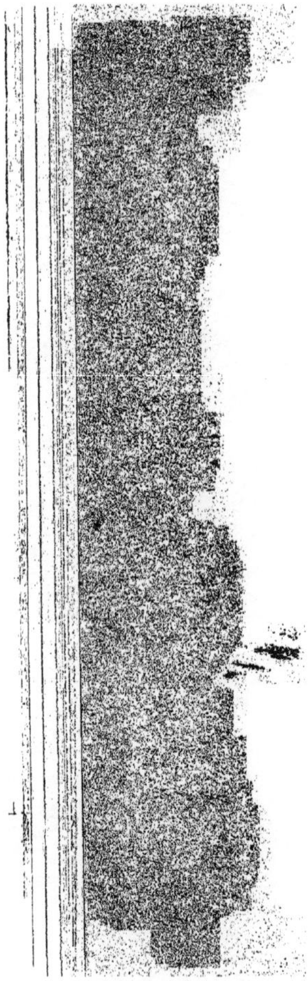

THE

THIRTY-THIRD

Annual Catalogue and Circular

OF

HANOVER COLLEGE,

AND

ELEVENTH TRIENNIAL

CATALOGUE OF THE ALUMNI.

JUNE 1865.

MADISON, INDIANA:
WM. P. LEVY, PRINTER AND BINDER.
1865.

THE

THIRTY-THIRD

Annual Catalogue and Circular

OF

HANOVER COLLEGE,

AND

ELEVENTH TRIENNIAL

CATALOGUE OF THE ALUMNI.

JUNE 1865.

MADISON, INDIANA:
WM. P. LEVY, PRINTER AND BINDER.
1865.

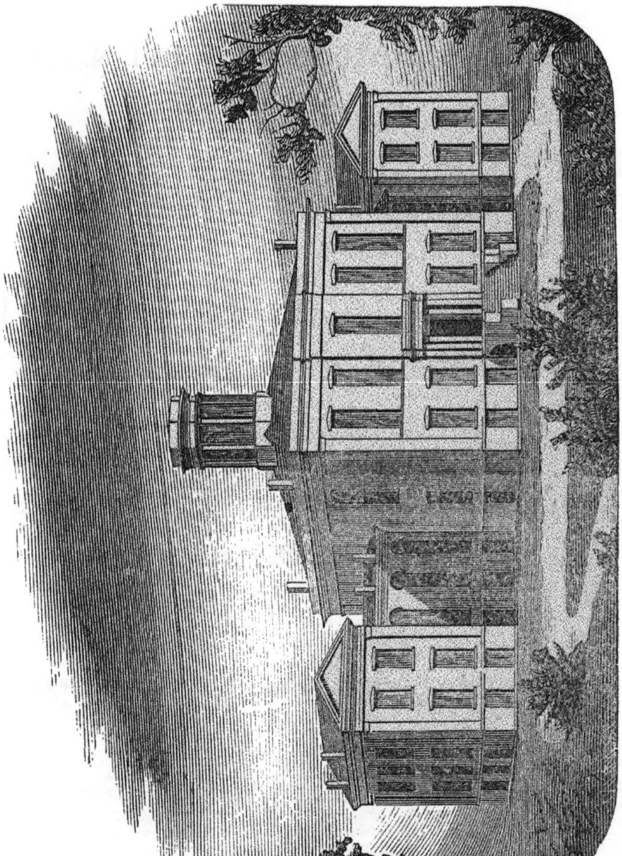

TRIENNIAL CATALOGUE.

OFFICERS OF THE COLLEGE.

PRESIDENTS.

1832—1836.	*Rev. James Blythe, D. D.
1836—1838.	*Rev. John Mathews, D. D. (pro. tem.)
1338—1838.	Rev. Duncan Macaulay, D. D.
1838—1843.	Rev. Erasmus D. McMaster, D. D.
1846—1849.	*Rev. Sylvester Scovel, D. D.
1849—1854.	Rev. Thomas E. Thomas, D. D.
1854—1855.	Rev. Jared M. Stone, (pro. tem,)
1855—1857.	Rev. Jonathan Edwards, D. D.
1857—1859.	Rev. S. Harrison Thomson, (pro. tem.)
1859—	Rev. James Wood, D. D.

VICE PRESIDENTS.

1832—1857.	*Rev. John Finley Crowe, D. D.

PROFESSORS.

1832—1837.	*Rev. John Finley Crowe, D. D., Rhet. Logic, Pol. Econ. and History.
1832—1836.	*Rev. Mark A. H. Niles, A. M., Prof. of Ancient Languages.
1832—1838.	John H. Harney, A. M., Prof. of Mathematics.
1833—1835.	Wm. McKee Dunn, A. B. Principal of Prep. Department.
1835—1838.	Charles K. Thompson, A. B., Principal of Prep. Department.
1835—1837.	Wm. McKee Dunn, A. M., Prof. Natural Science.
1836—1839.	Noble Butler, A. B. Prof. of Ancient Languages.
1838—1843.	Thomas W. Hynes, A. M., Prof. Math. and Nat. Science.
1839—1840.	Samuel Galloway, A. M., Prof. of Ancient Languages.
1840—1841.	*Minard Sturgus, A. M., Principal of Prep. Dep. and Acting Prof. of Ancient Languages.
1841—1852.	*Minard Sturgus, A. M., Prof. of Ancient Languages.
1841—1843.	Zebulon B. Sturgus, A. B., Principal of Prep. Department.
1843—1843.	Rev. Wm. C. Anderson, D, D., Prof. of Rhet. Logic, Political Economy and History.
1844—1850.	S. Harrison Thomson, A. M., Prof. of Math. and Nat. Science.
1844—1852.	Absalom C. Knox, A. M., Adj. Prof. of Ancient Lang. and Principal of Prep. Department.
1850—1856.	Rev. Jared M. Stone, A. M., Prof. of Nat. Science.
1850	S. Harrison Thomson, Prof. of Math. and Mech. Phil.
1852—1857.	Rev. Wm. Bishop, A. M., Prof. of Greek.
1852—1854.	Rev. William Hamilton, A. M., Prof. of Latin.
1854—1855.	Henry R. Lott, M. D., Prof. of Latin.
1857—1860.	*Rev. John Finley Crowe, D.D., Emeritus Prof. of Rhet. Logic, Pol. Economy and History,
1856.	Rev. Joshua B. Garritt, A. M., Prof. of Latin.
1860.	Rev. J. B. Garritt, A. M., Prof. of Greek.
1857—1859.	Augustus W. King, A. M., Prof. of Natural Science.
1858—1862.	*Minard Sturgus, A. M., Prof. of Greek.
1843—1844.	Frederick Eckstein, Teacher of French and German.
1845—1846.	Rev. F. Augustus Willard, A. M., Lecturer on Chemistry.
1851.	Mons. J. J. Piédfourck, Univ. of Paris, Teacher of French, Drawing and Civil Engineering.
1860.	Rev. J. W. Scott, D. D., Prof. of Natural Science.
1864.	Rev. Wm. A. Holliday, A. M., Prof. of Latin and Modern Languages.

*Deceased.

BOARD OF TRUSTEES.

Bd. REV. D. D. McKEE, Hanover..1869.
Bd. HON. JAMES Y. ALLISON, Madison...1869.
Bd. REV. WILLIAM A. HOLLIDAY, Hanover...................................1869.
Bd. JESSE L. WILLIAMS, Esq., Fort Wayne.....................................1869.
S. S. REV. GEORGE C. HECKMAN, Indianapolis................................1868.
S. S. REV. J. W. BLYTHE, Hanover..1868.
N. S. REV. THOMAS P. GORDON, D. D., Terre Haute........................1868.
N. S. REV. THOMAS WHALLON, Tipton...1868.
Bd. REV. G. D. ARCHIBALD, D. D., Madison,...................................1868.
Bd. DR. ANDREW SPEAR, Hanover...1868.
Bd. WILLIAM P. INSKEEP, Esq., Madison.......................................1868.
Bd. CHARLES N. TODD, Esq., Indianapolis.....................................1868.
S. S. REV. E. S. WILSON, Vincennes..1867.
S. S. JOHN H. VANNUYS, Esq., Franklin...1867.
N. S. REV. JOHN M. LOWRIE, D. D., Fort Wayne..............................1867.
N. S. REV. ISAAC N. SHEPHERD, Muncie..1867.
Bd. JOHN KING, Esq., Madison...1867.
Bd. REV. J. G. MONFORT, D. D., Cincinnati, Ohio.............................1867.
Bd. HON. W. McKEE DUNN, Madison..1867.
Bd. REV. JAMES WOOD, D. D., Hanover..1867.
Bd. JAMES M. RAY, Esq., Indianapolis...1866.
Bd. ROBERT DEAN, Esq., Hanover...1866.
Bd. HON. C. E. WALKER, Madison..1866.
Bd. COL. JAMES BLAKE, Indianapolis..1866.
S. S. SILAS C. DAY, Esq., New Albany..1866.
S. S. REV. THOMAS S. CROWE, Jeffersonville..................................1866.
N. S. REV. C. K. THOMPSON, Lebanon...1866.
N. S. REV. JAMES B. CROWE, Crawfordsville..................................1866.
S. S. JAMES H. McCAMPBELL, Esq., Jeffersonville...........................1865.
S. S. REV. DAVID MONFORT, Greensburg.......................................1865.
N. S. REV. E. W. WRIGHT, D. D., Delphi..1865.
N. S. REV. W. M. DONALDSON, Ossian..1865.

Officers of the Board.

JAMES M. RAY, Esq., *President.*   REV. G. D. ARCHIBALD, D.D., *Sec'y.*
REV. JAMES WOOD, D. D., *Treasurer.*

Executive Committee.

REV. JAMES WOOD, D. D.,   HON. C. E. WALKER,
JOHN KING, Esq.,   ROBERT DEAN, Esq.,
REV. W. A. HOLLIDAY, A. M.,   REV. G. D. ARCHIBALD, D.D.,
JAMES M. RAY, Esq.

Auditing Committee.

HON. C. E. WALKER,   JOHN KING, Esq.

FACULTY.

REV. JAMES WOOD, D. D., President,
Professor of Biblical Instruction, Psychology, Logic and Ethics.

REV. S. HARRISON THOMSON, A. M.,
Professor of Mathematics, Mechanical Philosophy, and Astronomy.

REV. JOSHUA B. GARRITT, A. M.,
Professor of the Greek Language and Literature.

REV. J. W. SCOTT, D. D.,
Professor of Natural Science.

REV. W. A. HOLLIDAY, A. M.,
Professor of the Latin and Modern Languages.

REV. JOSHUA B. GARRITT, A. M.,
Librarian.

WILLIAM BROWN,
Janitor.

HONORARY DEGREES.

L. L. D.

1834. Hon. Isaac Blackford, Judge of the Supreme Court of Indiana.
1838. John Delafield, *Cincinnati, Ohio.*
1840. *Hon. Charles Dewey,
" Hon. Jeremiah Sullivan, } Judges of the Supreme Court of Ind.
1863. Hon. Charles D. Drake, *St. Louis, Mo.*
1865. Rev. Lemuel G. Olmstead, Chaplain U. S. A., Military Hospital, Jeffersonville, Ind.

D. D.

1857. Rev. David McDill, *Hamilton, Ohio.*
" *Rev. Elihu W. Baldwin, *President of Wabash University, Indiana.*
1839. Rev. Stewart Bates, *Glasgow Scotland.*
1841. Rev. James Murphy, *Herkimer, New York.*
1843. William L. Breckinridge, *Danville, Ky.*
" Rev. Thomas C. Reed, *Prof. of Int. Philos. Union College N. Y.*
1845. *Rev. David Monfort, *Franklin, Ind.*
1846. *Rev. Sylvester Scovel, *New Albany, Ind.*
1847. Rev. Edward P. Humphrey, *Danville, Ky.*
" Rev. Robert C. Grundy, *Cincinnati, Ohio.*
1848. Rev. J. L. Yantis, *Missouri.*
" Rev. John C. Backus, *Baltimore, Md.*
1853. Rev. Leroy J. Halsey, *Chicago, Ill.*
" Rev. Elias Riggs, *Missionary at Smyrna, Asia Minor.*
" Rev. I. N. Candee, *Galesburg, Ill.*
1854. Rev. John M. Stevenson, *New York.*
" Rev. Thornton A. Mills, *New York.*
1858. *Rev. Josiah D. Smith, *Columbus, Ohio.*
1859. Rev. James Brown, *Keokuk, Iowa.*
" *Rev. J. C. Brown, *Valparaiso, Ind., Chaplain U. S. A.*
1861. Rev. N. C. Burt, *Cincinnati, Ohio.*
" Rev. J. W. Lowrie, *Fort Wayne, Ind.*
1862. Rev. E. W. Wright, *Delphi, Ind.*
1863. Rev. William Brand, *College Hill, Ind.*
" Rev. Robert C. Matthews, *Monmouth, Ill.*
1864. Rev. Samuel M. Hamill, *Lawrenceville, N. J.*
" Rev. Wm. Hamilton, *Ulsterville, N. Y.*
" Rev. W. C. Cattell, *Pres. Lafayette College, Easton, Pa.*
1865. Rev. G. D. Archibald, *Madison, Ind.*
" Rev. D. M. Maclise, *Montgomery, N. Y.*

A. M.

1833. *Rev. John Finley Crowe, *Vice Prest. of Hanover College Ind.*
" *Rev. M. A. H. Niles, *Professor of Languages, Hanover College, Ind.*
1834. Rev. John W. Cunningham, *Tennessee,*
1839. *Rev. David Monfort, *Franklin, Ind.*
1840. Samuel Reid, M. D., *Salem, Ind.*
" Leonard Bliss, jr., *Louisville, Ky.*
1843. Rev. Monroe T. Allen, *Raleigh, Tenn.*
" Samuel M. Elliott, M. D., *New York City.*
1845. *John L. Scott, Esq., *Cincinnati, Ohio.*
" James P. Holcombe, Esq., *Cincinnati, Ohio.*
" *Rev. Daniel Lattimore, *Vernon, Ind.*
" Rev. David V. Smock, *Sigourney, Iowa.*
" Rev. James Brownlee, *Livonia, Ind.*
1846. Rev. James C. Burt, M. D., *Vernon, Ind.*
1847. Rev. George J. Reed, *Chaplain, U. S. A.*
" *Rev. Mason D. P. Williams, *Louisville, Ky.*
" *Rev. Robert C. McComb, *London, Ohio.*
" *Rev. John C. Eastman, *Crawfordsville, Ind.*
1848. Rev. Thomas Brown, *Xenia, Ohio.*
" John W. Shields, Esq., *Cincinnati, Ohio.*
" Thomas H. Shreve, Esq., *Louisville, Ky.*
" *Ben Casseday, Esq., *Louisville, Ky.*
1849. Bland Ballard, Esq., *Louisville, Ky.*
1850. Dr. E. S. Cooper, *Knox Co., Ill.*
" Rev. Charles Axtell, *Knightstown, Ind.*
" John Orr, Esq., *Macon, Tenn.*
1852. Robert S. Knox, Esq., *Livonia, Ind.*
1853. William A. Churchman, Esq., *Indianapolis, Ind.*
1856. C. W. Kimball, *Lebanon, Ohio.*
" *Dr. James M. Logan, *Hanover, Ind.*
1857. Philip A. Emery, Esq., *Indianapolis, Ind.*
1858. John H. Tate, M. D., *Cincinnati, Ohio.*
1859. Ashley Pierce, Esq., *Valparaiso, Ind.*
1862. Ebenezer Neal, M. D., *Philadelphia, Pa.*
1865. John H. Blackburn, Esq., *Paris, Ill.*
" Hon. James Y. Allison, *Madison, Ind.*

A. B.

1846. Dr. John S. Burt, *Washington, Arkansas.*
1854. Dickerson B. Wayland, Esq., *Mt. Washington, Ky.*
1862. Rev. Geo. W. Hays, *McComb, Ill.*

ALUMNI.

1834.

NAMES.	PROFESSION.	RESIDENCE.
*William Hamilton Bruner, A. M.	Minister	
*Selby Harney	Teacher	
John Lyle Martin	Minister	Crawfordsville, Ind.
John Mason McCord, A. M.	Minister	Texas.
Isaac McCoy, A. M.	Farmer	Marion, Ill.
Isaac Newton Shepherd, A.M.	Minister	Muncie. Ind.
—Charles Kilgore Thompson, A. M.	Minister	Lebanon, Ind.

1835.

Robert Sherrard Bell, A. M.	Minister	Washington, Va.
James Brown, D. D.	Minister	Keokuk, Iowa.
†Jonathan Edwards, D. D.	Minister	Philadelphia, Pa.
Robert Simpson, A. M.	Minister	Newton, Ill.
‡Middleton Goldsmith, A. M., M. D.	Physician	Louisville, Ky.
*James Allen Watson	Teacher	

1836.

S. J. P. Anderson, D. D.	Minister	St. Louis, Mo.
?Noble Butler, A. M.	Teacher	Louisville, Ky.
*Andrew Fulton, M. D.	Physician	
‖Thomas Woodruff Hynes, A. M.	Minister	Pocahontas, Ill.
*Nathaniel T. Schillinger	Minister	
*David Edward Young Rice, A. M.	Minister	
*William Wylie McLain, A. M.	Minister	

*Deceased.

—Principal of Prep. Dep. 1834–8.
†President of Hanover College, 1855–57.
‡Prof. of Vermont Medical College, and Ky. Med. Coll.
?Prof. in Hanover College, 1836–39.
‖Prof. in Hanover College, 1838–43.

ALUMNI.

NAMES.	PROFESSION.	RESIDENCE.
*Amos Hynes Rogers, A. M.	Minister	Atlanta, Ill.
Samuel Frame Morrow, A. M.	Minister	Albany, N. Y.
Samuel Newell, A. M.	Minister	Paris, Ill.
Josiah Crawford, A. M.	Minister	New Washington Ind.
David Hays Commins, A. M.	Minister	Mountain, Tenn.
¶Minard Sturgus, A. M*	Teacher	S. Hanover, Ind.
S. Ramsay Wilson, D. D.	Minister	Louisville, Ky.

1837.

Thomas H. Alderdice	Minister	Scaffold Prairie, Ind.
Franklin Berryhill	Minister	Bellbrook, Ohio.
James Black	Minister	Cincinnati, Ohio.
*Samuel N. Evans, A. M.	Minister	
Edmund Waller Hawkins, A. M.	Lawyer	Covington, Ky.
John Macartney Hoge	Minister	Beech Bluff, Ark.
Braxton D. Hunter	Minister	
Sylvanus Jewett	Minister	
*John Wright McCormick, A. M.	Minister	
James A. McKee, A. M.	Minister	Minneapolis, Min.
Asahel Munson, A. M.	Minister	Jackson, Mo.
*William Cooper Scott, A. M.	Minister	
*Josiah D. Smith, D. D.	Minister	Columbus, Ohio.
†Samuel Harrison Thomson, A. M.	Minister	S. Hanover, Ind.
James F. Wood	Lawyer	Greensburg, Penn.

1838.

George B. Armstrong	Minister	Crittenden, Ky.
*William Blair	Minister	
*‡James E. Blythe, A. M.	Lawyer	Evansville, Ind.
William Kirkpatrick Brice, A. M.	Minister	Pleasant, Ohio.
Alex. Montgomery Brown, A. M.	Lawyer	Mound City, Ill.
William M. Cheever, A. M.	Minister	Troy, Ohio.
James Blythe Crowe, A. M.	Minister	Crawfordsville, Ind.
Thomas Searle Crowe, A. M.	Minister	Jeffersonville, Ind.
Joseph F. Fenton, A. M.	Minister	Washington, Mo.
James J. Gardiner, A. M.	Teacher	
Robert A. Gibson, A. M.	Farmer	Monmouth, Ill.
Abram T. Hendricks, A. M.	Minister	Petersburg, Ind.
John Jones		
James W. Mathews, A. M.	Clerk of Court	Macomb, Ill.
George Frederick Whitworth, A. M.	Minister	Olympia, W. T.

1839.

Samuel Stanhope Crowe, A. M.	Lawyer	New Lexington, Ind.
David M. Dunn	Lawyer	Logansport, Ind.

---

*Deceased.
¶Prof. in Hanover College, 1840–52, 1858.
†Prof. in Hanover College, 1844.
‡Member Indiana Const. Cony. and Ind. H. Rep.

(A)

ALUMNI.

NAMES.	PROFESSION.	RESIDENCE.
William W. Gilliland, A. M	Lawyer	Charlestown, Ind.
*Philander Hamilton	Lawyer	
Ephriam K. Lynn, A. M	Minister	Carlisle, Kansas.
Fielding G. Strahan, A. M	Minister	Danville, Ky.

1840.

Harleigh Blackwell, A. M	Minister	Snow Hill, Mo.
*Samuel G. Hass	Business	Valparaiso, Ind.
†Absalom C. Knox, A. M	Teacher	Vacaville, Cal.
Robert C. Mathews, D. D	Minister	Monmouth, Ill.
Robert S. Symington, A. M	Minister	Kansas City, Mo.

1841.

Charles M. Hays	Lawyer	Pittsburg, Penn.
John Lyle King	Lawyer	Chicago, Ill.
*George C. Lyon	Physician	

1842.

Alexander M. Johnston, A.M., M. D.	Physician	Cincinnati, Ohio.
*Thomas C. McCutchen, A. M	Farmer	
Alexander McHatton, A. M	Minister	Marion, Ind.
*George McMillan, A. M	Minister	
James Newton Sanders. A. M	Minister	Bloomfield, Ky.
*William W. Simonson, A. M	Minister	
‡Zebulon Barton Sturgus, A. M	Teacher	Washington, D. C.

1843.

Daniel Lambert Fouts	Farmer	Cal.
*James G. Hopkins, A. M	Minister	
George A. Irwin, A. M	Minister	Ind.
Samuel Barr Keys, A. M	Lawyer	Cincinnati, Ohio.
Joseph Chambers McKibbin, M. C.	Lawyer	——Cal.
Francis Peterson Monfort, A. M	Minister	Indianapolis, Ind.
John F. Read	Lawyer	Jeffersonville, Ind.
J. Franklin Trenchard, A. M., M.D.	Druggist	Philadelphia, Pa.

1844.

John C. Greer	Planter	Jackson, Tenn.

1845.

William T. Robinson, A. M	Lawyer	——Miss.
David R. Thompson,	Lawyer	——Miss.

1846.

*William H. G. Butler, A. M	Teacher	
John A. Frazier, A. M	Teacher	——Oregon.
Samuel Crothers Logan, A. M	Minister	Valparaiso, Ind.

1847.

Samuel Emmett Barr, A. M	Minister	Franklin, Ind.
Fauntleroy Senour, A. M	Minister	Rockport, Ill.

*Deceased.
†Prof. in Hanover College, 1844–52.
‡Principal of Prep. Department in Hanover College, 1841–43.

ALUMNI.

| NAMES. | PROFESSION. | RESIDENCE. |

1848.

Addison W. Bare, A. M...............Physician ....Bryantsville, Ind.
John Wesley Blake, A. M............Lawyer ....Lafayette, Ind.
John C. Caldwell, A. M..................Minister............Stillwater, Minn.
*†Moses S. Coulter, A. M............Minister......................
*Robert G. Jackson, A. M.............Teacher ....
Robert S. Shannon, A. M., M. D......Physician ....Lagrange, Texas.
Samuel C. Taggart, A. M., M. D......Physician ....Charlestown, Ind.
James Harvey L. Vannuys, A. M...Minister............Goshen, Ind.

1849.

Samuel C. Baldridge, A. M..............Minister............Friendsville, Ill.
*Jesse Y. Higbee, A. M. M. D.........Physician ....
Nathan S. Palmer, A. M................Minister............Franklin, Ind.
Xenophon Boone Sanders, A. M......Lawyer ....Memphis, Tenn.
Williamson D. Symington, A. M......Minister..............———Ky.
John White Taylor, A. M...............Lawyer ....Palestine, Texas.
Henry E. Thomas, A. M..................Minister............Augusta, Ky.

1850.

Wm. Maxwell Blackburn, A. M......Minister............Erie, Penn.
Joshua Selby Brengle..................Physician ....Lawrenceville, Ill.
*Avery Williams Bullock, A. M .....Lawyer ....Hampshire.
John Simpson Frierson ....Minister............Ashwood, Tenn.
*Samuel David Hawthorn ....
John Alexander Kimmons ....Minister............Saltilo, Miss.
Claudius B. H. Martin, A M..........Minister............Hamilton, Ohio.
Samuel Clark Mercer, A M............Editor ....Nashville, Tenn.
Robert Symington Reese, A M......Minister............Pleasant Hill, Mo.
William Harvey Rice..................Minister............Palestine, Texas.
William Walton Sickles, A M.........Minister............Indianapolis, Ind.
Alexander Stuart Walker............Lawyer ....Georgetown, Texas.
Austin Warner ....Minister............Moneka, Kansas.
Benjamin Rush Whitney..............Engineer............———Mo.
William Alexander Martin Young...Lawyer ....Salem, Ind.

1851.

James Madison Alexander, A M......Minister............Paris, Ill.
Henry Martyn Bayless..................Business............Chicago, Ill.
Joseph Boon ....Minister............Lagrange, Texas.
James Bruce, A M ....Minister............Mercersburgh, Pa.
James Huston Burns, A M ....Minister............Monroe, Ohio.
Theophilus Wilson Guy, A M ....Farmer ....Oxford, Ohio.
*James Simpson Jones..................Lawyer ....
James McEwen Kimmons, A M......   Miss.
Cornelius McKain, A M ....Minister............Washington, Ind.

---

*Deceased.

†Missionary to China.

12   ALUMNI.

NAMES.	PROFESSION.	RESIDENCE.

Hugh McHatton, A M ....Minister...............Cedarville, Ohio.
Archibald V. McKee, A M ....Lawyer ....Troy, Mo.
†Wm. James McKnight, A M.........Minister..........Danville, Ky.
Alexander Mayne, A M ....
Edward Ethel Porter, A M ....Minister............Memphis, Tenn.
Benjamin Niles Sawtelle, A M ......Minister............Batesville, Ark.
Joseph Gaston Symmes, A M ....Minister............Cranberry, N. J.
Robert Francis Taylor, A. M ....Minister............Colfax, Ind.
Joseph Greene Wells, A M ....Minister............Jackson, Mo.

1852.

Joseph Mayo Bachelder, A M.........Minister............Albia, Iowa.
Stephen James Bovell, A M ....Minister...........Palestine, Ill.
Jonathan Turner Carthel, A M ......Lawyer ....Trenton, Tenn.
John McCutchen Coyner, A M ......Teacher...........Centerville, Ind.
Benjamin Parke Dewey ....Lawyey ....Jeffersonville, Ind.
Henry Michael Giltner, A M ....Minister............Nebraska City, N. T.
Thomas Maise Hopkins, A M ....Minister............Bloomington, Ind.
Alexander Martin, A M ....Teacher ....U. S. A.
Robert Langdon Neely, A M ....Minister............Denmark, Tenn.
James Matlack Scovel, A M ....Lawyer ....Camden, N. J.
Francis Marion Symmes, A M........Minister............Bedford, Ind.
Daniel Price Young, A M..............Minister............——Ky.

1853.

*Lyman Beecher Andrews, A M......Teacher ....Cape Girardeau, Mo.
James Andrew Cunningham ....Business............Madison, Ind.
Lewis Isaac Drake, A M ....Minister............West Liberty, Ohio.
Jeremiah Mead Drake, A M ....Minister............—— Ohio.
‡Joshua Bolles Garritt, A M ....Minister............S. Hanover, Ind.
Edward John Hamilton, A M.........Minister............Oyster Bay, N. Y.
Henry Seymour Kritz, A M...........Teacher ....Waveland, Ind.
*Charles Lee, A M ....Minister............
Wm. Pope Lemaster, A M ....Farmer ....Memphis, Tenn.
Gideon Blackburn McLeary, A M ...Lawyer ....
James Alexander McRee, A M .....Minister............Dillsboro, Ind.
Joseph Warren Mahan, A M ....Teacher............Clermont Co., Ohio.
Henry Thomas Morton, A M ....Minister............
*Henry Spencer Scovel, ...Student Theology.
Sylvester Fithian Scovel, A M ......Minister............Springfield, Ohio.
*Jackson Jay Smith, A M ....Lawyer ....Louisville, Ky.
*Wm. Wheat ....Minister............

1854.

Stephen Cromwell Adair..............Lawyer ....Morganfield, Ky.
David Gilkerson Herron ....Teacher...........Canton, Miss.

†Prof. of Languages in Austin College, Texas.
‡Prof. in Han. College, 1856.
*Deceased.

ALUMNI.

NAMES.	PROFESSION.	RESIDENCE.
Robert Irwin, jr., A M	Minister	Waveland.
Robert Alexander Johnson,	Lawyer	Cincinnati, Ohio.
Isaac Brown Moore	Minister	Waveland, Ind.
Edwin Hubbard Rutherford	Minister	Vicksburg, Miss.
Edward Coles Sickles	Minister	St. Louis, Mo.
Wm. Rondeau Sim	Minister	Jordon's Grove, Ill.
Thomas Wallace, A M	Teacher	
James Edward Wilson		Concord, Tenn.
Jared Ryker Woodfil	Teacher	Near Madison.

1855.

James Robinson Evans	Teacher	Near Memphis, Tenn.
†Michael Montgomery Fisher, A M	Minister	Fulton, Mo.
James H. Hunter	Minister	Rockport, Ill.
Wm. Hall Huston	Farmer	Hamilton, Ohio.
Robert J. L. Matthews, A M	Minister	Jeffersonville, Ind.
Robert Clarke McGee	Minister	
John Quincy McKeehan, A M	Minister	Franklin, Ind.
Charles H. Park	Minister	Potts' Grove, Penn.
Wm. A. Sample, A M	Minister	Memphis, Tenn.
Wm. Bloomer Truax	Minister	Keosauqua, Wis.
Thomas Marion Tucker	Physician	N. Philadelphia, Ind.
Archibald Cameron Voris, A M	Lawyer	Bedford, Ind.

1856.

James Baillie Adams	Minister	Ohio.
James Wm. Allison, A M	Minister	Arcola, Ill.
Robert Brown Herron	Minister	Hillsborough, Ohio.
Henry Keigwin	Minister	Charlestown.
Harvey Lamb	Teacher	Texas.
‡James Kennedy Patterson, A M	Teacher	Lexington, Ky.
James Sanderson Rankin, A M	Teacher	Hanover, Ind.
Richmond Kelly Smoot	Minister	Bowling Green, Ky.
James Harvey Tedford	Minister	Michigan.
§Benjamin Dubois Wykoff	Minister	Allahabad, India.

BACHELOR OF SCIENCE.

Cyrus Alexander Johnson	Business	Memphis, Tenn.
James Edwin Rankin		

1857.

Leonard Fisk Andrews	Teacher	Cape Girardeu, Mo.
Wm. Cochrane, A M	Minister	Brantford, C. W.
Wm. Means Crozier		
John McMurray	Minister	Chapel Hill, Texas.
David McKnight Williamson	Minister	Olney, Ill.

BACHELOR OF SCIENCE.

Hiram Francis Braxton		Paoli.
David Taylor, jr		Columbus, Ohio.
John Newton Voris		Washington, D. C.

---

†Prof. in Westminster College, Mo., 1855.
‡Prof. in Stewart College.
§Missionary in India.

NAMES.	PROFESSION.	RESIDENCE.

1858.

Wm. Peter Baker..................*Teacher*............
*Jacob Reasoner Geyer..................*Minister*............U. S. A.
Horace Hovey Hanna ....*Business*............Ft. Wayne, Ind.
John David McClintock ....*Minister*............W. T.
James Baird McClnre, A M............*Minister*............Fulton, Ill,
Thomas Johnson McIlrath ....*Lawyer*............
David Wm. Moffit, A M ....*Minister*............Vernon, Ind.
James Alexander Piper, A M ....*Minister*............Quincy, Ill.
Robert Gaines Ross ....*Minister*............——Ill.
Augustus Taylor ....*Minister*............Amanda, Ohio.
James Harvey Vannuys ....*Minister*............
*Cornelius Pleasant Voris ....*Minister*............

1859.

Robert Long Adams.....................*Minister*............——Ohio.
Henry Ellet Crnwford ....*Minister*............Pleasant.
John Fox ....*Minister*............——Ill.
Columbus De Witt Huston ....*Minister*............New Philadelphia.
Samuel Finley Thompson................U. S. A............Nashville, Tenn.
John Bacon Vawter.....................*Minister*............

BACHELOR OF SCIENCE.

Charles Henry Johnson..................*Business*............Franklin, Ind.
Oliver Mulvey..........................*Artist*............Madison, Ind.
*George Martin Whitely.....................................

1860.

John McKnight Bloss ....U. S. A.
John W. Crawford......................*Minister*............Frankville, Iowa.
W. S. Coulter.........................*Teacher*............Jeffersonville.
R. F. Middleton.......................*Minister*............Frankfort, Ky.
W. G. Thomas ....*Minister*............
*Samuel D. Voris ....*Student of Theol*..Benington, Ind.
James Wilson..........................*Surgeon*............U. S. A.

BACHELOR OF SCIENCE.

W. A. Collins........................*Surgeon*............Madison, Ind.
George W. Cummins....................*Lawyer*............Logansport, Ind.
J. Marshall Story ....U. S. Army.

1861.

S. F. Denton..U. S. A.
S. H. Howe...........................*Minister*............Flemingsburgh, Ky.
S. M. Irwin..........................*Student of Theol.*
Stephen S. Lee..Vincennes.
Edward F. Reid..U. S. Army.
†B. F. Simpson ....
W. H. Smith ....*Student of Theol.* Allegheny, Penn.

BACHELOL OF SCIENCE.

J. B. Richardson ....Shelbyville, Ky.
J. W. Shrewsberry.....................................
S. *M.* Tilford ....Kent, Ind.

---

*Deceased.
†Killed in battle.

ALUMNI.

| NAMES. | PROFESSION, | RESIDENCE. |

1862.

Moses F. Dunn............................*Lawyer*............Bedford, Ind.
George P. Huckeby....................*Lawyer*............Rome, Ind.
George M. McCampbell................*Theo. Sem.*.........Princeton, N. J.
Samuel T. McClure....................*Theo. Student*......Allegheny, Pa.
James T. Patterson....................*Theo. Student*......Allegheny, Pa.
Wm. H. Sawtelle......................*Theo. Student*......Princeton, N. J.
Levi M. Schofield....................*Theo. Student*......Allegheny, Pa.
Henry C. Thomson....................*Theo. Student*......Princeton, N. J.
John C. Youngken....................*Theo. Student*......

1863.

Josiah Daugherty....................................Ladoga, Ind.
S. Addison Day......................*Student of Law*...New Albany, Ind.
Henry C. Donnell....................*Teacher*............Charlestown, Ind.
George Hippard......................*Student of Law*...Indianapolis, Ind.
Adam J. Johnson....................*Teacher*............
Augustus A. Joss....................*Theo. Student*......Princeton, N. J.
Hugh W. McKee......................*Theo. Student*......Princeton, N. J.
Amos W. Patterson..................*Student of Medicine* Cincinnati, O.
Emanuel N. Pires....................*Theo. Student*......Princeton, N. J.
Wm. C. Smock
Eberle Thomson....................*Theo. Student*......Princeton, N. J.
Wm. Torrance......................*Theo. Student*......
Benj. W. Tucker....................*Physician*..........New Philadelphia, Ind.

BACHELOR OF SCIENCE.

Felix J. Brandt....................................Hanover, Ind.

1864.

Samuel Brown......................*Farmer*............Shelby Co., Ky.
Wm. B. Chamberlin..................*Theo. Student*....Princeton, N. J.
James A. Dean......................................Hanover, Ind.
John H. Harbolt....................*Theo. Student*....Allegheny, Pa.
J. D. Harrington
John H. Holliday..................................Indianapolis, Ind.
Peter H. K. McComb
R. A. Mathes........................*Theo. Student*....Chicago, Ill.
Wm. A. Patton......................*Theo. Student*....Allegheny, Pa.
Arthur Rose........................*Theo. Student*....Princeton, N. J.
Robert A. Sturgus..................................Hanover, Ind.
Robert M. Webster..................................Fairfield, Iowa.
John Weston........................*Theo. Student*....Chicago, Ill.

BACHELOR OF SCIENCE.

John P. Armstrong..................*Student of Law*...Jeffersonville, Ind.
George Scoggan....................................Bedford, Ind.
Samuel M. Strader..................*Clerk in Bank*....Madison, Ind.

UNDERGRADUATES.

Seniors.

John G. Blake...Indianapolis,
Samuel P. Dale...Logansport.
Robert S. Dean...Hanover.
J. C. Eastman...Hanover.
W. H. Fullenwider...Waveland.
Charles L. Holstein..Madison.
John A. Kellar..St. Louis, Mo.
Robert M. Miller..Hanover.
Elias R. Monfort..Cincinnati, O.
Augustus T. Stone..Henry, Ill.
Martin V. B. VanArsdale......................................Washington.
Thomas Tracy..Jewett City, Ct.

Juniors.

Samuel Coleman...Cherry Fork, O.
Alexander Hail..Macomb, Ill.
John M. Lodge...Springfield, Ill.
George Wetherhold...McComb, Ill.

Sophomores.

Placide Boudreault..St. Anne, Ill.
W. N. Burt...Vernon.
J. C. Burt..Vernon.
George G. Dunn..Bedford.
Samuel W. Elliott...Dayton.
Daniel Lattimore...Liberty.
Alexander Peck..Omaha City, N. T.
Moses D. A. Steen..Youngsville, O.
C. S. Thomson..Camden.
Harvey W. Wiley..Kent.
Seth Woodruff...New Albany.

Freshmen.

James S. Blackwell	Henderson, Ky.
John Boyle	Albia, Iowa.
Silas Craig	Ghent, Ky.
T. B. Dean	Hanover.
Wm. Eastman	Hanover.
Edward Gilpin	Hanover.
Charles P. Mayhew	Rennselaer.
James F. McBride	Hanover.
Amos G. McCampbell	Louisville, Ky.
George G Reed	Hanover.
Oscar W. Shryer	Bloomfield.
George L. Spining	Highland, Kansas.
Frank Trigg	Freeborn, Min.
John L. Walker	Salines, W. Va.
Edward P. Whallon	Tipton.

SCIENTIFIC DEPARTMENT.

Third Year.

Samuel G. Gilpin	Hanover.
James M. Justice	Logansport.
Thad. S. Rollins	Logansport.
Andrew D. Wilson	Hanover.

Second Year.

James G. Boyle	Albia, Iowa.
Thomas J. Heady	Bennington.
John E. Henry	Pleasant.
Walter Roberts	Madison.
James Swan	Saluda.

First Year.

Charles W. Ewing	Jeffersonville.
Henry Hawley	Memphis, Tenn.
Elijah F. Hill	Salines, W. Va.
Jared C. Irwin	Hanover.
George Kester	Rockford.
Benj. A. Logan	Jefferson.
James H. Mathews	Hanover.
George W. McGee	Louisville, Ky.
Samuel McIlroy	Oak Dale.
George C. Monroe	Hanover.
J. H. Peters	Jeffersonville.
R. P. Shrewsberry	Salines, W. Va.
Joseph A. Southard	Frankfort
Edward Wedekamper	Louisville, Ky.
U. Z. Wiley	Kent.

(B)

PREPARATORY DEPARTMENT.

Seniors.

M. Amick	Scipio.
W. N. Amick	Scipio.
Wm. Boyle	Albia, Iowa.
Joseph C. Clore	Henderson, Ky.
J. S. Field	Jeffersonville.
Richard H. Rosseau	Louisville, Ky.
W. W. Taylor	Louisville, Ky.
J. H. Thomson	Hanover.

Juniors.

Albert G. Caldwell	Shawneetown, Ill.
Frank Compton	Springdale, O.
Wm. E. Drake	Bristow, Ky.
L. W. Lee	Hanover.
Charles H. Logan	Hanover.
Samuel Rogers	Hanover.
W. P. Shrewsberry	Salines, W. Va.
W. E. Truslow	Salines, W. Va.
W. A. Walker	Salines, W. Va.

SUMMARY.

Seniors	12	Scientific, 2d year	5
Juniors	4	Scientific, 1st year	15
Sophomores	11	Senior Preparatory	8
Freshmen	15	Junior Preparatory	9
Scientific 3d year	4		
Total			83

TEXT BOOKS.*

DEPARTMENT OF LANGUAGES.

LATIN.—Andrews' Grammar and Reader; Andrews' or Leverett's or Crooks & Schem's Lexicon; Andrews' Cæsar; Cooper's Virgil; Bojesen's Roman Antiquities; Butler & Sturgus' Sallust; Lincoln's Livy; Lincoln's Horace; Tyler's Tacitus; Chase's or Anthon's Tusculan Disputations.

GREEK—Hadley's Grammar; Liddell & Scott's, or Pickering's Lexicon; Owen's, or Boise's Anabasis; Bojesen's Grecian Antiquities; Owen's Homer; Woolsey's Greek Plays; Champlin's Demosthenes; Plutarch.

HEBREW—Stuart's Rœdiger's Grammar; Gesenius' Lexicon; Biblia Hebraica; Green's Hebrew Grammar

DEPARTMENT OF BELLES-LETTERS.

Blair's Rhetoric, (University Edition); Coppee's Logic; also for reference, Whately and Hamilton's Logic—the latter as reduced by Day; Wayland's Political Economy; Smith's Grecian History; Liddell's Rome; Lord's Modern History; American History and the Constitution of the U. S. A. For reference Day's Rhetorical Praxis.

DEPARTMENT OF MATHEMATICS.

Rays' Algebra, 2nd part; Davies' Legendre; Davies' Surveying, Coffin's Conic Sections; Loomis'. Analytical Geometry and Calculus; Olmsted's Natural Philosophy; Olmsted's Astronomy.

DEPARTMENT OF NATURAL SCIENCE.

Silliman's Chemistry; Cutter's Physiology; Wood's Botany; Lyell's Geology; Dana's Mineralogy; Agassiz & Gould's Zoology, Somerville's Physical Geography.

DEPARTMENT OF METAPHYSICS.

Walker's Reid on the Intellectual Powers; Sir William Hamilton's Philosophy, (Wight's Edition); Stewart's Active and Moral Powers; Wayland's Moral Science; Haven's Mental Philosophy.

DEPARTMENT OF RELIGIOUS INSTRUCTION.

English Bible, Hodge's, Alexander's or Jacobus' Notes; Greek Testament, Robinson's Greek Harmony; Old Testament Hebrew; Septuagint; Westminister Catechism; General Assembly's Psalm and Hymn Books; Butler's Analogy; Paley's Natural Theology; Coleman's Sacred Geography; Alexander's Evidences of Christianity.

---

*Several of these text books are for reference only. Those in use are occasionally changed, to meet the demands required by the improvements in Science and Literature.

SCIENTIFIC DEPARTMENT.

The three years' course of English, Mathematical and Scientific instruction pursued in this department, embraces all that is included in the College scheme, except the Classical Languages. Such as desire it, however, may pursue the study of Latin and French, in connection with a Scientific Course. We do not recommend it as in any sense an equivalent for a thorough Classical Course; nor is it intended for mere boys, since the subjects which it includes are entirely above their capacity; but to young men, who have attained a respectable common school education, including the elements of Algebra, and who have not time nor means to prosecute a Classical course, this system of studies will, it is hoped, commend itself as solid, comprehensive and practical. Those who shall complete the prescribed Scientific course, will receive a Diploma, certifying the extent of their attainments.

COLLEGE YEAR--EXAMINATIONS.

The College Year is divided into two Terms. The First Term begins on the Wednesday after the 25th day of August, and continues 16 weeks.— The Second Term begins on the first Wednesday in January and continues 24 weeks. The Annual Commencement occurs on Thursday before the 25th of June.

It is of great importance that students attend from the very beginning of the Term; especially since so considerable a portion of time is allotted to vacations. In most cases, the loss of a few weeks, or even days, seriously affects the future standing of the pupil. Absence during term time without special leave, is prohibited.*

Public Examinations will be held, hereafter, only at the close of the College year, when the Freshman and Junior Classes will be examined upon studies of the preceding year, and the Sophomore and Senior Classes on those of the two preceding years. These last examinations will be FINAL, for the studies pursued in those years. All the examinations will be THOROUGH and RIGID; and will be conducted, in part by the use of written questions, prepared by the Faculty and the Examining Committee, covering the whole field of study prosecuted during a given period, and entirely unknown to the Student until the moment of examination.— These questions must be answered in writing before the Committee; and correct answers to a definite portion of them will be the passport of admission to a higher standing. Similar examinations of a briefer and less decisive character, however, and by way of preparation for the final trial, may be conducted privately, at the pleasure of the Faculty.

*Parents are respectfully advised to give their sons no such permission to be absent, except in cases of NECESSITY.

Religious Instruction and Services.

The attention of a Christian community is respectfully invited to the system of Biblical Instruction which forms a characteristic feature of our course of Study. The Grammar School Classes recite stately in the English Bible; and every College Class has a daily or tri-weekly recitation in the Greek Testament, or the Hebrew. Proficiency in these, as in other studies, is tested by the usual examinations. In addition to this, Biblical Geography and Antiquities, Ecclesiastical History, Natural Theology, and the Analogy of Religion, Natural and Revealed, to the constitution and course of nature, are carefully and faithfully studied. There is also a Bible or Catechetical exercise on Sabbath mornings; a public service on Sabbath afternoon, appropriated to the Students; and daily morning prayers. The Students are expected to attend the Sabbath morning services of the congregation worshiping in the chapel, or of some other congregation in the vicinity, if their parents prefer any of the latter. The Methodist and United and Associate Presbyterian Churches have regular services in or near the Village.

ADMISSIONS.

Candidates for admission into the Freshman Class, are required to be proficient in Arithmetic and Algebra; Ancient and Modern Geography; History of the U. S. A.; the English, Latin, and Greek Grammars; Cæsar's Commentaries, and Greek Reader, or what is equivalent to these attainments. They must furnish testimonials of good character, and, if from another College, must bring certificates of honorable dismission.—Candidates for higher standing are examined upon that part of the course already studied by the Class, which they propose to enter.

No one can be admitted to the Freshman Class until he has completed his fourteenth year, nor to an advanced standing without a proportional increase of age.

Before a student shall be admitted to actual standing in any Class, he shall present to the President a receipt from the Treasurer, showing that he has complied with the Statutes relating to College Charges and Scholarships.

N. B. The regular examination for admission into College, commences on the Monday preceding the beginning of each Term.

Course of Instruction.

Preparatory Department.

Andrew's Latin Lessons, Grammar, Reader, and Exercises; Andrew's Cæsar; Butler and Sturgus' Sallust; McClintock & Crook's 1st and 2d Greek Books; Classical and Biblical Geography; Ray's Algebra, 2nd part, English Bible.

Scientific Department.

FIRST YEAR.

Algebra, Rays', 2nd part; Plane Geometry; Plane Trigonometry, Mensuration of Surfaces, Surveying and Navigation; History; English Bible; Historical Books; and Sacred Geography.

SECOND YEAR.

Solid Geometry; Analytical Plane Trigonometry; Mensuration of Solids; and Application of Algebra to Geometry; Spherical Trigonometry; Conic Sections, Rhetoric, Logic; Political Economy, English Bible, Poetical Books; Chemistry, Light, Heat, Electricity, and Botany.

THIRD YEAR.

Analytical Geometry and Calculus; Natural Philosophy, Astronomy, Anatomy, Zoology and Physiology; Mineralogy; Geology, Natural Theology, Butler's Analogy, Psychology, Moral Science, English Bible, Constitution of the U. S. A.

Collegiate Department.

Freshman Class.

FIRST TERM.

Greek Harmony of the Gospels............Robinson.
Biblical Antiquities............Nevin.
Sallust............Butler & Sturgus.
Latin Exercises............Andrews.
Greek Prose Composition............Boise.
Plane Geometry............Davies' Legendre.

SECOND TERM—SESSION FIRST.

Greek Harmony, continued............Robinson.
Sallust, continued............Butler & Sturgus,
Latin Exercises and Greek Composition, continued...
Practical Plane Trig. and Mensuration of Surfaces...Davie's Legendre.
This Session closes with the Spring Exhibitions, the last week in March.

SECOND TERM—SESSION SECOND.

Greek Harmony, completed............
Virgil............Cooper.
Xenophon's Memorabilia............Robbins.
Latin and Greek Exercises............
Surveying and Navigation............Davies.

SOPHOMORE CLASS.

FIRST TERM.

Greek Testament, Acts............Owen.
Livy............Lincoln.
Homer's Odyssey............Owen.
Greek History............Smith.
Solid Geometry............Davies' Legendre.

SECOND TERM—SESSION FIRST.

Greek Testament, Epistles..................................
Livy, continued..
Homer's Odyssey, continued...........................
Plato's Apology and Crito..........................Tyler.
Roman History...Liddell.
Roman Antiquities....................................Bojesen.
Analytical Plane Trigonometry.........................
Spherical Trigonometry, Mensuration of Solids, and
    Application of Algebra to Geometry.............

SECOND TERM—SESSION SECOND.

Greek Testament (Epistles)..............................
Horace ....Lincoln,
Greek Antiquities....................................Bojesen.
Apology and Crito, continued....................Tyler.
Modern History..Lord.
Conic Sections..Coffin.

JUNIOR CLASS.

FIRST TERM.

Hebrew Grammar and Hebrew—Genesis (optional)
Tacitus' Germania and Agricola..................Tyler.
Demosthenes' Select Orations................Champlin.
Analytical Geometry and Calculus.............Loomis.
Rhetoric..Blair.
Chemistry...Silliman.

SECOND TERM—SESSION FIRST.

Hebrew (Genesis continued)...........................
Tacitus (continued)..
Demosthenes' Select Orations (continued)........
Natural Philosophy, Mathematical part....Olmsted.
Logic..Coppee.
Chemistry (continued)....................................
Botany...Wood.

SECOND TERM—SESSION SECOND.

Hebrew (Psalms)..
Cicero's Tusculan Disputations...............Anthon.
Alcestis of Euripides..............................Woolsey.
Natural Philosophy—Applications.........Olmsted.
Political Economy..................................Wayland.
Optics and Electricity............................Olmsted.
Botany (continued)...................................Wood.

SENIOR CLASS.
FIRST TERM.

Anatomy and Physiology..................................Cutter.
Zoology..Agassiz.
Selections of the Hebrew Bible..............................
Psychology..Haven.
Cicero's Tusculan Disputations (continued)............
Greek Tragedies...Woolsey.
Astronomy and Review..................................Olmsted.

SECOND TERM—SESSION FIRST.

Select Hebrew (continued)...................................
Mineralogy and Geology...........................Dana and Lyell.
Butler's Analogy..
Natural Theology..Paley.
Moral Science..Wayland.
Greek Tragedies (continued)................................
Juvenal..Anthon.
Ouranography and Review...................................

SECOND TERM—SESSION SECOND.

Hebrew (continued)..
Geology (continued)..
Moral Science (continued).................................
Juvenal...
Plutarch...Hackett.
Constitution of the U. S. A............................Story.
Astronomy and Ouranography and Review..............

Department of English Literature and Philology.

The studies and exercises belonging to this Department are attended to by the Faculty. The Alumni Professorship, which was commenced some years ago, had in view the support of a separate Professor, who should devote his entire labors to this Department. The object contemplated is highly important, and the attention of the Alumni and other friends of the College is respectfully solicited to the endowment of this Professorship.

N. B. The Text Books needed for any part of the College Course will be furnished by one of the Professors, at Cincinnati prices.

(C)

EXPENSES &C.

The entire Expenditures of a Student need not much exceed $200, viz:
Tuition, per year..$30 00
Contingent fee.. 5 00
These are required in advance by the Term—first Term $14 second Term, $21.
Boarding with private families, and furnished room, at $4 00 to
$4 50 per week,......................................$144 00 to 162 00
Fuel, Light, Washing &c,..15 00
Books, &c.,..5 00 to 10 00

Boarding in Clubs will cost from one dollar and twenty-five cents to two dollars per week; and some board themselves even at a lower rate. The cost of clothing, and the amount spent as pocket money, will vary with the taste and habit of the Student, and with the wishes of his parents. As a general rule the more money allowed to a young man; beyond what is strictly necessary, the less likely he is to reflect honor upon his Parents and Instructors. Although Hanover presents comparatively few temptations to extravagance, yet parents are earnestly advised to require of their sons a detailed account of their expenditures, and to refuse the payment of any debt incurred by them, except for ordinary current expenses, without a written permission. It is also recommended that the funds of young pupils be deposited with some one of the Faculty, and expended under his direction. The younger Students are required to board where the Faculty may direct, and where they may exercise a more careful and frequent supervision.

N. B. Students placed upon Scholarships by the Faculty, are relieved in part, or wholly, as the case may be, from the payment of Tuition Fees. The Contingent Fee is required of those on Scholarships the same as others. This is now $2 00 for the first Term, and $3 00 for the second.

DISCIPLINE.

A record is kept by the Faculty, in which is entered weekly, the grades of scholarship of the Student, his absence from the exercises of the Institution, and such other facts as are worthy of notice with respect to his general deportment. From this record a report is made out at the end of each Session, and sent to the Parent or Guardian of each Student. In case of deficiency in scholarship, negligence in study, irregularity of attendance upon the exercises of the Institution, or improper conduct, the Student will be privately admonished, and the Parent or Guardian will be promptly informed of the fact.

The object of this arrangement is to keep Parents and Guardians accurately informed with regard to their sons and wards in this Institution, and thus to secure their co-operation with the Faculty in a mild system of discipline. Whenever it is ascertained that a Student is deriving no advantage from his connection with the Institution, or is pursuing a course injurious to himself or fellow-students, the Faculty will take decisive action, and his Parent or Guardian will be promptly addressed on the subject, and requested to remove him from the Institution.

Resolutions of the Faculty, Adopted Dec. 20, 1862.

As absence during the latter part of the College Term greatly injures the Scholarship of Students, impairs their habits of study, breaks the integrity of Classes, discourages study among students that remain, and thus lowers the literary standard of the Institute, therefore,

RESOLVED, 1st. That after this date, Dec. 20, 1862, all such absences (not made unavoidable by the Providence of God,) shall be recorded as unexcused.

RESOLVED, 2d. That this Resolution be published in the Catalogue and Quarterly Report.

SCHOLARSHIPS.

The endowment of this Institution is in the form of Scholarships, of which the Board has established several sorts. The sum of $400 paid, or secured to the Corporation by note payable within five years; and bearing six per cent. interest in advance upon principal remaining unpaid, purchases for the owner, his heirs and assigns, a perpetual right to the tuition of one Scholar in Hanover College. The sum of $200 paid, or subscribed under similar conditions, secures the right to twenty years' tuition; after which time the Scholarship is subject to the disposal of the Board for the gratuitous education of candidates for the Gospel Ministry. A Church Scholarship of $200, secures to the Church so contributing, a perpetual right to the tuition of one Student, who shall be a member of that Church; and appointed by the Session. A Presbyterial Scholarship of $200 secures a similar right to a Presbytery, in behalf of pupils who shall be candidates for the Ministry under its care. Principal paid on these Scholarships is invested by the corporation in some safe and productive Stock, and the Interest only can be expended for the support of the College.

Every person applying for admission as a beneficiary of a Scholarship under the control of the donors, shall present to the Treasurer, at the bginning of each Term, a written Certificate from those controlling the

Scholarship, of his right to such benefit;—when, after paying whatever interest may be due on said Scholarship, he shall receive an acknowledgment of his right, which he shall lodge with the President.

"The Scholorships subject to the disposal of the Corporation, may be occupied by such applicants as the Faculty may select, after inquiry into their circumstances, character, and attainments, the preference being ceteris paribus, to those who give the best evidence of Scholarship.

"There shall at no time be more than one Student upon each Scholarship."

ACCOMMODATIONS.

The community system of Boarding in Commons, or of rooming in large Lodging Halls, is not adopted in Hanover. Arrangements are made to accommodate the Students with board and rooms in respectable private families, where the number together can never be large; and where all shall be brought under domestic influence.

Settlement of Accounts.

No Diploma nor honorable dismission shall be granted until the Student shall exhibit a Receipt of Settlement of all his bills for boarding, room and washing.

Degrees.

No Degrees are conferred in Course. Candidates for Literary Honors are reported to the Board upon their ascertained or acknowledged merits.

Societies, Libraries &c.

There are two Societies connected with the College, the UNION LITERARY and the PHILALETHEAN, whose Libraries number each about twelve hundred volumes.

There is also a SOCIETY OF RELIGIOUS INQUIRY, which has begun to collect a Library, Maps, &c., and which receives regularly several valuable religious papers and periodicals.

The College Library contains near three thousand well selected volumes and is accessible to the Students.

The Cabinet contains several thousand specimens in Mineralogy and Geology.

The friends of the College are advised that contributions to the Library, to the Cabinet, or to the Laboratory, are much needed and will be thankfully received.

Public Literary Societies and Annual Commencement.

Ample opportuntiy is offered to the Students, once a week, to improve themselves in Composition and Elocution, and several times a year Literary entertainments are given in public, which furnish occasions for honorable competition among the Students, and an interesting and profitable repast to their friends. Three of these entertainments occur annually, viz : on the evening of Washington's birth-day ; on Tuesday and Wednesday evening, of the last week in March, and on the week of Commencement, when the two Literary Societies and the Society of Inquiry have addresses by gentlemen from abroad, and the Senior Class deliver their Graduating Orations,—altogether occupying over two days.

THE COMMENCEMENT DAY IS ON THE THURSDAY PRECEDING THE 25TH OF JUNE, after which there is a vacation till the last Wednesday of August.

Prohibited Secret Societies.

The following order was passed by the Board of Trustees, in July, 1858, viz:

"*Resolved*, That this Board disapprove of the existence among the Students of Hanover College, of any Society or Association of which the Faculty are not *ex-officio* Members, and will not permit the public exhibition of any such Society."

The following Resolution was adopted June, 1864.

"*Resolved*, By the Board of Trustees of Hanover College, that the Students of this Institution are prohibited from organizing and becoming members of secret, political or literary Societies of which the Faculty of the College are not honorary members; and, further, that a violation of this Resolution by any Student shall be disciplined by the Faculty in such manner as to them shall seem to be right.

Location, Buildings &c.

The Village of Hanover is situated upon an elevated bluff of the Ohio River, six miles below Madison, Indiana, in a region of remarkable salubrity and natural beauty. The village and neighborhood are characterized by morality, and the absence of all the ordinary temptations to vice, and idleness. The Ohio River, and the Railways from Madison, New Albany, and Cincinnati, place Hanover within twenty-four hours of all the principal points in Indiana, Kentucky, Western Ohio, and Eastern Illinois. A turnpike from Madison to Hanover, renders the village easy of access at all seasons of the year.

Hanover College is controlled by a Board of Trustees; one-half of whom are appointed by the Board itself, and the other half by the Synods of Indiana and Northern Indiana.

The Board purchased, some years ago, a farm of two hundred acres, lying between the Village and the Ohio River, upon a beautiful point of which,—overlooking the River from an elevation of four hundred feet,—they have erected a commodious College edifice, now completed and occupied. The new College consists of a center building nearly eighty feet square, with lateral and transverse wings. The whole length is about two hundred feet. It contains no dormitories for Students,—an undesirable provision,—but affords ample and convenient Halls, Library, Cabinet, Lecture, and Recitation Rooms, and a spacious Chapel.

The building commands an exceedingly diversified view of the River, for six miles up and ten miles down its course. A visitor of large acquaintance with our Country and the world, asserts that a more delightful prospect can not be found in America or Europe.

There is in Hanover, a Select School for young ladies under the care of the Rev. Wm. Oburn, and daughter. Gentlemen having daughters to educate as well as sons, can enter their sons in College, and their daughters in this Academy.

Mr. Oburn's school has been recently commenced, and it is thus far highly satisfactory to those who have given it their patronage.

A public school for boys and girls, is also usually taught in the village of Hanover, and if deemed exsedient a Grammar school for boys will be connected with the College. This measure is under consideration, for the benefit of those who are not far enough advanced to enter our regular prepapatory Department.

Form of Conveyances and Bequests.

The corporate name of this institution is "THE TRUSTEES OF HANOVER COLLEGE."

Donors residing in other States should also designate the place in which the college is located, thus: "*The Trustees of Hanover College, located at Hanover, in the State of Indiana.*"

The friends of Education in Indiana and elsewhere are respectfully solicited to make donations and legacies to this Institution. Since the College was chartered in 1832, about 3,000 have received all or part of their education here, and not less than 800 of these were candidates for the Gospel Ministry. The College has enjoyed 24 revivals of Religion. Over one half of the students in the present catalogue, are members of the Church, and one fourth or more have in view the sacred office.

THE

THIRTY-FOURTH

Annual Catalogue and Circular

OF

HANOVER COLLEGE,

INDIANA,

JUNE 1866.

MADISON, INDIANA:
WM. P. LEVY, PRINTER AND BINDER.
1866.

THE

THIRTY-FOURTH

Annual Catalogue and Circular

OF

HANOVER COLLEGE,

INDIANA,

JUNE 1866.

MADISON, INDIANA:
WM. P. LEVY, PRINTER AND BINDER.
1866.

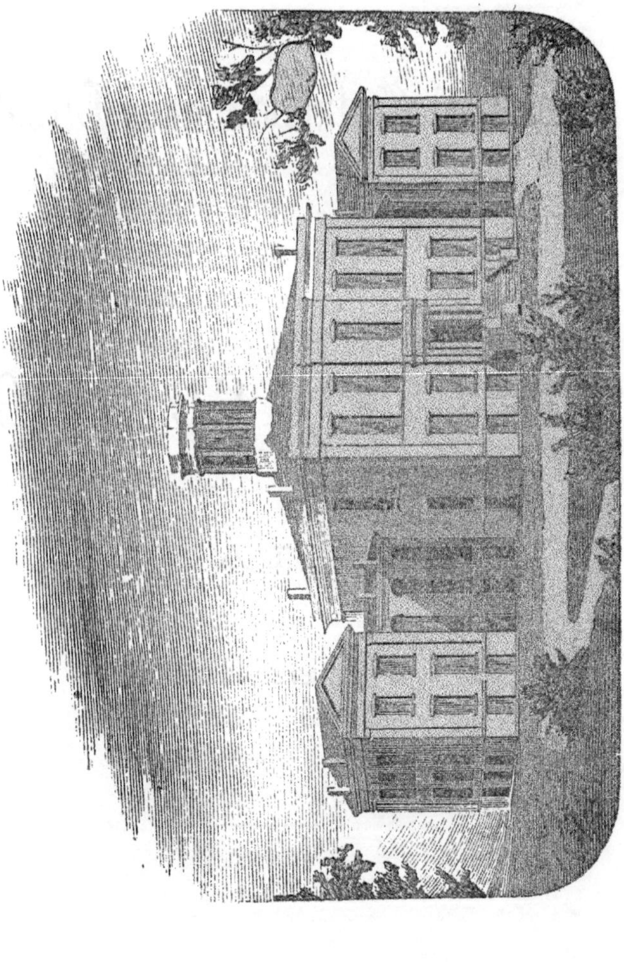

BOARD OF TRUSTEES.

Bd.	JAMES M. RAY, Esq., Indianapolis	1870.
Bd.	ROBERT DEAN, Esq., Hanover	1870.
Bd.	HON. C. E. WALKER, Madison	1870.
Bd.	COL. JAMES BLAKE Indianapolis	1870.
N. S.	REV. W. M. DONALDSON, Ossian	1869.
N. S.	R. P. DAVIDSON, Esq., Lafayette	1869.
S. S.	JAMES H. McCAMPBELL, Esq., Jeffersonville	1869.
S. S.	REV. J. P. SAFFORD, D. D., New Albany	1869.
Bd.	REV. D. D. McKEE, Hanover	1869.
Bd.	H. JAMES Y. ALLISON, Madison	1869.
Bd.	REV. WM. A. HOLLIDAY, Indianapolis	1869.
Bd.	JESSE L. WILLIAMS, Esq., Fort Wayne	1869.
S. S.	REV. GEORGE C. HECKMAN. Indianapolis	1868.
S. S.	REV. J. W. BLYTHE, Hanover	1868.
N. S.	REV. ROBERT IRWIN, Jun., Waveland	1868.
N. S.	REV. J. H. NIXON. Indianapolis	1868.
Bd.	REV. G. D. ARCHIBALD, D. D., Madison	1868.
Bd.	DR. ANDREW SPEAR, Hanover	1868.
Bd.	WILLIAM P. INSKEEP, Esq., Madison	1868.
Bd.	CHARLES N TODD, Esq, Indianapolis	1868.
S. S.	REV. E. S WILSON, Vincennes	1867.
S. S.	JOHN H. VANNUYS, Esq, Franklin	1867.
N. S.	REV. JOHN M. LOWRIE, D. D., Fort Wayne	1867.
N. S	REV. ISAAC N. SHEPHERD, Muncie	1867.
Bd.	JOHN KING, Esq., Madison	1867.
Bd.	REV. J. G. MONFORT, D. D., Cincinnati, O.	1867.
Bd.	HON. W McKEE DUNN, Madison	1867.
Bd.	REV. JAMES WOOD, D. D., Hanover	1867.
S. S.	SILAS C DAY, Esq, New Albany	1866.
S. S.	REV. THOMAS S. CROWE, Jeffersonville	1866.
N. S.	REV. C. K. THOMPSON, Lebanon	1866.
N. S.	REV. JAMES B. CROWE, Crawfordsville	1866.

Officers of the Board.

JAMES M. RAY, Esq., *President.*   REV. G. D. ARCHIBALD, D. D., *Sec'y.*
REV. JAMES WOOD, D. D., *Treasurer.*

Executive Committee.

REV. JAMES WOOD, D. D.,   HON. C E. WALKER,
JOHN KING, Esq.,   ROBERT DEAN, Esq.,
JAMES M. RAY, Esq.,   REV. G. D. ARCHIBALD, D. D.

Auditing Committee.

HON. C. E. WALKER,   JOHN KING, Esq.

FACULTY.

Rev. JAMES WOOD, D. D., President.

Professor of Biblical Instruction, Psychology, Logic and Ethics.

Rev. S. HARRISON THOMSON, A. M.,

Professor of Mathematics, Mechanical Philosophy, and Astronomy.

Rev. JOSHUA B. GARRITT, A. M.,

Professor of the Greek Language and Literature.

Rev. J. W. SCOTT. D. D.,

Professor of Natural Science.

Rev. W. A. HOLLIDAY, A. M.,*

Professor of the Latin and Modern Languages.

Rev. JOSHUA B. GARRITT, A. M.

Librarian.

WILLIAM BROWN,

Janitor.

* Resigned.

UNDERGRADUATES.

Seniors.

Preston McKinney..................................Livonia, Ind.
George M. Lodge..................................Wilton, Iowa.
George Wetherhold.................................Macomb, Ill.

Juniors.

Placide Boudreault................................St. Anne, Ill.
W. N. Burt..Vernon, Ind.
I. C. Burt..Vernon, Ind.
Irwin M. L. Caton.................................Cincinnati, O.
George G. Dunn....................................Bedford, Ind.
V. L. Mack..Columbia, Tenn.
Alexander Peck....................................Omaha City, N. T.
J. S. Thompson....................................Camden, Ind.
Harvey W. Wiley...................................Kent, Ind.
Seth Woodruff.....................................New Albany, Ind.

Sophomores.

James S. Blackwell................................Henderson, Ky.
William Eastman...................................Hanover, Ind.
Edward Gilpin.....................................Hanover, Ind.
Jeremiah Long*....................................Franklin, Ind.
Charles P. Mayhew.................................Logansport, Ind.
George G. Reed....................................Hanover, Ind.
James Spear.......................................Hanover, Ind.
George L. Spining.................................Highland, Kansas.
Frank Trigg.......................................Freeborn, Min.
Edward P. Whallon.................................Lexington, Ind.
James Williamson..................................Greenfield, Ind.

---

* Sophomore except in Mathematics.

Freshmen.

W. N. Amick	Scipio, Ind.
Ebenezer Gilpin	Hanover, Ind.
Thomas R. Paxton	Princeton, Ind.
Henry Robb	Hanover, Ind.
J. H. Thomson	Hanover, Ind
Thomas V. Thornton	Bedford, Ind.

SCIENTIFIC DEPARTMENT.

Third Year.

Thomas J. Heady	Bennington, Ind.
James Swan	Saluda, Ind.

Second Year.

M. Amick	Scipio, Ind.
Thomas J. Charlton	Pleasant, Ind.
James H. Matthews	Hanover, Ind.
James Edson McClelland	Vernon, Ind.
George C. Monroe	Hanover, Ind.
William Oburn	Hanover, Ind.
George Phelps	Greenville, Ill.
Oscar W. Shryer	Bloomfield, Ind.
John L. Walker	Salines, W. Va.
U. Z. Wiley	Kent, Ind.

First Year.

James D. Aberdeen	Hanover, Ind.
John Arnold	Rushville, Ind.
Alexander Blackburne	Macomb, Ill.
C. Bollinger	Seymour, Ind.
William B. Brandt	Hanover, Ind.
Champ Eugean Buel	Valparaiso, Ind.
Kennedy F. Clapp	Scipio, Ind.
D. Frank Clark	St. Louis, Mo.
Mark H. Dale	Connersville, Ind.
John R. Dickey	Hanover, Ind.
William Douglass*	Frankfort, Ind.
John A. Douglass	Frankfort, Ind.
William A. Duckwall	Portland, Ky.
James Huston Faris	Connersville, Ind.

* Deceased.

Robert L. Graham...N. Washington, Ind.
James N. Kimball..Livonia, Ind.
Willie C. Levi..Louisville, Ky.
George M. Logan..Hanover, Ind.
William M. Pelan..Connersville, Ind.
E. S. Phillips..Hanover, Ind.
J. T. Sandefur..Henderson, Ky.
Jacob F. Scudder..Washington, Ind.
Charles T. Shannon..Carlisle, Ind.
James Edward Talbott......................................Bloomfield, Ind.

PREPARATORY DEPARTMENT.

Seniors.

Frank Compton...Springdale, O.
John M. Coulter..Hanover, Ind.
J. Albert Devin..Princeton, Ind.
James Nelson Huston..Connersville, Ind.
L. W. Lee..Hanover, Ind.
John Thomson Stevenson..................................Grenada, Miss.
William A. Walker..Salines, W. Va.

Juniors.

Sylvester S. Bergen...Franklin, Ind.
Stanley Coulter...Hanover, Ind.
H. F. McCullough...Livonia, Ind.
M. Wade Luckett..Edwardsville, O.
J. M. Oburn..Hanover, Ind.
George T. Thomin...Venice, O.
Henry Thomson..Greensburgh, Ind.
Williell Thompson..Hanover, Ind.
Henry C. Thornton..Bedford, Ind.
William H. Tolbert..Venice, O.
Andrew Harvey Young......................................Hanover, Ind.

SUMMARY.

Seniors................................	3	Scientific, 2d year..................	10
Juniors................................	10	Scientific, 1st year..................	24
Sophomores.........................	11	Senior Preparatory.................	7
Freshmen.............................	6	Junior Prepartory...................	11
Scientific, 3d year................	2		
Total.............................			84

TEXT BOOKS.*

DEPARTMENT OF LANGUAGES.

LATIN.—Harkness' Grammar and Reader; Andrews' or Leverett's or Crook's & Schem's Lexicon; Andrews' Cæsar; Cooper's Virgil; Bojesen's Roman Antiquities; Butler & Sturgus' Sallust; Lincoln's Livy; Lincoln's Horace; Tyler's Tacitus; Chase's or Anthon's Tusculan Disputations.

GREEK—Hadley's Grammar; Liddell & Scott's, or Pickering's Lexicon; Owen's, or Boise's Anabasis; Bojesen's Grecian Antiquities; Owen's Homer; Woolsey's Greek Plays; Champlin's Demosthenes; Plutarch.

HEBREW—Stuart's Rœdiger's Grammar; Gesenius' Lexicon; Biblia Hebraica; Green's Hebrew Grammar.

DEPARTMENT OF BELLES-LETTERS.

Blair's Rhetoric, (University Edition); Coppee's Logic; also for reference, Whately and Hamilton's Logic—the latter as reduced by Day Wayland's Political Economy; Smith's Grecian History; Liddell's Rome; Lord's Modern History; American History and the Constitution of the U. S. A. For reference Day's Rhetorical Praxis.

DEPARTMENT OF MATHEMATICS.

Rays' Algebra, 2nd part; Davies' Legendre; Davies' Surveying, Coffin's Conic Sections; Loomis' Analytical Geometry and Calculus, Olmsted's Natural Philosophy; Olmsted's Astronomy.

DEPARTMENT OF NATURAL SCIENCE.

Silliman's Chemistry; Cutter's Physiology; Wood's Botany; Lyell's Geology; Dana's Mineralogy; Agassiz & Gould's Zoology, Somerville's Physical Geography.

DEPARTMENT OF METAPHYSICS.

Walker's Reid on the Intellectual Powers; Sir William Hamilton's Philosophy, (Wight's Edition); Stewart's Active and Moral Powers; Wayland's Moral Science; Haven's Mental Philosophy.

DEPARTMENT OF RELIGIOUS INSTRUCTION.

English Bible, Hodge's, Alexander's or Jacobus' Notes; Greek Testament, Robinson's Greek Harmony; Old Testament Hebrew; Septuagint; Westminister Catechism; General Assembly's Psalm and Hymn Book; Butler's Analogy; Paley's Natural Theology; Coleman's Sacred Geography; Alexander's Evidences of Christianity.

---

*Several of these text books are for reference only. Those in use are occasionally changed, to meet the demands required by the improvement' in Science and Literature.

SCIENTIFIC DEPARTMENT.

The three years' course of English, Mathematical and Scientific Instruction pursued in this department, embraces all that is included in the College scheme, except the Classical Languages. Such as desire it, however, may pursue the study of Latin and French, in connection with a Scientific Course. We do not recommend it as in any sense an equivalent for a thorough Classical Course; nor is it intended for mere boys, since the subjects which it includes are entirely above their capacity; but to young men, who have attained a respectable common school education, including the elements of Algebra, and who have not time nor means to prosecute a Classical Course, this system of studies will, it is hoped, commend itself as solid, comprehensive and practical. Those who shall complete the prescribed Scientific Course, will receive a Diploma, certifying the extent of their attainments.

COLLEGE YEAR--EXAMINATIONS.

The College Year is divided into two Terms. The First Term begins on the Wednesday after the 25th day of August, and continues 16 weeks. The Second Term begins on the first Wednesday in January, and continues 24 weeks. The Annual Commencement occurs on Thursday before the 25th of June.

It is of great importance that students attend from the very beginning of the Term; especially since so considerable a portion of time is allotted to vacations. In most cases, the loss of a few weeks, or even days, seriously affects the future standing of the pupil. Absence during term time without special leave, is prohibited.*

Public Examinations will be held, hereafter, only at the close of the College year, when the Freshman and Junior Classes will be examined upon the studies of the preceding year, and the Sophomore and Senior Classes on those of the two preceding years. These last examinations will be FINAL, for the studies pursued in those years. All the examinations will be THOROUGH and RIGID; and will be conducted, in part by the use of written questions, prepared by the Faculty and Examining Committee, covering the whole field of study prosecuted during a given period, and entirely unknown to the Student until the moment of examination. These questions must be answered in writing before the Committee; and correct answers to a definite portion of them will be the passport of admission to a higher standing. Similar examinations of a briefer and less decisive character, however, and by way of preparation for the final trial, may be conducted privately, at the pleasure of the Faculty.

---

* Parents are respectfully advised to give their sons no such permission to be absent, except in cases of NECESSITY.

(A)

Religious Instruction and Services.

The attention of a Christian community is respectfully invited to the system of Biblical Instruction which forms a characteristic feature of our course of Study. The Grammar School Classes recite statedly in the English Bible; and every College Class I as a daily or tri-weekly recitation in the Greek Testament, or the Hebrew. Proficiency in these, as in other studies, is tested by the usual examinations. In addition to this, Biblical Geography and Antiquities, Ecclesiastical History, Natural Theology, and the Analogy of Religion, Natural and Revealed, to the constitution and course of nature, are carefully and faithfully studied. There is also a Bible or Catechetical exercise on Sabbath mornings; a public service on Sabbath afternoon, appropriated to the Students; and daily morning prayers. The Students are expected to attend the Sabbath morning services of the congregation worshipping in the chapel, or of some other congregation in the vicinity, if their parents prefer any of the latter. The Methodist and United and Associate Presbyterian Churches have regular services in or near the Village.

ADMISSIONS.

Candidates for admission into the Freshman Class, are required to be proficient in Arithmetic and Algebra; Ancient and Modern Geography; History of the U. S. A.; the English, Latin and Greek Grammars; Cæsar's Commentaries, and Greek Reader, or what is equivalent to these attainments. They must furnish testimonials of good character, and, if from another College, must bring certificates of honorable dismission. Candidates for higher standing are examined upon that part of the course already studied by the Class which they propose to enter.

No one can be admitted to the Freshman Class until he has completed his fourteenth year; nor to an advanced standing without a proportional increase of age.

Before a student shall be admitted to actual standing in any Class, he shall present to the President a receipt from the Treasurer, showing that he has complied with the Statutes relating to College Charges and Scholarships.

N. B. The regular examination for admission into College, commences on the Monday preceding the beginning of each Term.

Course of Instruction.

Preparatory Department.

Andrew's Latin Lessons ; Harkness' Grammar, Reader, and Exercises; Andrew's Cæsar ; Butler and Sturgus' Sallust ; Arnold's 1st Greek Book ; Boise's Greek Prose ; Classical and Biblical Geography; Ray's Algebra, 2d part; English Bible.

Scientific Department.

FIRST YEAR.

Algebra, Rays', 2nd part; Plane Geometry; Plane Trigonometry, Surveying and Navigation; History; English Bible, Historical Books; and Sacred Geography.

SECOND YEAR.

Solid Geometry; Analytical Plane Trigonometry; Mensuration of Surfaces and Solids; Spherical Trigonometry; Analytical Geometry; Rhetoric, Logic, Political Economy; English Bible, Poetical Books; Chemistry, Light, Heat, Electricity, and Botany.

THIRD YEAR.

Analytical Geometry and Calculus; Natural Philosophy, Uranography, Astronomy, Anatomy, Zoology and Physiology; Mineralogy; Geology, Natural Theology, Butler's Analogy, Psychology, Moral Science, English Bible, Constitution of the U. S. A.

Collegiate Department.

Freshman Class.

FIRST TERM.

Greek Harmony of the Gospels	Robinson.
Biblical Antiquities	Nevin.
Sallust	Butler & Sturgus.
Latin Exercises	Andrews.
Greek Prose Composition	Boise.
Plane Geometry	Davies' Legendre.

SECOND TERM—SESSION FIRST.

Greek Harmony, continued	Robinson.
Sallust, continued	Butler & Sturgus,
Xenophon's Anabasis or Memorabilia	Robbins or Anthon.
Latin Exercises and Greek Composition, continued...	
Practical Plane Trig. and Mensuration of Surfaces	Davies' Legendre.

This Session closes with the Spring Exhibitions, the last week in March.

SECOND TERM—SESSION SECOND.

Greek Harmony, completed	
Virgil	Cooper.
Xenophon's Memorabilia	Robbins or Anthon.
Latin and Greek Exercises	
Surveying and Navigation	Davies.

SOPHOMORE CLASS.

FIRST TERM.

Greek Testament, Acts	Owen.
Livy	Lincoln.
Homer's Odyssey	Owen.
Greek History	Smith.
Solid Geometry	Davies' Legendre.

SECOND TERM—SESSION FIRST.

Greek Testament, Epistles..
Livy, continued...
Homer's Odyssey, continued...
Plato's Gorgias...Woolsey.
Roman History...Liddell.
Roman Antiquities...Bojesen.
Analytical Plane Trigonometry.....................................
Spherical Trigonometry, Mensuration of Surfaces and Solids........

SECOND TERM—SESSION SECOND.

Greek Testament (Epistles)..
Horace..Lincoln,
Greek Antiquities...Bojesen.
Plato's Gorgias...
Modern History...Lord.
Analytical Geometry..Loomis.

JUNIOR CLASS.

FIRST TERM.

Hebrew Grammar and Hebrew—Genesis (optional)
Tacitus' Germania and Agricola................................Tyler.
Demosthenes' or Aeschines' Orations........................Champlin.
Analytical Geometry and Calculus............................Loomis.
Rhetoric...Blair.
Chemistry..Silliman.

SECOND TERM—SESSION FIRST.

Hebrew (Genesis continued)..
Tacitus (continued)...
Demosthenes' or Aeschines' Orations (continued)...
Natural Philosophy, Mathematical part........................Olmsted.
Logic...Coppee.
English Literature...Spaulding.
Chemistry (continued)...
Botany...Wood.

SECOND TERM—SESSION SECOND.

Hebrew (Psalms)...
Cicero's Tusculan Disputations or De Officiis..............Anthon.
Demosthenes' or Aeschines' Orations...............................
Natural Philosophy—Applications.............................Olmsted.
Political Economy..Wayland.
Optics and Electricity......................................Olmsted.
Botany (continued)...Wood.

SENIOR CLASS.

FIRST TERM.

Anatomy and Physiology..................................Cutter.
Zoology..Agassiz.
Selections of the Hebrew Bible.................................
Psychology..Haven.
Cicero's Tusculan Disputations, or De Officiis (continued)..................................
Greek Tragedy..Woolsey.
Uranography and Review.......Burritt and Olmsted.

SECOND TERM—SESSION FIRST.

Select Hebrew (continued).................................
Mineralogy and Geology..........................Dana and Lyell.
Butler's Analogy ....
Natural Theology..................................Paley.
Moral Science..................................Wayland.
Greek Tragedy (continued).................................
Juvenal..................................Anthon.
Astronomy and Review.................................

SECOND TERM—SESSION SECOND.

Hebrew (continued).................................
Geology (continued).................................
Moral Science (continued).................................
Juvenal.................................
Greek Tragedy.................................
Constitution of the U. S. A..................................Story.
Astronomy and Uranography and Review.................

Department of English Literature and Philology.

The studies and exercises belonging to this Department are attended to by the Faculty. The Alumni Professorship, which was commenced some years ago, had in view the support of a separate Professor, who should devote his entire labors to this Department. The object contemplated is highly important, and the attention of the Alumni and other friends of the College is respectfully solicited to the endowment of this Professorship.

N. B. The Text Books needed for any part of the College Course will be furnished by one of the Professors, at Cincinnati prices.

EXPENSES, &C.

The entire Expenditures of a Student need not much exceed $200, viz:
Tuition, per year... $30 00
Contingent fee... 5 00
These are required in advance by the Term—first Term, $14. Second Term, $21.
Boarding with private families, and furnished room, at $4 00 to $4 50 per week.........................$144 00 to $162 00
Fuel, Light, Washing, &c................................. 15 00
Books, &c..5 00 to 10 00

Boarding in Clubs will cost from one dollar and twenty-five cents to two dollars per week; and some board themselves even at a lower rate. The cost of clothing, and the amount spent as pocket money, will vary with the taste and habit of the Student, and with the wishes of his parents. As a general rule, the more money allowed to a young man, beyond what is strictly necessary, the less likely he is to reflect honor upon his Parents and Instructors. Although Hanover presents comparatively few temptations to extravagance, yet Parents are earnestly advised to require of their sons a detailed account of their expenditures, and to refuse the payment of any debt incurred by them, except for ordinary current expenses, without a written permission. It is also recommended that the funds of young pupils be deposited with some one of the Faculty, and expended under his direction. The younger students are required to board where the Faculty may direct, and where they may exercise a more careful and frequent supervision.

N. B. Students placed upon Scholarships by the Faculty, are relieved in part, or wholly, as the case may be, from the payment of Tuition Fees. The Contingent Fee is required of those on Scholarships the same as others. This is now $2 00 for the first Term, and $3 00 for the Second.

DISCIPLINE.

A record is kept by the Faculty, in which is entered weekly, the grades of scholarship of the Student, his absence from the exercises of the Institution, and such other facts as are worthy of notice with respect to his general deportment. From this record a report is made out at the end of each Session, and sent to the Parent or Guardian of each Student. In case of deficiency in scholarship, negligence in study, irregularity of attendance upon the exercises of the Institution, or improper conduct, the Student will be privately admonished, and the Parent or Guardian will be pomptly informed of the fact.

The object of this arrangement is to keep Parents and Guardians accurately informed in regard to their sons and wards in this Institution, and thus to secure their co-operation with the Faculty in a mild system of discipline. Whenever it is ascertained that a Student is deriving no advantage from his connection with the Institution, or is pursuing a course injurious to himself or fellow-students, the Faculty will take decisive action, and his Parent or Guardian will be promptly addressed on the subject, and requested to remove him from the Institution.

Resolutions of the Faculty, Adopted Dec. 20, 1862.

As absence during the latter part of the College Term greatly injures the Scholarship of Students, impairs their habits of study, breaks the integrity of classes, discourages study among those that remain, and thus lowers the literary standard of the Institution, therefore,

RESOLVED, 1st. That after this date, Dec. 20, 1862, all such absences (not made unavoidable by the Providence of God,) shall be recorded as unexcused.

RESOLVED, 2d. That this resolution be published in the Catalogue and Quarterly Report.

Scholarships.

The endowment of this Institution is in the form of Scholarships, of which the Board has established several sorts. The sum of $400 paid, or secured to t Corporation by note payable within five years; and bearing six per cent. interest in advance upon principal remaining unpaid, purchases for the owner, his heirs and assigns, a perpetual right to the tuition of one Scholar in Hanover College. The sum of $200 paid, or subscribed under similar conditions, secures the right of twenty years' tuition; after which time the Scholarship is subject to the disposal of the Board for the gratuitous education of candidates for the Gospel Ministry. A Church Scholarship of $200, secures to the Church so contributing, a perpetual right to the tuition of one Student, who shall be a member of that Church; and appointed by the Session. A Presbyterial Scholarship of $200 secures a similar right to a Presbytery, in behalf of pupils who shall be candidates for the Ministry under its care. Principal paid on these Scholarships is invested by the corporation in some safe and productive Stock, and the Interest only can be expended for the support of the College.

Every person applying for admission as a beneficiary of a Scholarship under the control of the donors, shall present to the Treasurer, at the beginning of each Term, a written Certificate from those controlling the Scholarship, of his right to such benefit, when, after paying whatever interest may be due on said Scholarship, he shall receive an acknowledgment of his right, which he shall lodge with the President.

"The Scholarships subject to the disposal of the Corporation, may be occupied by such applicants as the Faculty may select, after inquiry into their circumstances, character and attainments, the preference being ceteris paribus, to those who give the best evidence of Scholarship.

"There shall at no time be more than one Student upon each Scholarship."

ACCOMMODATIONS.

The community system of Boarding in Commons, or of rooming in large Lodging Halls, is not adopted in Hanover. Arrangements are made to accommodate the Students with board and rooms in respectable private families, where the number together can never be large; and where all shall be brought under domestic influence.

Settlement of Accounts.

No Diploma nor honorable dismission shall be granted until the Student shall exhibit a Receipt of Settlement of all his bills for boarding, room and washing.

Degrees.

No Degrees are conferred in Course. Candidates for Literary Honors are reported to the Board upon their ascertained or acknowledged merits.

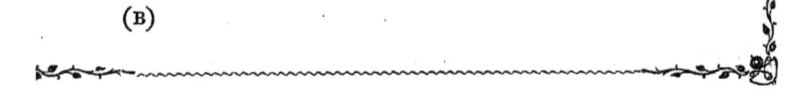

(B)

Societies, Libraries, &c.

There are two Societies connected with the College, the UNION LITERARY and the PHILALETHEAN, whose Libraries number each about twelve hundred volumes.

There is also a SOCIETY OF RELIGIOUS INQUIRY, which has begun to collect a Library, Maps, &c., and which receives regularly several valuable religious papers and periodicals.

The College Library contains near three thousand well selected volumes and is accessible to the Students.

The Cabinet contains several thousand specimens in Mineralogy and Geology.

The friends of the College are advised that contributions to the Library, to the Cabinet, or to the Laboratory, are much needed and will be thankfully received.

Public Literary Societies and Annual Commencement.

Ample opportunity is offered to the Students, once a week, to improve themselves in Composition and Elocution, and several times a year Literary entertainments are given in public, which furnish occasions for honorable competition among the Students, and an interesting and profitable repast to their friends. Three of these entertainments occur annually, viz: on the evening of Washington's birth-day; on Tuesday and Wednesday evening of the last week in March, and on the week of Commencement, when the two Literary Societies and the Society of Inquiry have addresses by gentlemen from abroad, and the Senior Class deliver their Graduating Orations,—altogether occupying over two days.

THE COMMENCEMENT DAY IS ON THE THURSDAY PRECEEDING THE 25TH OF JUNE, after which there is a vacation till the last Wednesday of August.

Location, Buildings, &c.

The village of Hanover is situated on an elevated bluff of the Ohio River, six miles below Madison, Indiana, in a region of remarkable salubrity and natural beauty. The village and neighborhood are characterized by morality, and the absence of all the ordinary temptations to vice and idleness. The Ohio River, and the Railways from Madison, New Albany, and Cincinnati, place Hanover within twenty-four hours of all the principal points in Indiana, Kentucky, Western Ohio, and Eastern Illinois. A turnpike from Madison to Hanover, renders the village easy of access at all seasons of the year.

Hanover College is controlled by a Board of Trustees; one-half of whom are appointed by the Board itself, and the other half by the Synods of Indiana and Northern Indiana.

The Board purchased, some years ago, a farm of two hundred acres, lying between the village and the Ohio River, upon a beautiful point of which,—overlooking the River from an elevation of four hundred feet,—they have erected a commodious College edifice, now completed and occupied. The new College consists of a center building nearly eighty feet square, with lateral and transverse wings. The whole length is about two hundred feet. It contains no dormitories for Students,—an undesirable provision,—but affords ample and convenient Halls, Library, Cabinet, Lecture, and Recitation Rooms, and a spacious Chapel.

The building commands an exceedingly diversified view of the River, for six miles up and ten miles down its course. A visitor of large acquaintance with our country and the world, asserts that a more desirable prospect can not be found in America or Europe.

There is in Hanover, a Select School for young ladies, under the care of the Rev. Wm. Oburn, and daughter. Gentlemen having daughters to educate, as well as sons, can enter their sons in College, and their daughters in this Academy.

Mr. Oburn's School is highly satisfactory to those who have given it their patronage.

A public school for boys and girls, is also usually taught in the village of Hanover, and during the past year a Grammar school for boys was connected with the College. This will be continued, if a suitable teacher can be obtained, for the benefit of those who are not far enough advanced to enter our regular Preparatory Department.

Form of Conveyances and Bequests.

The corporate name of this Institution is "THE TRUSTEES OF HANOVER COLLEGE."

Donors residing in other States should also designate the place in which the College is located, thus: *"The Trustees of Hanover College, located at Hanover, in the State of Indiana."*

The friends of education in Indiana and elsewhere are respectfully solicited to make donations and legacies to this Institution. Since the College was chartered in 1832, about 3,000 have received all or part of their education here, and not less than 800 of these were candidates for the Gospel Ministry. The College has enjoyed 24 revivals of Religion. Over one-third of the students in the present catalogue, are members of the Church, and one-fourth or more have in view the sacred office.